RESTRUCTURING WORLD POLITICS

Social Movements, Protest, and Contention

Series Editor: Bert Klandermans, Free University, Amsterdam

Associate Editors: Ron R. Aminzade, University of Minnesota
David S. Meyer, University of California, Irvine
Verta A. Taylor, The Ohio State University

RESTRUCTURING
WORLD POLITICS

Transnational Social
Movements, Networks,
and Norms

Sanjeev Khagram, James V. Riker, and Kathryn Sikkink, Editors

Social Movements, Protest, and Contention
Volume 14

University of Minnesota Press
Minneapolis • London

Published by the University of Minnesota Press
111 Third Avenue South, Suite 290
Minneapolis, MN 55401-2520
http://www.upress.umn.edu

Library of Congress Cataloging-in-Publication Data

Restructuring world politics : transnational social movements, networks, and norms / Sanjeev Khagram, James V. Riker, and Kathryn Sikkink, editors.
    p.   cm. — (Social movements, protest, and contention ; v. 14)
Includes bibliographical references and index.
ISBN 0-8166-3906-X (HC : alk. paper) — ISBN 0-8166-3907-8 (PB : alk. paper)
1. Social movements.   2. International organization.   3. World politics. I. Khagram, Sanjeev.   II. Riker, James V.   III. Sikkink, Kathryn, 1955– IV. Series.
HM881 .R47 2002
303.48'4—dc21
                                                                    2001006775

Printed in the United States of America on acid-free paper

The University of Minnesota is an equal-opportunity educator and employer.

12 11 10 09 08 07 06 05 04 03   10 9 8 7 6 5 4 3 2

Contents

Preface

This volume grew out of a series of conversations over many years among a group of faculty and students participating in the MacArthur Consortium on Peace and International Cooperation that linked the University of Minnesota, the University of Wisconsin at Madison, and Stanford University. We also invited practitioners and activists to join our conversations and present their views and concerns. Our discussions started at a MacArthur Consortium workshop, "Democracy, Popular Empowerment, and Development," held in Minneapolis in 1994, when a small group of us discovered that we had many common intellectual agendas and questions. Although our research focused on different issue areas and different parts of the world, we were all interested in trying to explain and understand transnational processes that involved nonstate actors as central players.

We called these actors transnational networks, coalitions, or movements, and we understood that they have the potential to transform both domestic political systems and international politics, especially by creating issues, mobilizing new constituencies, altering understandings of interests and identities, and sometimes changing state practices. In particular, these forms of transnational collective action helped bring new norms into politics and instantiate them through their practices. Because our disciplines provided relatively little theoretical guidance to help us with our research, we used our mutual discussions to explore issues, share ideas, suggest approaches, and develop elements of a common framework in which to situate our work.

The early group included people working on human rights and environmental nongovernmental organizations (NGOs) in Indonesia, democratization in Senegal, international norms around women and children's rights, the growth of Esperanto organizations, the internationalization of capital markets, NGOs and the World Bank, human rights in Chile, and transnational campaigns against big dams. Reading one another's work and talking among ourselves convinced us that the transnational connections among nonstate actors we observed in our research were not unique to the cases we knew well, but also existed in other parts of the world and in other policy or issue arenas.

Strikingly, several of these cases foreshadowed and highlighted future outcomes. When the Collective Actors in Transnational Space (CATS) project began in 1994, many of the issues addressed in this volume had not yet played themselves out. For example, while limited action on the debt issues was occurring at the time, it was not until June 1999 that the Group of Eight (G-8) nations agreed to pursue debt relief for the poorest countries of the developing world. Who would have predicted that grassroots and transnational campaigns against dam projects in the developing world would give birth to the World Commission on Dams? Who would have suspected that the Pinochet case would lead to a transnational and domestic convergence to challenge his immunity from prosecution for human rights abuses in Chile? Finally, few scholars at the time would have predicted that President Suharto would step down in May 1998 and give way to a relatively smooth democratic transition in Indonesia. Clearly no one had a crystal ball, but each contributor has had a finger on the pulse of key events and the possible trajectories for future outcomes.

Because our first meeting took place in the context of a workshop focusing on democracy and popular empowerment, it was inevitable that we would ask about what has been (and can be) the influence of transnational social movements and networks on international democratization. Promoting democracy and human rights has been a common theme or "master frame" for most of the transnational efforts we study. But it also led us to ask questions about internal democratic practices within transnational networks and coalitions, questions we take up in more depth in the conclusions.

The volume offers a new model by deliberately drawing on the insights of both scholars and practitioners. We first invited practitioners to a speaker series on transnational social movements held in the fall of 1994 at the University of Minnesota. Smitu Kothari, activist, scholar, and founding member of the Lokayan (Dialogue of the People) spoke on global alliances and the Narmada movement. Arvonne Fraser, a Minnesota-based transnational women's rights activist, spoke on violence, women, and the World Conference on Human Rights. At each subsequent meeting of the research networks, we asked a practitioner to participate in our deliberations. Sidney Jones, director of Human Rights Watch–Asia, labor rights activist Mary McGinnis, and

Mark Ritchie, president of the Institute for Trade and Agricultural Policy and international activist on trade and labor issues, participated and made key contributions to our workshops. Kothari, Ritchie, and Charles Call agreed to provide short written comments to be included in this volume, giving their thoughts and insights about how the issues raised by chapters in the volume relate to their ongoing work.

But the longer the project continued, the more blurred the distinction became between scholar and practitioner. Sidney Jones pointed out that the distinction between activists and academics is misleading. She suggested instead that the distinction is rather organizational location, between those who work full time in advocacy organizations and those who are involved in university-based research and teaching. Using this distinction, many participants in the volume (especially James Riker, Sanjeev Khagram, Thalia Kidder, Paul Nelson, and Charles Call) have experienced professional shifts as some of the original scholars moved on to activist jobs, and some of the early activists returned to academic life. The extraordinary mobility and flux of the core group of writers (in addition to being one of the reasons this volume took so long to move from inception to print) reflect a new model of informed scholar-activism.

In the post–cold war world and in the context of an increasingly globalized political economy, we expect that collective actors in transnational space will be a feature of the contemporary world and will continue to expand in numbers and importance. Even so, we recognize that most transnational networks and coalitions are crucial but imperfect vehicles for contributing to the goals articulated in the MacArthur Consortium—popular empowerment, democratization, sustainable development, human rights and the rule of law, and security. One practical application of our research could be to contribute to the discussions about how to enhance the ability of transnational networks and coalitions to empower and amplify the voice of less powerful sectors in society, to facilitate access to transnational justice, and to improve their own representativity, internal democracy, and effectiveness.

We wish to thank all the many people who helped stimulate our discussions and support our work: foremost among them is the MacArthur Foundation, particularly Kennette Benedict, whose vision and ongoing support made the consortium and its research networks possible. The directors and associate directors of the three MacArthur programs at Minnesota, Madison, and Stanford provided crucial support: Allen Isaacman, Raymond Duvall, Amy Kaminsky, Lynn Eden, David Holloway, David Trubek, Gay Seidman, and Leigh Payne. We especially want to recognize the contributions of the participants in the various workshops whose work is not included in this volume but whose comments and participation were central to shaping our thinking about these issues, including David Trubek, Linda Beck, Young S. Kim, Federico Besserer, Raymond Duvall, Francisca James-Hernandez, Gili Drori, Mary McGinn, and Pauline Chakravarty. We have also benefited greatly from the incisive comments and hard work of our research assistants: Ann Holder, Helen Kinsella, Jennifer Pfeifer, and Ann Towns.

Sanjeev Khagram, James V. Riker, and Kathryn Sikkink

Abbreviations

AAP	Association of American Publishers
ACFOA	Australian Council for Overseas Aid
ACFOD	Asian Cultural Forum on Development
ACTWU	Amalgamated Clothing and Textile Workers Union
ADB	Asian Development Bank
AFRODAD	African Network and Forum on Debt and Development
ANGOC	Asian NGO Coalition for Agrarian Reform and Rural Development
APEC	Asia Pacific Economic Cooperation Forum
CASA	Citizen Assessments of Structural Adjustment
CATS	Collective Actors in Transnational Space
CCC	Communist Correspondence Societies
CEDAW	Convention on the Elimination of All Forms of Discrimination Against Women
CGAP	Consultative Group to Assist the Poor
CGI	Consultative Group on Indonesia
CIP	Commission on International Policy
CIPAF	The Center for Research for Feminine Action
CJM	Coalition for Justice in the Maquiladoras
CMC	Coordinator of Cibao Women
CODEMUH	Collective of Honduran Women
CONAR	The National Committee to Aid Refugees
COPACHI	The Committee of Cooperation for Peace

CSCE	The Conference on Security and Cooperation in Europe
CSW	Commission on the Status of Women
CTU	United Workers Confederation
DONGO	donor-organized NGO
DPI	Democratic Pluralism Initiative
ECOSOC	United Nations Economic and Social Council
EDF	Environmental Defense Fund
EU	European Union
EURODAD	European Network on Debt and Development
FDC	Philippines Freedom from Debt Coalition
FES	Friedrich Ebert Stiftung
FIRE	Feminist International Radio Endeavor
FIRR-US	Federation for Industrial Retention and Renewal
FLACSO	Facultad Latinoamericana de Ciencias Sociales
FNS	Friedrich Naumann Stiftung
FONDAD	Forum on Debt and Development
FTZ	Free Trade Zone
G-8	Group of Eight nations
GC	General Council
GDP	gross domestic product
GONGO	government-organized NGO
HIPC	Heavily Indebted Poor Countries initiative
IACHR	Inter-American Commission on Human Rights
IATP	Institute for Agriculture and Trade Policy
ICCR	Interfaith Center on Corporate Responsibility
ICFTU	International Confederation of Free Trade Unions
ICG	international coordinating group
IDA	International Development Association
IDB	Inter-American Development Bank
IFI	international financial institution
IGGI	Inter-Governmental Group on Indonesia
ILO	International Labour Organization

IMF	International Monetary Fund
INFID	International NGO Forum on Indonesian Development
INGI	International NGO Forum on Indonesia
INGO	international nongovernmental organization
IR	international relations
ITS	International Trade Secretariat
IUF	International Union of Food, Agricultural, Hotel, Restaurant, Catering, Tobacco, and Allied Workers' Association
IWMA	International Working Men's Association
IWRAW	International Women's Rights Action Watch
IWTC	International Women's Tribune Center
IWY	International Women's Year
JANNI	Japan NGO Network on Indonesia
KBRI	Kedutaan Besar Republik Indonesia
KIPP	Komite Indepen Pemantau Pemilu (Independent Committee to Monitor the Elections)
LBH	Legal Aid Institute
LC	League of Communists
LPHAM	Lembaga Pembela Hak-Hak Azasi Manusia (Institute for the Defense of Human Rights)
MAI	Multilateral Agreement on Investment
MFN	most favored nation
MPR	People's Consultative Assembly
NAFTA	North American Free Trade Agreement
NBA	Narmada Bachao Andolan
NCEPC	National Committee on Environmental Planning and Coordination
NGO	nongovernmental organization
NRDC	Natural Resources Defense Council
OD	operational directives
OECD	Organization for Economic Cooperation and Development
OMS	Operational Manual Statement
PAN	National Mandate Party

PCJP	Pontifical Council on Justice and Peace
PDI	Indonesian Democracy Party
PDI-P	The Struggle for Indonesian Democracy Party
PKB	Nation's Revival Party
PPP	United Development Party
PRSP	Poverty Reduction Strategy Paper
QUANGO	quasi-NGO
RMALC	Red Mexicana de Acción Frente al Laibre Comercio
SAP	structural adjustment program
SAPRI	Structural Adjustment Participatory Review Initiative
SDRF	Swiss Debt Reduction Facility
SSP	Sardar Sarovar Project
TIE	Transnationals Information Exchange
TIRN	Tennessee Industrial Renewal Network
TLN	transnational labor network
TSMO	transnational social movement organization
UAI	Union of International Associations
UAW	United Auto Workers
UDHR	Universal Declaration of Human Rights
UNCED	UN Conference on Environment and Development
UNDP	United Nations Development Programme
UNESCO	United Nations Educational, Scientific, and Cultural Council
USAID	United States Agency for International Development
WB	World Bank
WCC	World Council of Churches
WCD	World Commission on Dams
WEDO	Women's Environment and Development Organization
WTO	World Trade Organization
YLBHI	Indonesian Legal Aid Institute

Part I
Theoretical Framework and Issues

1

From Santiago to Seattle: Transnational Advocacy Groups Restructuring World Politics

Sanjeev Khagram, James V. Riker, and Kathryn Sikkink

The chapters in this volume take us from Santiago to Seattle, covering over twenty-five years of the most recent wave of transnational advocacy. When Chilean activists, exiled by the repressive Pinochet regime in the mid-1970s, took their human rights campaign abroad and requested the support of governments, international organizations, and nongovernmental organizations (NGOs) around the world to bring pressure to bear on the Chilean government to improve its human rights practices, they initiated a form of transnational advocacy that has become increasingly common in the last two decades. This campaign came full circle in 1998, when General Pinochet was arrested in London for human rights violations committed during his government.[1]

At the close of the twentieth century, transnational advocacy groups gave a visible and startling manifestation of their power in the massive demonstrations against the World Trade Organization (WTO) meetings in Seattle, Washington, where they contributed to shutting down global negotiations and captured world attention for their cause. The protest in Seattle was not an isolated, spontaneous event but rather a conscious tactic of an increasingly coordinated and powerful movement against globalization that often targets international organizations such as the WTO, the World Bank (WB), and the International Monetary Fund (IMF).

In this volume, we argue that what links the episodes in Santiago and Seattle, and the many other cases explored here, is that all are forms of transnational collective action involving nongovernmental organizations interacting with international norms to restructure world politics. The chapters in this volume focus on this novel, but increasingly important process and its effects in issue areas from labor to human rights and gender justice to democratization and (sustainable) development. We contribute to a broader debate in the social sciences over the role of transnational relations involving nonstate actors of various kinds, including epistemic communities, professional groups, and foundations, but in particular we highlight the role of nongovernmental organizations and social movements.

One of the primary goals of transnational advocacy is to create, strengthen, implement, and monitor international norms. How they go about doing this, when they are successful, and what the problems and complications are for this kind of transnational advocacy and international norm work are the main themes of this book. In it, we have chosen to look at a wide range of cases around the world where nongovernmental actors attempt to change norms and practices of states, international organizations, and private sector firms. We have also invited leaders from activist organizations to join the dialogue and critically comment on the lessons and challenges for restructuring world politics that emerge from this volume.

We join other scholars and policymakers who now assert that international nongovernmental organizations and transnational social movements are emerging as a powerful new force in international politics and are transforming global norms and practices (see, for example, Risse-Kappen 1995a; Smith, Chatfield, and Pagnucco 1997; Lipschutz 1992; Keck and Sikkink 1998; Boli and Thomas 1999; Stiles 1998; Risse, Ropp, and Sikkink 1999; Peterson 1992; Florini 2000). Others see these nonstate actors as sources of resistance "from below" to globalization that challenge the authority and practices of states and international institutions that shape the parameters for global governance (Falk 1997; Waterman, Fairbrother, and Elger 1998; Mittelman 2000; Naim 2000; O'Brien et al. 2000). Indeed the networks, coalitions, and movements we study in this volume have, in some cases, become active participants in "de facto global governance" (Shaw 2000). Some analysts even herald the emergence of a global civil society and its corresponding notion of global citizenship (Dorsey 1993; Wapner 1995; Lipschutz 1992, 1996; Falk 1993, 1998; Commission on Global Governance 1995, 1999; Naidoo 2000; Reinicke and Deng 2000). Many different terms are now used to describe these new forms of global governance—"complex multilateralism," "heterarchic governance," "multi-level structures of transnational governance," or "networked minimalism" (O'Brien et al. 2000; Knight 2000; Smith 2000; Nye and Donahue 2000). All stress a similar phenomena—the increase in new nonstate actors, new arenas for action, and the blurring of distinctions between domestic and global levels of politics.

This volume contributes to this dynamic, ongoing dialogue. We provide additional quantitative evidence of the growth of international nongovernmental and transnational social movement organizations, and qualitative case studies that explore the dynamics and appraise the effectiveness of the transnational networks, coalitions, and movements in which they are members. The chapters in this volume tell some inspiring yet puzzling stories of historically weak coalitions and networks that contributed to unexpected changes in norms, policies, and practices.

In India, for example, a coalition of local, national, and international nonstate organizations has been able to reform and even stall the construction of a huge set of large dams on the Narmada River. Relatedly, in Washington, D.C., networks of nongovernmental organizations around the globe compelled the World Bank to alter its lending policies and priorities to take social and environmental concerns into account.

But we also examine cases of transnational collective action involving nonstate actors that have been less successful. A campaign to change the conditionality policies of the IMF has, as yet, made little impact. In the 1990s, women around the world convinced policymakers that violence against women was a serious violation of human rights that governments needed to address, but they have had less success in actually helping to reduce the incidence of such violence in domestic contexts.

The chapters in this volume attempt to bridge at least two sets of theoretical literatures: the literature on transnationalism, regimes, and norms in the international relations subfield of political science, and the literature on social movements in sociology and political science. Scholars in these two fields often have not addressed or even acknowledged one another.[2] For international relations scholars and social movement theorists to enter into a theoretical dialogue with each other requires both translation—because sometimes they are talking about similar phenomena but using different words—and grappling with each other's empirical frames of reference.

The social movements literature has developed intermediate theoretical propositions about when social movements emerge, what forms they take, the roles they play in social life, the types of impacts they have, and (to a lesser extent) the conditions under which they can be effective. Because this literature has always focused directly on nonstate actors, its emerging synthesis of theoretical concepts and propositions provides a potentially rich source of insights for the international relations student of transnational collective action (for example, McAdam, McCarthy, and Zald 1996; Tarrow 1998). There is an emerging subfield of social movement theory devoted to theorizing transnational collective action and as this type of study develops, it could benefit from insights from international relations (IR) theory.

But if social movement scholars have been "myopically domestic,"[3] IR scholars have been equally myopically state-centric, so each can benefit from the insights of the other. The (neo-)realist and (liberal-)institutionalist paradigms that have dominated the study of IR until very recently focused exclusively, and in a self-conscious way, on the predominant role of states in world politics (Waltz 1979; Krasner 1985; Keohane 1989; Katzenstein, Keohane, and Krasner 1998). Even the recent challenge from many self-described "constructivist" scholars of IR has been primarily focused on ideas and norms and not so much on the role of nonstate actors in shaping those ideas and norms.

We believe strongly that dialogue between the two sets of scholars is potentially fruitful: First, the debates about norms and ideas in international relations could benefit from engagement with older debates over framing and collective beliefs in the social movements literature. Second, the political opportunity structure debates in social movement theory could be usefully informed by IR literatures that explore the dynamic interaction of domestic politics and the international system. After describing the main forms and dimensions of transnational collective action in this volume, we will turn to these two potential theoretical dialogues.

Forms of Transnational Collective Action

We argue that the essential types or forms of transnational collective action or contentious politics are *international nongovernmental organizations (or transnational nongovernmental organizations), transnational advocacy networks, transnational coalitions, and transnational social movements.*[4] As a starting point we present a typology of these forms of transnational collective action because we believe that the form that transnational collective action takes may influence its goals and effectiveness. For the purposes of this volume, *nongovernmental organizations (NGOs)* are private, voluntary, nonprofit groups whose primary aim is to influence publicly some form of social change.[5] Generally, NGOs are more formal and professional than domestic social movements, with legal status and paid personnel. *Domestic nongovernmental organizations* draw membership from one country, though the focus of their efforts may be directed internationally. *International nongovernmental organizations (INGOs)* have a decision-making structure with voting members from at least three countries, and their aims are cross-national and/or international in scope.[6]

Domestic and international NGOs are primary actors that constitute the transnational collective action that is the focus of this volume. We will discuss three types of configurations—transnational networks, transnational coalitions, and transnational movements (and associated transnational movement organizations)—involving different degrees of connection and mobilization.

Transnational advocacy networks are the most informal configuration of nonstate actors. Networks are sets of actors linked across country boundaries, bound together by shared values, dense exchanges of information and services, and common discourses (Keck and Sikkink 1995, 1998). While some networks are formalized, most are based on informal contacts. The essence of network activity is the exchange and use of information. Networks do not involve either sustained coordination of tactics, as with coalitions, or mobilizing large numbers of people in the kind of activity we associate with social movements. Advocacy networks are the most common form of transnational collective action found in this volume. All the chapters involve some transnational network activity, with information exchange and shared values being central features to much of the collective action that the authors discuss. Several chapters discuss transnational collective action that goes beyond network advocacy.

A *transnational coalition* involves a greater level of transnational coordination than that present in a transnational network. Transnational coalitions are sets of actors linked across country boundaries who coordinate shared strategies or sets of tactics to publicly influence social change. The shared strategies or sets of tactics are identified as *transnational campaigns,* which are often the unit of analysis used when researching and analyzing transnational collective action. Such coordination of tactics requires a more formal level of contact than a network because groups usually need to meet to identify and agree upon these shared tactics, to strategize about how to implement the campaign, and to report regularly to each other on campaign progress. The coordinated strategy or tactic can be "noninstitutional," such as a boycott, but transnational coalitions, like domestic social movements, frequently blend institutional and noninstitutional tactics (Tarrow 1998; Meyer and Tarrow 1998).

Sanjeev Khagram discusses the emergence and work of two transnational anti-dam coalitions that attempted to reform or halt the Sardar Sarovar dam project, developing a campaign with coordinated activities to meet this goal. The transnational network around violence against women, discussed by Karen Brown Thompson, became a transnational coalition prior to the 1993 Vienna Human Rights conference when women's groups developed and coordinated transnationally two tactics: an international petition drive and the "sixteen-day" campaign of coordinating activism in diverse countries in the same sixteen-day period.

Transnational social movements are sets of actors with common purposes and solidarities linked across country boundaries that have the capacity to generate coordinated and sustained social mobilization in more than one country to publicly influence social change.[7] In contrast to transnational networks and coalitions, transnational social movements mobilize their (transnational) constituencies for collective action, often through the use of protest or disruptive action. This definition of transnational social movements fits with definitions of domestic social movements that stress mobilization and/or disruption as a defining characteristic of movements (Tarrow 1998; Rucht 1996; Kriesi 1996). Social movement theorists argue that a movement's effectiveness in bringing about social change is linked to its ability to disrupt or threaten a social order (McAdam 1982; Tarrow 1998). We would, then, expect transnational social movements, with their capacity for mobilization and disruption, to be more effective than other forms of transnational collective action. We would also expect transnational movements to have a higher level of transnational collective identity.

But transnational social movements are also the most difficult and rare form of transnational collective action. In order to speak of a truly transnational social movement, we suggest that groups in at least three countries must exercise their capacity to engage in joint and sustained mobilization. What often occurs in practice is that members of transnational networks or coalitions are linked to domestic movements in different countries but the domestic social movements themselves are not directly linked to each other. Other times, a cross-national diffusion of ideas occurs between domestic social movements in similar issue areas without efforts at coordinated mobilization.

While we have many examples in this volume of domestic social movements that link up to transnational networks and coalitions, we have few examples of full-fledged transnational social movements. Karen Brown Thompson speaks of an international women's movement, and this example may be the closest case in the volume to a transnational social movement. The other case that comes close was the short-lived but dramatic example of the First International. Though it carried out network activities like dispensing and exchanging information, the International Working Men's Association was certainly more than a network because it met periodically to develop and coordinate common strategies and tactics. Among the common tactics it used were active strike-support activities and coordinated antiwar actions. The transnational activists who protested at the WTO meeting in Seattle in

1999 certainly engaged in disruptive mobilization that may portend the formation of a transnational social movement targeting globalization.

These three forms can be viewed as ascending levels of transnational collective action. Often, a transnational coalition will emerge only after a network of communication has first developed, and a transnational movement will add the mobilizational element to an existing transnational coalition. Conversely, a sustained transnational network may be initiated from a shorter-term campaign of transnational coalition. It is difficult to imagine a movement emerging without prior network or coalition activity, and we do not have examples of it in this volume. While the definitions of transnational networks, coalitions, and movements are not necessarily comprehensive or mutually exclusive, they do highlight the dominant modality of each type of transnational collective action:

Form	Dominant Modality
transnational network	information exchange
transnational coalition (campaign)	coordinated tactics
transnational movement	joint mobilization

The members of transnational networks and coalitions can be identified *expansively* to include all the relevant actors working to influence social change in an issue area. This more inclusive definition would mean that although nongovernmental organizations and social movements are the primary actors of transnational collective action, (parts of) states and intergovernmental organizations, as well as other nonstate actors such as foundations, research institutes, epistemic communities, corporations, domestic interest groups, and social movements could also be included. This is what is sometimes referred to as "mixed actor coalitions" (Shaw 2000). Some of the authors in this volume use this more expansive definition. So, for example, Daniel Thomas, in his chapter on Helsinki norms, makes the surprising (from a social movement perspective) assertion that the U.S. Congressional Commission on Security and Cooperation in Europe became a "network bastion" within the U.S. government.

On the other hand, transnational coalitions, networks, and social movements can be defined more *restrictively* to include only domestic and international NGOs and social movements. Some scholars believe that this narrower conceptualization helps focus on the conscious linkages made to other actors as factors conditioning the emergence and/or effectiveness of transnational collective action rather than as a part of the network by definition.

Thus foundations might be critical to the formation of transnational net-works by providing financial resources; transnational coalitions that ally with particular state agencies, intergovernmental organizations, political parties, and/or dominant domestic groups might increase their chances of impact; and the knowledge provided by epistemic communities or research institutes could provide a common discourse for the persistence of trans-national networks. Activists may also believe that a restrictive definition is necessary to preserve the character or autonomy of the movement or net-work. In this volume, for example, August Nimtz discusses how the First International limited membership to societies of workers to free it from middle-class or aristocratic patronage.

All our cases have a transnational dimension but the cases differ on whether they involve transnational *sources* of problems, transnational *processes* of collective action, and/or transnational *outcomes* (Imig and Tarrow 1999). In this volume, all the cases involve some kind of transnational process, either the transnational exchange of information or tactics and mobilizations coor-dinated across borders. Some of our cases also involve transnational sources and transnational outcomes, such as the debt and structural adjustment net-works discussed by Elizabeth Donnelly and Paul Nelson. But in many cases, activists use transnational processes to generate domestic outcomes—such as improved human rights practices in Chile, a stop to dam building in India, or the promotion of sustainable development and democracy in Indonesia.

In two cases in the volume, Paul Nelson's chapter on the World Bank and Elizabeth Donnelly's chapter on debt issues, the focus of the campaign is an international organization—the World Bank and the IMF. Donnelly also examines private transnational banks. These campaigns demand policy changes at international institutions that would have far-ranging implica-tions for a wide range of countries. The sources of the campaign, its targets, and its outcomes are intrinsically international. In Thalia Kidder's chapter on transnational labor organizing, the source of organizing is both the trans-national nature of the target, in this case, transnational corporations, and the emergent structures of a tri-national trade agreement, NAFTA. The source of the campaign is transnational, but the demands are often quite local—activists frequently ask for specific collective bargaining outcomes in par-ticular plants. Two chapters focus primarily on bringing about change in a single country, Darren Hawkins's chapter on Chile and James Riker's on Indonesia. The transnational campaign has domestic sources or origins in the practices of a particular state. The international dimension emerges from the tactics and processes used to try to influence the target actor, not by the nature of the actor itself.

Makers and Managers of Meaning: Norms and Framing in Transnational Collective Action

The emergent transnationalist research program is intrinsically linked to concerns with the influence of ideas and norms on world politics (see Katzenstein 1996; Finnemore and Sikkink 1998; see also Kratochwil 1989; Lumsdaine 1993; Klotz 1995; Thomson 1990; Finnemore 1993). Because most transnational nongovernmental actors are relatively weak, their ability to influence international politics is often based on the use of information, persuasion, and moral pressure to contribute to change in international institutions and governments. As Daniel Thomas argues in his chapter, the "deployment and engagement of competing justifications becomes a highly significant political process, and justifications themselves become a source of political power." Most of the chapters also highlight the important role that key individuals and movements have played as "moral entrepreneurs" in instigating campaigns around particular normative demands (Nadelman 1990).

The nongovernmental sector is an increasingly important and distinctive actor in this international society. As an ideal type, it represents a third sector distinct from but interacting with government and business, in which the characteristic form of relation is neither authority or hierarchy (as in government and bureaucracy), nor the market, but rather the informal and horizontal network.[8] If the business sector has been characterized by the drive for profit and the government sector by the use of authority, the third sector, or nongovernmental sector, could be characterized by the search for meaning. The individuals and groups in this sector are primarily motivated to shape the world according to their principled beliefs. Of course, many government and business activities are also involved in managing meanings, but for NGOs and movements it is their raison d'être, rather than an ancillary motivation for action.

International arenas such as intergovernmental organizations are key meeting places where governments and businesses interact with transnational nongovernmental actors. These interactions are often far from harmonious, as they represent a clash, not only of forms of organization, as vertical hierarchy encounters horizontal network, but also a clash of purposes, as the purposes of states encounter and conflict with (or converge with) those of businesses and nongovernmental organizations. While most accounts of international organizations succeed in conveying the conflicts of interest, few have captured the role of these organizations as arenas for "consensus mobilization" or the "battle of justifications," nor have they understood the unique role of the nongovernmental sector in these struggles.

All of the chapters in this volume describe and analyze these struggles over meaning. These struggles are not divorced from power politics, but are rather enmeshed in them. The efforts to get Chile or Indonesia to accept international human rights and democracy norms, discussed by Darren Hawkins and James Riker, were not only about the power of those norms and the role of international institutions in enforcing them, but also about the survival of the Pinochet and Suharto regimes. But the struggle cannot be understood if we use only the lens of state power and interest to analyze it. Nor are issues of individual or collective self-interest unrelated to struggles for meaning. For example, the transnational campaign for norms on violence against women, discussed by Karen Brown Thompson, was in the "self-interest" of women around the world who could use these norms to protect themselves from bodily harm, but it also involved new ways of thinking about their roles and relationships to family, culture, and the state.

Analyzing the third sector has been so difficult exactly because of the intractability of sorting out these kinds of struggles over meaning. Yet we cannot understand transnational networks or coalitions unless we grasp that a significant amount of their activity is directed at changing understandings and interpretations of actors or, in other words, the creation, institutionalization, and monitoring of norms. International relations theorists have tried to conceptualize these processes by thinking about persuasion, legitimacy, socialization, and communicative action (Finnemore 1996; Risse 2000; Risse and Sikkink 1999). Social movement theory can be quite useful in this regard, because scholars from this tradition have been working for decades on these issues, although usually within the bounds of a single state.

Social movement theorists have long been preoccupied with the process of meaning creation, and in the 1990s "the social construction of meaning has become a central part of social movement theory" (Klandermans 1997, 204). Movements help to create and recreate meanings through "framing" or "the strategic efforts by groups of people to fashion shared understandings of the world and of themselves that legitimate and motivate collective action."[9] According to Sidney Tarrow, frames are not ideas, but ways of packaging and presenting ideas. Movements then use these frames to attempt the "mobilization of consensus," that is, persuasive communication aimed at convincing others to take their side.

The notion of "framing" from the study of social movements is similar to the process called "strategic social construction" recently identified in IR (Klandermans 1997). Social movements and NGOs often take new ideas and turn them into frames that define issues at stake and the appropriate strategies for action. Carrying this task out transnationally is far more daunting than doing so domestically, but where successful, such activity can have far-reaching effects. Framing occurs not only through what movements say, but also through what they do—through their choices of tactics and the connections between their actions and their rhetoric (McAdam 1996, 354). Sanjeev Khagram's chapter on big dams makes this point. In the course of a little more than a decade, transnational coalitions have succeeded in altering common understandings of big dams, so they have gone from being seen as obvious and natural tools for (and symbols of) development and modernity to being seen as increasingly controversial and problematic projects. But these movements successfully changed policy not only through their ideas and speeches, but also through mobilizing thousands of tribal peoples who were to be displaced by dams, helping them to bring their plight dramatically to the attention of the media and domestic and international publics.

Social movement scholarship suggests that it will be particularly difficult to form transnational social movements. In particular, social movement theories suggest that the conditions contributing to the emergence and effectiveness of social movements will be difficult to find and sustain transnationally (Tarrow 1999). For example, they argue that the framing processes critical to social movements will happen among "homogenous people who are in intense regular contact with each other" (McAdam, McCarthy, and Zald 1996, 9). But transnational social movements usually start with participants who are not homogenous. How do we explain why and how non-homogeneous people sometimes engage in transnational collective action?

Likewise, few examples exist of truly transnational collective identities. Social movement theory suggests that social movements emerge from "mobilizing structures" in communities—families, friendship networks, and the "informal structures of everyday life," including schools and churches (McAdam 1988; McCarthy 1996). Yet such mobilizing structures and interpersonal networks are largely absent from the transnational arena. In one sense, these arguments are consistent with our finding, and that of others, that there are very few examples of true transnational social movements. But we still need to explain the emergence of the many international NGOs, transnational networks, and transnational coalitions we discuss in this book. Can certain aspects of social movement theory be modified to help explain the emergence and effectiveness of these other forms of transnational collective action?

One of the main ways these efforts at transnational collective action work is by creating and enforcing international norms. Norms in the IR literature are defined as shared expectations held by a community of actors about appropriate behavior for actors with a given identity (Katzenstein

1996; Finnemore 1996). They are standards for how different actors "ought" to behave. Three aspects of this definition merit attention when specifying norms: (1) What are the shared expectations about appropriate behavior, or how do we know a norm when we see one? (2) Who are the actors that hold these expectations? (3) To which actor identities do these norms apply?

The IR literature also distinguishes between ideas (beliefs held by individuals) and norms (intersubjective beliefs about proper behavior) and makes the useful distinction between causal and principled ideas: causal ideas are ideas about cause and effect, while principled ideas are about right and wrong. Causal ideas are supported by evidence, often scientific evidence; principled ideas may be related to causal ideas, but cannot easily be resolved by appeals to evidence (Goldstein and Keohane 1993).[10] When principled ideas are accepted by a broad range of actors, they become "norms," which are intrinsically intersubjective and held by communities. Like social movement theorists, norms scholars are very interested in the processes through which beliefs held by individuals are transformed into collective beliefs and norms.

In this volume, we will reserve the use of *international norms* to speak of the shared expectations or standards of appropriate behavior accepted by states and intergovernmental organizations that can be applied to states, intergovernmental organizations, and/or nonstate actors of various kinds. Most often states work together to make norms in the context of international organizations. Other transnational actors that promote or accept international norms may be international epistemic communities, multinational corporations, transnational professional groups, and so forth.

Many international norms serve the needs of states for coordination and stability of expectations. But there is a subset of international norms that are not easily explained. They do not promote economic and political coordination and the stability of states. They do not necessarily serve the interests of private firms in maximizing profits. It is this subset of somewhat puzzling norms that is the topic of this book. Why would public authorities adopt norms that limit their own ability to treat individuals, groups, or their physical environment the way they please? Why would public authorities (or for that matter private firms) alter their practices?

We argue that you cannot understand the emergence and effectiveness of this subset of international norms without paying attention to the crucial role of transnational networks, coalitions, and movements. A critical mass of actors must accept the standards of behavior before they can be considered as norms. Because we are concerned about international norms, a certain number of states must accept principles before we can refer to them as norms.

In the international arena, different states have more weight than others when it comes to promoting new norms. Nevertheless, as a working operational definition, we suggest that approximately one-quarter to one-third of the actors must support and accept new standards of behavior before we can speak of the existence of new norms (Finnemore and Sikkink 1998).

How do we operationalize these definitions of norms? We can think of norms as having a "life cycle" with a continuum from norm emergence to a norm threshold or tipping point, followed by a "norms cascade" and ending in a situation of norm internalization. Different measures are necessary for different stages in the life cycle (Finnemore and Sikkink 1998). Emergent international norms are often signaled by international declarations or programs of action from international conferences. The entry of a treaty into force or the adoption of new policies by intergovernmental organizations can often be used as an indicator of a norm reaching a threshold or tipping point. Widespread and rapid treaty ratification can be a signal of an international norms cascade. Not all issue areas, however, are governed by treaties, and soft law and other policy guidelines and statements may serve as indicators of international norms.

Where international relations theorists talk of norms, social movement theorists tend to talk of collective or shared beliefs (Klandermans 1997). We distinguish between international norms (standards of appropriate behavior held by a critical mass of states) and collective beliefs (or transnational norms) held by transnational networks, coalitions, and movements. This distinction allows us to inquire about the relationship between the collective beliefs of linked NGOs and movements, and international norms. Groups must first work to develop "collective beliefs" or collective action frames for the movement.

In the transnational arena, transnational networks, coalitions, and movements share some collective beliefs or collective action frames. In this process international norms can form part of the "resources" and "political opportunities" from which actors draw to develop their collective beliefs. Other times transnational networks, coalitions, and movements may attempt to transform their collective beliefs into international norms.

This focus on norms is one main distinction among the cases in this volume. In some cases, for example the case of Chile or the Helsinki case, activists draw on already existing international norms to help construct their collective action frames. In some of the other cases, strong international norms did not exist and the first task of the activists was to build new international norms by mobilizing international consensus around their collective action frames. This is what the anti-dam coalition attempted to do when it urged the World Bank to change its policies regarding large dam building. In a recent, self-conscious attempt at international norm building, a World Commission on Dams was set up to generate new international criteria and guidelines on planning, implementing, operating, and decommissioning large dams (Khagram 2000b). The success of these efforts to create new norms varies greatly. Other groups engage in "frame bridging" or "frame amplification" by building on already existing norms but attempting to expand the domain to which these norms apply (Snow and Benford 1988). This framing process is what women's rights groups did when they worked to get their campaign about "women's rights are human rights" accepted as an international norm.

Once international norms are in place they empower and legitimate the transnational networks and coalitions that promote them. Daniel Thomas argues that "nonstate actors that are otherwise weak can exploit the legitimacy inherent in international norms to construct transnational networks and transform prevailing conceptions of state interests." In this way, he says, "networks serve . . . as 'teachers of norms' to reluctant states." A number of the chapters stress the constitutive aspects of the norms. Networks promote norms that not only stress the appropriate behavior, but help define the very notion of what a state is. Thus, Karen Brown Thompson stresses the ways in which the norm about women's human rights reconstitutes the boundaries between the public and the private spheres. Human rights norms also demarcate the boundaries of the appropriate limits of international intervention and define the behavior that constitutes the necessary attributes of the liberal state.

One way that networks assist in "teaching norms" is by internationalizing domestic policy disputes (Finnemore 1993). In the issue of the environmental networks in the World Bank, for example, Paul Nelson argues that NGOs amplify, interpret, and legitimate local claims by appealing to international norms. Networks use the international arena as a stage or mirror to hold state and international organization behavior up to a global judgment about appropriateness. They attempt to display or publicize norm-breaking behavior to embarrass public authorities and private firms so they will conform to norms. Human rights activists have called this action the "mobilization of shame." Activities that might have stayed hidden before the advent of transnational networks are exposed to the glare of international scrutiny. In these efforts to publicize norm breaking, the media can be a crucial outlet and an ally of networks and much network activity is directed at gaining media attention.

The chapters in this volume generally do not pose normative arguments against rationalist arguments, but rather suggest that norms are present in most debates in world politics. In any discursive terrain, there are always contradictory norms present, and over time certain norms are increasingly emphasized while others lose influence. This dynamic process is what Dan Thomas refers to when he says that "[s]tates whose practices are delegitimated by international norms find that the political terrain has been tilted in favor of political challengers (both state and nonstate) committed to implementation of the new norms." Transnational networks, coalitions, and movements are not the only normative actors in world politics, but rather they lend their weight to certain normative positions vis-à-vis others.

Domestic and International Opportunity Structures and Transnational Collective Action

One of the fundamental insights from social movement theory is that certain features of the political opportunity structures within which movements operate affect their chances of success (Tarrow 1998; Kitschelt 1986). Political opportunity structures are those consistent dimensions of the political environment that provide incentives for or constraints on people undertaking collective action (Tarrow 1998). Political opportunities often provide resources for leverage and spaces for access.

We also need to keep in mind that political opportunities are not only perceived and taken advantage of by social movements, but they are also created. There are numerous examples of how social movement activists have helped create political opportunities at the international level. A number of chapters argue that international norms, in particular, are key examples of political opportunities created in part by activists that in turn empower and create more opportunities for social movement activity.

Many social movement theorists examine social and political opportunity structures in liberal democracies.[11] Thus, the phrases "open" or "closed" opportunity structures generally refer to a continuum within liberal democracies, depending on how porous they are to social organizations (Kitschelt 1986). These studies thus overlook the "really closed" opportunity structure of the authoritarian or semiauthoritarian regime, as compared to the "relatively open" structures of most democratic regimes. The ultimate "closed" domestic political opportunity structure is the repressive authoritarian or totalitarian regime. Not only is the regime "not porous" to societal influences, but it may be actively engaged in physically eliminating its opponents, or actively undermining their capacity to organize. The Chilean government under Pinochet is the most obvious example in this volume, but the actions of the Suharto government toward domestic social movements in Indonesia is another example of an essentially closed opportunity structure.

This volume includes diverse cases and allows us to make the basic but often overlooked comparison between democratic and authoritarian regimes (see Khagram 2000a, b). So, for example, Sanjeev Khagram argues in his chapter on the Narmada Dam that the effectiveness of coalition pressures was enhanced by the procedurally democratic institutions in India, so that internal groups had direct access to and influence on state and national governments. Likewise, in Daniel Thomas's chapter on Helsinki norms and U.S. foreign policy, the democratic structure of the U.S. Congress made it more open to the influence of the human rights networks. Network influence in Chile and Indonesia took a longer time to develop because the authoritarian nature of these states made it more difficult for domestic groups to have influence. Yet recently, both cases have shown remarkable breakthroughs due to persistent action where international norms have led Chile's courts to reject Pinochet's immunity and Indonesia to embrace democratic forms of governance.

However, it is not enough to think about the effectiveness of transnational collective action only in terms of domestic opportunity structures. In addition, we need to think systematically about transnational political opportunity structures—that is, what are the consistent dimensions of the international or transnational political environment that provide incentives or constraints for collective action? Social movement theorists are increasingly aware that social movements operate in both a domestic and an international environment: they speak of "multilayered" opportunity structure, including a "supranational" layer or a "multilevel polity," or they highlight how international pressures influence domestic opportunity structures (Oberschall 1996; Klandermans 1997; Marks and McAdam 1996; McAdam 1996; Tarrow 1998, 1999).

But international pressures are still mainly seen as some form of "exogenous shock" to primarily domestic processes. Social movement theorists have been skeptical about the existence of a true transnational political opportunity structure. Doug McAdam, for example, argues that social movements target institutionalized power and since such institutionalized power is rare in the transnational arena, we cannot speak of a true transnational political opportunity structure, with a few exceptions like the European Union.

We argue that international institutions indeed present clear political opportunity structures for transnational advocacy (see also Tarrow 1999). An international opportunity structure will not displace a domestic political opportunity structure, but will rather interact with it. To understand the effectiveness of transnational collective action, we must understand the dynamic interaction between an international opportunity structure and the domestic structure. This dynamic interaction may be similar to the logic of two-level games spelled out by Robert Putnam, but without the chief negotiator sitting as the linchpin in the center of negotiations (1988).

There appear to be characteristic patterns in this interaction of domestic and international opportunity structures. The "boomerang" pattern and the "spiral model" could both be thought of as models of the interaction between domestic opportunity structures and international opportunity structures (Keck and Sikkink 1998; Risse and Sikkink 1999). Both models suggest that it is blockage in the domestic society that sends domestic social movement actors into the transnational arena. This blockage is often due to repression, authoritarianism, or both. The combination of a closed domestic opportunity structure and an open international opportunity structure initiates the boomerang and the spiral. The interaction in the "spiral model" is more complex. Closed domestic polities generate transnational linkages as domestic activists are "pushed" outward, often to protect their existence. But one of the main goals of the move to the international arena is to liberalize and open domestic regimes. So the spiral model generated sustained change only when it was able to help create a more open domestic opportunity structure—usually through regime change (Risse and Sikkink 1999).

Thus, a two-level interacting political opportunity structure produces outcomes that would be counterintuitive for those only looking at domestic political opportunity structure. For example, it is generally assumed that the state's capacity or propensity for repression will diminish domestic social movement activity (Tarrow 1995; McAdam 1996). But the boomerang model suggests that repression may simultaneously move actors into international arenas to pursue their activities. Repression is the most obvious form of blockage, but a lack of responsiveness may also compel groups to work internationally. For example, feminist groups and groups of indigenous peoples have often found the international arena to be more receptive to their demands than domestic political institutions are.

The perceived degree of openness of international opportunity structures is not absolute, but is rather relative to the openness of domestic structures. For a Chilean human rights activist, the international arena was permissive and open compared to harsh repression at home. But activists in countries with very open domestic opportunity structures may perceive a move to an international institution as one that provides less room for influence. This is the basic argument about the democratic deficit in the European Union. Similar arguments are being made by labor rights activists like Mark Ritchie, who writes in this volume about the WTO and NAFTA. Some activists charge that governments prefer to move policy decisions to some multilateral institutions exactly because those institutions are less open to societal influence. In many cases transnational activists have developed strategies to try to influence these more closed international institutions, but they see this action as a necessary defensive response, rather than as a desirable strategic move. Where domestic groups have open domestic opportunity structures and responsive national governments, they will not seek out international institutional access, even though the source of their problems is transnational in nature. Rather they will pressure their own governments to represent their interests in international arenas (Tarrow 1995).

Some have asked about the long-term effect of internationalization on domestic actors—"Does it empower them or disempower them?" (Tarrow 1999). Our volume suggests there is no single answer to that question because it depends on the nature of the domestic opportunity structure and the issue area. For the NGOs and movements in the repressive society (the examples of Chile, Eastern Europe, and Indonesia in this volume) it seems unambiguous that internationalization of the movement empowered them, and, to the degree that it contributed to democratization, opened previously closed space domestically for action. But this unambiguous empowerment is only relative to the very disempowered position they originally occupied in their societies. For the labor activists discussed by Thalia Kidder and Mark Ritchie, globalization has disempowered them locally, and the move to transnational arenas is more of a defensive move to try to reclaim lost levels of empowerment.

The possibilities for dynamic interactions among domestic and political opportunity structures are far reaching. For example, one basic aspect of the domestic opportunity structure is the presence of elite allies and support groups. By considering international opportunities, the universe of potential allies and support groups is dramatically expanded. At the same time, however, these allies may be more difficult to mobilize in transnational space because of distance, language, and cultural differences. Just as potential allies multiply, so too do potentially antagonistic sectors. In other words, the "multiorganizational fields" within which the transnational networks, coalitions, and social movements operate are more complex than those of their domestic counterparts (Klandermans 1997).

Chapter Overview

The chapters in this volume point to a very diverse set of cases and relations between transnational collective action and international norms. As August Nimtz's historical chapter on the formation of transnational workers networks in the First International makes clear, transnational organizing is not a new phenomena. NGOs have been involved in international governance since the 1800s and have experienced a continuous, though uneven, growth since that time (also Charnovitz 1997). By looking at a case from this early period, we see the role of transnational nongovernmental actors in an atmosphere prior to the formation of formal international organizations. By contrasting this case with Thalia Kidder's charter on transnational labor organizing across the Mexico-U.S. border in the 1980s and 1990s, we see the differences in transnational advocacy in the dense international institutional context of the late twentieth century compared to the thin context of the mid-nineteenth century.

In chapter 2, Jackie Smith and Kathryn Sikkink highlight the significant growth in transnational advocacy international NGOs (TNGOs) or transnational social movement organizations (TSMOs) since the 1950s. This growth has occurred across all issues, but to varying degrees in different issue areas. At the same time as the overall number of international NGOs has increased, they have also increased and diversified their contacts with intergovernmental organizations and with other NGOs. Although the networks discussed in this book represent only a subset of the total number of networks, these include the issue areas around which the largest number of international nongovernmental social change organizations have organized. Together, human rights, women's rights, and the environment account for over half of the total number of international nongovernmental social change organizations.[12]

Daniel Thomas's chapter on the Helsinki accord examines how transnational nongovernmental actors used "soft international law" in the area of human rights to help successfully alter and influence the foreign policy of a superpower, the United States, vis-à-vis its major competitors, the USSR and Eastern Europe. In Darren Hawkins's chapter on the influence of transnational actors in promoting human rights in Chile, nongovernmental actors call on existing international human rights norms embodied in international treaties and in international organizations, such as the UN Human Rights Commission and the Inter-American Commission on Human Rights, to pressure the Chilean government to improve its human rights practices. Karen Brown Thompson discusses the role of transnational actors and international organizations in instigating and institutionalizing new global norms about women's rights as human rights.

In the chapters by Elizabeth Donnelly on the IMF and Paul Nelson on the World Bank, transnational nongovernmental actors direct their campaigns and strategies at international financial institutions to attempt to alter their policies and practices. In Sanjeev Khagram's chapter on big dam construction, transnational coalitions influence international organizations like the World Bank and in turn use the leverage of these international organizations to change the domestic politics of dam construction in India. Likewise, with the creation of a transnational nongovernmental forum to parallel the annual meeting of donor countries providing aid to the Indonesian government, James Riker's chapter examines how NGOs, transnational networks, and international development agencies have strengthened civil society and reshaped the discourse about sustainable development and democracy in Indonesia.

Together these cases highlight the changing dynamics, policy arenas, and possibilities for restructuring world politics through transnational collective action. At the same time, the growing role of nonstate actors at both the state and international levels raises fundamental questions about their authority, legitimacy, and accountability. International nongovernmental organizations increasingly play an advocacy role in a wide range of global public policy networks that define and shape global policy and practice from human rights to human development and security (Reinicke 1999/2000; Bryer and Magrath 1999; Brown et al. 2001). The derailing of the World Trade Organization meetings in Seattle in November 1999 has prompted much debate about whether and how such nonstate actors should have a voice and participate in these forums (Economist 1999; Cardoso 2000, 42). These fundamental issues are highlighted and addressed in the volume's conclusions.

Notes

1. The British government eventually determined General Pinochet was too ill to stand trial and allowed him to return to Chile, but only after several pathbreaking legal decisions establishing that he did not have immunity from prosecution for human rights violations committed during his government. The Chilean Supreme Court has likewise ruled that Pinochet does not have immunity from prosecution.

2. With the exception of Sidney Tarrow (1995; 1999), whose recent work is serving as a bridge between these two fields. See also Brysk 1994; Keck and Sikkink 1998; Smith, Chatfield, and Pagnucco 1997; Smith 2000; Schmitz 2000; and Khagram 2000a, b.

3. Doug McAdam, presentation at the University of Minnesota, 17 November 1999.

4. These distinctions are based on Khagram 1999.

5. The emphasis here is on those NGOs engaged in transnational advocacy for the public interest (see Gordenker and Weiss 1995b). For other definitions of NGOs, see the World Bank (Malena 1995), the United Nations (UNDP 2000), the

work of The Johns Hopkins Comparative Nonprofit Sector Project (Salamon 1994, Salamon et al. 1999), and Uvin 2000.

6. *The Yearbook of International Organizations* identifies international NGOs as organizations where there is voting participation from at least three countries. See chapter 2 in this volume for a more detailed description of a data set of international NGOs from the *Yearbook*.

7. See a similar definition of a transnational social movement by Doug McAdam: "organized, coordinated transnational collective action designed to promote change in more than one country with active and equal participation of actors from multiple countries." Presentation at the University of Minnesota, 17 November 1999.

8. On the distinction between hierarchy, market, and network, see Powell 1990; on the notion of NGOs constituting a "third sector," see Drucker 1989 and Schweitz 1995.

9. David Snow and his colleagues have adapted Erving Goffman's concept of framing. Definition from McAdam, McCarthy, and Zald 1996 (6).

10. On the distinction between ideas and norms see Finnemore and Sikkink 1998.

11. There are notable exceptions such as Escobar and Alvarez 1992.

12. They constitute about half of the INGOs listed in the *Yearbook of International Organizations* (see Sikkink and Smith, this volume).

2

Infrastructures for Change: Transnational Organizations, 1953–93

Kathryn Sikkink and Jackie Smith

It is now common in the literature on transnational social movements and networks to assert that they have expanded dramatically in recent years. But few researchers have provided strong quantitative evidence or analysis of this growth and its relevance for transnational movements and networks. Researchers have shown significant growth in international nongovernmental organizations (INGOs) of all types, but only a small portion of these organizations are engaged in the kinds of social change activities typical of social movements and networks (see, for example, Skjelsbaek 1971). Jackie Smith presented clear evidence of the growth of INGOs established for the explicit purpose of promoting social or political change. Drawing from the *Yearbook of International Organizations* for the years 1983, 1988, and 1993, Smith examined the population of what she labeled "transnational social movement organizations" or "TSMOs," demonstrating their parallels with research on national social movements.[1] This chapter presents the results of an expanded collaborative effort at data collection and coding from the *Yearbook,* using Smith's coding procedures, to include the years 1953, 1963, and 1973.[2] This long-term perspective can offer insights about the nature of the subset of INGOs working across national borders to promote social and political change, and it can tell us about change in this sector over time. This allows us to relate the arguments made in this book derived from case studies of particular transnational social change efforts to a broader understanding of the organizations that help compose such movements.

We cannot measure the growth of transnational movements and networks using the definition presented in the first chapter of this volume because there is no source that systematically documents such organizations and networks. Accounting for the extent of contemporary transnational networks would prove a time-consuming and difficult task, given the informal and fluid nature of these networks. As a proxy for such a measure, however, we use the changing number and characteristics of international nongovernmental organizations that are explicitly devoted to social and political change goals. For consistency with other chapters and research, we refer to the organizations we examine as "social change INGOs." A subset of INGOs whose organizational missions involve the promotion of some form of social and/or political change, these organizations serve as social infrastructures for change, and they represent more or less routine efforts to generate resources and collective action for social change efforts. Moreover, they provide opportunities for individuals to participate in international politics in ways that would otherwise be impossible. International organizations and their member states provide few formal channels of access to international policy-making arenas. But transnational social change organizations have worked to expand citizens' access to the global polity by creating structures that convey information and ideas between individuals and groups within societies and the institutions that structure interstate relations (see, e.g., Smith 1997). We can therefore expect these particular actors—in contrast to actors whose principal objectives, instructions, or routines lie outside the sphere of social change work—to be *routine,* though by no means the *only* participants in transnational advocacy networks and transnational social movements. Understanding the nature of this organizational infrastructure can help us anticipate the issue arenas most likely to attract transnational advocacy efforts.

As we know from work on the precursors to modern transnational social movements and networks, including the chapter by August Nimtz in this volume, transnational social movements are not a new phenomenon (see also Keck and Sikkink 1998; Chatfield 1997). We find numerous early examples including the transnational campaign against slavery, transnational labor organizing, and campaigns for women's suffrage. The oldest social change INGO in the *Yearbook*'s current listing, the Anti-Slavery Society for the Protection of Human Rights, was founded in 1839. The International Working Men's Association (1864–72), discussed by August Nimtz, was short-lived but was also the forerunner of diverse networks, movements, and political parties. Other early social change INGOs include the World Woman's Christian Temperance Union (1883), the World Zionist Organization (1897), and the International Bureau for the Suppression of Traffic in Persons (1899). Nevertheless, the vast majority of social change INGOs emerged in the latter half of the twentieth century, and our data suggest that their number and size, as well as the density and complexity of international linkages, have grown dramatically in the last three decades. More than 60 percent of all social change INGOs active in 1993 were formed after 1970. This is consistent with the material from our case chapters, where many of the organizations in the networks we discuss were formed in the 1970s and 1980s.

Data

The Union of International Associations (UAI), based in Brussels, produces an account of international nongovernmental organizations as part of its annual *Yearbook of International Organizations,* published since 1950.[3] International organization scholars have long referred to the *Yearbook* to document trends in international organization and international nongovernmental activity (see Skjelsbaek 1971; also Jacobson 1979, appendix B, 435–39). The Union of International Associations was commissioned by a United Nations resolution to keep track of international organizations, which it does by consulting relevant UN records, and by seeking out information directly from INGOs themselves. The *Yearbook* is the only source of systematic annual data on international NGOs.

For scholars and activists interested in social movements or networks, however, the *Yearbook* data poses some problems. The *Yearbook* only collects information about *international* nongovernmental organizations, and they use a quite stringent criteria to determine if an organization is international. Members, officers, voting, and substantial budgetary contributions have to come from at least three countries for the organizations to be included. This creates a list of formal and bureaucratized INGOs. But many of the organizations that scholars and activists would consider transnational social movements or networks would not be listed in the *Yearbook.* The *Yearbook* only lists those organizations that are formally international, not all networks with substantial, but informal international linkages. Moreover, the groups most likely to respond to the UAI's census survey are those that wish to have information about their group made public. This would likely exclude groups working for political and social change that is seen as illegitimate, as well as groups using illicit means to advance their change goals. Thus any data set based on information from the *Yearbook* will underestimate the absolute number of transnational social movement organizations. This suggests that data from the *Yearbook* can provide only a partial picture of transnational network sectors. Nevertheless, the dynamics and patterns of this particular subset of formally organized actors may be helpful to help us understand general patterns in transnational networks.

Second, and perhaps more troubling for the social movement theorist, the *Yearbook* does not distinguish between different types of international nongovernmental organizations. It lumps together in a single INGO category all different types of international NGOs, such as international professional organizations like the International Political Science Association (IPSA) and international medical associations, with what we would call more genuine social movements or networks. Smith overcame this problem by drawing from sociological research on social movement organizations to introduce a "political or social change" criteria in her coding scheme. Coders identified organizations whose specified goals (or "aims" under *Yearbook* headings) indicated that their principal purpose was to work for some form of social or political change.[4] It is this social change subgroup that we refer to as social change INGOs. Coders also excluded the following types of organizations outright: funds, foundations, institutes or organizations primarily devoted to research, groups that seek world peace through spiritual transformation (e.g., yoga, transcendental meditation), organizations whose primary mission is the promotion of a particular religious tradition, exchange programs, and service delivery and general education organizations. In addition, because the *Yearbook* did not indicate whether they were autonomous from government control, labor organizations were excluded from the data set. However, labor organizations working principally on workers' rights and protection from forced labor were included, since their social change emphasis was more apparent. Religious organizations were excluded, except when their *principal* organizational focus went beyond the propagation of a particular religious ideology to include the promotion of social or political change. The idea here is that churches and other religious institutions—while frequently supportive actors within transnational social movements—have organizational missions that are not primarily for the promotion of social change, and thus their work toward movement goals may vary substantially across time and place.

These distinctions were necessary to exclude the large number of INGOs that do not fit our definition of transnational social movements in any sense. Nevertheless, these criteria do exclude some organizations that are a critical part of some of the networks in this volume. For example, the coding scheme excluded groups whose primary aim is the promotion of religion, yet in her chapter on the debt network, Elizabeth Donnelly describes the significant activity of the hierarchy of the Catholic Church, including the pope himself, on behalf of debt forgiveness. Though not formally a part of the debt networks, the Catholic Church and Catholic bishops were some of the most active and influential actors on these issues. Likewise in his chapter on Chile, Darren Hawkins argues that international church organizations, like the World Council of Churches (WCC), played a crucial role in the human rights network in Chile, but the WCC is not in our list of INGOs whose specific purpose is promoting social change. In addition, funds and foundations are excluded from the database, yet most of the chapters in the volume point to the extremely important role that some funds and foundations play in supporting transnational social movements and network activity. Some of the transnational labor networks discussed by Thalia Kidder and Mark Ritchie would not appear in our database because they are listed primarily as labor unions. Finally, sometimes parts of a government become members of a transnational network, as in Daniel Thomas's discussion of the Helsinki network, where the Congressional Helsinki Commission and even Ambassador Goldberg himself often seemed to be more identified with transnational network principles than with U.S. government policy, eventually succeeding in changing U.S. policy to bring it in line with network goals.

Given these problems, we emphasize that what we present here is a look at the population of international nongovernmental *organizations* with social or political change aims or both, rather than a comprehensive portrait of transnational social *movements* or *networks* discussed in the empirical chapters of this book. Nevertheless, since organizations are major components of movements and networks, many of the specific transnational organizations mentioned in the chapters here appear in this data set as well.

In addition to analyzing the trends in the growth of social change INGOs, we examine the data in light of some of the hypotheses proposed in this volume. Authors in this volume make a series of arguments about the explanations for the growth and effectiveness of networks in their issue area. Many of these arguments have to do with the impact of international institutions, including international norms, on social movement activity (see Tarrow 1999). More specifically, as noted in chapter 1, authors discuss how specific aspects of international institutions, or international opportunity structures, facilitate the growth and effectiveness of networks. For example, a number of authors argue that issue areas where preexisting well-institutionalized norms exist are more likely to lead to network growth and successful network action. For example, in his chapter on Chile, Darren Hawkins argues that "preexisting domestic and international human rights norms acted as a 'pull factor' to facilitate the emergence and growth of the transnational advocacy network." Without such preexisting norms, he says, "it is difficult to imagine the formation and growth of such a dense network in such relatively short time periods."

This raises the question of what exactly we mean by norms, and how we know a norm when we see one. In chapter 1 we stressed that although international norms are manifest in complex ways, for many research purposes it is possible to operationalize international norms using international treaties, or declarations of "soft law," such as the Helsinki Final Act. Looking at the entry into force of a treaty as a threshold in norm institutionalization may provide a starting place for talking about the influence of norms on the growth of networks and network success. In this chapter we will briefly look at the relevant treaties in a handful of issue areas and discuss whether there is any apparent relation between treaty ratification and social change INGO growth. In some cases, we also need to look at "soft law." For example, Daniel Thomas suggests that the preexisting Helsinki norms were essential for the mobilization and strength of that network, and yet Helsinki was not a treaty, but rather soft law. In any case, both Hawkins and Thomas argue that norms legitimate the work of change advocates operating in networks and/or movements and thereby encourage network growth and success.[5] We shall briefly explore this in relation to available data.

In the case of human rights, such an argument would suggest that network growth would occur after the mid-1970s, because both the Covenant on Civil and Political Rights and the Covenant on Economic, Social, and Cultural Rights entered into force in 1976. Some regional human rights treaties and laws also date to this period: the Helsinki Final Act was passed in 1975, and the American Convention on Human Rights entered into force in 1978. In the women's rights area, this argument would anticipate social change INGO expansion after 1981, when the Convention on the Elimination of All Forms of Discrimination Against Women (CEDAW) entered into force. The environmental area is more difficult to evaluate because there is not a single treaty, but a set of several specific treaties. Some issue areas we deal with in the volume—for example the area of debt forgiveness—have virtually no strong preexisting or institutionalized treaty norms. If institutionalized norms lead to the growth of networks, we would expect slight growth of social change INGOs in this issue area. Elizabeth Donnelly points out that the Catholic Church has a "jubilee" tradition of periodic debt forgiveness, but this has not been translated into any international treaties. Likewise, in other areas, such as development, Paul Nelson suggests that multiple and contradictory norms exist, some stressing economic rights and basic needs, and others stressing fiscal austerity and the need to balance budgets.

A second hypothesis is that large international conferences created the impetus for network growth. In the area of women's rights, this would lead us to expect that the large UN conferences associated with the International Women's Year in 1975 and International Women's Decade (1975–85) would lead to the growth of networks and movements. In the environmental area, it suggests we would see network growth after the 1972 Conference in Stockholm and the UN Conference on Environment and Development (UNCED) in 1992 in Rio de Janeiro. Likewise, we might expect human rights network growth in response to the 1968 International Conference on Human Rights in Tehran and the 1993 World Conference on Human Rights in Vienna.[6]

Growth in the Number of Social Change INGOs

The data support the general view presented in this book and elsewhere that there has been a significant increase in the total number of international nongovernmental organizations. The total number of social change INGOs listed in the *Yearbook* increased almost six times between 1953 and 1993. The growth has been particularly dramatic in the ten-year period from 1983 to 1993 (see Table 2.1).

Types of Issues around Which Social Change INGOs Organize

The data also tell us about the kinds of issues around which social change INGOs organize and how this has changed over time. The story here is one of both remarkable stability in some issues and some significant changes. Table 2.1 shows that the number of social change INGOs has increased across all issues, though to varying degrees in different issue areas. This variance across issue areas suggests that social change INGO growth is not just an epiphenomena of more generalized growth of organizations internationally. The number of social change INGOs working on some issues has increased dramatically, while those working on other issues has stagnated, and in a relative sense, declined.

Table 2.1. Number of Transnational Organizations by Issue Focus

Issue	1953 (N = 110)	1963 (N = 141)	1973 (N = 183)	1983 (N = 348)	1993 (N = 685)
Human rights	33	38	41	79	190
Peace	11	20	14	22	81
Women's rights	10	14	16	25	62
Environment	2	5	10	26	123
World order/ international law	22	23	37	57	80
Development/ empowerment	3	3	7	13	47

Note: These six issues account for approximately 70 percent of all organizations in each time period.

Human rights has been a predominant focus of transnational social change organizations since the 1950s. The issue has been the focus of roughly a quarter of all groups in each decade studied. There were five times as many organizations working primarily on human rights in 1993 as there were in 1953, but human rights groups are about the same proportion of total groups in 1993 as they were in 1953. The number of groups focusing on human rights has grown in each period, although the issue areas declined proportionally in the 1973 and 1983 period, only to recover again by 1993.

Two of the chapters in this volume focus on these human rights organizations: the chapter on Chile by Darren Hawkins and the chapter on U.S. policy toward Eastern Europe and the Soviet Union by Daniel Thomas. Both Hawkins and Thomas argue that these networks were relatively more effective because they could identify their case with well-institutionalized international norms. The United Nations General Assembly passed the first clear statement of international human rights norms, the Universal Declaration of Human Rights, in 1948. The relatively large numbers of human rights INGOs in 1953 could reflect this early declaration on emergent international norms. Indeed, some human rights groups' efforts to press for rights protections in the wake of World War II's atrocities were critical to achieving the Universal Declaration. These norms became increasingly detailed and institutionalized in 1976, when the Covenant on Civil and Political Rights and the Covenant on Economic, Social, and Cultural Rights entered into force, and in 1975 when the Helsinki Final Act was signed. The data on the number of human rights INGOs seems to reflect the increasing institutionalization of international norms: between 1973 and 1983 the number of transnational human rights NGOs nearly doubled. The World Conference on Human Rights in Vienna in 1993 also coincided with an increase in both the absolute number of human rights INGOs and their proportion of all social change INGOs. This might be explained by the convergence of this conference with the end of the cold war and the subsequent expansion of the global agenda to include issues and voices that had been excluded in the bipolar struggle that had dominated global affairs.

The second largest proportion of social change INGOs active in 1953 worked to promote the development of international law and institutions. These organizations made up 13 percent of the population in the period 1953 through 1973, but by 1983 the numbers remained steady as the total number of social change INGOs grew. By 1993, this issue focus accounted for only 4 percent of all organizations. This does not mean that international law has become an irrelevant concern for these organizations. Many international human rights, women's rights, and increasingly environmental organizations pay significant attention to international law, but they do so from the vantage point of their particular issue. It is likely that the growth in the quantity and complexity of international law and international institutions in the postwar period have made the INGOs that serve them less viable as they compete with other, more focused groups for funding and other resources.[7] None of the chapters in this volume focuses on transnational movements or networks dedicated to promoting the development of international law or institutions. Indeed, as Paul Nelson's chapter on the World Bank, Elizabeth Donnelly's chapter on the International Monetary Fund, and Mark Ritchie's comments about campaigns against NAFTA and the WTO point out, today's transnational social movements are more likely to critique the practices of international institutions than they are to promote their development. It is interesting to note that there were no major attempts to write treaties or hold conferences to institutionalize or deal with general norms about international law or international institutions.

Groups working on women's rights accounted for about 9 percent of all groups in 1953 and in 1993. Like human rights, the women's rights issue area grew very slowly before 1973, but has grown much more rapidly since 1983. This is somewhat surprising, because as Karen Brown Thompson points out in chapter 5, histories of the international women's movement have signaled the UN International Women's Year in 1975 and the UN International Women's Decade (1975–85) as a major growth period for international women's rights NGOs. Likewise the early 1980s saw the emergence for the first time of clear treaty norms on women's rights. CEDAW was adopted in 1979, and entered into force in 1981. Yet, despite all this activity around norms and conferences, 1983 was the year when the women's rights issue accounted for the lowest proportion of the total groups since 1953 (7.2 percent). In some cases there appears to be a significant lag time between the founding of organizations and their appearance in the *Yearbook*. So, for example, the parallel NGO meeting at the International Women's Year Conference in Mexico City in 1975 encouraged a group of women to found the International Women's Tribune Center, which used the mailing list generated at Mexico City to keep in touch with individuals and groups around the globe. By 1990, the Tribune Center was a communication link for sixteen thousand individuals and groups working on behalf of women in 160 countries. The Tribune Center, though founded in the mid-1970s, does not show up on the *Yearbook* list until 1993. We do not know whether this lag is more characteristic of women's groups than other groups. It could be that the feminist movements that came to the forefront in the 1970s and 1980s, which eschewed hierarchical forms of organization, avoided setting up the kind of formal international groups that met the *Yearbook* criteria. In general, it appears that the full effect of the Women's Decade from 1976 to 1985 may not have been reflected in the data until the 1993 *Yearbook.*

Transnational environmental organizations have grown most dramatically in absolute and relative terms. In 1953, only two organizations worked to promote environmental change. By 1973, the year following the UN Conference on the Human Environment in Stockholm, their number rose to ten, and it more than tripled between 1983 and 1993, the year following the Earth Summit, or the UN Conference on Environment and Development in Rio. This growth supports Khagram's point in chapter 10 that the Stockholm conference in 1972 contributed to the growth of international networks.

Proportionally, environmental INGOs rose from 1.8 percent of total groups in 1953 to 14.3 percent in 1993. Forty-two percent of all environmental INGOs active in 1993 were formed after 1985, and 80 percent were formed after 1970. Some of this growth might be the result (or even the partial cause) of UN meetings on the environment in 1972 and 1992 (see Willetts 1999). This dramatic growth parallels the expansion of national and locally based environmental movements. If this is the case, it is perhaps not surprising that some of the more successful social movements and network activity discussed in this volume, such as the anti-dam transnational social movements discussed by Sanjeev Khagram and movements pressuring the World Bank to consider the developmental impact of major infrastructural projects, discussed by Paul Nelson, are linked to international environmental activism.

The percentage share of groups in the development issue area has also grown (from 2.7 percent in 1953 to 5.4 percent in 1993), but not as dramatically as the growth in the environmental issue area. Groups focusing on development still account for a relatively small percentage of the social change INGOs recorded in this data set.[8] In this volume, the poverty and structural adjustment networks discussed by Paul Nelson and the debt networks discussed by Elizabeth Donnelly are the groups most engaged in the development issue area. Some of the major development NGOs (such as Church World Service, Community Aid Abroad, CARE, Christian Aid, Oxfam International, Save the Children Federation, and World Vision International) not only advocate policy positions, but also carry out significant development projects on their own. To carry out these projects, they may seek funding from the very institutions they are pressuring for policy changes. Paul Nelson suggests that this creates tensions within some major development NGOs between "their desire to advocate for new policy and practice" and "their dominant organizational need to secure funding from major aid donors."

Other groups that might be considered "development" organizations have found that they are more effective if they "frame" their demands in human rights or environmental terms. Thus a number of the organizations discussed by Jim Riker, Sanjeev Khagram, Paul Nelson, and Thalia Kidder might be characterized as "development" NGOs but also frequently use the frames of the environment or human rights (and workers' rights in the case of labor networks) because they have found that these frames have more resonance than the development frame. These are examples of strategic venue shift, as activists frame issues in certain ways in the search for more support and a more receptive political venue (Baumgartner and Jones 1991; Keck and Sikkink 1998). Even more far reaching than simple venue shift is what occurs, as Sanjeev Khagram describes, when new norms on indigenous peoples, human rights, and the environment "restructur[e] the global politics of development."

The percentage share of groups in such issue areas as peace, ethnic unity, and Esperanto has declined. None of the chapters in this volume looks at international organizing in these issue areas. To the initial U.S. observer, the inclusion of Esperanto organizations in social change INGOs and the high number of Esperanto organizations in our database may seem puzzling. But for many internationalists around the world, the desire to learn a "world language" such as Esperanto was an expression of a desire for an international identity that transcended national identities. In parts of the world where more explicit international political activity was limited, Esperanto organizations became the depository of internationalist norms and aspirations, as well as an opportunity to join together with organizations elsewhere. These organizations were frequently organized along the lines of occupation or interest/identity, so we find such organizations as the International Federation of Esperantist Railwaymen, the League of Homosexual Esperantists, and the World Esperantist Vegetarian Association. None of the chapters in this volume examines such organizations, but the steady presence of such international language organizations in our data set provides support for the argument we present in the conclusions that transnational social movements and networks are harbingers of the emergence of international identities that coexist with, and in some cases transcend, national identities.[9]

Although the networks discussed in this book represent only a subset of the total number of networks, these include the issue areas around which the largest number of social change INGOs have organized, and/or the ones that are currently experiencing the greatest growth. Together, groups working on human rights, women's rights, the environment, and development account for well over half of all total social movement and network activity.

As pointed out above, many labor organizations have not been included in the data set. In summary, the issues dealt with in this volume are not an unusual or marginal form of social movement activity, but a sample of the most important issues to which the majority of modern social change INGOs devote themselves.

Finally, although coders of the data set were obliged to choose the "major focus" of an organization, in the cases in this book many social movements and campaigns work simultaneously on a number of different issues, or they work on issues that are at the intersection of issue areas. This may be increasingly true as economic and political globalization make the connections among issues more obvious, as with the NAFTA and WTO effects on environmental and human rights concerns. Perhaps the clearest example of this is described in Sanjeev Khagram's chapter on the Narmada Dam campaign, where activists worked on issues involving the protection of indigenous or tribal people, human rights, environmental preservation, and development. Paul Nelson also points to the overlapping of three networks, poverty, the environment, and structural adjustment, in his focus on the World Bank.

Geographic Dispersion of Social Change INGOs and Networks

One common criticism of transnational social movements and networks is that they tend to be disproportionately based in the countries of the North. Critics claim that this physical location in the most developed countries has led these social change INGOs to reflect primarily the sensibilities of citizens or governments in the developed world.

Our data supports the general understanding that the great bulk of social change INGOs are based in the developed world and primarily have branch offices and membership from the North (see Tables 2.2 and 2.3). This is the closest indicator in the data set to what we have referred to as "asymmetries" of power and influence within the networks and transnational social movements. Of course, the physical location of an INGO is only one possible indicator of the points of view held by network members. Hosting the secretariat of an international NGO is a costly and complex administrative operation. There are examples of efforts made to locate secretariats of social change INGOs in Southern countries that failed because Southern NGOs were hesitant to take on the large financial and administrative burden of serving as the secretariat.

Another explanation for the geographic distribution of social change INGO headquarters is that it makes practical sense for these groups to base their organizational operations near the political targets they seek to influence.

Table 2.2. Regions of TSMO Membership

Region	1953 (91)	1963 (117)	1973 (134)	1983 (214)	1993 (525)
Europe	92%	91%	89%	87%	84%
North America (except Mexico)	69	73	72	64	68
Latin America and Caribbean	59	65	68	61	61
Asia	55	67	63	59	60
Africa	53	61	61	56	59
Oceania	45	51	55	52	53
USSR/Eastern Europe	49	46	53	43	50
Middle East	32	55	57	50	43

Note: The numbers in parentheses after each year indicate the number of organizations able to provide valid data.

Table 2.3. Locations of TSMO Secretariats

Region	1953 (N = 110)	1963 (N = 141)	1973 (N = 179)	1983 (N = 343)	1993 (N = 679)
Western Europe, Canada	83%	77%	73%	68%	58%
United States	9	8	10	11	14
USSR and Eastern Europe	2	5	4	3	4
Any global south country	5	6	12	17	23
Latin America	3	1	2	5	6

Locating in sites near international organizations facilitates access to information on international negotiations and it enables organizational staff to monitor negotiations, to lobby government delegations and members of international organization secretariats, and to otherwise facilitate communications between geographically dispersed memberships and global institutions. Thus, it is not surprising that we found some of the largest concentrations of social change INGOs near major IGO headquarters in Brussels and Geneva. This pattern holds throughout the time periods we examined.

Another consideration is that a transnational organization is likely to choose a site for the international secretariat that dispersed members can readily communicate with—electronically, by telephone, or in person. Cities with good physical infrastructures and frequent nonstop airline service facilitate global networking and thus make logical candidates for headquarter siting. Figure 2.1 shows the percentage of groups whose headquarters were located in one of four key cities of Europe, cities that are among what Sassen calls "global cities," or centers of commercial and professional activity that enjoy high concentrations of specialized service industries and supportive infra-structures (e.g., telecommunications and transportation), which reinforce their centrality as global centers (Sassen 1991).[10]

Despite the overrepresentation of developed countries among social change INGO memberships and among the secretariat headquarters, these

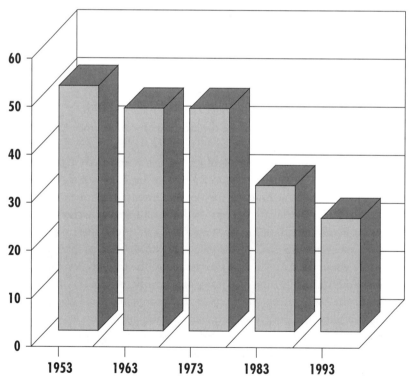

Figure 2.1. TSMOs headquartered in "global cities." The Y axis indicates the percentage of all TSMOs headquartered in Brussels, Geneva, London, or Paris. Source: Saskia Sassen, The Global City: New York, London, Tokyo *(Princeton: Princeton University Press, 1991).*

data show a trend over the past forty years away from this predominance of Northern and European representation and toward more geographically dispersed membership. Developing areas are somewhat better represented among the memberships of social change INGOs today than they were in the past. Of the developing areas, Latin Americans and Asians are most networked with social change INGOs, with Africans running a close third. While Europeans are most likely to have memberships with social change INGOs, their relative proportions have declined somewhat (from 92 percent in 1953 to 84 percent in 1993), reflecting the more rapid growth in participation from other regions. The proportion of social change INGOs reporting members in the United States and Canada remained fairly constant at around 70 percent. Middle Eastern countries were least likely to have representation in social change INGOs in most years of the study. Participation in the sector by Eastern European and former Soviet countries was generally low, although it expanded between 1983 and 1993, and may continue to grow as the cold war recedes further into history. Much more dramatic is the decline in the percentage of social change INGOs based in global cities, from more than half of all groups in 1953 to roughly one-quarter of all groups in 1993. While the absolute numbers of groups based in global cities have grown, these groups represent a smaller proportion of the transnational social movement sector than they once did.

With this shift in membership, the location of social change INGO secretariats has also shifted to reflect greater participation from developing countries. While only 5 percent of all secretariats were based in developing countries in 1953, this figure rose to 23 percent by 1993. Of these, nearly one-fourth were in Latin America. To a certain extent, modern communication technologies have made secretariat location a less constraining issue than it once was, because all network members can receive information rapidly through electronic mail. Nevertheless, the kinds of geographic concentration shown in the data set were also present in the case studies. Both Paul Nelson and Elizabeth Donnelly, writing on network pressures on the World Bank and the IMF, respectively, report that groups based in Washington, D.C., have had disproportionate influence in campaigns. This led in turn to complaints that the Washington-based activists were not more representative or accountable, but had more influence because they had "loud voices and resources." Likewise, the close cooperation between some networks, especially environmental and human rights networks, and the U.S. government strengthens the perception that networks are guided by an "essentially Northern agenda" (Nelson). When the World Bank set up the standing NGO–World Bank Committee it attempted to circumvent the advantages of geographical concentration by mandating representation from each of the five major global regions. Other Southern-based networks have proposed establishing their own Washington offices, but the chapters in this volume provide only one example where such an office has been created (an African consortium cited in Nelson).

The *Yearbook* does not provide significant data on the financial resources of organizations. We suspect that such data would suggest that the process of geographic dispersal of membership and of secretariats has not been accompanied by substantial dispersal of the sources of funding for social change INGOs. Many of the authors in this volume point to the problems that funding creates for their movements, which suggests that asymmetries in transnational networks and movements is more a result of concentration of funding sources than of the location of secretariats.

U.S. and European foundations increasingly provide very significant financial support for social change INGOs, including those based in and drawing their membership from the developing world. Funding from international organizations and agencies is also increasingly important. Not surprisingly, financial difficulties were by far the most significant obstacle reported by Southern (and Northern) groups in recent surveys of transnational human rights groups and affiliates of EarthAction, a large transnational organization working for environment, peace, and human rights (Smith, Pagnucco, and Lopez 1998; Smith 1999). However, most groups (in both surveys) still report that a substantial portion (approximately half of operational budgets, on average) of their funding is raised from internal sources, such as dues or fees paid for services or materials.

Despite this concentration in the developed world and the great dependence on financing from U.S. and European foundations, it is interesting to note that the issues around which social change INGOs organize do not simply reflect the issues that are most prominent in domestic social movement organizations in Western countries. For instance, while human rights is the most predominant issue for social change INGOs, human rights organizations are a relatively small part of the social movement sector in Western countries. Likewise, women's organizations are important both domestically and internationally, but the issues they focus on differ (Keck and Sikkink 1998).

Network Density: Countries of Membership, Linkages among Social Change INGOs, and between Social Change INGOs and IGOs

Chapter 1 of this volume argues that to understand transnational social movement activity, one must look not only at single social change INGOs and social movements, but also at campaigns organized by loosely affiliated networks, coalitions, and movements. In general, we and others have argued, denser networks and coalitions are likely to be more effective in achieving their goals, especially if they have significant network, coalition, or movement participants within the country or countries targeted by the campaign. So, for example, Darren Hawkins argues that the density of the transnational networks working on human rights in Chile was an important part of the explanation for human rights change in that country. Especially important, however, was that social movement activity was often initiated and sustained by significant domestic human rights organizations within Chile and by networks of Chilean exiles working abroad.

The best measure of network scope and density that one can glean from the *Yearbook* data is the number of countries reported among social change INGO membership and their reported links with IGOs and other NGOs.

Table 2.4 shows that there has been some growth in the geographic expansion of social change INGO memberships. The number of groups reporting members in twenty-five or fewer countries remained fairly constant, at least between 1963 and 1993. But between 1953 and 1993, we see some clear growth in the scope of social change INGOs as the proportion of groups reporting fewer than twenty-five countries of membership declined from 68 to 55 percent while the numbers reporting more than forty membership countries grew from 15 to 28 percent. Of these, 8 percent of the organizations now report members in more than eighty countries, up from 2 percent in 1953. The average number of countries of membership for all the social change INGOs in the data set increased from twenty-six in 1953 to thirty-four in 1993.

Table 2.4. Geographic Dispersal of Members

Number of Countries of Membership	1953 (N = 90)	1963 (N = 125)	1973 (N = 153)	1983 (N = 233)	1993 (N = 528)
3–10	19%	14%	12%	20%	17%
11–25	49	38	32	34	38
26–40	17	23	24	21	18
41–80	13	21	27	20	20
More than 80	2	4	4	5	8
Average number of member countries (median)	26 (21)	30 (24)	34 (28)	31 (23)	33 (23)

Social change INGO contacts and formal relations with IGOs and NGOs remained constant between 1953 and 1983. By 1993, however, groups reporting any ties with other intergovernmental or nongovernmental organizations were more likely to have broader ranges of ties. The proportion of groups reporting having ties with more than three IGOs more than doubled from 17 percent in 1953 to 37 percent in 1993. The expansion of ties with NGOs is most dramatic after 1983. In 1983, 90 percent of the groups reporting any NGO ties said that they had fewer than four links to other NGOs. By 1993, only 53 percent of such groups had fewer than four links to other NGOs. The proportion of social change INGOs reporting links with four or more other NGOs grew nearly fivefold, from 10 percent in 1983 to 47 percent in 1993. This pattern clearly supports our claim that network density, especially among NGOs, has increased significantly. Also, we would argue that these figures still significantly underestimate the number of network links, since many informal ties exist and these might not be reported on the UAI questionnaire that asks about significant organizational contacts.

Table 2.5. Contacts with IGOs and NGOs

	IGOs				
Number of links with IGOs	1953 (N = 48)	1963 (N = 60)	1973 (N = 80)	1983 (N = 126)	1993 (N = 360)
1–3	83%	76%	70%	78%	62%
4–10	17	24	30	21	30
More than 10	0	0	0	0	7
Average	—	—	—	1.3	2.3
(Standard deviation)	—	—	—	(1.9)	(4.4)
	NGOs				
Number of links with NGOs	1953 (N = 61)	1963 (N = 48)	1973 (N = 68)	1983 (N = 123)	1993 (N = 489)
1–3	88%	87%	91%	90%	53%
4–10	10	10	9	8	32
11–20	0	2	0	2	10
More than 20	2	0	0	0	5
Average	—	—	—	0.98	4.88
(Standard deviation)	—	—	—	(1.8)	(7.28)

Organizations were not asked to report on their funding links to foundations, nor on kinds of linkages to governments, so the total number of network linkages is not represented in the data set. A number of chapters suggest that informal linkages, based on personal trust and ties among individuals in different groups, may be key linkages in some cases, but these would not be reported here.

Conclusions

This chapter outlines the broad shifts in the organizational infrastructure that supports global social change efforts. While these organizations are not the only actors behind important global changes, the fact that their principal reason for existing is to promote some social or political change means that they are likely to be key figures that activate and sustain transnational advocacy networks. Unlike governments and foundations, these organizations are collections of individuals who care deeply about the social change goals of their organization and who spend large amounts of their time and energy working to promote these goals. Thus, understanding this infrastructure helps us better understand the changes in and potential for transnational networks, coalitions, and movements.

The data we have analyzed suggest that the population of transnational social movement organizations is expanding both numerically and in geographic scope. The number of organizations grew more than sixfold between 1953 and 1993. While there are still gaps between the participation of citizens of less industrialized countries and their Northern counterparts, this gap appears to be shrinking as more developing countries are represented among social change INGO memberships and as more social change INGOs locate their organizational headquarters outside the global North and its global cities. These trends suggest that transnational advocacy work is more likely now than in the past to incorporate more globally representative voices. They also suggest that such networks are more likely to be accounting for the needs and interests of people from regions outside the industrialized nations as they advocate for global change.

In addition to noting expanding size and scope of the transnational social movement infrastructure, we found a trend toward greater density in the linkages among social change INGOs and other actors, such as other NGOs and international agencies. This reflects the success of past work by social change INGOs to defend and expand their access to IGOs and it demonstrates the extent to which these groups have become routine actors in international affairs. Moreover, it shows that through decades of work in the international system, social change advocates have learned to cultivate networks among themselves in order to share information and coordinate strategies.

We did not find unambiguous support, however, for either of the two arguments about the impact of international institutions on the growth of social movement organizations. In none of the cases did the entry into effect of the relevant treaty appear to contribute to a significant increase in the number of social change INGOs, at least in the short term. Preexisting international norms do seem important for the effectiveness of networks and movements, but they do not lead immediately to the growth of movements. In some cases, such as the two environmental conferences and the 1993 World Conference on Human Rights in Vienna, large international conferences appear to contribute to the growth in the number of social change INGOs in the same issue area. In other issues, such as women's rights and the 1968 International Conference on Human Rights in Tehran, international conferences did not contribute immediately to growth in the number of social change INGOs organized on the issue.

In summary, parallel to the expansion of economic and political globalization we find that nongovernmental actors have worked to expand and develop global social infrastructures. Seeking to shape the character of globalization and its policies are a larger number of more geographically diverse organizations with stronger and denser communications networks than were present at the founding of the United Nations. This sector of society has proven influential in shaping global changes in the past, and it is likely to continue to be a voice (however discordant) for principled change.

Notes

1. For other discussions of the population of transnational social movement organizations, see Smith 1995, 1997, and 1999. For discussions of the applications of sociological research on social movements for the study of international NGOs, see Smith, Chatfield, and Pagnucco 1997, and Smith 2000.

2. As far as we are aware, this data set spanning fifty years is the only effort to provide quantitative historical data on social change INGOs from the same source.

3. The data in the *Yearbook* is the most complete census of international organizations, which included information on organizations' founding dates, goals, memberships, and interorganizational ties. The Union on International Associations uses UN records on nongovernmental organizations (NGOs), self-reports, referrals, and the media to identify organizations and compile organizational profiles for the *Yearbook*. Editors consistently check this reported information against other sources, such as periodicals, official documents, and the media. We have confidence in this data because it has been gathered by the same organization using the same methods

over time. Nevertheless, some of the increases we see in the total numbers of social change INGOs may be the result of more complete methods of identifying and surveying international nongovernmental organizations in the current period.

4. For more details on coding, see Smith 1995.

5. Transnational movements and networks have also been catalysts for the establishment and elaboration of international norms; see, e.g., Risse-Kappen 1995a, Finnemore 1996, and Chatfield 1997.

6. On NGOs at these meetings, see Clark, Friedman, and Hochstetler 1998.

7. Many private and government funders require groups seeking resources to propose specific projects. This may help explain the pattern we find, as organizers are encouraged to specialize their groups' work around key issue areas or legal/institutional arenas, such as the Human Rights Sub-Commission or the Commission on Sustainable Development. Also, during the latter half of the twentieth century, the number of United Nations functional agencies and treaty bodies grew tremendously, enabling more specialized work in very focused arenas.

8. Many of the larger international relief organizations that would be considered important players in transnational networks (e.g., CARE) are excluded from this data set because they are not international in structure or because their organizational missions are focused more on relief or charity than on social change.

9. For a more detailed discussion of Esperanto groups, see Kim 1999.

10. Unfortunately, we were not asking this question when we recorded information on these groups and we did not code separate cities within the United States. We are certain, however, that a substantial portion—if not a majority—of these groups are located in New York or Washington D.C., for the same reasons outlined above.

Part II
Influencing Human Rights Discourse, Policy, and Practice

3

Human Rights Norms and Networks in Authoritarian Chile

Darren Hawkins

Well we know that the action of our internal adversaries is connected with important political and economic centers in the international world, which complicates even further the situation just described.
—General Augusto Pinochet to Army Corps of Generals, 1977[1]

Though once confined largely to the domestic realm, in recent years the politics of human rights have become increasingly internationalized and transnationalized. It has become routine for states to sign and ratify human rights treaties, for intergovernmental organizations to monitor rights abuses, and for nongovernmental organizations (NGOs) to mobilize campaigns on behalf of the oppressed all over the world. Domestic groups and individuals suffering repression frequently seek political and financial support from international patrons and provide the international community with crucial information on the nature of repression. Human rights groups join hands with philanthropic foundations, concerned individuals, churches, and others to create transnational human rights networks that span the globe.

These activities were not always commonplace. Most of them developed gradually and without much fanfare in the 1970s and 1980s. They have become, however, an important feature of the international arena and have altered the ways in which states must deal with human rights issues. In consequence, repressive states must consider not only domestic responses to their terrorism, but also international reactions. The victims of state terror find important political allies abroad and use them to strengthen their own position and to bring more pressure on the repressive state (Khagram, Riker, and Sikkink, this volume; Keck and Sikkink 1998, 12–13). States that embrace the rhetoric of human rights internationally may find themselves in a greater bind when carrying out repression domestically.

Authoritarian Chile, 1973–90, marked a crucial case in the development of transnational human rights activities and efforts to restrict state human rights abuses. While international human rights norms were developed on paper from the 1940s to the 1960s, the 1973 Chilean military coup triggered one of the first and most extensive efforts to translate those norms into practice (Sikkink 1996, 155). International and domestic human rights groups formed a well-known transnational advocacy network that set key precedents for later human rights networks. The Chilean transnational network pioneered activities that are now standard practice, including a variety of monitoring efforts, international funding for domestic opposition groups and research centers, an activist role for intergovernmental organizations, and lobbying powerful Western states to take action.

This chapter examines the emergence, growth, and impact of the Chilean transnational human rights network. In Khagram, Riker, and Sikkink's conceptualization, the Chilean case involves a domestic problem—gross and systematic human rights abuses—and a domestic outcome—a gradual easing of some of the abuses and eventually a transition to democracy. Yet the process of responding to the problem and producing the outcome was fundamentally transnational. Prior to the 1970s, international human rights consisted of all talk and no action. The transnational network that emerged from the 1973 Chilean coup dramatically changed that pattern. Even in the face of harsh repression inside Chile and strong initial U.S. support for military rule, the network grew rapidly and reached remarkable size inside Chile as well as in the international arena.

As I discuss in the first section, a combination of the push and pull factors conceptualized by Khagram, Riker, and Sikkink accounts for the rapid emergence and substantial growth of the Chilean network. Repression pushed many Chileans into international exile where they naturally made contact with each other, and simultaneously pushed those living in Chile to appeal to the international community for help. At the same time, preexisting domestic and international human rights norms acted as a "pull factor" to facilitate the emergence and growth of the transnational advocacy network. In the absence of preexisting human rights norms, it is difficult to imagine the formation and growth of such a dense network in such relatively short time periods. In contrast to most of the other chapters in this volume, networks did not have to create international norms before or while attempting to hold states accountable to those norms. States themselves, under pressure from earlier generations of human rights activists, had formulated international norms protecting civil and political rights. Likewise, earlier generations of Chilean politicians and social groups had created strong and widespread human rights norms in the domestic arena. These preexisting norms facilitated the rapid emergence and growth of the network.

In the second section, I argue that the Chilean network enjoyed some important successes. Network actors helped mitigate some of the worst effects of the human rights abuses, opened political space for opposition groups, and dramatically increased the size and scope of the network over time. Network actors raised Chilean human rights abuses into a pressing international issue and successfully lobbied intergovernmental organizations and Western states to take action. Under intense transnational scrutiny, the Chilean military regime adopted the discourse of human rights and gradually ended some of its more heinous practices. At the same time, network actors also faced important shortcomings: the regime endured seventeen years in power and remained repressive to the end. In terms of the levels of influence outlined by Khagram, Riker, and Sikkink in chapter 1, the Chilean network put human rights on the agenda and influenced the military regime's discourse, policy, and practices. Yet this influence was gradual and partial, much less than the network hoped for and more than the regime preferred.

What accounts for the network's success? Authoritarian Chile presented a difficult case for network influence due to its closed opportunity structure. As a result, the network created its own success by utilizing preexisting international and domestic norms through extensive monitoring, as I argue in the third section. The Chilean case essentially confirms Khagram, Riker, and Sikkink's hypothesis that strong norms and strong networks together produce the most significant changes in targeted states. Human rights activists generally lacked material resources and only rarely mobilized widespread domestic protests due to the military regime's effective repression. Instead, they drew on moral authority, as discussed in Sikkink's concluding chapter, and utilized extensive monitoring to bring about changes. Detailed monitoring was crucial in the following four ways: (1) it conveyed information out of Chile; (2) it legitimized the substance of that information and delegitimized the military regime; (3) it motivated and justified widespread international pressure; and (4) it was a means to remain engaged with military regime officials and to press for improved behavior. The expansive scope and high quality of these monitoring efforts contributed significantly to the network's successes.

Network Emergence: Preexisting Norms and Repression

International reaction to the Chilean coup and the subsequent human rights abuses was unexpectedly swift, strong, and widespread from the outset. Rarely, if ever before, in world history had so many international actors reacted so strongly to a military coup and human rights abuses.[2] The reactions mushroomed into what was probably the largest international network against human rights abuses in the 1970s, one that rivaled the massive effort against South Africa in the 1980s (Klotz 1995). Prior to the 1973 Chilean coup, states began to establish human rights norms, but action on behalf of human rights was confined largely to the domestic realm. The coup and subsequent abuses pushed activists to form one of the world's first transnational advocacy networks centered on modern conceptions of human rights. Preexisting human rights norms offered network groups a set of values and beliefs around which they could rally and which they could easily employ as standards in condemning Chile's behavior.

The Development of Norms

To explain the emergence of the network, one must first understand the importance of human rights in Chilean history. Ideals of democracy and human rights enjoy a long pedigree in Chilean history, and they traditionally limited the state's authority over its citizens' free expression, participation, group affiliations, and so on (Valenzuela 1989, 159–71). Elites initiated civilian constitutional rule in Chile in 1833, and the military intervened only twice prior to the 1973 coup—once in 1891 and again between 1924 and 1932. During those 140 years, stable political parties grew and flourished, suffrage was gradually extended, and each Chilean president was followed by an elected successor. On a variety of indicators, Chile was more democratic throughout its history than many Western European states (159–61).

Domestic human rights ideals played an important role in Chile's democratic tradition. In 1925, Chileans adopted a new constitution that included significant human rights guarantees, such as the right to residence and movement, the right to due process, and the right to personal freedom and security (Inter-American Commission on Human Rights 1985, 24–25). Chile's strong and independent judiciary helped enforce these rights, and the state generally respected them. While the constitution recognized that the state could restrict human rights under state of siege conditions, it also ensured that such restrictions would be temporary and would only affect some rights. In practice, government-sponsored terror was largely unknown and virtually unthinkable prior to the 1973 military coup.

Due to a series of widely discussed problems, Chile's political system became increasingly polarized in the mid-1900s between left, center, and right, each with a highly charged, ideologically driven political agenda (Valenzuela 1978; Sigmund 1977). In 1970, the socialist Salvador Allende was elected president despite the best efforts of the United States and Chile's conservatives to stop him. Unfortunately, his election simply increased the intensity of the polarization in Chile. Strong pressure from the United States, unyielding opposition among the major political parties, paramilitary activity on the right and left, and severe economic shortages combined to create general social disorder. While the government lurched from crisis to crisis, it became increasingly unable to prevent the violence breaking out in the streets and in the countryside. In this rapidly degenerating context, the armed forces perceived a deep internal security crisis requiring immediate, forceful, and violent action. Proclaiming the need to restore law and order, Chile's military seized power and imposed strict authoritarian rule on 11 September 1973.

In contrast to Chilean domestic human rights norms, international human rights norms are of more recent vintage.[3] States first incorporated the principle of human rights into the charter of the United Nations by committing themselves to promote "universal respect for, and observance of, human rights and fundamental freedoms for all without distinction as to race, sex, language or religion" (UN Charter, Article 55). In 1948, the UN General Assembly unanimously passed the Universal Declaration of Human Rights (UDHR)—a fairly comprehensive statement of human rights ranging from the rights to life, personal security, and civil liberties, to the rights to work, food, clothing, and education.

The effort to establish international human rights norms bore additional fruit in the 1960s when two international covenants were signed—one dealing with civil and political rights and the other with economic, social, and cultural rights. These covenants catalogued a wide variety of human rights standards in greater detail than the UDHR, empowered international committees to monitor violations, and required states to report their compliance. By 1976, dozens of states, including Chile, had ratified one or both of these covenants and they entered into force as binding agreements. Similarly, Latin American states negotiated and signed a regional human rights treaty, the Inter-American Convention on Human Rights, in 1969. It affirmed extensive political and civil rights and set up a regional human rights court. The human rights norms articulated in these documents inform expectations of state behavior and set widely accepted standards that can be used to measure state noncompliance.

The development of international human rights norms—even if they existed only rhetorically and on paper—was still a surprising step for states to take. Human rights agreements potentially entail a loss of sovereign authority and open the possibility that human rights standards would be used against those who created them. Suggesting that all human beings possess inherent rights and deserve certain standards of treatment sets important limits on the state's authority over its citizens. Enshrining human rights principles at an international level also suggests that international actors have a right or even an obligation to "intervene" in the domestic affairs of other states to protect those rights. International human rights principles thus serve as a very useful tool for states who wish to condemn their enemies or to justify intervention. They are a very dangerous tool, however, as no state has an unblemished human rights record.

Not surprisingly, states at first made little effort to monitor compliance or to ensure human rights norms would be enforced. States established intergovernmental commissions to monitor human rights abuses, but then allowed (or required) them to languish in obscurity—sometimes even preventing them from reading the complaints sent by abuse victims. The Inter-American Commission on Human Rights (IACHR), for example, dates to 1959, but it began actively investigating systematic human rights abuses (as opposed to isolated cases) only in the early 1970s (Farer 1997). The UN Commission on Human Rights was established even earlier and yet did not authorize investigations of human rights abuses until 1970. Prior to the Chilean coup, human rights norms existed but were not acted upon.

Repression, Norms, and Network Formation

The military coup marked a radical turning point in Chile's tradition of human rights and democracy. A weak, disintegrating state unable to retain order was transformed overnight into a strong, predatory state seeking to destroy and then rebuild basic social institutions. Although nearly everyone in Chile had expected a coup and many had pleaded for it, few had envisioned the brutality and long years of terror that would follow. Virtually every social and political institution that could resist this campaign was destroyed within a few weeks of the coup or quietly acquiesced to the climate of fear. Arguing that they were afflicted with decay from Marxist infiltration and required complete rebuilding, the new military rulers disbanded Congress, censored the media, and repressed political parties, labor organizations, student groups, and neighborhood organizations. By conservative estimates, more than two thousand Chileans disappeared or were killed by state security forces, mostly within the first four years of military rule (Chilean National Commission on Truth and Reconciliation 1993). Although no firm numbers exist, estimates suggest that tens of thousands were tortured, hundreds of thousands arrested or detained, hundreds of thousands exiled, and untold numbers scarred emotionally or psychologically by government terror.

With Chilean groups reeling from state terror, international human rights groups sprang into action. They used international and domestic human rights norms to call for monitoring, to lobby Western states for sanctions, and to motivate UN action. Two international NGOs—Amnesty International and the International Commission of Jurists—were among the first to react. They cabled the intergovernmental IACHR just three days after the coup, urging that people be allowed to request asylum and to leave the country, and that the newly installed government respect human rights (Medina Quiroga 1988, 263). Within a month of the coup, the IACHR sent an observer to Chile to gather information on human rights. After a six-day visit, the observer returned with reports of torture, disappearances, illegal arrests, and murders, and recommended further action (263–64). This visit marked the first in a long series of international efforts to monitor human rights abuse, as discussed later in this chapter.

International human rights groups also played an important role in motivating Western states to take action (Schoultz 1981). Although the United States generally supported Chile's new rulers, U.S. human rights groups and widespread media attention helped influence Congress to condemn the military regime and its abuses from the start. Within a month of the coup, Congress took up a proposal to sanction Chile, marking one of the first times that human rights issues entered the U.S. foreign policy agenda (Sigmund 1993, 89; Salzberg and Young 1977, 251–66). Under strong lobbying from domestic and international human rights groups within the network, Congress imposed sanctions on Chile in 1974 and in subsequent years, cutting both military and economic aid (Sigmund 1993, 98–102). These actions represented one of the first successful congressional efforts to tie foreign aid to human rights anywhere in the world. In early 1977 Jimmy Carter took office and with the strong support of human rights groups, he substantially increased the pressure on Chile as a centerpiece of his emphasis on the foreign policy of human rights.

International human rights groups also helped focus UN attention on Chile, which created important precedents for UN action in other countries. Prior to the early 1970s, the United Nations addressed repression in a country only when domestic human rights abuses threatened international peace and security (Kamminga 1992, 88). The Chilean case was the first to break this precedent. UN General Assembly resolutions condemning the military regime—which began in 1974 and continued uninterrupted for fourteen more years—made no reference to threats to regional peace (Sánchez 1990, 91–97). Likewise, when the UN Human Rights Commission began investigating human rights abuses in Chile in 1974, it relied for the first time solely on human rights procedures without invoking the existence of an international threat (Kamminga 1992, 94; Vargas 1990). No longer did the international community require a threat to international peace to justify action against a repressive state.

International and domestic human rights norms shared among Western states and Chilean social groups facilitated this flurry of activity. The strength of Chilean human rights norms contributed to international shock and motivated international action. States and organizations that might have otherwise been reluctant to condemn human rights abuses felt justified in a case where the actions so clearly violated domestic norms. Intergovernmental organizations appealed to recently developed international norms to justify their monitoring missions. States appealed to the same norms when condemning Chile in the United Nations and when imposing sanctions. Organizations within the transnational human rights network used international and domestic norms as baselines by which to judge the Chilean regime. Their reports and the resulting media attention spelled out the nature of the expectation and the nature of the violation in clear and compelling ways.

At an even deeper level, the existence of human rights norms created the possibility of international action.[4] It is difficult to imagine much international action against Chile in the absence of international human rights norms. After all, the Westphalian state system had existed for hundreds of years without such an international outcry. Sustained international action on behalf of human rights was inconceivable prior to World War II. Newly developed human rights norms created a social basis of understanding in which international action was conceivable, permissible, and even expected. New international organizations were identified by their commitment to these norms. Human rights norms thus played a constitutive role in the formation of the network by articulating the types of understandings that made network formation possible.

Effects of the Transnational Network

The turmoil of the Allende years and the brutality of the military's first months in power decimated Chilean social and political groups. Yet Chileans' commitments to human rights ideals and democratic traditions did not simply vanish in the chaos of 1973, nor did they evaporate along with the smoke of the bombs that fell during the coup. Human rights organizations were among the first social groups to emerge from the ashes of the coup, and human rights issues provided an important rallying cry for the first weak attempts to oppose the military regime.

Transnational ties quickly formed between domestic human rights groups and international actors. International organizations provided financial aid and international recognition to struggling domestic groups, making it more difficult for the military regime to repress them entirely. In turn, domestic Chilean organizations offered information about the nature of human rights abuses to international actors. Over time, these linkages flourished, allowing groups to rapidly transfer information, money, and ideas within the network. Although network groups never coordinated strategies, as with the anti-dam coalition in Sanjeev Khagram's chapter, or engaged in multicountry mobilizations, as with the women's movement in Karen Brown Thompson's chapter, they did learn from each other and reinforce each other's work.

The transnational human rights network achieved three types of success in Chile. First, transnational linkages mitigated the impact of human rights abuses by providing aid for victims. Although human rights activists never won any important court cases or direct concessions from the military regime, they helped untold numbers of victims through legal, financial, and psychological aid. Second, the network preserved some political space for domestic human rights groups and academic institutions, allowing them to function during periods of intense repression. Transnational ties were crucial to the survival of domestic groups during the darkest days of state terror in the mid-1970s. Third, the transnational human rights network grew over time and took on a more overtly political cast. Ultimately, transnational ties strengthened political opposition groups and enabled them to mount serious challenges to military rule in the 1980s. As a result, the network successfully pressured the regime to guarantee free and fair conditions for a 1988 plebiscite on President Augusto Pinochet's rule. So fair were the conditions that Pinochet lost the plebiscite and was forced from office.

In order to illustrate these network successes, I focus on three aspects and periods: (1) the first human rights groups affiliated with Chilean churches in the early to mid-1970s; (2) the emergence and importance of social science academic centers in the 1970s; and (3) the growth of the network from human rights issues into a more overtly political network in the 1980s that openly and actively worked to end the military regime.

Churches and Human Rights Groups

At first, the transnational human rights network was centered around the Catholic Church and other churches that could build on preexisting international ties, high visibility, apolitical credentials, and wide social respect.[5]

Churches were the first domestic actors to set up human rights groups and to funnel information about repression in Chile to the outside world (Fruhling 1983, 1989; Fruhling and Orellana 1991; and Hutchison 1991). While the Argentine and Uruguayan Catholic Churches guarded their silence in the face of repression, the Chilean Catholic Church—historically more progressive than its counterparts—responded relatively quickly to human rights abuses (Fruhling 1989).

In the weeks following the coup, Jewish, Catholic, Orthodox, and Protestant church leaders created two human rights organizations: the National Committee to Aid Refugees (CONAR) and the Committee of Cooperation for Peace (COPACHI). Both groups did the best they could to help refugees leave the country and to provide minimal legal, financial, and emotional assistance to human rights victims. They mitigated some of the worst human rights abuses and created small political spaces on which later organizations could build. Despite the limited scope of its activities, COPACHI attracted the attention of the military regime, which condemned it publicly and pressured privately for its dissolution (Fruhling 1983, 516–23).

Under extreme pressure, church leaders disbanded COPACHI in 1975 but quickly replaced it with the Vicariate of Solidarity—an organization that became an international symbol of humanitarian resistance to state terror (Lowden 1996). While COPACHI had been an ecumenical institution, the Vicariate was an ecclesiastical body placed under the personal protection of Santiago Archbishop and Cardinal Raúl Silva Henríquez. When the regime attempted to move against the Vicariate as it had against COPACHI, Catholic bishops and the international church closed ranks on its behalf (Smith 1982, 318–19). The Vicariate survived and played a crucial role by distributing information on human rights abuses to international and domestic audiences, by providing institutional and political space for opposition groups, and by aiding several thousand victims of human rights abuse. For example, between 1974 and 1979, COPACHI and the Vicariate sent an estimated 1,720 human rights petitions to international organizations on behalf of 1,928 individuals (Detzner 1991, 92–96).

International financial support for the Chilean Catholic Church was absolutely essential to these human rights activities. As Brian Smith has noted, "None of the new projects begun under the auspices of the Chilean Church since 1973 could have been inaugurated or sustained over time without very considerable outside support" (325). International actors donated an estimated hundred million dollars to the Chilean Church from 1974 to 1979, dwarfing the total of $4 million dollars the church received during the same period from its domestic tithing campaigns (325–26).

Nearly all of the international grant money targeted economic development and human rights programs. The money came from a mixture of private and public sources, mostly North European and West German church organizations and the U.S. and West German governments (Smith 1982). Thus, Chile offers some case study support for Sikkink and Smith's general claim in chapter 2 that U.S. and European organizations are fundamentally important in financing social change organizations in developing countries.

The international ties of Chilean churches offered visibility and legitimacy to their human rights efforts and helped protect them in the face of repression. In 1977, Pinochet publicly accused the World Council of Churches of sending more than two million dollars annually to the Vicariate to be used for subversive purposes. The Chilean Church responded with vigorous denials and praised the work of both the Vicariate and the World Council. Military regime officials soon ceased public criticisms of this type of international currency transfer (Smith 1982, 328). In 1978, the military regime took stronger action when it froze funds being transferred from the U.S.-based Inter-American Foundation to Catholic Church–sponsored programs. The ensuing outcry over the illegitimacy of this move from church officials and international actors soon forced the military regime to back down (328–29). In this case the military regime certainly had the legal authority to stop the transfer of funds and the ability and desire to do so, but the transnational and religious status of these groups helped protect them.

The military regime's reluctance to do away with human rights groups completely and the church's success in protecting them reflects both the social and political weight of the Catholic Church in Chile and its transnational status. The Chilean Catholic Church had created a series of strong transnational ties long before the coup occurred, receiving funding, information, and education abroad (287–94). These ties helped sustain the church in the face of heavy regime pressure in the 1970s. Additionally, most church leaders carefully avoided any political stances, arguing that they were engaging in purely humanitarian activities to protect the well-being of individuals in a chaotic situation. Their religious status provided them with a normative position that enabled them to survive repression and pursue human rights work. As a result, government officials did not completely crush church-related human rights organizations as they did labor unions, leftist parties, and other groups.

Social Science Research

International financial support for Chilean social scientific research institutions during the 1970s and 1980s offers a second example of a transnational activity that fostered small political spaces in the midst of repression. Soon after the coup, the military regime outlawed student organizations; named high-ranking military officers to run the universities; purged faculty, staff, and students from university rolls; and implemented a climate of fear that brought most research to a halt (Constable and Valenzuela 1991, 251–56). The Catholic Church and international donors responded by setting up small independent research institutes where many social scientists sought refuge. During the 1970s, these institutes carefully limited their scholarship to relatively noncontroversial topics and restricted the circulation of their ideas. Over time, the repressive climate eased and international donors poured more money into social science in Chile. By the late 1980s, at least fifty social science research institutes openly published a wide range of analyses. Collectively, they received as much as 95 percent of their budgets from abroad, an estimated three million dollars annually (Angell 1994, 23; Puryear 1991, 7).

This international funding of independent research centers in the 1970s and 1980s helped protect important political and social space in Chile. During periods of severe repression, as in the mid-1970s, academic institutes provided one of the few safe havens in which intellectuals and opposition leaders could exchange information, articulate their ideas, and even circulate critical analyses as academic work. Although these analyses and ideas were not distributed to a wider audience, research centers provided a home in which elites could preserve dissident thought and build a base for more open critiques should the political winds shift.

As with church-sponsored human rights organizations, the military regime was reluctant to crack down on research institutions protected by transnational ties and by formally apolitical agendas. Junta records show that in March 1979 the military regime debated what to do with Facultad Latinoamericana de Ciencias Sociales (FLACSO), a social scientific institution headquartered in Santiago, set up under the auspices of the United Nations Educational, Scientific, and Cultural Council (UNESCO) and financed by Latin American governments and international private donor foundations. FLACSO had become a well-known gathering place for scholarly critics of the military regime and also provided a place for leaders of opposition political groups to gather and exchange ideas. In 1978–79, military regime officials attempted to force FLACSO out of Santiago by withdrawing from the international agreement establishing FLACSO, cutting off more than $100,000 in annual funds that the Chilean regime had committed to provide FLACSO and passing a law that would take away FLACSO's legal personality in Chile as an international organization (Act de la Junta

No. 365-A, 21 March 1979). Despite these efforts, FLACSO survived and became one of the leading research institutions in Chile and an important political actor itself in the 1980s.

If Pinochet preferred to terminate FLACSO's stay in Santiago, why did the regime fail to do so? The regime was certainly militarily capable of shutting down FLACSO and was legally capable of exiling its chief scholars. After all, regime officials had previously outlawed the powerful Christian Democratic party and exiled or imprisoned many of its top leaders. One key difference between FLACSO and the Christian Democratic party was that FLACSO was clearly a transnational organization and was protected by its international status. A second key difference is that FLACSO was an educational institution dedicated to scientific knowledge. Although the Junta's legal advisors drafted legislation that took away all of FLACSO's benefits under Chilean law, they failed to take the final step and simply disband FLACSO.

The existence of human rights and academic groups during the harshest periods of repression stood as a beacon of hope for other groups. Human rights and academic groups survived state terror in part because of their strong transnational ties and in part because they could use religion and knowledge as a way to partially deflect regime repression. In the 1970s, these groups constituted the nucleus of the human rights network inside Chile. Although it posed a long-term threat to Pinochet's power, the network did not exist with the express purpose of gaining power. Rather, network groups shared principled moral beliefs in the importance of human rights and acted on that basis. As Khagram, Riker, and Sikkink note in the first chapter and as Kidder emphasizes in the context of labor unions, these principled beliefs distinguish networks from other kinds of transnational organizing.

From Human Rights to Politics

In the mid-1980s, the network broadened its scope to include new groups and began to focus on a seminal political event, the looming plebiscite on Pinochet's rule. Human rights groups realized that winning the plebiscite offered the single best opportunity to dramatically improve the human rights situation. As a result, they linked hands with labor unions, opposition media sources, political parties, and international actors of all sorts to ensure a free and fair vote and to win the plebiscite. In short, the network in the mid-1980s became more explicitly focused on a political goal, although that goal also had a moral character, and the network retained its essential nature as an exchange mechanism for information and money.

International funding moved in tandem with the broadening of the network. While in the 1970s international actors had focused on church-related human rights and research groups, in the 1980s donors broadened their support to include more overtly political organizations. These funds, which may have totaled as much as fifty-five million dollars a year between 1985 and 1988 (Angell 1994), helped rebuild the strength of political parties, labor unions, and media organizations that had been decimated by years of repression.[6]

New kinds of international donors helped provide these new funds. Significantly, foreign governments became major donors of political aid in the 1980s, in part because churches and international human rights groups were reluctant to tarnish their nonpartisan images.[7] German political foundations funded by the German government and closely affiliated with German political parties and trade unions provided a large part of this aid (Pinto-Duschinsky 1991, 33–35). From 1983 to 1988, German political foundations funneled twenty-six million dollars to Chilean trade unions, political parties, neighborhood self-help organizations, media sources, and other social groups. The United States also provided $6.8 million in political aid between 1984 and 1988, much of it to ensure that Chile held a free and fair plebiscite in 1988 (Pinto-Duschinsky 1991, 40). Additionally, political parties, trade unions, political foundations and NGOs in Italy, Holland, and elsewhere provided an unknown amount of money for the Chilean opposition during this same period.[8]

Transnational social and ideological ties helped determine which network actors received international financial assistance and which did not. Many Chilean human rights activists and opposition politicians had been educated or worked professionally in the United States, Europe, and elsewhere prior to the coup. Additionally, tens of thousands of Chileans were exiled to dozens of countries after the coup. Exiles and domestic opposition actors alike used their international contacts to lobby foreign governments and to funnel aid to selected domestic groups.

Although it is difficult to judge with certainty, center-left groups probably benefited the most from transnational ties. Nearly two-thirds of the German money, for example, was provided by the Konrad Adenauer Foundation, affiliated with the Christian Democrats. The foundation directed about 90 percent of the aid to a coalition of moderate-left groups, while the remainder went to moderate-right groups who supported Pinochet but called for a quick and complete transition to democracy (Pinto-Duschinsky 1991, 38–40). The moderate wing of the Chilean Socialist Party, which had strong ties to Western Europe, likely received more assistance than the leftist wing, with its ties to Eastern Europe (Angell 1994). The moderate wing undoubtedly had greater access to the Western media and to key actors in Western states, offering it a higher profile and a greater opportunity for influence. Labor unions, research institutions, and media sources affiliated with Christian Democrats all gained prominence among opposition actors and were presumably well-funded from abroad.

Although differences in funding and ideology created asymmetries within the network, as Sikkink suggests in the concluding chapter, the consequences of these asymmetries are unclear. Domestic network actors retained a certain level of unity in the face of the threat posed by the military regime. This unity was most in evidence during the 1988 electoral campaign to unseat Pinochet. Only the Communists dissented from the opposition's electoral strategy, and even they switched tactics at the last minute. A certain plurality may have even helped the network, as different actors pursued different strategies and tactics that all worked toward the same goal of improving human rights and removing Pinochet. At the same time, groups affiliated with well-established actors like the Christian Democrats, the Socialists, and the Catholic Church undoubtedly received more attention and funding than grassroots human rights organizations or shantytown protesters. It is not surprising that the strategies of well-established actors—dialogue, patience, playing by electoral rules—won out over the preferences of popular-based organizations for confrontation and high levels of mobilization (Schneider 1995; Oxhorn 1995).

The politicization and expansion of the network is also illustrated by the explicitly political tone of social science research in the mid- to late 1980s. Research institutes served as meeting places for opposition leaders, allowed intellectuals to articulate and communicate dissident thought, and provided an academic platform useful in openly criticizing the military regime (Angell 1994, 21–24; Puryear 1991, 16–25). For example, in the mid-1980s, foreign funding enabled researchers at academic centers to carry out extensive public opinion polls (Puryear 1991, 10–21). Opposition leaders soon realized the strategic importance of these polls for winning the scheduled 1988 plebiscite on Pinochet's rule. Drawing on foreign funding, Chilean academics and opposition politicians brought the U.S. political consulting group Sawyer/Miller to Chile to teach them modern political campaign techniques. In consultation with Sawyer/Miller, opposition groups used public opinion polls and in-depth focus groups to formulate a campaign strategy that was then used to unseat Pinochet (Puryear 1991, 10–21).

Finally, international political aid helped ensure that free and fair voting procedures would be respected in the 1988 plebiscite. Widespread doubts that the regime would hold a fair plebiscite led international actors to provide money for voter registration drives, the training of poll watchers, and election-night monitoring activities (Puryear 1991, 6; Sigmund 1993, 167–74). Most significantly, foreign funding allowed the opposition parties to install a nationwide system to tabulate votes that would provide an independent check on the regime's vote tally (International Human Rights Law Group 1989). The night of the plebiscite, opposition parties announced accurate election results, taking away any regime opportunity to announce fraudulent numbers (Cavallo, Salazar, and Sepúlveda 1989, 566–88). The presence of hundreds of international election monitors also helped ensure that the plebiscite would be clean. International political aid, in short, placed strong constraints on the regime and gave the opposition the resources needed to win the 1988 plebiscite.

Engaging the State: International Monitoring

Monitoring played a central role in the growth and success of the transnational network. Chile lacked the relatively open political opportunity structure available to groups such as anti-dam activists in India, as discussed by Khagram in chapter 10. As a result, the Chilean network developed monitoring as the crucial mechanism by which human rights norms could be translated into action. Network actors possessed few material resources, but excelled at gathering and communicating information about the nature of human rights abuses in Chile. Monitoring helped make the networks effective by (1) facilitating the flow of information out of Chile; (2) legitimizing the substance of that information thanks to the reputations of impartiality of the monitors; (3) motivating Western states to pressure the military regime; and (4) providing a way for international actors to engage the military regime despite its closed nature.

While monitoring to ensure compliance with international agreements was scarcely a new idea in the 1970s, Chile represented one of the first efforts to monitor human rights issues in a country on an ongoing, intensive basis. In the months following the coup, international human rights observers, both governmental and nongovernmental, traveled to Chile to investigate reported abuses. For intergovernmental human rights organizations such as the IACHR and the UN Human Rights Commission, their consideration of Chile represented a sharp break from the traditional practice of avoiding specific cases and opting instead for general statements in support of human rights norms. Both organizations produced numerous reports and condemnations over the life of the military regime, opening the door for similar action in other countries.

During the first several months following the coup, Chilean military regime officials surprised observers by cooperating, to a certain extent, with international monitoring. The military regime did not, of course, simply throw open its prisons and secret files for all who wished to see. However, regime officials cooperated with the IACHR by accepting two commission-sponsored visits to Chile in 1973–74, by allowing delegates access to detention centers and military trials, by facilitating interviews with alleged human rights victims, and by maintaining open and cooperative communication with the commission (Medina Quiroga 1988, 263–66). Similarly, the military regime allowed visits in 1974 by the International Labor Organization and other issue-specific groups.

Although it is difficult to say what motivated the military regime to cooperate with international monitors, two factors appear to have played a key role. First, legal advisors within the military regime argued that Chile was legally obligated to respond positively to these requests. Second, regime officials were eager to show the world their triumph over Marxism and seemed convinced that monitors would find nothing wrong. Even after international human rights NGOs strongly criticized the regime, military officials, gambling on the strong anticommunist sentiment in the Organization of American States, continued to hope that the IACHR report would turn out differently.

Soon after the IACHR issued its first report in October 1974 condemning the military regime, Chile abruptly closed its doors to international monitors. In early 1975, the military regime apparently changed its mind and invited an ad hoc investigative committee from the UN Commission on Human Rights to Chile. However, when committee members met in Lima, Peru, in July 1975, prior to traveling to Chile, Pinochet announced that they would not be allowed into the country. Likewise, the military regime throughout 1975 ignored repeated requests from the IACHR for information on the human rights situation. Other international actors interested in human rights continued to be denied access to Chile.

During the late 1970s and early 1980s the military regime continued to deny access to monitors while simultaneously arguing that the principle of international monitoring was in fact valid. Regime officials argued that monitors were denied access because their methodology was biased, not because they lacked the right to monitor. In their response to the 1974 IACHR report, for example, Chilean officials argued that the IACHR neglected important evidence favorable to the Chilean regime in reaching its conclusion, failed to appreciate the circumstances of civil war that Chile was experiencing, and relied upon undocumented evidence (Medina Quiroga 1988, 272–74). None of these statements challenged the authority of the

IACHR to carry out human rights inspections in Chile or to issue its report. Rather, they focused on complaints about the way in which the IACHR conducted its investigation. This behavior illustrates the strength of human rights norms. Even when regime officials did not buy into those norms, they felt compelled to endorse the substance of those norms and to accept the fact that human rights violations were indeed an international issue.

Chile continued to find fault with international monitoring on procedural grounds until it again opened its doors to limited monitoring in 1985. In late 1978, the United Nations had appointed a special rapporteur to monitor and investigate human rights abuses in Chile. Regime officials had steadfastly refused to cooperate with the rapporteur until mid-1985, when they changed positions and invited him to Chile. He visited Chile a total of four times before the October 1988 plebiscite, receiving some cooperation from the military regime and issuing a number of human rights reports.

Why did Chile once again allow international monitoring? Three factors appear to have influenced the regime's decision. First, regime officials came to believe they could better control the content of international reports by working with the process instead of against it.[9] Second, by the mid-1980s the military regime had embarked on a search for legitimacy at both the domestic and international levels. Third, regime decision makers finally realized that, no matter what their response, they would continue to be targeted for international investigations. Their strategic response was to accept this fact and work to ensure that other state actors would be subjected to the same treatment. Thus, in the 1980s, Chilean diplomats introduced initiatives in the Organization of American States to standardize and systematize the monitoring process. They hoped that other states, such as Cuba and Mexico, would be subjected to the same treatment as Chile, thus diluting the stigma of condemnation.

International efforts to monitor the regime's human rights abuses produced four broad impacts on the military regime. First, international monitoring facilitated the flow of information out of Chile. Even with the protection of the Catholic Church, domestic groups found it very difficult to gather and communicate information on human rights abuses in Chile. Human rights groups risked severe penalties for their activities, operated on extremely limited resources, and routinely failed to overcome widespread fear in Chile, which discouraged people from discussing human rights issues. International actors, by contrast, possessed more significant organizational and financial resources, did not risk retribution, easily communicated the information around the world, and sometimes even enjoyed access to prisoners or officials willing to divulge information.

Second, international monitoring legitimized the substance of that information. Reports of torture and disappearances from domestic opposition groups may not be given much credibility in the international arena unless substantiated by more impartial observers. The IACHR and the UN Commission on Human Rights both carefully cultivated an image of impartiality during their Chilean investigations in the 1970s and 1980s. Investigative teams were composed of professional jurists acting as international civil servants rather than as government representatives. Because they possessed valuable reputations as impartial judges, they spoke with greater authority in the eyes of Western states. International NGOs like Amnesty International also cultivated a careful image of impartiality. The periodic reports of these groups lent credibility to charges of human rights abuses that could otherwise have been seen as politically motivated.

Third, the information gathered through monitoring efforts helped motivate and justify international sanctions on Chile and international financial support for the regime's opposition. Reports issued by the IACHR and UN investigators garnered a wide international audience and provided ammunition for domestic human rights groups in other states. Human rights investigations and subsequent media reports were instrumental in pressuring the U.S. Congress and others to sanction Chile (Salzberg and Young 1977; Schoultz 1981, 74–88). Further, these reports provided a way for information on human rights abuses to work its way back into Chile, thereby completing the boomerang pattern (Keck and Sikkink 1998, 12–13). The Vicariate and other Chilean human rights groups found it nearly impossible to disseminate in the domestic media the information they collected on human rights abuses. Once the information was included in international reports, however, the military regime found it difficult to obstruct its distribution in Chile. The Chilean media often summarized the content of IACHR and UN reports in stories about international condemnations of the military regime. As a result, tales of human rights abuses authenticated by international actors threatened to erode the legitimacy of the military regime in the mid-1970s.

Finally, monitoring provided a way for international actors to engage Chilean officials on human rights issues and to exert political pressure for improved behavior. International actors requested information, compiled reports, and generally used their monitoring authority as a way of demonstrating to the Chilean regime the importance of human rights issues. U.S. executive branch officials and members of Congress would sometimes submit requests to travel to Chile and receive firsthand information on the human rights situation. These requests and subsequent journeys (when allowed) served as not-so-subtle threats that sanctions might be implemented if the human rights situation did not improve.

This analysis illustrates the importance of norms as rules for state behavior. Chilean officials themselves recognized that international actors had a right to inquire into the state of human rights in Chile. Although retaining ultimate authority to allow monitoring only with their assent, regime officials thereby conceded the legitimacy of human rights norms. Twenty years previous, virtually any state in the world would have denounced an international investigation of human rights abuses as intolerable intervention in domestic affairs. In Chile, in the 1970s and 1980s, that argument was rarely used, and regime officials themselves often understood international investigations to be legitimate and legal, though undesired. This legitimation of monitoring provided a way to judge the military regime not only by international standards, but by its own.

In response to constant monitoring, the Chilean regime generally endorsed human rights standards in its official discourse. The regime's chief ideological statement, the Declaration of Principles issued in March 1974, declared that "man has natural rights prior to and superior to the state." According to subsequent regime statements, these rights included virtually every civil and political right generally respected in Western states. Government officials repeatedly insisted that individual liberty formed an integral part of Western, Christian society, of which Chile was a part. In 1976, the Junta drafted constitutional articles guaranteeing human rights, although they never took legal force, and the new 1980 constitution produced by the military government contained impressive human rights guarantees that were nevertheless widely violated. Even when government officials justified human rights abuses, they did so in a way that did not deny the underlying validity of the concept of human rights. They argued, in fact, that they were laying the groundwork for the better protection of rights by instilling stability and order.

Traditional human rights standards, in short, did not simply disappear from Chile in the midst of widespread violations. They were endorsed and kept alive not only by international and domestic actors, but paradoxically by the Chilean military regime itself. Again, this underscores the power of the human rights norms. Government justifications for repression did not question the legitimacy of human rights standards themselves, but rather offered reasons why the standards did not apply to Chile at that time. Government officials in fact encouraged expectations that they would some day wholly respect human rights.

This rhetorical strategy had paradoxical consequences. In the short run, it served the military regime well. Given the deeply ingrained nature of human rights norms in Chile, it would have been counterproductive to simply reject those standards out of hand or to offer substitute norms. Further, regime supporters (including U.S. officials) could cite the official rhetoric to justify their support for military rule. In the long run, however, the strategy worked against the military regime by opening it to charges of hypocrisy. Having endorsed human rights standards and having promised to implement them, the regime was bound to some extent by its own rhetoric if it wished to retain credibility. As order and stability returned to Chile, it became increasingly difficult for regime officials to continue justifying human rights abuses. In the 1980s, continuing repression and the regime's double standard became easy targets for opposition forces.

Conclusions

The Chilean case illustrates both remarkable changes in human rights issues in the past thirty years and important limitations to those changes. Perhaps the most fundamental change is the shift in human rights from being a domestic issue to being an international one. At a different historical moment, there might have been no international reaction to the human rights abuses that followed the Chilean military coup. Human rights norms established in the two decades following World War II made it possible for human rights groups to put Chile's abuses on the international agenda. As a result, the military regime was constantly forced to consider the international repercussions of its human rights abuses and to contend with international actors concerned about human rights.

The emergence and growth of numerous transnational human rights networks similar to the Chilean network constitutes another important change in international affairs. The Chilean case demonstrates that a human rights network can emerge and grow rapidly in response to events in one particular country, but suggests that such rapid growth is more likely after international norms have been established. By creating a social context that sanctioned and made possible the activities and identities of key actors, the human rights norms developed after World War II helped produce the Chilean network. In Khagram's, Riker's, and Sikkink's terminology, both the "push" of Pinochet's repression and the "pull" of international norms facilitated the emergence and growth of the network.

The Chilean network achieved some important successes. Over time, the military regime altered its agenda, discourse, policies, and practices in ways that brought it closer to the demands of human rights groups. It is important not to overstate the nature of this success; the military regime remained repressive until the end. Yet in the absence of the network, it seems likely the regime would have been even more repressive and would have endured even longer. Even this limited success is surprising when compared with other cases, such as Indian dams (Khagram) or U.S. foreign policy (Thomas) because it occurred in the context of a closed domestic political opportunity structure.

Two factors account for the network's success. First, intensive monitoring allowed the network to bypass the domestic limitations and appeal to international actors who could pressure the regime from outside. Thus, a relatively open international political opportunity structure had important domestic political repercussions, as discussed by Khagram, Riker, and Sikkink in chapter 1. The Chilean case demonstrates that monitoring is one of the most powerful tools of network actors because the information can be used simultaneously to delegitimize the targeted regime and encourage international action against it. As Sikkink phrases it in her concluding chapter, impartial and verifiable monitoring offered moral authority to the Chilean network, and thus explains how the network could influence an otherwise closed regime.

Second, networks benefited from strong human rights norms and utilized them to produce changes in the regime. This result confirms Khagram, Riker, and Sikkink's central hypothesis that a combination of strong networks and strong norms will produce the largest changes in targeted states. It seems unlikely that international norms alone, absent the concerted effort of the Chilean human rights network, would have put many constraints on the authoritarian regime in Chile. Authoritarian regimes facing less developed networks but the same set of international norms—for example, Mexico—were under far less pressure to change in the 1970s and 1980s (Khagram, Riker, and Sikkink this volume; Keck and Sikkink 1998, 110–16). At the same time, the network alone—absent strong human rights norms—would not have been as effective. In this respect, it is significant that the network focused on rights related to personal integrity and civil liberties, which are more well-established internationally than other kinds of rights. In particular, it is difficult to imagine that a network focusing on economic and social rights would have had the same level of success as the Chilean network. In fact, some Chilean and international NGOs did focus on the individual costs to the poor of Pinochet's neoliberal economic program, but without much success.

It is equally important to stress that advocacy networks found fertile soil in Chile. In many countries international actors seeking to promote human rights have found few domestic actors receptive to their pressure and few opposition groups able to push a domestic human rights campaign. In Chile, however, several decades of democracy and respect for human rights created strong normative expectations that the state would continue to respect individual rights. These norms facilitated the emergence of a domestic opposition around human rights issues and a set of linkages between the opposition and international actors. These findings suggest that the effectiveness of networks depends on the normative structure of each country. Where domestic norms are stronger, historically grounded, and congruent with international norms, transnational networks are likely to have greater impact.

The recent transnational and domestic prosecution of Pinochet illustrates the long-term impact of the network that existed in the 1970s and 1980s, and its changing character in the 1990s and early 2000s. When Pinochet stepped down as president of Chile in 1990, he had built a strong system of protection against prosecution that included constitutional guarantees, friendly appointees in the court system, an electoral system that favored conservative parties, and social and legal taboos on prosecuting military officials. Since then, human rights groups have worked hard to bring Pinochet and other Chilean officials to justice. Stymied at the domestic level, they organized transnationally by filing complaints and compiling documentation in Spanish courts (Wilson 1999). An activist Spanish judge drew on domestic and international law to request Pinochet's extradition. Many of the documents essential to this effort were originally compiled by network groups using standard monitoring procedures in the 1970s and 1980s. A British court then drew on new international norms—in particular, the torture treaty of the mid-1980s—to authorize extradition. Ultimately, Pinochet was returned to Chile, where the intense international activity helped break down the domestic barriers to prosecution. The once unthinkable—prosecuting Pinochet in Chile for human rights abuses—became possible. Networks and norms were responsible for this change, just as they were in the 1970s and 1980s. As in previous decades, however, results fell short of expectations as Pinochet's legal defense team found new ways to prevent prosecution.

More broadly, human rights norms and networks have succeeded in opening an international political contest over the location of authority for individual well-being. Seen from an international perspective, states have held exclusive authority over individuals for centuries. To a large extent, states still retain that authority. Individuals still depend on the state as the primary guarantor or violator of human rights. As Ruggie argues, human rights issues have not revolutionized the nature of international relations by breaking down the fundamental authority of states (1983, 104–6). At the same time, human rights norms and networks have begun to challenge those authority claims in successful ways. Even if no revolution has occurred, a gradual evolution is well underway. Human rights networks and norms are restructuring world politics by creating stronger rules by which states must abide, and by holding them accountable to those rules. In this way, states no longer hold exclusive authority over their citizens to do as they wish with their lives. Rather, states share that authority with transnational human rights groups who help enact and enforce human rights norms.

Notes

I would like to thank my fellow participants in the MacArthur Consortium, and especially Kathryn Sikkink and Dan Thomas, for helpful comments on previous versions of this paper. In addition, Helen Kinsella and Ann Holder offered useful comments at the final stages of the revision. I acknowledge the generous financial support of the John D. and Catherine T. MacArthur Foundation, provided through the Global Studies Program at the University of Wisconsin, and the support of the Latin American and Iberian Studies Program at the University of Wisconsin.

1. A copy of this speech is located in the Fundación Jaime Guzmán, Santiago, Chile.

2. For a general overview of pariah states in international history, see Geldenhuys 1992.

3. Useful overviews of the evolution of international human rights norms may be found in Donnelly 1986 and 1989 and in Forsythe 2000.

4. On the constitutive role of norms and social understandings, see Kratochwil 1989 and Wendt 1992.

5. For more on the importance of the Catholic Church in transnational networks, see Donnelly in this volume.

6. Finding data on international support for political groups is even more difficult than for academic and human rights organizations. A particularly comprehensive account may be found in an article titled "Money: Black, White . . . and Political" in *El Mercurio,* 24 January 1988.

7. Political aid may be defined as a form of funding that "aims to exercise a direct influence on the working of politics within a foreign country. Frequently the objective is to encourage a change from military or one-party government to an elective democracy" (Pinto-Duschinsky 1991).

8. For example, Italian political groups apparently provided twenty million dollars to Chilean NGOs between 1987 and 1992, including nine million that Chilean leftist parties allegedly spent directly on campaign expenses during the 1989 parliamentary and presidential elections. See *Que Pasa,* 14 May 1994.

9. Interview with a high-level cabinet minister of the mid-1980s, Santiago, Chile, April 1994.

4

Human Rights in U.S. Foreign Policy

Daniel C. Thomas

This chapter argues that transnational networks of nonstate actors gain greater access and influence over states when they identify their cause with prevailing international norms, defined as standards of appropriate behavior for actors with a given identity in world politics. To illustrate the importance of international norms for network influence, the chapter explains the rise of human rights in U.S. foreign policy toward Eastern Europe and the Soviet Union during the mid-1970s, when human rights activists living under repressive communist regimes used the norms of the Helsinki Final Act to network with sympathetic legislators, journalists, and activists in the United States. The "Helsinki network" documented the East bloc's violations of human rights, highlighted the U.S. government's failure to press for compliance with the Final Act, and thus overcame powerful forces within the White House and State Department favoring a traditional realpolitik agenda in relations with the Soviet Union and Eastern Europe. This movement of human rights from a peripheral concern to the center of American policy began before the arrival of the Carter administration, which is often credited with introducing human rights to U.S. foreign policy, and accelerated after Carter's inauguration despite the reluctance of his senior advisors.

Analysis of this historically significant shift in U.S. foreign policy thus demonstrates that international norms can empower transnational network actors even in the absence of any initial intention by states to implement or monitor the norm in question. The weakness of alternative explanations is discussed before the chapter's conclusions.

The Argument

International norms enable transnational networks to mobilize and achieve influence beyond their command of traditional power resources because world politics is as much about authority and legitimacy as it is about material resources. As Inis Claude points out, "politics inevitably requires that power be converted into authority, competence be supported by jurisdiction, and possession be validated as ownership" (1967, 74). Max Weber spoke likewise of "the generally observable need of any power, or any advantage of life, to justify itself" (1968, 953). Even Hans Morgenthau, elaborating on his famous claim that "states pursue interests defined as power," acknowledges that power that can be justified in terms of international law or morality (which he called "legitimate power") is far more useful than that which lacks normative justification (1993, 32; see also Beetham 1991). "The principle is the same," Claude adds, "whether we are dealing with those who want the *is* to be recognized as the *ought*, or those who are setting out to convert their *ought* into a newly established *is*" (1967, 74, emphasis in original). As a result, the deployment and engagement of competing justifications becomes a highly significant political process, and justifications themselves become a source of political influence. In the quest for international authority and legitimacy, though, not all justifications or reasons for action are created equal.

International norms have special authority as issue frames and justifications for action in international society because they are established by groups of states, rather than asserted by a single state and reducible to its ideology or preferences.[1] International norms are thus the preeminent vocabulary of international society, which both state and nonstate actors use to justify their existence, their goals, and their behavior. They enable state actors to pressure other states to change their behavior without appearing to be acting unilaterally or arbitrarily. They provide state actors with political justifications that increase the credibility of sanctions and undermine the ability of target states to escape via third-party alliances.[2]

The ability of nonstate actors to exploit this "language of state action" (Ruggie 1983, 196) helps us explain both the emergence of particular transnational networks and their surprising influence over states, which otherwise remain far more powerful (see Hawkins, this volume). International norms promote the emergence of transnational networks by expanding the actual or expected political opportunities available to nonstate actors (see Tarrow 1998). First, state actors are more likely to respond positively to the demands of nonstate actors that identify with international norms. This is true both because most states value the legitimacy they gain by appearing to comply with international norms, and because they value the material goods that others may link to certain behaviors.[3] Second, formal acceptance of international norms by state actors whose actual behavior contradicts the norms can signal the possibility of a tentative or internally contested move toward policy change, which nonstate actors may seek to encourage, resist, or exploit. In either case, anything that appears to limit the willingness of state actors to exercise their advantage in material power over nonstate actors encourages transnational mobilization.

International norms also increase the potential effectiveness of transnational networks whose purposes coincide with the purposes of the norms.[4] States whose practices are delegitimated by new international norms find that the political terrain has been tilted in favor of political challengers (both state and nonstate) committed to implementation of the new norms. Likewise, states that once accorded low priority to a particular issue find it more difficult to resist appeals for support from transnational networks whose position on the issue is consistent with international norms. The creation of a new international norm will thus expand the political clout of sympathetic nonstate actors by enabling them to build new domestic and transnational coalitions, by legitimizing their claims, and by enhancing their access to state decision makers and international organizations. Finally, transnational network actors sometimes appeal directly to the international organizations or conferences that monitor and assess compliance with the norms that interest them. Nonstate actors committed to the implementation of a particular international norm by one state may even use another state's rhetorical commitment to the norm to engage its influence when that state would otherwise prefer to remain uninvolved.

This dynamic is complicated by the fact that a particular international norm may not be interpreted the same way by all relevant actors, and by the fact that political confrontations often engage coexisting but contradictory international norms. As a result, when state and nonstate actors refer to a norm to justify pressure against another state, the target state is likely to try to reinterpret the norm or to use another norm consistent with its purposes to justify its noncompliance with the first norm (Kratochwil and Ruggie 1986, 768). Transnational networks of nonstate actors thus seek to ensure that their confrontations with state actors are framed in terms of the norm most favorable to their purposes, and to influence the collective interpretation of any contested norms. For nonstate actors dependent upon international norms, to neglect the dynamics of issue framing would be akin to an army allowing its adversary to select the battlefield and the weapons.

As the following case study demonstrates, the empowerment of transnational networks through international norms is sometimes an unintended result of traditional diplomacy between states. This feedback from traditional diplomacy to transnational network effectiveness may involve a three- or four-step process. In the simple model, state actors negotiate to create new international norms, even though some of these state actors may have no intention of complying or promoting the new norm; the new norms facilitate the formation of transnational networks by nonstate actors sympathetic to the purposes of the norm; and finally, network actors use the political justifications provided by the norm to persuade state actors to change their behavior or even to revise the understandings of state interests that drive policy. Sometimes, though, as in the case presented in this chapter, nonstate actors seeking to shape the behavior or identity of one state use the international norms to affect the foreign policy of another state, whose influence is then brought to bear on the initial target state.[5]

Case Study: East-West Relations and Helsinki Norms

The Conference on Security and Cooperation in Europe (CSCE) was launched in 1972 as a multilateral forum to bridge the East-West divide in Europe and to improve relations in a broad range of issue areas.[6] On 1 August 1975, the heads of the thirty-five participating states came to Helsinki to sign a "Final Act" establishing basic norms for relations among European states and identifying opportunities for continued cooperation. Among the ten basic norms established by the Helsinki Final Act, one committed the CSCE states to practice "non-intervention in internal affairs" of other states, while another committed them to ensure "respect for human rights and fundamental freedoms" within their borders. Other portions of the Final Act reinforced the human rights norm by committing the CSCE states to expand cooperation in "humanitarian" fields, including the freer flow of people, ideas, and information across borders. These normative references to human rights represented a clear departure from several decades of diplomatic rhetoric and political practice on both sides of the divide that explicitly excluded such issues from the agenda of East-West relations.[7]

While the Helsinki agreement seemed to give unprecedented legitimacy to reviews of human rights implementation in any East-West negotiations, including subsequent CSCE meetings, the interpretation and relative salience of the human rights and nonintervention norms remained to be determined. This was where a transnational network of nonstate and eventually substate actors became significant. Almost immediately, longtime dissidents and newly inspired activists in Eastern Europe and the Soviet Union showered their governments with appeals for political reform and the protection of human rights. Interpreting their governments' relatively lenient response to these protests as evidence of a desire to be seen as compliant with Helsinki norms, domestic opposition activists across the East bloc began in mid-1976 to move toward the creation of truly independent groups, or social movement organizations. This mobilization of opposition is especially noteworthy in light of the near absence of dissent in the early 1970s. Given the entrenched nature of communist regimes, though, the influence of Western governments was required to produce any substantial change in East bloc practice.

Creating the Transnational "Helsinki Network"

At the same time that they were testing the limits of dissent within the communist bloc, East European activists also established new, transnational ties to substate and nonstate actors in the West. As word about Helsinki violations and Helsinki-oriented movements reached the West, private transnational actors began to pressure East bloc regimes for compliance. In June 1976, for example, the Italian and Spanish communist parties lobbied successfully for a recommitment to Helsinki's human rights norms at the Conference of Communist and Workers' Parties in East Berlin. Later that summer, Catholic bishops in the West called on the Czechoslovak government to adhere to Helsinki principles by releasing political prisoners and protecting the freedom of religion (UPI/Reuters newswire item, Bonn, Linz, 19 August 1976). Meanwhile, within Protestant circles, the World Council of Churches and its affiliate, the Conference of European Churches, continued to focus on the meaning of Helsinki norms for "the service of human beings in Europe" (Conference of European Churches 1976, 15). This private pressure afforded some measure of protection for Helsinki activists within the communist bloc. What these Helsinki activists really wanted, though, was the protection to be gained by engaging the attention of foreign governments.

Following the Helsinki summit, the U.S. State Department continued with its implicit policy, in place since the beginning of negotiations, that the CSCE should be tolerated, but not emphasized in East-West relations. Overall, U.S. policy downplayed the CSCE and the human rights issue. In fact, when one of the U.S. negotiators at Geneva returned to the State Department after the summit and initiated measures to monitor compliance with the Helsinki Final Act, he was instructed by senior officials that the CSCE was now completed and no longer required attention.[8]

There was also little reason to expect that the U.S. Congress would take a substantially different position. Except for the politically charged issue of emigration and refuseniks, which catalyzed the Jackson-Vanik amendment of 1973, the U.S. Congress was not especially engaged with human rights issues in the East bloc during the early and mid-1970s.[9] Most members of Congress viewed the CSCE negotiations in Geneva, at best, as a necessary evil for the maintenance of détente, and at worst, as a concession to continued Soviet hegemony. When the Congress's Committee on Foreign Affairs held hearings during the CSCE negotiations, not a single member asked executive branch officials about the CSCE's human rights content, or its likely effects in that area (U.S. House 1972).

In August 1975, several weeks after the Helsinki summit, a congressional delegation went to the Soviet Union for a routine visit. One member of the delegation, Representative Millicent Fenwick of New Jersey, was particularly struck by the lengths to which Soviet refuseniks (those refused emigration visas by the authorities) would go to meet the delegation. "We would meet them at night in hotels in Moscow and Leningrad," she later recalled, "and I would ask, 'How do you dare to come see us here?'" under the eyes of the KGB. "Don't you understand?" they replied. "That's our only hope. We've seen you. Now they know you've seen us" (Albright and Friendly 1986, 291).

This expression of the power of international oversight on behalf of human rights deeply moved the first-term representative. Her interest took concrete shape during a subsequent meeting, organized by an American newspaper correspondent, with longtime dissident Yuri Orlov and refusenik activist Vaniamin Levich at the home of Valentin Turchin, head of the Moscow chapter of Amnesty International. Orlov in particular expressed his belief that the recently signed Helsinki Final Act could provide leverage against the Soviet regime, and urged Fenwick and her colleagues to take advantage of this opportunity.[10]

Representative Fenwick had no prior experience in foreign policy and did not represent a particularly East European constituency, but these encounters in Russia had a powerful effect on her. Brezhnev described Fenwick as "obsessive" after she pressed him on several humanitarian cases during a meeting before the delegation's departure (Korey 1993, 23). She returned to Washington committed to using the Helsinki Accords and American influence on behalf of those whom she had met.

Establishing a Network Bastion within the U.S. Government

On 5 September, within days of her return, Fenwick introduced a bill proposing that the U.S. Congress establish a Commission on Security and

Cooperation in Europe, which would monitor compliance with the Helsinki Final Act, particularly in the human rights field.[11] Twelve days later, Senator Clifford Case, a fellow Republican from New Jersey, introduced a parallel bill in the other chamber.

The executive branch immediately opposed Fenwick's CSCE monitoring initiative. President Ford had been heavily criticized from all sides for his participation in "another Yalta," and, with the summit past, his political advisors hoped to let the CSCE issue fade away. Within the State Department, the Final Act was considered "yesterday's news."[12] Senior officials continued to view Eastern Europe as part of the Soviet Union's natural sphere of influence.[13] Henry Kissinger, who was never a CSCE enthusiast or a proponent of human rights in foreign policy, viewed the proposed commission as an intrusion into the prerogative of the executive branch and as an obstacle to the highly personalized method of "shuttle diplomacy" that he preferred.

The proposed commission did represent a major new congressional foray into foreign affairs, reaching well beyond the 1973 Jackson-Vanik amendment which linked most favored nation (MFN) status to the emigration policies of communist states, but did not involve detailed congressional oversight into conditions abroad. The Department of State also argued that the proposed commission would violate the Constitution by subordinating the executive branch to legislators in the making of foreign policy. Assistant Secretary of State for Congressional Relations Robert J. McCloskey testified that the commission's "extraordinary composition would not seem to provide an appropriate or effective means for coordinating or guiding our efforts" (U.S. Senate 1976).

As the months went by, more and more news reached the West about this new, Helsinki-focused wave of human rights activity in the East. Human rights and émigré organizations in Washington, New York, and Chicago (as well as in Paris, London, Rome, and elsewhere in Western Europe) became transit stations for Helsinki-oriented petitions and appeals from Eastern Europe and the Soviet Union. On the 22 October 1975 Op-Ed page of the *New York Times,* Soviet dissident Andrei Amalrik criticized the U.S. government's tendency to favor good relations with the Kremlin over frank discussion of human rights conditions and compliance with Helsinki norms.

Many of the ethnic lobbies in the United States that had once opposed or been skeptical about the Helsinki Final Act began to reconsider their position in light of the positive response it had evoked in the "home country." Influential Polish, Hungarian, and Czechoslovak émigré organizations endorsed the Case-Fenwick bills, as did the Baltic-American Committee, which had only recently criticized the Final Act for legitimating Soviet rule in

Latvia, Lithuania, and Estonia. At a February 1976 meeting in Brussels on the problem of Jewish emigration from the Soviet Union, members of Congress heard delegates from around the world call on the United States to monitor implementation of the Helsinki Final Act (*Cong. Rec.* 1976, 14051–52).

Though Representative Dante Fascell, chair of the House Foreign Affairs Committee, was initially "skeptical about the wisdom of setting up yet another governmental entity for such a specific purpose," he was eventually won over by the arguments and political might of the various groups within the Helsinki network (*Cong. Rec.* 1976, 14049). With Fascell's support, bills to create the U.S. Commission on Security and Cooperation in Europe passed the Congress in late May and became law on 3 June 1976.

Still unresigned to the existence of the commission, President Ford then threatened to "pocket veto" the necessary financing legislation. By this point, the Helsinki network of human rights and ethnic solidarity groups in the West was regularly receiving materials from its counterparts in the East, and was experienced in using that material to pressure the U.S. government. For example, on the first anniversary of the Helsinki Final Act, they delivered to Capitol Hill a translation of the Moscow Helsinki Group's recent evaluation of the influence of the Final Act. This firsthand account of Soviet violations reinforced the congressional argument that strict monitoring was absolutely necessary.[14] Faced with such arguments, and a second round of lobbying from the ethnic organizations, President Ford conceded and signed the bill authorizing funds for the U.S. Helsinki Commission (as it was coming to be known). When Yuri Orlov and his fellow activists across the communist bloc concluded that Helsinki norms offered them a new opportunity for transnational lobbying, they never dreamed that their appeals would result in the creation of a new agency within the U.S. government!

Reshaping U.S. Foreign Policy

As indicated above, the initial U.S. policy after the Helsinki summit was to deemphasize the CSCE. Though more positively inclined than their American allies, the West European governments intended to pursue a nonconfrontational approach to the implementation of the Final Act. This combination of policies within the NATO alliance produced a December 1975 North Atlantic Council communiqué whose tone was remarkably similar to East bloc commentaries on the Final Act:

> In the political sphere, détente requires tolerance and mutual understanding, and accordingly demands that the natural contest of political and social ideas should not be conducted in a manner incompatible with the

letter and spirit of the Final Act of Helsinki. (North Atlantic Council 1980, 38–39)

As for implementation, the communiqué stated only that the allies expected progress in relations between states, in confidence-building measures, in economic cooperation, and in "lowering barriers between peoples"—an early NATO formula that fell far short of the more specific norms already established by the Final Act.

As the months went by, though, Western foreign ministries were flooded with massive documentation of human rights violations submitted by members of the Helsinki network.[15] As a result of this pressure, American and NATO policy on the CSCE began to reflect the prioritization of human rights advocated by dissidents in the East and their supporters in the West. Pressured from all sides, the White House and the State Department began to take Helsinki compliance seriously. The North Atlantic Council's May 1976 communiqué struck an entirely new tone:

> Ministers . . . emphasised the importance they attach to full implementation of all parts of the Helsinki Final Act by all signatories, so that its benefits may be felt not only in relations between states but also in the lives of individuals. (North Atlantic Council 1980, 45)

The communiqué continued, acknowledging some progress in the area of human contacts and working conditions for journalists, but pointing out "the importance of what still remains to be done," and expressing the hope for rapid progress on implementation of the basic principles, including human rights.

During a trip to Europe organized by the Helsinki Commission, a U.S. congressional delegation heard East bloc dissidents and sympathetic human rights activists speak of "the need to base détente between East and West on the progress of internal change inside the Soviet Union" and repeat the importance of Helsinki monitoring and issue-linkage in U.S. policy.[16] Such reports only bolstered the commission's argument within U.S. government circles that Helsinki norms were not being respected in the East bloc. Though still diplomatic in style, the North Atlantic Council's December 1976 communiqué expressed this growing concern (North Atlantic Council 1980, 61).

The fact that this reorientation of Western and especially U.S. policy toward the CSCE clearly began in late 1975 and accelerated through 1976—all before the election of Jimmy Carter—is additional evidence for the independent influence of the transnational Helsinki network on foreign policy.

East Bloc Reactions to the Helsinki Network

The shift in Western policy did not go unnoticed in the Kremlin. On 24 February 1976, Brezhnev's report to the Twenty-Fifth Communist Party Congress acknowledged "certain difficulties in our relations with a number of capitalist European states" during the seven months since the Helsinki summit. In response to the unexpected salience of human rights, Brezhnev focused again on the principle of nonintervention in internal affairs, as he had done in his speech at the Helsinki summit:

> Certain quarters are trying to emasculate and distort the very substance of the Final Act adopted in Helsinki, and to use this document as a screen for interfering in the internal affairs of the socialist countries, for anti-Communist and anti-Soviet demagogy in cold-war style. (Brezhnev 1979, 106)

Notwithstanding these frustrations, Brezhnev remained committed to the Helsinki Final Act as the instrument by which the Soviet Union and its allies could achieve greater economic ties with the West: "The main thing now is to translate all the principles and understandings reached in Helsinki into practical deeds. This is exactly what the Soviet Union is doing and will continue to do" (106). Communist authorities nonetheless became less and less patient as East European dissidents became more active, the U.S. Congress more assertive, and U.S. policy slowly more confrontational.

Throughout the summer of 1976, official Soviet media criticized the formation of the U.S. Helsinki Commission as a violation of Soviet internal affairs and as an act aimed not at the promotion of détente, but at "fouling up the process" (*Izvestia* 17 June, 7 and 29 August). In September, Polish Ministry of Foreign Affairs' counselor Jerzy Nowak warned that "[f]or the good of all-European cooperation the capitalist states should cease trying to force the socialist side to accept a different interpretation of some concepts" (Nowak 1976, 12). As Western governments strengthened their rhetoric on human rights that autumn, the postsummit luster disappeared from Brezhnev's rhetoric on the CSCE.[17]

New Opportunities and Challenges: The Early Carter Administration

Feedback from the Helsinki process actually contributed to Jimmy Carter's narrow election victory and then pushed his new administration further than it intended to go on the human rights issue. During the campaign, Carter's speeches combined support for human rights as an element in foreign policy with a decidedly negative view of the Helsinki process, calling the Final Act a "tremendous diplomatic victory" for Leonid Brezhnev (Buncher 1977, 77–78). Hearing his criticisms of the Helsinki process, the U.S. Helsinki Commission contacted the Carter campaign and urged that the governor adopt a more positive view (Albright and Friendly 1986, 303–4).

The first opportunity to do so came four days later, during a televised debate, when Ford claimed that Eastern Europe was not subject to Soviet domination. Carter quickly rebutted that many Americans felt otherwise and, for the first time, criticized Ford's failure to uphold the human rights components of the Helsinki Final Act. Pollster George Gallup called this the "most decisive moment in the campaign" (Hyland 1987, 173). In the end, Carter's narrow margin of victory over Ford, especially in some traditionally Republican areas, depended in part on the conservatives and East European ethnic and émigré voters whom Ford had alienated by his apparent commitment to détente over human rights or Helsinki compliance.

The newly created Helsinki Commission also made its voice heard before Jimmy Carter took office. As Carter's staff prepared for the inauguration, Commission Chairman Dante Fascell wrote to Secretary of State–elect Cyrus Vance urging a strong reference to human rights in the inaugural address.[18] Though surely not the only source, Fascell's message was closely reflected in the inaugural's declaration, "Because we are free, we can never be indifferent to the fate of freedom elsewhere." The same is true of a second inaugural statement, broadcast the same day by the U.S. Information Agency, in which Carter promised listeners around the world, "You can depend on the United States to remain steadfast in its commitment to human freedom and liberty."[19] This rhetoric was noticed in Eastern Europe, by regime and opposition forces alike.

The question was whether, and how, the Carter administration would implement this commitment, especially when it appeared to conflict with other priorities. Senior officials in the new administration, especially in the State Department, set out to avoid a human rights confrontation in CSCE that would upset its broader détente agenda, including nuclear and conventional arms control with the Soviets (Hyland 1987, 203; Garthoff 1994, 627–33). Marshall Shulman, the State Department's new chief Soviet specialist, had long argued that U.S. policy should not become preoccupied with human rights (*New York Times,* 31 October 1975; Shulman 1977).

Before long, though, East European and Soviet dissidents, along with their allies in the U.S. Congress, forced the administration to take a far more confrontational approach to human rights than it initially intended. Almost immediately after the inauguration, reports began to reach the West through Helsinki network channels about a crackdown in Czechoslovakia against signatories of the new human rights initiative, Charter 77. On 26 January, the State Department harshly criticized the government of Czechoslovakia for violating its commitment in the Helsinki Final Act (*New York Times,* 27 January 1977). Though the statement had apparently been issued without prior authorization from the White House or the Secretary of State (Hyland 1987, 204), it was seen publicly as a landmark action by the new administration. Editorial pages across the country quickly praised the break from past failures to insist on Helsinki compliance.[20]

Soon thereafter, Soviet dissident Andrei Sakharov wrote to President Carter, praising his commitment to human rights and calling his attention to human rights violations in the Soviet Union. (Sakharov was closely affiliated with the Moscow Helsinki Group, but not officially a member.) Carter felt obligated to respond to this appeal from the Soviet Union's most famous scientist and dissident, but National Security Advisor Zbigniew Brzezinski and Secretary of State Cyrus Vance tried to draft the letter in a way that would avoid provoking the Kremlin (Brzezinski 1983, 156).

Even after the criticism of the Czechoslovak authorities and Carter's personal correspondence with Sakharov, the administration sought to maintain the possibility of quiet diplomacy for human rights. When the Soviets complained in late January 1977 about Washington's contact with Sakharov, Vance responded that "[w]e do not intend to be strident or polemical" and predicted that the human rights dispute would not affect U.S.-Soviet arms negotiations (Buncher 1977, 116). One week later, in his first letter to Brezhnev, Carter expressed his hope that all Helsinki commitments would be observed, but tried to reassure the Soviet leader, saying that "it is not our intention to interfere in the internal affairs of other nations" and offering "private, confidential exchanges on these delicate matters" (Brzezinski 1983, 156). Brezhnev responded brusquely, indicating that he would not "allow interference in our internal affairs, whatever pseudo-humanitarian slogans are used to present it," and strenuously objected to Carter's correspondence with Sakharov, whom he called a "renegade who has proclaimed himself an enemy of the Soviet state" (Brzeszinski 1983, 155). All sides in this debate recognized, however, that it was merely a rehearsal for the forthcoming CSCE conference in Belgrade held to review progress on Helsinki principles and to consider future areas of cooperation.

Setting the Belgrade Conference Agenda

Pressure from the Helsinki network had a significant impact on U.S. planning for the Belgrade conference, including the preparatory talks set to begin

June 15. As Representative Dante Fascell, chair of the U.S. Helsinki Commission, recalls,

> [P]reparations for Belgrade elicited surprising public attention. Western journalists in Moscow, Berlin, Warsaw, Bucharest and Prague began to write about the Helsinki-related demands of workers, writers, religious believers, Jews and Germans seeking to emigrate from the Soviet Union, and of human rights activists. The Communist regimes reacted critically and sometimes violently to these activities, but—by their repressive measures—only aggravated the concerns of private and official groups in the West. (Fascell 1978)

Human rights activists and Helsinki watch groups from across Eastern Europe and the Soviet Union submitted detailed reports of human rights violations by East bloc regimes and argued strenuously that the United States should press for greater compliance as a prerequisite to progress in the CSCE: "Although the Belgrade Conference should discuss all sections of the Helsinki Agreement, it is 'basket three' [on "humanitarian cooperation"] which is the most urgent and which therefore should form the central part" (Pelikan 1977, 2). Encouraged by these NGOs and armed with their documentation of developments in Eastern Europe, the Helsinki Commission continued its battle with the State Department and the White House to ensure that human rights became the focus of U.S. CSCE policy. In particular, the commission argued that the Belgrade conference should be used for a detailed review of compliance with the Final Act, especially on the issue of human rights. It issued numerous reports and held hearings on East bloc violations related to human contacts, religious liberty and minority rights, information flow, and other human rights issues.[21]

Though the State Department resisted the inclusion of Helsinki Commission members in pre-Belgrade policy planning meetings, this domestic and transnational lobbying produced results.[22] In April, Secretary of State Cyrus Vance told an audience at the University of Georgia: "Our belief is strengthened by the way the Helsinki principles and the UN Declaration of Human Rights have found resonance in the hearts of people of many countries" (Buncher 1977, 181–82). On 6 June, just nine days before the preparatory negotiations for Belgrade were to begin, National Security Advisor Zbigniew Brzezinski noted in his journal that congressional pressure had forced the White House to issue a report on CSCE compliance that he considered imprudently critical of the East bloc (Brzezinski 1983, 126).[23] The State Department's Coordinator for Humanitarian Affairs acknowledged privately that the commission was responsible for the report.[24]

The State Department nonetheless remained uncomfortable with human rights as a diplomatic issue and preferred to give it a lower profile. To this end, Albert Sherer, head of the U.S. delegation to the CSCE from 1973 to 1975, was appointed as ambassador to the Belgrade meeting and sent to Europe to consult with the NATO allies. Suddenly, at the end of the preparatory negotiations in August, Sherer was replaced as U.S. ambassador to the Belgrade conference by Arthur Goldberg, a former Supreme Court justice and an outspoken UN ambassador with no prior CSCE experience.

This unexpected appointment provides further insight into the impact of network pressure on the Carter administration's CSCE policy. Goldberg had already accepted President Carter's invitation to serve as special envoy to the Middle East when Brzezinski and Vance objected, apparently on policy grounds. A senior official then suggested that Goldberg be offered the equally prestigious CSCE ambassadorship, in place of Sherer.[25] Given mounting pressure on the White House to emphasize human rights at Belgrade, Goldberg's career-long interest in civil rights and labor issues would be seen as a "dramatic demonstration of the U.S. commitment to human rights, and particularly of President Carter's determination to give it the highest priority" (Korey 1993, 69). Over the following months, Goldberg came to champion the high-profile position on human rights within the CSCE demanded by the nonstate actors who had helped bring about his appointment.

Meanwhile, the Soviets and their allies had followed the growth of the Helsinki network and its influence on the gradual turnaround in U.S. policy since 1976 and were preparing for a confrontation at Belgrade over the issue of human rights (Maximov 1976). Kremlin conservatives were increasingly unhappy with the evolution of the Helsinki process. One result was that Ambassador Anatoly Kovalev, who had faithfully executed Brezhnev's policy in two years of CSCE negotiations in Geneva, was denied an expected promotion to the party's Central Committee. His replacement, Ambassador Yuli Vorontsov, was instructed to refuse any further concessions on human rights at Belgrade (Shevchenko 1985, 264–67).

Shaping the Belgrade Conference

The approach to reviewing human rights implementation at Belgrade favored by the U.S. State Department and the West Europeans was "to be frank and detailed in listing those points in the record of other States which required criticism and called for improvement, but to avoid heightening the tension by concentrating on individual cases where practical results were unlikely" (Secretary of State for Foreign and Commonwealth Affairs 1978, 7). Some argued that emphasizing human rights might actually cause more hardship to those living under communist rule, especially political prisoners. Even West European NGOs concerned about human rights were sensitive to this possibility (Helsinki Review Group n.d., 18–19).

The strong preference among Western delegations for a nonconfrontational approach to human rights, especially when the issue appeared to conflict with other strategic interests, was reinforced by competing predictions about the effects of pressure on human rights (see Fall 1977; Birnbaum 1977).

By the time the conference opened on 4 October 1977, the NATO countries had agreed among themselves to insist on a frank review of human rights implementation, but not to "name names" or otherwise upset the balance of issues embodied in the Helsinki Final Act. Through the first two weeks of talks, all of Goldberg's references to East bloc violations were indirect, as required by NATO agreement and diplomatic protocol.

This diplomatic protocol was remarkably robust, even to the point of absurdity. At one point, a French diplomat at Belgrade criticized the human rights record of an East bloc country by saying "I won't name names because the person in question is sitting right in front of me, but in his country the practice is. . . ." In turn, an East German diplomat criticized a "country whose language is English with a population of over two hundred million which only published seven thousand copies of the Final Act" (Goldberg n.d., 99, 104).[26]

Before long, though, protocol was overturned by a combination of impassioned appeals from East European dissidents and political pressure from the U.S. Congress, both framed in terms of Helsinki norms. On the eve of the Belgrade conference, forty-eight human rights activists in Moscow announced a one-day fast to protest repression against the Moscow Helsinki Group. The protest was covered in the Washington press (*Washington Star,* 5 October 1977). At about the same time, Andrei Sakharov sent a personal appeal to the West emphasizing the importance of human rights in détente.

On 6 October, the day of Ambassador Goldberg's first speech to the Belgrade conference, Sakharov's letter appeared in the *International Herald Tribune.* It was pointed and powerful:

> The Soviet and East European representatives have always tried to neutralize the humanitarian principles of the Helsinki accords by emphasizing the principle of non-interference in the internal affairs of other countries. . . .
> Every person serving a term in the hell of present-day Gulag for his beliefs, or open profession of them—every victim of psychological repression for political reasons, every person refused permission to emigrate, to travel abroad—represents a direct violation of the Helsinki accord. . . . We are

going through a period of history in which decisive support of the principles of freedom of conscience in an open society, and the rights of man, has become an absolute necessity. . . . Is the West prepared to defend these noble and vitally important principles? Or, will it, little by little, accept the interpretation of the principles of Helsinki, and of détente as a whole, that the leaders of the Soviet Union and of Eastern Europe are trying to impose?

Ambassador Goldberg was impressed by Sakharov's letter (and the other appeals sent to the West over the preceding months) and conveyed this impression to allied delegations (Korey 1993, 79). In fact, Sakharov's letter was crucial in persuading Goldberg to reject the one argument against emphasizing human rights that he had found plausible over the preceding months: that it might cause greater hardship to those living under communist rule (Goldberg n.d., 86).

The State Department, however, including deputy head of the U.S. delegation, Albert Sherer, remained unconvinced (*Washington Post,* 17 October 1977). Then, on 17 October Goldberg received a copy of a letter addressed to President Carter from a bipartisan group of 127 representatives and 16 senators calling for the U.S. delegation in Belgrade to forcefully criticize all violations of Helsinki norms. Entitled "Make Human Rights a Central Issue," the letter highlighted the repression of the Moscow Helsinki Group and argued that "if the Soviets are allowed to blatantly violate the human rights provisions of the Helsinki Agreement, the credibility and effectiveness of the agreement, and any other bilateral negotiations could be undermined" (Goldberg n.d., 174–75).

Goldberg was emboldened by evidence of congressional support. The following day, he replaced his deputy in the Basket Three caucus and surprised the assembled diplomats by reading an article from the French Communist Party newspaper *L'Humanité* about how the Czechoslovak authorities had denied Western reporters access to a trial of Charter 77 activists. This move broke the diplomatic taboo against naming names, while publicizing the plight of Helsinki monitors and Czechoslovakia's violation of its commitment to the free flow of information.

These initiatives were not well received by the West Europeans, who still favored a nonconfrontational approach. A member of one NATO delegation complained, "We seem to spend more time negotiating with Goldberg than negotiating with the Russians" (cited in Cook 1978, 10). Even after breaking the diplomatic taboo on names, Goldberg remained frustrated by what he saw as the U.S. State Department's and West European foreign ministries' tendency to place NATO unity and friendly East-West relations over frank discussion of human rights. As the weeks wore on, though, the Soviets' absolute refusal to engage in serious discussion about human rights produced a renewed unity of purpose among Western delegations.[27]

The meeting ended on 9 March 1978. Reflecting the deadlock in substantive negotiations, the final document from Belgrade merely recorded the dates and formalities of the meeting and stipulated that the participating states would meet again in Madrid in November 1980.[28] The priority of human rights in U.S. policy toward the East bloc and the means by which that objective should be advanced, however, had not been settled.

Sustaining the Helsinki Network's Influence

The Belgrade meeting's failure to achieve a frank discussion of human rights by all parties called into question the new salience of the Helsinki process and especially the focus on human rights. European members of NATO expressed their fear that another stalemated meeting would endanger the CSCE and even détente itself (Helsinki Review Group 1977; von Gesau 1980). Other West European voices recognized that East European activists had changed the terms of debate within the CSCE and East-West relations, but doubted the efficacy of Goldberg's approach to promoting human rights: "[O]utside the context of the Belgrade meeting there are dangers that stressing individual cases in public too frequently not only distracts attention from the plight of others, but induces confrontation" (Helsinki Review Group n.d., 19). First privately and then publicly, U.S. diplomat Albert Sherer criticized Goldberg's approach as a threat to NATO unity and called for a less confrontational policy at Madrid (Sherer 1980). Influential American columnist William Safire urged the United States to denounce the entire Helsinki process and blasted the Helsinki Commission as "a group with a vested interest in meeting and junketing and tut-tutting at the way the Russians ignore the treaty" (*New York Times,* 19 June 1978).

This post-Belgrade threat to the salience of human rights in U.S. policy was the occasion for a second crucial development in the Helsinki network: the creation of a nongovernmental organization in the United States devoted entirely to the Helsinki process. As discussed above, private human rights groups in the United States had begun to monitor compliance with Helsinki norms two years earlier in response to appeals from activists in the East. Subsequent reports of repression against Helsinki monitors in the East only increased their commitment to raise the priority of human rights in U.S. foreign policy toward Eastern Europe and the Soviet Union. One of these groups, the International Freedom to Publish Committee of the Association of American Publishers (AAP), had announced in December that it would not sign any formal trade protocol with the Soviet book-publishing industry until the Kremlin improved its human rights record (U.S. Department of State 1978, 25). During the Belgrade conference's winter break, representatives of the AAP met in New York with Ambassador Goldberg, who agreed that only concerted public pressure in the West would keep the CSCE focused on human rights.[29]

In testimony before the Helsinki Commission less than two weeks after the end of the Belgrade meeting, Goldberg spoke about the need for pressure from the nongovernmental sector to support human rights:

> Private individuals have a lot to do, outside of government. It's a great anomaly to me that while in the Soviet Union, in Czechoslovakia, in Poland, under conditions of repression, private individuals have had the courage to organize private groups but that in our country individuals have not organized a monitoring group. I would hope they would, as an indication that individuals in our country, in addition to government, have a great interest in the implementation of the Final Act. (U.S. Commission 1978, appendix F, 18–19)

After Goldberg's testimony, members of Congress affirmed his call for a private organization that could supplement the work of the Helsinki Commission.

Meanwhile, governmental and nongovernmental members of the Helsinki network worked to maintain the salience of human rights in the East. In late April, the Helsinki Commission convinced the Carter administration to convey to the Kremlin its interest in the trials of several members of the Moscow Helsinki Watch Group.[30] In June, the AAP and the International Publishers Association issued a statement reiterating concern for the fate of Yuri Orlov, who had recently been sentenced to seven years imprisonment (U.S. Department of State 1978, 26). When two leading members of the group, Aleksandr Ginzburg and Anatoly Sharansky, were nonetheless found guilty of treason several months later, the Carter administration responded by canceling the sale of an advanced computer to the Soviet news agency Tass and by requiring validated licenses for all exports of oil technology to the Soviet Union (Martin 1992). All members of the network nonetheless knew that consistent public pressure would be necessary to sustain U.S. pressure for human rights and Helsinki compliance.

During a series of discussions between members of the AAP committee, other human rights activists, Ambassador Goldberg, and McGeorge Bundy, president of the Ford Foundation, the decision was made to create an independent Helsinki watch committee in the United States.[31] The U.S. Helsinki

Watch Committee was formally established in February 1979 with a $400,000 grant from the Ford Foundation as an "independent, non-governmental organization composed of a representative group of private U.S. opinion leaders" to monitor domestic and international compliance with the human rights provisions of the Helsinki Final Act and to provide "moral support for the activities of the beleaguered Helsinki monitors in the Soviet bloc" (U.S. Helsinki Watch Committee 1980, 3–4). This was, of course, just what Orlov and his fellow activists had called for two years earlier when they established the Moscow Helsinki Group.

The Watch Committee immediately became a major fixture in the transnational Helsinki network and gained a voice in U.S. policymaking on the CSCE, Eastern Europe, and the Soviet Union. With its reputation for reliable information about human rights conditions in the East and its ability to organize political pressure within the United States, Helsinki Watch played an especially important role in the early 1980s, when the Reagan administration's initial skepticism about détente and multilateral institutions led to talk of withdrawing from the CSCE.

Alternative Explanations

While Helsinki norms and the transnational network that emerged around them were certainly not the only factors shaping U.S. foreign policy in the mid- and late 1970s, potential alternative explanations for the rise of the human rights agenda in U.S. policy toward Eastern Europe and the Soviet Union are all less persuasive than the norms-network connection. For example, one might argue that the salience of human rights in U.S. policy toward the communist bloc depended on the status of East-West geopolitics: as long as détente was healthy, Washington would downplay the sensitive issue of human rights, but when détente soured, Washington would use the rights issue as an additional stick with which to beat its adversary. The first problem with this hypothesis is that the change in U.S. policy began in the fall of 1975, before détente had truly deteriorated—if anything, the new U.S. focus on human rights was a cause, not a result of the decline of détente. Moreover, as documented above in great detail, the focus on human rights in Eastern Europe entered U.S. policy not through the geostrategic calculations of the executive branch (as the hypothesis leads one to expect), but through political pressure from private groups and the Congress.

Likewise, suggestions that the declining influence of Henry Kissinger in this period permitted U.S. foreign policy to return to its "normal" tendency to support freedom and human rights, based on assumptions about American political culture and institutions, are no better at explaining this case.[32] First of all, they offer no explanation for why Kissingerian realpolitik should have declined while he was still in office. And while the argument that U.S. foreign policy reflects fundamental aspects of American political identity is certainly plausible, it is logically inconsistent with the ability of an individual to impose a contrary agenda on U.S. policy for half a decade. Above all, numerous examples of U.S. support for repressive and murderous regimes during this period and the State Department's stubborn resistance to the agenda of the Helsinki network are entirely inconsistent with the claim that human rights is a "normal" priority in U.S. foreign policy.

A more common explanation for the rise of human rights in U.S. foreign policy during the period is the influence of Jimmy Carter and the "globalist" outlook prevalent in his early administration (Muravchik 1991; Rosati 1991). Yet notwithstanding the innovations of the Carter administration, the power of this explanation is seriously undermined by the fact that U.S. policy toward the East began to change before Carter's election and inauguration, and by the fact that leading figures in his administration then resisted the focus on human rights demanded by the Helsinki network.

Others have suggested that the Congress had its own reasons in the early and mid-1970s, unrelated to Helsinki norms or transnational networking, for asserting its voice in U.S. foreign policy and raising the salience of human rights (Franck and Weisband 1979; Sikkink 1993b). Vietnam and Watergate had weakened the executive branch and discredited the principles of realpolitik, which had long justified overlooking human rights. Moreover, the Voting Rights Act and other domestic civil rights accomplishments of the 1960s had reduced the internal political obstacles to emphasizing human rights in U.S. foreign policy. Ever anxious to expand its authority, and more sensitive to public opinion than was the executive branch, some members of Congress seized the human rights issue in the early 1970s as a means to assert its independence from the White House and relegitimize U.S. foreign policy at home and abroad. This much is undeniable.

What the simple domestic political explanation cannot account for, though, is why the Congress began to press for human rights conditionality in U.S. aid to Latin America, but largely ignored Eastern Europe until 1975, despite U.S. financial assistance to both regions. One might hypothesize that the Congress ceded East European policy to the White House because the stakes of East-West relations were higher, but that argument is undermined by the Congress's dramatic about-face after 1975. More persuasive is the argument that congressional interest in human rights conditions in Eastern Europe and the Soviet Union was catalyzed by the Helsinki network after 1975, just as it had been several years earlier by a transnational network focused on the "dirty wars" in Argentina and Chile (Sikkink 1993a).[33]

In short, the change in U.S. policy documented in this paper cannot be simply attributed to other factors, such as geopolitical trends, an enduring "national interest," a change of government, or domestic political pressure unconnected to transnational networking. The fortunes of détente, American liberalism, the election of Jimmy Carter, and the assertiveness of Congress all mattered, but none provides a sufficient explanation for this historically significant development in U.S. foreign policy and East-West relations.

Conclusions

As seen above, dissidents and human rights activists in the East used the human rights norms of the Helsinki Final Act to attract support from sympathetic forces in the West, including private groups and a dynamic member of the U.S. Congress. The resulting Helsinki network conveyed information and mobilized political pressure, which brought about a sharp turn in U.S. policy toward Eastern Europe and the Soviet Union. This impact on U.S. policy included raising human rights from a low-priority issue that the Ford White House and State Department preferred to ignore, to a high priority in U.S. relations with the East, creating a new governmental commission dedicated to the implementation of Helsinki norms, and forcing the new Carter administration to adopt more confrontational policies than it originally wanted or intended to.

The international attention and diplomatic pressure produced by the new salience of human rights in U.S. policy toward Eastern Europe after 1975 created unprecedented space for opposition in Eastern Europe and the Soviet Union through the late 1970s and 1980s and contributed both directly and indirectly to the eventual overthrow of communist rule (Thomas 2001). Equally important, it helped transform the contemporary meaning of state sovereignty by consolidating respect for human rights as a fundamental norm of world politics that all states recognize and few entirely ignore. The maximal concession to the power of normative ideas possible within the Realist paradigm—the claim that norms "have been used to codify existing practices rather than to initiate new forms of order"—is thus seriously challenged by the Helsinki case (Krasner 1993, 238).

In fact, it demonstrates how nonstate actors that are otherwise weak can exploit the legitimacy inherent in international norms to construct transnational networks and transform prevailing conceptions of state interests. Transnational networks thus serve, like international organizations, as "teachers of norms" to reluctant states.[34] As this case clearly demonstrates, though, the learning process is predominantly political. The transformation of state behavior, identity, and interests through transnational collective action must be understood as a politically contested process in which careers, deeply held values, and even lives are sometimes at stake.

The Helsinki case also demonstrates why the politics of international norms is often not explicable in terms of relations between unified states or by focusing purely on state actors. As one member of Congress recalled, U.S. policy on the Helsinki Accords was transformed by the arguments and examples of nonstate actors:

> [F]ew suspected that the Helsinki Accords would become a subject of lively political interest. Most thought the agreements were no more than footnotes to the complex, often contradictory history of détente. . . . Now the verdict has been reversed. . . . The changed perception is not of our making. For the first to recognize—indeed, to exalt—the innovative content of the accords were men and women in the Soviet Union and the other Warsaw Pact states. (Council of Europe 1977, 168)

In this as in many other cases, nonstate and substate actors played a major role in the reconstruction of state interests. Further research promises to yield important new insights into the relationship between the causal power of norms and the causal power of transnational networks, and their joint relationship to the transformation of state interests.

Of course, for all the heuristic advantages of this case study, one may still ask whether it was a hard or an easy test of the proposition that international norms empower transnational networks in their confrontation with states. After all, the Helsinki network's success in reorienting U.S. policy toward a focus on human rights during the mid- to late 1970s surely benefited from the fact that its ultimate targets—the communist regimes of Eastern Europe and the Soviet Union—were already vilified in U.S. political discourse. Resistance to emphasizing human rights in U.S. policy toward the region persisted in inner circles of government, but lacked broad popular support. Moreover, the Helsinki Final Act emphasized civil and political rights, rather than the economic, social, and cultural rights that have never thrived within American political culture. In contrast, transnational human rights networks seeking to influence U.S. policy today have a much harder job, as economic, social, and cultural rights gain prominence and human rights increasingly competes with lucrative trade interests for priority on the foreign policy agenda.

On the other hand, there are strong reasons to conclude that the Helsinki network was fighting an uphill battle to change U.S. policy. First of all, there is considerable evidence that the multiplicity of voices and political pressures in decentralized states like the United States actually renders them less susceptible to the influence of any given transnational campaign (Risse-Kappen 1995a). In addition, if Realist claims about the priority of state survival have any validity, then an elite commitment to nonconfrontation with the East bloc would pose a serious obstacle to the Helsinki network's campaign. In fact, senior foreign policymakers in the Ford and early Carter administrations were convinced that nonconfrontation was the best means of avoiding nuclear war with the Soviet Union, and that this policy would be endangered by a move to raise the profile of human rights in East-West relations.

Prior to 1975, neither the Congress nor the NGO community had displayed any inclination to engage and press the East bloc for improvements in human rights. During the early 1970s, appeals from human rights activists in Eastern Europe had been largely ignored in the West. The Helsinki network thus had to overcome significant resistance in the executive branch, a lack of interest in the legislative branch, and a human rights NGO sector whose limited resources were focused elsewhere. Without the salience and legitimacy gained through their identification with the normative commitments of the Helsinki Accords, it is hard to imagine that activists in Eastern Europe would have attracted the attention of private groups and substate actors in the West, and thereby reoriented the foreign policy priorities of a superpower.

The evolution and effectiveness of transnational networks are thus best understood as the product of a continuous exchange of ideas, information, and resources among nonstate and substate actors unified and politically empowered by their identification with international norms. Without the political justifications offered by international norms, transnational networks would find it much harder to overcome the superior power of states. Without the political agency or pressure applied by these networks, many outcomes we take for granted would never have occurred. The interaction of transnational networks and international norms thus deserves greater attention in all areas of world politics, whether our goal is explaining, understanding, or designing policy.

Notes

1. On legitimation by international institutions, see Claude 1967 (chap. 4) and Krasner 1985.

2. On norms and sanctions, see Martin 1992 and Klotz 1995.

3. For discussion of when state actors respond to material incentives versus the intrinsic lure of international legitimacy, see Thomas 2001.

4. On social purpose, see Ruggie 1983 (198).

5. This feedback is discussed as a "boomerang effect" in Keck and Sikkink 1998 (12).

6. All the states of Europe participated, except Albania, plus the United States and Canada.

7. The inclusion of human rights in the Final Act was insisted upon by the member-states of the European Community, who had recently defined respect for human rights as a fundamental part of the "European identity." For more, see Thomas 2001 (chaps. 1–2).

8. Guy Coriden, interview by author, Washington, D.C., 31 March 1994.

9. On the history of congressional interest in human rights in U.S. foreign policy, see Franck and Weisband 1979 (83–97).

10. Yuri Orlov, interviews by author, Ithaca, N.Y., 1990–92; confirmed in telephone interview with Christopher Wren, 22 August 1995.

11. Despite the timing of the congressional visit to the Soviet Union and the speed with which Fenwick introduced the bill after her return, there is no evidence from any source that she or any other member of the delegation contemplated in advance the creation of such a commission.

12. Coriden, interview.

13. State Department counselor Helmut Sonnenfeldt expressed this view in a private meeting with U.S. ambassadors in Europe in December 1975. See *New York Times*, 6 April 1976.

14. "An Evaluation of the Influence of the Helsinki Agreements as They Relate to Human Rights in the USSR, 1 August 1975–1 August 1976," unpublished mimeo. In the Belgrade Conference files of the U.S. Commission on Security and Cooperation in Europe (henceforth "U.S. Commission").

15. Interviews by author with former American and West European CSCE policy-makers, 1993–95.

16. Working Meeting of the Commission on Security and Cooperation in Europe, Washington, D.C., 8 January 1977, unpublished transcript. In U.S. Commission files.

17. See his 25 October 1976 address to a plenary meeting of the C.P.S.U. Central Committee, in Brezhnev 1979 (131–36).

18. Correspondence from Dante Fascell to Cyrus Vance, 11 January 1977. In U.S. Commission files.

19. For the full text of both statements, see Buncher 1977 (80–81).

20. For a sample of editorials, see Buncher 1977 (111–15).

21. See "Soviet Helsinki Watch, Reports on Repression" and "U.S. Policy and the Belgrade Conference" in U.S. Commission 1977.

22. Correspondence from Dante Fascell to Cyrus Vance, 4 February 1977. In U.S. Commission files.

23. The report in question was U.S. House 1977—the president's second semi-annual report to the U.S. Helsinki Commission prepared by the State Department.

24. Correspondence from Patricia Derian to commission Deputy Staff Director Alfred Friendly, 20 July 1977. In U.S. Commission files.

25. Brzezinski (1983) and Kampelman (1991, 221) report that Deputy Secretary of State Warren Christopher recommended Goldberg for the CSCE, while Brzezinski (1983, 300) takes personal credit for the idea.

26. Dorothy Goldberg, the wife of Ambassador Arthur Goldberg, accompanied him to Belgrade and took careful notes on the proceedings.

27. "Weekly Summaries of Belgrade meetings." Photocopied memos from the U.S. State Department delegation to the Belgrade CSCE. In Harvard Law School International Legal Studies Library.

28. For the text of the Belgrade document, see Bloed 1990 (101–3).

29. Robert Bernstein, interview by author, New York, 12 January 1994.

30. Correspondence between commission chair Dante Fascell, Secretary of State Cyrus Vance, and Assistant Secretary of State for Congressional Relations Douglas Bennet. In U.S. Commission files.

31. Jeri Laber, executive director, Helsinki Watch, interview by author, New York, 11 January 1994; Robert Bernstein, former head of the AAP Freedom to Publish Committee, interview by author, New York, 12 January 1994; and McGeorge Bundy, telephone interview by author, 24 January 1994.

32. On Kissinger as an exception to American exceptionalism, see Huntington 1982 and Smith 1994.

33. On how the transnational antiapartheid network catalyzed congressional interest in human rights in South Africa in the 1980s, see Klotz 1995.

34. On international organizations as "teachers of norms," see Finnemore 1993.

5

Women's Rights Are Human Rights

Karen Brown Thompson

Women's local, national, and international organizations have for decades, and most intensively in the last quarter of the twentieth century, demanded accountability for gendered human rights violations. These claims have constituted new expectations about the relationship among state authority, family practices, and women's rights. This chapter explores various meaningful global practices related to women's rights from the perspective of state-citizen relations. I examine specifically how the practices of IGOs, states, and NGOs with respect to international women's rights challenge, reconstitute, and reinforce certain aspects of the authority relations between states and the people who live in them.

This chapter illuminates the importance of attending to the very processes of global norm institutionalization, in particular through transnational advocacy networks composed of NGOs, international institutions, and individual activists.[1] The processes by which women's human rights came to inform international discourse and state practices provide valuable insight into the highly politicized, and often diverse, constructions of a global norm. The processes themselves, and not simply the resultant norm, are socially consequential in that they construct particular kinds of state-citizen relations. The historical contingency and the socially constructed character of state-citizen relations can be seen in examining the gendering of the international human rights discourse. Specifically, I focus on the kinds of social knowledge about states and women-as-citizens invoked or silenced in the process of gendering international human rights. I highlight the ways in which transnational activism and the social knowledge undergirding it can be both politically empowering and disempowering in this process. This tension between empowerment and exclusion is expressed in divisions, disagreements, and asymmetries within transnational movements for women's human rights.[2] Despite this tension, transnational advocacy has served to foster the rapid emergence and development of a norm of state responsibility for protecting women's human rights (even within the family).

In the case of women's rights, the circulation and articulation of the norm of state responsibility for mitigating gender inequality both destabilized the dominant human rights discourse and reinforced its international political centrality. As gender oppression was increasingly identified with women's human rights violations, international norms and understandings about human rights were reconfigured to include private actor violations. At the same time, though, "framing" gender inequality as a human rights issue strengthened and reproduced human rights discourse in new fields and among a new set of transnational actors.

Gendering the Human Rights Discourse: The Historical Process

The notion that "women's rights are human rights" went from being virtually unknown in the 1970s to being widely circulated by the 1990s. The process by which women's rights came to constitute one aspect of a global human rights discourse highlights changing social knowledge in two areas: bringing women into public life and bringing state authority into family relations. Each involves distinct challenges to the boundaries between states and families, public and private. Several categories of practice were crucial in this process: the establishment of relevant United Nations institutional structures, the United Nations Decade for Women, and the adoption of the Women's Convention. These international institutional developments were in essence outcomes of transnational collective action spanning a wide range of actors.

The international framing of women's status within the rubric of human rights and citizenship was first formally institutionalized in the United Nations with the Commission on the Status of Women (CSW) (Lutz, Hannum, and Burke 1989, 27). The CSW served mainly to prepare reports to the UN Economic and Social Council (ECOSOC) on promoting women's rights[3] and draft international treaties and declarations. International conventions promoted by the CSW further codified women's rights as international legal and political issues. In 1957, for instance, the UN General Assembly adopted the Convention on the Nationality of Married Women, which framed the issue of married women's nationality in terms of human rights by referencing Article 15 of the Universal Declaration on Human Rights (United Nations 1957).

This early stage of work, of establishing the responsibility of states for women's human rights and of rearticulating women's citizenship within the expressly political frame of human rights, culminated within the United Nations in the 1979 adoption by the General Assembly of the Convention on the Elimination of All Forms of Discrimination Against Women (Women's Convention or CEDAW) (Lutz, Hannum, and Burke 1989, 27). The establishment of the CSW and the participation of governments in sending representatives to serve as commission members involved a minimal commitment in terms of state activity and resources. However, this initial commitment had paved the way for future state involvement in granting and protecting the human rights of women, while simultaneously offering a means through which international organizations and individuals, both public and private, could lobby states and the United Nations system for improvements in the status of women. Thus United Nations institutions, and United Nations–sponsored activities around the world, represented another facet of the process of global norm formation by facilitating discursive and institutional accountability to women's rights as human rights. As Khagram, Riker, and Sikkink note in this volume, IGOs such as the United Nations are often primary targets for transnational activism. In this case, the CSW, the Women's Convention, and related changes offered women's rights activists an opening or opportunity for both forging transnational networks and transforming human rights discourse.

Women's Rights as a Global Issue: The UN Decade and Three World Conferences

At the international level, the institutionalization of women's rights and status as global political issues took on more definable contours with the United Nations International Women's Year (1975), or IWY, and Decade for Women (1976–85). The IWY represents a concrete starting point from which to trace the international institutionalization of the norm. The events of the IWY and the ensuing Decade for Women constituted not merely isolated events, but elements of a process of development and institutionalization of global norms. In particular, my analysis of this process highlights the global dimension of relations between states and families, of authority in public and private realms.

A series of global conferences on women were focal events during the UN International Women's Year and the Decade for Women. The first (1975) World Conference on Women took place in Mexico City, where over six thousand people met for the largest-ever gathering on women. One hundred and twenty-five of 133 United Nations member states from all regions of the world sent representatives to this meeting to discuss and debate the status and concerns of women (Fraser 1987, 18). This conference, together with the subsequent conferences in Copenhagen (1980) and Nairobi (1985), saw several key developments. First, they focused state attention on both the legal status of women and the family practices that reproduced structures of gender inequality and domination. For example, the report from Mexico City asserts that "it is *the task of all States to create the necessary conditions* for the attainment" of women's equality with men, suggesting that states are responsible actors for guaranteeing women's rights. The World Plan also explicitly connects women's rights with family relations: "The family is also an important agent of social, political, and cultural change. If women are to enjoy equal rights, the functions and roles traditionally allotted to each sex within the family will require constant re-examination."[4] This emphasis on private realm equality was echoed in the 1985 *Nairobi Forward-Looking Strategies for the Advancement of Women,* which admonished governments to publicize the formerly private issue of gender-based abuse.

A second accomplishment was the recognition of the global character of women's inequality. The secondary status of women virtually everywhere could no longer be overlooked, but would now be a subject of debate and discussion among governments and citizens. The official report and program of action adopted in Copenhagen both recognized the contextual specificity of inequality between men and women and referred to a global historical process. The Copenhagen conference also put forward the now widely used statement incorporating some of the research on women conducted as a result of the IWY and the Decade for Women. "The effects of these long-term cumulative processes of discrimination [noted to be within and outside of the family] have been accentuated by underdevelopment and are strikingly apparent in the present *world profile of women:* while they represent 50 percent of the world adult population and one-third of the official labour force, they perform nearly two-thirds of all working hours, receive only one-tenth of the world income and own less than 1 per cent of world property" (United Nations 1980, 243). After the end-of-decade Nairobi conference, the contents of the Forward-Looking Strategies were widely disseminated to women around the world. Teresita Quintos-Deles, a CEDAW member and a peace and women's rights activist in the Philippines, contends that even if women don't know the Forward-Looking Strategies in detail, they know the basic themes because "there were enough women in Nairobi who took it home and said, 'This is ours.'"[5]

The Decade and its world conferences added a third important element to transnational women's human rights movements with the establishment of a number of prominent women's rights NGOs. These NGOs provided concrete institutional expression of and support for the idea that women's rights were global in scope, as well as the elements for a transnational network around women's human rights. The International Women's Tribune Center (IWTC) grew out of the Mexico City conference,[6] while International Women's Rights Action Watch (IWRAW), an international network of individuals and groups monitoring implementation of the Women's Convention, has its roots in a series of workshops on the Women's Convention held at the Nairobi conference in 1985.

In a sense, both IWTC and IWRAW are formalized transnational networks that focus on the gathering, exchange, and persuasive use of information on women's human rights violations and resources. Each of these formal, umbrella networks is in turn supported by a vast informal network of domestic women's NGOs. When IWRAW prepares a country report on women's rights for CEDAW, the staff of the NGO draws upon extensive, informal networks of contacts with NGOs to gather and later disburse information. IWRAW then compiles and channels this information to CEDAW and back to activists as part of a multilayered, multidirectional transnational network. Many of the women's NGOs forming this network (which includes women's crisis centers and shelters, women's political and educational organizations, and other NGOs focusing much of their energy domestically, yet definitely connected into transnational women's rights networks) would not be "counted" in the *Yearbook of International Organizations,* which helps to explain Sikkink and Smith's findings that periods of strong transnational activity around women's rights (1970s–80s) appeared not to show a comparable increase in international women's NGOs. At the same time, these apparently domestic NGOs clearly meet Sikkink and Smith's definition of a TSMO in "creating structures that convey information and ideas between individuals and groups within societies and the institutions that structure interstate relations." Nowhere is this more clear than in the list of NGOs approved for participation in the 2000 Beijing+5 Special Session at the UN. The list of groups participating in the global event includes women's NGOs such as the Kenyan Coalition on Violence against Women, the Women Workers' Union of Denmark, the Congress of Black Women of Canada, the U.S. Family Violence Prevention Fund, the Albanian Family Planning Association, and the Zambia National Women's Lobby Group. Many or most of these certainly fail to meet the *Yearbook*'s criteria for "international" NGOs.

Divisions and Disagreements within Transnational Women's Rights Movements

Despite agreement on many of the recommendations for states at the Mexico and Copenhagen conferences, disagreement and division over the appropriate strategies for women's activism highlighted cleavages and power struggles at the international level. Cheryl Johnson-Odim summarizes the widely held sentiment that "the battle lines were often drawn between First and Third World feminists over what constituted a feminist issue, and therefore what were legitimate feminist foci and goals" at both Mexico City and Copenhagen (1991, 317). One significant aspect of this First World–Third World cleavage was the debate over the appropriateness and effectiveness of pursuing a strategy emphasizing individual human rights, based on equality before the law and an end to gender discrimination. This debate can also be characterized as an opposition between the priority of collective or group rights vis-à-vis individual human rights (Donnelly 1989).

Many Third World women (including those geographically located in First World states) object to this interpretation of rights on the grounds that it is impossible for them to separate their struggle as women from the struggle of their community (race-, ethnicity-, and/or class-based). Hilary Charlesworth points out that these "third generation"[7] or group rights have been "only cautiously accepted by the mainstream international human rights community because of their challenge to the western, liberal model of individual rights invocable against the sovereign" (1994, 75). Third World women have frequently charged white, Western women with dominating and controlling the agendas of international women's conferences through disproportionate funding and attendance. As Sikkink and Smith note, this stems in part from the geographic concentration of NGOs in North America and Western Europe, as well as the inequitable distribution of funds and other resources skewed toward these regions of the world. Transnational activism in fact requires particular kinds of material resources, including travel funds, computer and Internet access, and the financial ability to take time away from day-to-day responsibilities to participate in meetings and conferences. Because such resources are often limited, a kind of funneling process can result in which only a handful of representatives can attend meetings or access information, raising questions about the representativeness and accountability of NGOs. The organizations with the greatest access to resources are most able to engage in transnational activism and influence the development of norms and institutions.[8] Conversely, though, changing international institutions and norms relating to women's rights have had the effect of bringing new voices into international human rights activism.

Women's Rights Are Human Rights: Breaking the Silences of the Human Rights Discourse

The discourse of international politics, long structured to focus on inter-state practices such as war, alliance formation, and trade, has recently been affected by the efforts of human rights groups. Human rights NGOs have worked to change the presumptive meaning of international relations as the realm of sovereign states. Human rights principles have emerged in a series of post–World War II international agreements and actions, solidify-ing the sense that the manner in which governments treat their own citi-zens represents a legitimate item on international political agendas (as Hawkins, this volume, describes).[9] The practices of human rights activists offered alternative interpretations of the domestic/international division of responsibility and authority. It is not an exaggeration to say that the social knowledge that structures international practice now includes the notion that human rights must at least be acknowledged as a legitimate issue of concern. "Authority" outside the boundaries of the state must now figure into the domestic ruler-ruled or state-citizen relation. Human rights norms represent political resources for global or regional institutions, citizen movements, or individuals to use to challenge statism. This is not to say that these resources are evenly distributed or equally effective in all cases (see Smith and Sikkink, this volume), only that they are increasingly avail-able and often effective.

Gendered Silences in the Dominant Human Rights Discourse

Beginning in the late 1980s, women's rights organizations and individual women from many countries recognized the potential of framing women's rights as human rights. However, the gendered nature of human rights dis-course required reformulation in order to attend to gender oppression. Much of the social knowledge drawn upon by international women's rights activists comes from the practices of mainstream human rights activists and organizations, as well as from their own experiences organizing women for change in their local and national communities. The dominant construction of international human rights issues was silent on gender-specific violations, especially in the private or family realm. One international women's rights activist notes that "[c]learly the interpretation and the development of the human rights mechanisms and processes and framework from that point had failed women in particular by not taking seriously the kinds of systematic discrimination and violence that they faced in different spheres."[10] This approach suggests that the human rights framework required modification in order to address the violation of women's rights, but retains the conventional understanding of the state as the primary actor responsible for implementing human rights—in this case, women's rights.

The 1948 Universal Declaration of Human Rights, one of the fundamental documents underpinning the global human rights discourse, decries distinctions based on sex.[11] However, it also describes the private sphere of the family as "the natural and fundamental group unit of society . . . entitled to protection by society and the State." Some women's rights activists argue that this "protection" of the family implies that the family is under the jurisdiction of a (male) head, relegating women to control in the private sphere. While individuals have rights, the family is a "natural" group unit (Fraser 1993, 31). Silence on human rights within the family stemmed in part from the historical legal status of women in many countries, under which women and children appear as legally and socially dependent within a patriarchal family unit. The "legal story" about women in some national contexts portrays them as legal minors or incompetents, making independent political claims on the state virtually impossible, and supporting state/public silence on the treatment of women and children within families.

The view of women's rights as somehow legally and politically distinct from men's rights was reinscribed in the separate establishment of United Nations commissions on human rights and women's rights (geographically separate and with differential allocation of resources and authority), sharpening the distinction between women's and human rights. In addition, as human rights declarations purport to be contracts between states and their citizens, women's ability to use these contracts has been limited because of the gendered nature of state-citizen relations (Kerr 1993, 5). This is largely because women in every country are "socially and economically disadvantaged in practice and in fact and in many places by law," restricting their capacity to participate in public life.[12] Even where women's de jure citizen relation to the state is the equivalent of men's, women's relationship to the state often, as Georgia Ashworth describes, "remains mediated by men, be they husbands, fathers, brothers or sons" (Kerr 1993, 5). While international human rights claims based on the traditional framework may serve as a resource in resisting certain forms of state repression, they did not offer women an effective resource for enhancing their security in the key site of the family.

Breaking the Silence: Gendering the Walk and Talk of Human Rights Activism

Mainstream human rights organizations have in recent years begun to rec-ognize how the traditional human rights framework perpetuates the invisi-bility of violations of women's human rights, in part because of a focus on violations by state agents (and of those, primarily civil and political rights violations). This emphasis on civil and political rights excludes many gender-based violations because "[m]any of the violations suffered by women are bound up with the disadvantages they suffer in the economic and so-cial field" (Byrnes 1990, 20). In the late 1980s, some mainstream human rights NGOs (including Amnesty International, Human Rights Watch, the Lawyers Committee for Human Rights, and the International League for Human Rights) started to consider more explicitly incorporating gender into their framework (Byrnes 1990, 33). Thus far, I have provided overviews of the introduction of women's rights and human rights to international in-stitutions and politics, and described debates among activists responsible for this introduction. This section specifically examines the institutionalization of the norm that the state is the site of responsibility and authority for women's rights.

This increasing attention to women's rights as human rights by main-stream groups was due to two factors. The 1979 United Nations adoption of the Convention on the Elimination of All Forms of Discrimination Against Women (Women's Convention) provided a comprehensive international normative statement of women's rights. The Women's Convention fits the traditional human rights mandate in that it calls upon states to alter their be-havior toward citizens, referring to the treaty obligations of "states parties" (United Nations 1984, 3). For articles of the Women's Convention such as those on granting nationality without regard to gender (Article 9) and allow-ing women to represent their governments at the international level on equal terms with men (Article 8), states represent the explicit agents of practices that need to be changed. However, it is not necessarily states that are the im-mediate agents of women's rights violations. The convention requires states parties not only "to ensure that public authorities and institutions" conform to the treaty, but also to act to "eliminate discrimination against women by any person, organization or enterprise" (5). The drafters of the convention recognized that implementation of this mandate demanded not only the conventional human rights standards of nondiscriminatory state conduct, but also the modification of "social and cultural patterns of conduct" and "family education" (Article 5, 6). In other words, not only public institutions and practices needed to be changed to ensure women's human rights; private or family practices also needed to be addressed, and addressed by states. In this way, the Women's Convention (as well as those activists encouraging mainstream human rights groups to take up the cause of the Women's Convention) suggested the need for a rejection of the public/ private boundary in human rights discourse. States should be viewed as responsible agents for violations of women's rights, whether in "public" or "private." In a process similar to that explicated by Daniel Thomas (this volume) in his analysis of the political opportunities created for East European human rights activists by the inclusion of human rights in the 1975 Helsinki Final Act, the alteration of the international human rights discourse to include gender-specific violations created the conditions of possibility for transnational women's rights activism and an emphasis on private-sphere violations.

The construction of the private sphere as a site of violations of women's human rights as well as a realm in which the state can legitimately intervene represents an important contribution of women's rights activists to the human rights discourse, and one of the ways in which the human rights discourse has been "gendered." To mitigate the gendered effects of focusing on public human rights violations or on state agents as rights violators, activists and governments suggested that the "rules of the game" in the domain of international human rights be altered in ways that challenged the boundaries between public and private responsibility. Particular articles of the Women's Convention, including Article 15 (legal capacity) and Article 16 (family law) can pose particular barriers for states because "[i]mplementation of these articles requires an examination of relationships between men and women, between family members, and between family and state, that affects every citizen personally as well as theoretically" (Freeman 1993, 95). This is a case where the unintended consequences of state action appear most strikingly. As one CEDAW member put it, governments have not yet understood the convention in that they don't consider rights in the family as human rights. The convention broadens the human rights concept.[13] State policy toward the institution of the family and women's roles within the family have been of major concern to CEDAW members (Byrnes 1989, 30).

A variety of practices contributed to this discursive and legal authorization of states to protect women within the family. There were explicit efforts on the part of women's rights activists to convince mainstream organizations that they ought to expand their mandate to include women's rights issues. A number of meetings and exchanges occurred between women's rights and human rights groups. For instance, in 1988, International Women's Rights

Action Watch hosted a meeting at the Carnegie Foundation in New York for representatives of human rights groups to persuade them of the importance of the Women's Convention as a human rights document.[14] While this meeting involved primarily U.S.-based activists, at least one Finnish human rights activist attended. Her presence helped to disseminate these concepts through the European human rights network. A 1992 consultation on international women's human rights sponsored by the Ford Foundation included lawyers from Africa, the Americas, Asia, Australia, and Europe (Cook 1992). Such meetings had the effect of both disseminating human rights norms and drawing geographically underrepresented voices into the discussion of women's rights as human rights.

In addition to the pressure from women's rights activists to broaden their mandate, activists within mainstream human rights organizations began to focus on new understandings of state responsibility for women's rights. Amnesty International, Human Rights Watch, and other organizations have long documented certain kinds of human rights violations against women, such as mass killings by soldiers. However, sex-specific and gender-based violations (such as rape) were generally not addressed. The structure of the international human rights framework precluded a focus on gender-based violations by highlighting civil and political rights violations by state agents. In the case of Human Rights Watch, the Women's Rights Project was established in 1990 to address this oversight. However, this project continues to use the same tools as the human rights framework, such as identifying violators, documenting abuses, and petitioning states for change. This dominant pattern of advocacy is evidenced by all the chapters in this section of the volume. As a result, for the most part, the first report of the Women's Rights Project dealt with "private actor" violations in examining violence against women in Brazil. The emphasis was on the failure of the state to prosecute crimes against women, even though those crimes were not committed by state agents. This report represented one of the early efforts to include domestic violence in the human rights accountability framework by evaluating the protections that the state offers to women.[15] The Women's Rights Project emphasizes the need to hold governments accountable for abuses of women's rights, monitoring "violence against women and discrimination on the basis of sex that is *committed or tolerated by governments*" (Human Rights Watch 1994, 1). Human rights NGOs such as Amnesty International and Human Rights Watch became part of the transnational network around women's human rights, contributing significantly to information development and exchange in the area of state practices.

The new focus of the human rights discourse being introduced through this kind of practice by human rights NGOs affects the relationship between states, female citizens of states, and international organizations. John Mathiason, who served as deputy director of the UN Division for the Advancement of Women and worked on the United Nations' first systemwide strategy for activities relating to women from 1990 to 1995, explained the novelty of this approach:

> [W]hen one began to look at the human rights of women, you have a very hard time under most of the human rights instruments to find violations of women's rights—women's rights and men's rights are the same. But, as our [Women's] Convention tends to show, what happens is that it's not rights violation in the usual sense of the state going out and doing something. It's the state *failing* to do something. And that's hard, that's always been harder in the human rights regime. That's why the human rights regime had a hard time dealing with women's rights. You just couldn't go out and find a state that was beating up on its women.[16]

States are being called upon not only to stop committing violations against women, but also (and more fundamentally in terms of the experiences of women in many countries) to stop tolerating violations by nonstate actors.

Amnesty International's 1991 report entitled "Women in the Front Line: Human Rights Violations against Women" represents another case of the increasing attention to women as social actors with human rights vis-à-vis their states. Amnesty International, however, chose to keep the boundaries of state responsibility more or less intact. On the one hand, the report recognized that women "face human rights violations solely or primarily because of their sex" (Amnesty International 1991, 52). The stories of human rights violations in the report, however, focus not on so-called "private" rights violations. Instead, "[i]t covers only those human rights violations which fall within Amnesty International's strictly defined mandate." This mandate focuses on prisoners of conscience, political prisoners, the death penalty, extrajudicial executions, and torture—all actions of state agents (Amnesty International 1991, 1–2).

In the context of gendering the human rights discourse and related political practices, the 1993 Vienna World Conference on Human Rights represents a key event in solidifying and entrenching "women's rights as human rights" in both governmental and nongovernmental institutions and practices.[17] While some objectives of human rights activists at the Vienna Conference were not achieved, most observers agreed that women's organizations dramatically and effectively placed women's rights on the international human rights agenda. This success came about in large measure because of effective transnational networking (information exchange) and coalition building (for coordinated campaigns). "Women's human rights are integrated into the mainstream of human rights; this theme is emphasized repeatedly in the Vienna Declaration. Most of the NGO reform proposals, such as an elaboration of an Optional Protocol to the Women's Convention introducing the right of petition, the immediate adoption of the Draft Declaration on Violence Against Women, and the appointment of a Special Rapporteur on this important issue, can be found in the Declaration."[18]

The Vienna Conference was viewed by many international women's rights activists as "a crucial opportunity to address women's rights as a human rights concern" (Kerr 1993, 159). A wide variety of national, regional, and international women's activities built momentum and support for putting women's rights on the 1993 Vienna Conference agenda, transforming less formal transnational networks into a more clearly defined, multitiered, transnational campaign. Working groups, conferences, lobbying, petition drives, demonstrations, and media campaigns were among the practices undertaken by women's NGOs from 1991 to 1993 in preparation for Vienna.

A key issue animating a transnational campaign around Vienna was violence against women. For example, during the first annual international "Sixteen Days of Activism against Gender Violence" campaign, a petition drive began in which activists coordinated in part by the Center for Women's Global Leadership called on the World Conference on Human Rights "to comprehensively address women's human rights at every level of its proceedings." The Sixteen Days Campaign temporally and conceptually links violence against women with human rights as it begins on 25 November, International Day for an End to Violence against Women, and ends 10 December, anniversary of the Universal Declaration of Human Rights.[19] The petition was eventually translated into twenty-three languages and over one thousand sponsoring groups had collected nearly half a million signatures from 124 countries (Bunch and Reilly 1994, 4–5). Activities at the Vienna Conference included a Global Tribunal on Violations of Women's Human Rights. A variety of practices by activists built on the beginnings of global social knowledge about women's human rights. One striking result of the pre-Vienna organizing by women was the gender composition of the NGO participants at the conference—nearly half were women, "an unprecedented number for a UN World Conference that was not focused specifically upon women or children" (Bunch and Reilly 1994, 94–95). Women's media groups disseminated information, including the Radio Tribunal on women's human rights conducted by FIRE (Feminist International Radio Endeavor). Daily women's caucuses, women activists in each of five conference working groups preparing text of the unified NGO document, and a report on the Global Tribunal were among the events and practices that spread knowledge of women's rights as human rights (Bunch and Reilly 1994, 96–104).[20] The Working Group on Women's Rights at the NGO Forum identified women's subordination on a global scale as a human rights issue: "Women's subordination throughout the world should be recognized as a human rights violation with due account to those structures of oppression that intersect and compound such subordination."[21]

The final document adopted by consensus of the 171 United Nations member states, the *Vienna Declaration and Programme of Action,* unequivocally situates women's rights within the broader terrain of human rights by claiming that "[t]he human rights of women and of the girl-child are an inalienable, integral and indivisible part of universal human rights . . . and the eradication of all forms of discrimination on grounds of sex are priority objectives of the international community" (United Nations 1993, 7).

Beijing: Holding States Accountable

While the events of preceding years clearly defined the contours of a *global* women's rights discourse, the 1995 UN Fourth World Women's Conference (FWCW) and parallel NGO forum held in Beijing served to make this globalization more concrete. It did so in several ways. First, the sheer number of participants at the FWCW was staggering. Each previous world conference on women—Mexico City, Copenhagen, and Nairobi—had grown progressively larger in terms of number of participants. None compared to the unexpectedly large number of participants at Beijing—approximately forty-six thousand in all (at both the official and the NGO conferences). Representatives of over 150 states negotiated to reach consensus on the Platform for Action, the blueprint for future action by states and other organizations to fulfill the promises made at Beijing. The NGO forum was also by far the largest ever—over twenty-six thousand people (mainly women) participated in the forum activities. The conference participants were also a more diverse group than at previous meetings, with five thousand participants from the host country of China alone. While women from the West and Japan still made up a disproportionately large number of conference goers, more countries and groups of women were represented.[22] This resulted in part from an effort to direct scholarship monies to enable poor and working-class women to attend the conference. In spite of the predominance of women from the United States and Europe, walking the streets of the NGO forum site was truly a "global experience."

The "critical areas of concern," or themes for the Platform for Action and the NGO forum, reflected the issues that had emerged as priorities in regional preparatory meetings. They included separate themes of violence against women, women's human rights, and the girl-child, among others. The regional preparatory meetings were another practice contributing to globalization, as women had the opportunity to meet on a smaller scale to identify their most pressing concerns. The Beijing conference was the first to organize regional NGO forums paralleling the regional intergovernmental preparatory meetings. These regional NGO meetings were well attended (a total of about ten thousand women attended the five regional meetings, at least double the expected number) (United Nations 1995a, 10). The Latin America and the Caribbean NGO Forum included twelve hundred participants from forty-one countries, while the Africa NGO Forum in Senegal attracted four thousand NGO delegates from fifty-two countries. The United Nations also hosted an NGO consultation in New York to report on the regional meetings and develop an "NGO lobbying document to the draft Platform for Action based on the regional documents" (United Nations 1995b, 3). These regional meetings built in another layer to the process of globalization, further concretizing women's rights norms as global in scope.

Examining some of the contentious issues and central themes at the FWCW illustrates how global norms do not simply emerge and affect actors, but are (and must be) constantly made and remade in the practices of women and men. It is these practices that form the process of normative change. Women's rights as human rights, the persuasive slogan of the Vienna World Conference on Human Rights, was one of the issues of concern to states and activists. The Women's Human Rights Caucus at the conference, composed of NGO representatives seeking to lobby and influence state representatives deciding on the final Platform for Action (PfA), fought to include strong language on "women's rights as human rights" in the PfA. Activists were concerned that diluting the language of women's human rights represented "backsliding" on commitments previously made by states at the Vienna human rights conference, the Cairo population conference, and the Copenhagen social summit. The clear attempt by a number of states to "backslide" shows the ongoing "work" of norm construction and reproduction—norms are established only through practice. While the institutional spaces provided by the United Nations, state agencies, and NGOs offer more coherence and material resources for a global discourse on women's rights, it is the practices of states, citizens, and organizations that give the norms material expression. In fact, I argue that the way we know a norm exists is through its reflection in the practices of these actors.

Violence against Women at Beijing

Another striking feature of the FWCW was the emphasis on violence against women, especially family violence, as both a global and a human rights issue. Violence against women was a priority issue emerging from all the regional conferences, and violence against women, including family violence, was one of the twelve priority issues framing the conference. Getting the issue on the governmental agenda, however, was not always automatic. The European Economic Commission (the UN regional body that held the Europe–North America regional preparatory meeting for Beijing) document to be used as a regional input for the Beijing platform initially did not include language on violence against women, but ultimately did as a result of women's lobbying efforts.[23] The practices of NGOs again proved critical to constructing a norm of state responsibility for private, as well as public, rights violations.

The PfA, the concluding document coming out of the Beijing conference, strongly linked violence against women with human rights: "Violence against women is an obstacle to the achievement of the objectives of equality, development and peace. Violence against women both violates and impairs or nullifies the enjoyment by women of their human rights and fundamental freedoms." The PfA language also clearly supports the normative construction of state responsibility for private acts of violence, defining violence against women as "any act of gender-based violence . . . whether occurring in public or private life" and as including "violence perpetrated or condoned by the State, wherever it occurs" (*Beijing Declaration and Platform for Action,* sections 113, 114). The norm of women's rights to make claims on states for protection against "private" violence, and the responsibility of states to prevent such violence, were strongly rearticulated in this document.

Gender-based violence was also a prominent theme at the NGO forum, with typically at least twenty events (seminars, workshops, tribunals) per day dealing specifically with violence against women or family violence. In the first two days of the forum alone, over forty workshops and events on violence against women were held. Women from all regions of the world met to discuss definitions, causes of, and strategies against gender-based violence. Protests against violence at the forum included a demonstration involving hundreds of women. The widespread attention to violence against women was in some ways a globalizing and unifying theme for women's rights activists, contributing to a construction of women's rights emphasizing gender-based commonality and globalism.

Beijing saw a call for a transnational campaign to end violence against women, based in large part on the fact that all the regional preparatory conferences agreed that violence represents a common global issue for women. As the organizer of the Women's Human Rights and Violence against Women thematic workshop at the Vienna regional preparatory forum explained, "When you look at human rights through women's eyes, gender-based violence is the most personal and fundamental everyday violation that occurs throughout the world, to women of every color and class."[24] This commonality was reflected in the many pieces of women's art at the conference site, including quilts, t-shirts, and paintings, that spoke to the issue of gender-based violence. The Center for Women's Global Leadership organized a Global Tribunal on Women's Human Rights that prominently featured gender-based violence, based on the testimony of women from all areas of the world. The global "Sixteen Days" campaign against gender violence was also actively promoted at Beijing.

Holding States Accountable through the International Legal Framework

Beijing did not see the development of a new international convention on women, but it did provide the site for NGOs and citizens to articulate claims on states through the already-established legal and institutional framework. The above-referenced work of NGO activists to retain in the PfA commitments made by states at previous conferences is one example of these practices. The designation of Beijing as the "conference of commitments" was critical to solidifying the legal framework and to strengthening the material effects of the discursive construction of women's rights as human rights. A proposal by the Australian delegation at the preparatory CSW session to make Beijing the "conference of commitments" was strongly supported by NGOs, and the slogan was concretized by states announcing their commitments to women at the Beijing conference. While many states did announce their commitments at the FWCW, there was also a successful opposition to the recording of state commitments for inclusion in the FWCW report. In a clear-cut example of NGO practices to reassert the responsibility of states, NGOs tracked the commitments made during states' plenary speeches.[25] The Women's Environmental and Development Organization (WEDO) has subsequently coordinated a transnational campaign by women's NGOs to track and monitor the actual practices of states with regard to commitments of support and resources made at Beijing and to monitor implementation of the PfA.[26] The June 2000 Beijing+5 assessment of progress made toward Beijing commitments served a similar purpose, with a political declaration by special session of the General Assembly strongly reaffirming that states are responsible for implementing the PfA.[27] When states acted to resist the material implications of their rhetorical commitments to implement women's rights at the national level, NGOs stepped in and engaged in practices to reinforce global norms about state responsibility. This supports both the centrality of NGOs to the process of developing global norms about women's rights and the ways in which state practices with regard to norms may have unintended effects (in this case, ongoing monitoring by citizens of their commitments). The PfA and other commitments made by governments at Beijing were recognized as crucial to the strength of the international legal and institutional framework for women's rights—they are means to support and reinforce that framework.

Other practices by NGOs at the FWCW served to establish state accountability for women's rights through the international legal framework of women's rights as human rights. Among them was a movement to incorporate "gender perspectives" into all UN-based human rights work. An expert group meeting held just prior to Beijing produced a set of recommendations distributed at the FWCW on "gendering" the United Nations human rights system not just through CEDAW and the CSW, but through "a comprehensive integration of gender perspectives into all parts of the United Nations," including other human rights bodies and individual complaints under optional protocols.[28] This would expand the range of state, IGO, and NGO practices relevant to the representation of women's rights as human rights. One NGO, International Women's Rights Action Watch, has recently expanded its mandate beyond reporting on women's rights violations to CEDAW—it now prepares gender-specific reports on rights violations for other UN human rights bodies, including the Committee on the Rights of the Child. In practical terms, the mere existence of a legal framework served to establish the conditions of possibility for holding states accountable. The work of NGOs through this framework now offers the possibility of strengthening norms about state responsibility in concrete ways.

Demands for a mechanism to allow individual women or NGOs to make direct claims for rights violations found expression at Beijing. A campaign among NGOs called for the adoption of an optional protocol to the Women's Convention to allow the right to petition CEDAW for specific cases of rights violations. For instance, among the many NGOs supporting the optional protocol, Human Rights Watch notes: "Member states should adopt and ratify a protocol to CEDAW that would allow women whose *domestic legal systems have failed them* to submit complaints directly to the Committee on the Elimination of Discrimination Against Women" (Human Rights Watch 1995, xxi). A number of NGOs held sessions at the Beijing

NGO forum for the purpose of educating women on the use of international law in domestic contexts. Ultimately, the Optional Protocol campaign was successful, with the protocol adopted and opened for signature on International Human Rights Day in December 1999. This process represents an attempt for citizens to hold states and private rights violators responsible for their actions. This kind of practice is critical to institutionalization—it builds on the previous developments (globalizing, framing in international laws and institutions) to make private violations public and to make states responsible for women's rights.

Women's Rights as Human Rights: The New Sounds of Silence

Gendering the discourse of human rights places women's rights on international political agendas and establishes the norm of state responsibility for the status of women. This construction of state authority, while popular, has its own empowering *and* exclusionary political effects. The move toward incorporating state responsibility for women's rights came not only as a result of women's groups persuading human rights organizations that they should broaden their vision of human rights; it also stemmed from an increasing focus on the state as a critical agent for improving women's lives and from the recognition that the state already controlled many aspects of women's lives. As Anne Phillips explains, "All contemporary states have an agenda for women and the family, but it is often covert and contradictory, and hard to expose to the public gaze" (1991, 86). Arvonne Fraser argues that by the early 1990s, "the international women's movement had learned that in organizing there can be strength and that the state can be a friend as well as an enemy" (1993, 32). Activists at the Center for Women's Global Leadership, for example, explicitly sought out "some of the frameworks that exist in the world, that would facilitate linkages globally, that have potential and possibilities for the advancement of women. So, we began wondering about using the human rights framework to facilitate and to be an umbrella framework around which women would link and work together internationally."[29] This increased focus on framing gender inequality in terms of human rights was one of the ways in which the relationship between international women's rights advocacy and male-dominated state structures was changing.

Transnational organizing around women's human rights should be understood as global in nature. While many women's human rights activists are based in the West, the use of the social knowledge and resources contained in the historically male-dominated human rights practices has not been confined to Western women's rights NGOs. For instance, the international network "Women Living under Muslim Laws," created in 1986, undertakes to "[a]ctively support women's initiatives in Muslim countries and communities and defend women's human rights" (Helie-Lucas 1993, 57). Many other transnational women's rights organizations strive for similar goals in other communities, including ISIS-International (Philippines), Third World Movement against the Exploitation of Women, Asian Women's Human Rights Council, Caribbean Association for Feminist Research and Action, Comité Latinoamericano para la Defensa de los Derechos de la Mujer, and Women in Law and Development Africa, to name only a few. The Global Campaign for Women's Human Rights links these groups and other groups and individuals together in a loosely formed, worldwide coalition working for women's human rights (Bunch and Reilly 1994, 3). Activists self-consciously identify an international women's movement in relation to a global political space. Khunying Supatra Masdit, the Convener of the Beijing NGO Forum on Women 1995, explained in a 1994 speech in Vienna that it is important to strengthen the international women's movement because many of the "local and national problems we struggle with have their roots in global structures."[30] This view of women's rights as a global political issue implies particular kinds of political strategies and global commonalities. It suggests that many of the common issues faced by women must be addressed in terms of the global structures underlying them—local or national action alone cannot resolve them. This understanding also implies fundamental common qualities of the subordination of women in very different national, economic, and cultural contexts.

Despite extensive transnational organizing and cooperation among women's rights NGOs, including the emergence of transnational networks and coalitions around specific issues such as gender-based violence, the tensions among women's groups from different areas of the world cannot be overlooked. Transnational social movements produce not simple coherence, but complex and conflictual relationships, often clearly in evidence at international events and conferences. Such tensions often reflect disparities in terms of power and resources that influence whether and how women participate in transnational women's rights activism. The dominance of women from the United States and Western Europe, as well as of upper- and middle-class educated women, suggests that other voices have not been heard.[31] Women living in poverty, working-class women, women of color, and Third World women have often not participated in international women's rights activism. The 1995 Beijing conference was the site of numerous attempts (with mixed results) to incorporate the largely unheard voices of these women, not only within the larger international human rights framework, but specifically within the linked discourse of women's human rights.

Understanding gender-based oppression in terms of a human rights framework is itself an issue, as was briefly mentioned earlier in the context of the debate over the priority of collective versus individual rights. There is a uniquely gendered aspect to this debate as well. As one analyst of women's rights in southern Africa put it, "No attempt to analyse the position of women in African customary law from the standpoint of rights is immune from the suggestion that the whole process is a 'Western-inspired' exercise and therefore irrelevant at best and, at worst, traitorous. In this connection it is often argued that the whole notion of human rights is foreign to Africa and is an inappropriate standard against which to judge political and social arrangements on the continent" (Nhlapo 1991, 139). The very use of legalistic discourse is at the least not empowering and at the worst disempowering for some women, depending on their social context. For example, human rights activist Tokunbo Ige from Nigeria pointed out that legal reforms of the kind typically pursued under human rights approaches can be ineffective and irrelevant in a case such as her country, where the court system is not regarded as an effective problem-solving institution (Kerr 1993, 160–61). Making use of laws that protect women's rights also requires resources and capacities (money, literacy, time) unavailable to many women, especially (but not only) in developing countries. The rights-based approach, because of its affinity with a Western liberal political project and the modern European states system, provokes criticism from state officials and women alike. Women activists may be understood as cultural traitors or sellouts to Western, bourgeois feminism. These diverging views of the usefulness of a human rights framework may reflect different forms of state-citizen relations in different countries, and also clearly suggest the resistance to the identification of the West in general and the United States in particular as the standard setters for international women's movements.

Second, because of the above-mentioned limitations and silences of the international human rights discourse, it cannot provide the conditions of possibility for eradicating many forms of gender oppression such as those involving global economic processes and racism. The human rights discourse has limited capacity to address questions of global distributive justice. This is not to say that women should abandon the notion of women's human rights, because it can serve as a useful tool in many instances. However, the discourse of human rights contains particular kinds of social knowledge about causes of gender oppression and appropriate remedies for this oppression. This knowledge focuses on states and legal rights.

Activists participating in transnational organizing have argued for alternative knowledge about gender oppression focusing on economic or community-based strategies for change. Self-identified indigenous women meeting at Beijing, for example, suggested that equality and rights could not address many forms of gender oppression:

> [The Beijing Platform for Action's] recommended "strategic objectives" and actions focus on ensuring women's equal access and full participation in decision-making, equal status, equal pay, and in integrating and mainstreaming gender perspectives and analysis. These objectives are hollow and meaningless if the inequality between nations, races, classes, and genders is not challenged at the same time. Equal pay and equal status in the so-called First World is made possible because of the perpetuation of a development model which is not only unsustainable but causes the increasing violation of the human rights of women, indigenous peoples, and nations elsewhere. The Platform's overemphasis on gender discrimination and gender equality depoliticizes the issues confronting indigenous women.[32]

Instead of discursively linking women's human rights and equality with social change, the declaration suggests that the rights of indigenous peoples to *self-determination* represent the most central goal.[33] Rigoberta Menchu, a prominent transnational activist in the area of indigenous peoples, questioned the ability of a forum such as the Beijing conference to address the concerns of indigenous women: "It's a fact that the immense majority of the organizations that planned the Beijing World Congress [on Women] have marginalized indigenous women" and because of this "indigenous women will not be taken into account in the women's agenda."[34]

Other groups emphasized economic inequality and the exclusion of grassroots women as obstacles to eradicating gender oppression, in lieu of a focus on protecting human rights. Dr. Nandini Azad of the GROOTS delegation to Beijing suggested that "[g]rassroots women are neither weak nor defenceless. . . . What they need therefore is self-initiated, integrative and gender equitable planning *instead of protection*. . . . Resources have to be used differently."[35] These alternative formulations have common elements with dominant women's rights discourses, but significantly different emphases and prescriptive force.

Contestations around the dominant global women's rights discourse are crucial not only for the resistance and power struggles they connote, but also for the ways in which they influence the development of global norms as they rearticulate them in slightly different ways. Poverty and economic exploitation, for example, were central issues at Beijing. The efforts made to bring a more diverse group of women to Beijing brought new voices to the task of articulating global norms about women's rights.

Despite disagreements and debates over how to focus international activism around the advancement of women, practices have increasingly converged around some form of women's human rights. This reshaping of understandings about the appropriate means for achieving gender equality and addressing gender hierarchies shifted the emphasis to human rights mechanisms and state responsibility. This move cannot be underestimated, nor should it be misunderstood as merely a challenge to existing state practices. While international women's rights activists self-consciously draw on human rights discourse as a resource for pressing women's claims against often nonresponsive states, these practices could serve also to reinforce state power over all citizens. The kind of global connection being made in international women's rights networks and practices has often been understood in the human rights literature as strictly a challenge to state authority.

In the case of international women's human rights, citizens and transnational NGOs and IGOs are *asking states to assume additional responsibility and obligation in the so-called private sphere of the home and family.* This construction of the state as the site of responsibility for protecting women within the family, as a "state party" to international laws obligating the governmental apparatus to be aware of and to establish practices for eliminating gender oppression with families, has the additional effect of strengthening the state as the predominant political actor in the global political system. The human rights discourse is part and parcel of the broader discourse of states as fundamental political actors. Claims are made on states. In this case, state authority is challenged and potentially reinforced. Whereas states may not have understood themselves as obligated to intervene in family situations in the past, international law and citizens' groups now demand that they do so. Through these demands and changing practices, the boundary of responsibility and authority between state and family is altered in a global sense. In the case of women's human rights, this reinforcement of states as key actors is critical precisely because it suggests that transnational collective action should aim to influence the development and enforcement of international norms (i.e., norms about appropriate state behavior) as opposed to focusing efforts on local or community-based strategies. An emphasis on state responsibility also tends to encourage legal and/or electoral strategies for change, as these are the primary means for many citizens to affect their states. Such strategies can have limited effectiveness for women who lack legal or political resources, and for those economic and political issues with their roots in global processes. For instance, it is well documented that women are adversely affected by certain aspects of structural adjustment programs (SAP). Yet, activism targeted at changing a state structure would fail to address the transnational source of much SAP policy.

The preceding exploration of transnational organizing around women's rights and relevant state practices suggests several key elements of the process of institutionalization of global norms. The norm of state responsibility for women's rights, in particular for addressing gender oppression in both public and private settings, is increasingly and repeatedly invoked. This analysis of expressed understandings about women's rights is suggestive of how the boundaries between state and families, public and private can change in part through transnational activism, and how normative influences can be global as well as national.

What lessons can be drawn from this case? First, the importance of international institutions such as the United Nations as a forum for transnational networks to develop, in part through the personal contacts and shared experiences of participating in global conferences and campaigns, cannot be underestimated. Second, NGOs clearly have a great deal of persuasive ability (what Sikkink terms "soft power") in promoting state adherence to international norms. NGO monitoring and publicity in the case of women's rights have resulted in a greater degree of accountability for states to the commitments they have made. But, as some observers pointed out at the Beijing conference, the transnational women's human rights movement itself must be accountable to women, and cannot be so without including a broad range of voices and perspectives.

Notes

This chapter is based largely on research funded by the MacArthur Program on Peace and International Cooperation, the University of Minnesota, and the Institute for the Study of World Politics. I am grateful to members of the Minnesota-Stanford-Wisconsin MacArthur Consortium Research Network on Globalization and Global Governance for their critical reading and helpful comments on this work.

1. My use of the term *global norms* in this chapter is intended to convey a sense of shared understandings beyond the *international norms* defined in chapter 1 of this volume as "standards of appropriate behavior held by a critical mass of states." I look to the broad normative terrain encompassing both international norms evidenced by state practices and related understandings expressed by a range of other actors including individual activists, NGOs, and units of INGOs. For a comparison of the role of international networks in establishing institutional nodes, see Daniel Thomas on the Helsinki network (this volume).

2. Here *transnational movements* is appropriate because it is difficult to define a singular transnational women's rights movement. However, I argue that it is possible

to outline a dominant global women's rights discourse as well as its companion alternative discourses that make up the terrain of global women's rights norms.

3. "ECOSOC resolution establishing the Commission on the Status of Women (CSW)," E/RES/2/11, 21 June 1946. In United Nations 1995d (102).

4. *World Plan of Action for Implementation of the Objectives of the International Women's Year,* 126, 131–32, as cited in Fraser 1987 (44–45).

5. Teresita Quintos-Deles, CEDAW member, interview by author, 24 January 1994.

6. Anne Walker, director, International Women's Tribune Center, interview by author, 1 September 1994. This is an example that clearly draws the linkages between the UN conferences and the growth of international organizing around women's issues.

7. "First generation rights" are widely understood to encompass civil and political rights; "second generation rights" are those economic, social, and cultural rights promoted most strongly by non-Western activists and governments; and "third generation rights" are collective, group, or "people's" rights.

8. Kidder and Nelson (this volume) note similar tensions in the cases they analyze.

9. For example, the adoption of the Universal Declaration of Human Rights and the concomitant establishment of the United Nations Human Rights Commission, the Council of Europe's European Convention on Human Rights, and the OAS Declaration of Human Rights.

10. Niamh Reilly, program associate, Center for Women's Global Leadership, Rutgers University, New Brunswick, N.J., interview by author, 4 April 1995.

11. Cook 1993 points out that the legal obligation to eliminate discrimination against women is a fundamental tenet of international human rights law. Sex discrimination is prohibited not only by the Universal Declaration, but also by the International Covenant on Civil and Political Rights, the International Covenant on Economic, Social, and Cultural Rights, and regional human rights conventions (the European Convention for the Protection of Human Rights and Fundamental Freedoms, the American Convention on Human Rights, and the African Charter on Human and People's Rights).

12. Legal inequalities include nationality and marriage laws; see Thomas and Beasley 1993 (39).

13. Dr. Hanna Beate Schopp-Schilling, CEDAW member, interview by author, 19 January 1994.

14. Arvonne Fraser, former director, International Women's Rights Action Watch, and former U.S. representative to the UN Commission on the Status of Women, interview by author.

15. This discussion on the development of the Women's Rights Project comes

from an interview by the author with Regan Ralph, acting do-director of the Women's Rights Project of Human Rights Watch, Washington, D.C., 29 August 1994.

16. John Mathiason, deputy director of UN Division for the Advancement of Women, interview by author, New York City, 25 August 1994.

17. The Vienna Conference was also a turning point on the issue of violence against women.

18. *World Conference on Human Rights, Vienna/Austria, 14–25 June 1993, NGO Newsletter No. 4,* Vienna, Ludwig Boltzmann Institute of Human Rights, 5.

19. Women attending the First Feminist Encuentro for Latin America and the Caribbean in Bogota, Colombia, in July 1981 proposed the designation of 25 November as International Day for an End to Violence against Women to commemorate the 1960 assassination of the Miraval sisters by the Dominican Republic security forces.

20. The development of this web of communications opportunities, common campaigns (such as the Sixteen Days Campaign against gender-based violence), and shared adherence to the promotion of women's human rights norms created what Keck and Sikkink term a *transnational advocacy network* around women's rights (Keck and Sikkink 1998); see also Smith and Sikkink, this volume.

21. "Statement by the Working Group on Women's Rights of the NGO Forum at the World Conference on Human Rights" (1993), mimeo.

22. According to forum organizers, the NGO forum registered participants were distributed regionally as follows: Europe and North America, 40 percent; Asia and Pacific, 45 percent; Africa, 8 percent; Latin America and the Caribbean, 5 percent; Western Asia, 2 percent.

23. Observation at Vienna regional conference, October 1994.

24. Charlotte Bunch, Center for Women's Global Leadership, speech at Vienna ECE regional meeting, October 1994. At the thematic workshop, participants defined six areas of violence against women for consideration: (1) domestic violence; (2) religious traditions; (3) trafficking in women; (4) war, migration, and conflict situations; (5) rape; and (6) female genital mutilation.

25. "Summary of Fourth World Conference on Women," *Earth Negotiations Bulletin* 14, no. 21 (18 September 1995).

26. WEDO is an international advocacy network focusing on women's power in policymaking processes.

27. "Preliminary Analysis of the Beijing+5 Outcome Document," Division for the Advancement of Women, United Nations, http://www.un.org/womenwatch/daw/followup/analysis.html, accessed 28 August 2000.

28. "Working Paper on Development of Guidelines to Incorporate Gender Perspectives into the Human Rights Work of the United Nations," Report of Expert

Meeting, Palais des Nations, Geneva, 3–7 July 1995 (UNIFEM and Centre for Human Rights), 9.

29. Reilly, interview.

30. Khunying Supatra Masdit, convener of NGO Forum on Women 1995, speech to Opening Plenary Session of Vienna Regional NGO Forum on Women, 13 October 1994.

31. In a quite literal example, a number of French-speaking women left a 1994 regional preparatory meeting for Beijing in protest over the dominance of English as a working language and their consequent inability to make their voices heard.

32. *Beijing Declaration of Indigenous Women,* para. 16. Transmitted via e-mail 13 September 1995 from femisa@csf.colorado.edu.

33. *Beijing Declaration of Indigenous Women,* para. 17.

34. Rosa Rojas, "Menchu: The Indigenous Woman Is Being Marginalized at the Beijing Conference," *La Jornada,* Mexico City, 4 September 1995 (translated for NY Transfer News by Michael Pearlman, transmitted electronically via NY Transfer News Collective by zapata@together.net).

35. Dr. Nandini Azad, "Statement Made by Dr. Nandini Azad, chairperson, GROOTS [Grassroots Organisations Operating Together in Sisterhood]," 10 September 1995 (electronically transmitted by the United Nations Development Programme (UNDP) in collaboration with the UN Fourth World Conference on Women Secretariat).

6

A Human Rights Practitioner's Perspective

Charles T. Call

Darren Hawkins, Daniel Thomas, and Karen Brown Thompson each provides an excellent illustration of how activists—most notably victims—have transformed world politics. Acting through advocacy networks, victims of gender oppression and political repression by the Left and the Right have organized themselves, stimulated advocacy networks, and ultimately reshaped state interests, undermined regimes, and strengthened international norms on which they drew. These case studies are illustrative of constraints on governmental behavior that were unthinkable only thirty years ago.

At the same time, human rights activists are daily aware of the abiding limits on their ability to curb violations of widely accepted international human rights norms. As someone with one foot in academia and the other in the policy world, including my work with human rights NGOs, I have been asked to comment on these three chapters. Two recent personal experiences as a consultant to Human Rights Watch are immediately pertinent. In 1999, I documented violations of the laws of war in Chechnya, and in 2000 I documented similar violations in Colombia's guerrilla-held territory. These different situations exemplify the continuing limits facing transnational advocacy networks in their efforts to influence powerful states on the one hand, and nonstate perpetrators on the other. Russia, for instance, continued to use methods and arms that drew strenuous objections from human rights groups and Western governments, even as the latter proved unwilling to adopt sanctions they might have enacted against weaker countries.

In the face of academic analysis that shows the impact of human rights ideas and advocacy, it is important to recognize the continued resistance to these ideas and efforts, especially among powerful governments. Certainly the international climate for enforcing and advancing human rights norms is vastly improved. And rights activists, perhaps because of the daily obstacles they encounter, tend to overstate the constraints posed by powerful countries, bureaucracies, and public apathy. Nevertheless, frustrations among activists seeking to improve human rights in China, Russia, the United States, and Turkey signify the continued importance of material power and the need to integrate such considerations into analysis of norms.

Hawkins's and Thomas's accounts closely parallel my own experience in human rights advocacy during the 1980s and 1990s. One of the main strategies of the little-known Washington Office on Latin America was to bring Latin American victims of human rights violations to Washington to press congresspersons and U.S. officials to more vigorously enforce human rights standards. Hearing directly from repression's victims, either through such visits or through congressional delegations to the region, elicited moral outrage that was translated into political action. As these two chapters depict, the impact of this advocacy was meaningful but not fully satisfactory. Activists from Latin America often guided our strategies and tactics, and many Latin American political actors eventually knew the ways of Washington better than some U.S. analysts.

The universality inherent in human rights has permitted multiple marginalized and oppressed groups to draw on the language and legitimacy of the human rights legal regime. In responding to their denunciations of human rights violations, many astute actors with more directly political concerns have successfully framed those concerns in the rubric of "human rights." As the book's first chapter notes, "framing" is one way that advocates achieve acceptance of their claims. On this point, I believe that Hawkins omits an important element of why Chile became a "crucial case": Pinochet's regime was not only brutal, but also represented the overthrow of the hemisphere's first elected Socialist government. This political dimension helped Chilean human rights activists garner more resources and political support from international allies acting out of a political context as well as a humanitarian one. Many NGOs within the "Chile network" saw human rights advocacy not only as a means of protecting lives, but also as a tool against a repressive capitalist order. Similarly but more cynically, once the Reagan administration failed in its efforts to dismantle human rights bureaucracies erected during the Carter administration, it determined to use those bureaucracies to confront socialism rather than friendly right-wing repressive regimes. Ironically, when actors with questionable commitment to human rights norms and language draw upon them, they strengthen those norms, often in unforeseen ways that "entrap" them. Thomas's account of Soviet acceptance of the Helsinki Act shows how a regime reaching for the cloak of legitimacy can become entangled in a lethal net. So does Pinochet's decision to ratify the UN Convention against Torture, which eventually snared him in Britain.

Thomas provides an illuminating account of the eventual impact of the Helsinki Final Act, showing how East European activists stimulated Western governmental responses that had far-reaching impact on rights, governments, and even international relations. His account of the creation of the U.S. Helsinki Commission shows how the causal arrow can point both ways: most academics and practitioners focus on the influence of nongovernmental actors on government human rights practices, but government strategies also shape the playing field for nongovernmental human rights activities.

Human rights advocates don't often step back and reflect on their work, and rarely think in terms of "international norms" and "regimes." Nevertheless, many transnational rights networks and NGOs seek to go beyond the implementation of human rights norms by bolstering those norms. Hawkins and Thomas stress how nongovernmental activists helped translate extant human rights norms into Western pressure and policies. Yet those very activities in turn strengthened rights norms and even helped constitute new ones. Hawkins's case of Chile is a perfect example. The British Court's rejection of immunity in 1999 for General Pinochet not only reflected the lingering effects of the "Chile network," but also contributed to an emergent international norm that former heads of state are not immune from prosecution for crimes against humanity. Increasingly global human rights standards have enabled advocates to think far beyond old boundaries. NGOs now self-consciously plan to create new norms (e.g., banning weapons like land mines) and new instruments (e.g., the international criminal court, truth commissions) for rights protections.

Brown Thompson's chapter richly shows how women's rights activists have broadened the definition of human rights and expanded state action in the private sphere. What strikes me about her contribution is how differently women's rights evolved relative to the networks around physical integrity and political rights described by Hawkins and Thomas. The role of UN conferences, statements, and declarations that marked work on gender rights contrasts sharply with my own experiences of contentious efforts to educate and pressure congressional offices and government officials in the United States and abroad. Perhaps the process of developing new norms and regimes around certain group rights follows different paths than efforts to get powerful governments and international organizations to implement previously agreed-upon commitments.

Brown Thompson superbly shows how women's rights activists have "gendered" the human rights discourse. "Gendering" not only has brought human rights NGOs into the private sphere, but it also holds important substantive implications for all sorts of outcomes. In early 1994, for example, the Clinton White House approached several human rights and advocacy NGOs to seek their public and decisive support for the use of military force to oust Haiti's brutal military regime. Although religious and human rights NGOs had lobbied insistently for stronger U.S. action against the military regime, most were reluctant to call for military intervention given their objections to past U.S. interventions in the hemisphere. At a meeting of sixteen heads of NGOs to discuss the question of military force, two directors strongly opposed intervention, and the remaining fourteen opted not to oppose U.S. intervention. I believe it is no coincidence that the two dissenting directors were also the only two women in the room. This example shows how gendering human rights advocacy is likely not to simply add new concerns to an agenda, but to have far-reaching implications for the process and outcomes of transnational advocacy.

Brown Thompson raises some serious and well-founded critiques of the human rights movement and its foundations. She shows how international human rights instruments helped make women's rights invisible. Those of us who worked with self-denominated "human rights NGOs" in Washington during the 1980s and 1990s were too slow to organize action on women's rights, indigenous rights, gay rights, and children's rights. Most "traditional" human rights NGOs eventually embraced these group rights and helped strengthen their place in human rights instruments and discourse. They often did so because of education and even pressure from specialized groups and others dedicated to various group rights. I recall being lectured by two Senate aides who said that my office was not doing enough on indigenous rights. Funders, especially Western foundations, helped bring group rights (e.g., children's rights) into mainstream human rights concerns by channeling their funding accordingly. Brown Thompson brings out an overlooked point: that NGOs and advocacy networks often need to be educated and pressed—even by governments, the United Nations, or foundations—to reexamine their scope of work and to expand participation in coalitions on diverse rights issues.

Rights-related NGOs and networks enjoy greater influence than they ever imagined three decades ago. Greater power brings greater responsibility. The rights-friendly post–cold war environment and the unprecedented influence of human rights groups yield new challenges for those groups on a number of levels. First, rights-related NGOs must make sure they practice what they preach. NGOs, be they wealthy and Geneva-based or young and poor in developing countries, often ignore internal patterns of discrimination based on gender, ethnicity, sexual preference, or class. They often fail to provide minimum health and retirement benefits. Greater scrutiny of these issues by fellow NGOs and even funders will inevitably be perceived as unwarranted interference, but may be helpful to prevent advocacy for some rights from undermining other rights. NGOs must take steps to address growing critiques of their lack of accountability.

Second, as Brown Thompson suggests, NGOs will increasingly have to confront new and diverse concerns, identify new advocacy targets, and develop new methods. Campaigns over repressive authoritarian regimes have largely been supplanted by more diverse struggles over different types of rights. Consequently, the nature and composition of the "transnational human rights advocacy network" has itself changed. Tensions abound between South and North, East and West, social/economic/cultural rights versus civil/political rights, individual versus group rights, local level versus national level strategies, and so forth. None of these cleavages necessarily coincides with others. Human rights advocates everywhere will increasingly need to consider strategies and tactics in light of this more diverse community.

The proliferation of "rights networks" has spawned multiple competing agendas. Now that most governments in the world must at least take human rights into consideration in formulating policies, political battles have shifted from the *recognition* of rights to the *ranking* of rights—from "whether" rights to "which" rights. In many post-transition societies, for instance, "victims' rights" movements have called for tougher criminal justice laws and enforcement, directly contradicting the positions held by most international and national human rights NGOs. These are some of the tensions signaled by Brown Thompson.

Globalization poses a third challenge for NGOs internationally: how to carry out advocacy aimed at targets beyond the more conventional "governments." Brown Thompson's chapter illustrates several ways in which women's rights advocates changed state behavior by successfully targeting, and benefiting from, international organizations. As power over the conditions of labor, capital, and even coercion is accumulated in intergovernmental organizations, regional and international organizations, and multinational corporations, transnational advocacy networks will have to continue to develop new strategies and tactics. The chapters presented here provide useful concepts and experiences for NGOs seeking effectiveness in this complex transnational environment.

Part III
Promoting Development, Environmental Protection, and Governance

7

Agendas, Accountability, and Legitimacy among Transnational Networks Lobbying the World Bank

Paul J. Nelson

The World Bank has been dragged into the world of participatory–public-interest politics and may never be the same.
— Bruce Stokes, *National Journal*

Within the institution the U.S. non-governmental organizations are taken too seriously.
— Evelyn Herfkens, executive director to the World Bank

Scholars and practitioners interested in the expanding role of nonstate actors, including NGOs, have labored to demonstrate their relevance to governmental policy processes and to catalog the variety of methods NGOs use to influence governmental and corporate behavior (Keck and Sikkink 1998; Sikkink 1993a; Wapner 1995; Clark 1991; Florini 2000).

But with NGOs' place as political actors, often through transnational advocacy networks, becoming established, scholars and practitioners are raising issues about the networks' accountability and efficacy. Hulme and Edwards (1997), for example, explore these issues specifically regarding NGOs concerned with development, while Nelson (1996a), Fox and Brown (1998), and Jordan and Van Tuijl (2000) focus on transnational networks and the World Bank. Görg and Hirsch (1998) pose profound theoretical concerns about whether NGO participation in intergovernmental decision making should be thought of as a democratic gain. They emphasize the importance of relationships between NGOs operating internationally and the social movements and NGOs working at the national level. This paper pursues these themes by examining transnational networks' efforts to change policy and practice at the World Bank (WB) and by analyzing the role of these networks in representing views and interests otherwise excluded from policy formation.

NGOs based in the industrial countries have largely led transnational advocacy networks in three distinct issue areas: one dealing with the environmental and social impacts of major infrastructure projects; a second focused on World Bank–sponsored structural adjustment programs; and a third focused on antipoverty and social policy.[1] There are important differences among these networks' origins, claims to legitimacy, and advocacy strategies: the three networks, in fact, represent an array of strategic responses to the growing authority of international financial institutions such as the World Bank, from accepting and exploiting WB authority in the environmental network to opposing and contesting it in the structural adjustment network.

Unlike chapters in this volume that emphasize issue-specific networks (Brown Thompson, Donnelly, Khagram), I examine NGO advocacy, sponsored by multiple networks, focusing on the World Bank as an institution. This analysis reveals dynamics that arise when multiple networks with distinct issue priorities and strategies seek to influence the same international governmental organization. This specificity also affords a perspective on the outcome of NGO advocacy on institutional and policy issues in the international arena.

The chapter advances four broad arguments. First, NGOs have organized and mobilized themselves differently to influence the WB in different issue areas: environment and infrastructure (major dam and road projects), poverty, structural adjustment, and governance. But I argue that while the networks and their targets are international, the networks have in common the strong influence of U.S.-based NGOs and their strategies, agendas, and principles.

Second, these diverse networks, while all critical of the World Bank, embody fundamentally different strategic approaches to the World Bank and its borrowing governments. The environmental network, while critical of WB lending, has in effect worked to strengthen its regulatory obligations and its power to regulate borrowing country governments. The environmental network seeks a more benign, even activist, international lending authority.

The antipoverty network has sought to redirect WB lending priorities and to introduce participatory methodologies that would strengthen neither the WB nor its borrowers, but the individuals and communities affected by project loans. It aims to make the WB, in effect, a more egalitarian, more benign development aid agency. The structural adjustment network treats the WB as a manifestation of expanding global authority—of globalization—and opposes both the substance of its economic prescriptions and the expanding role it has taken in shaping national economic policies. The World

Bank's adjustment lending is an artifact of globalization to be exposed, opposed, and reduced.

Given these different orientations to the World Bank as an international authority, the three networks pursue sometimes contrasting strategies. They rely less consistently on transnational norms than do the other networks discussed in this volume. The most important role of norms in these networks' advocacy is the successful encouragement and creation of new norms of practice by the environmental campaign; around treatment of (especially indigenous) populations to be resettled for WB-financed projects (see Khagram, this volume); and around transparency and accountability. Their records in influencing the WB are widely varied, and, in general, their calls for the WB to expand its roles, responsibilities, and mandates have been more successful than strategies that seek to limit its mandates or influence.

Third, NGOs participating in the networks make distinct (and sometimes competing) claims to legitimacy in the international policymaking process. While these claims often stress the networks' transnational nature, asserting their roles as representatives of some otherwise underrepresented population, there are also three other kinds of legitimacy claims: claims based on expertise, on a strong U.S. political constituency, and on designation.

Fourth, while networks are held together by shared commitments, participants are sometimes also sharply at odds over fundamental issues of agenda and strategy. Networks involve relatively new international political actors who manifest power relations and differences as well as shared values and solidarity. The networks themselves generally have few internal arrangements to ensure accountability, broad participation, and democracy in their own planning and practice. As their influence grows and as governments respond to them more actively, these concerns are becoming more important to their future effectiveness.

This chapter's four sections discuss (1) the three networks (environment, poverty, and adjustment), their campaigns, and the bases of their international relationships; (2) the legitimacy claims they articulate; (3) the management of conflict within and among these networks; and (4) issues for the networks' future development, including their relations to governments.

The Networks: Origins, Participants, Strategies

This section traces the origins and strategies of the three networks with the longest history of transnational advocacy with the World Bank: environment, poverty, and adjustment.[2]

The three networks discussed are loosely coordinated and of diverse origins, organized to influence policy and practice at the World Bank, with activities that together amount to a common, collective agenda. They have varied claims to legitimacy, use diverse forms of action, and respond to a variety of constituencies. They are held together variously by shared values, shared political experience, partnership arrangements in development project funding, and joint participation in international gatherings. But they are also sharply divided over key issues, and the presence of real conflict within the networks is a factor that calls for more careful attention. While they are by definition not hierarchies, Washington-based participants have privileged access to the World Bank and have tended to take initiatives that guide the networks' joint work.

Each network appeals to norms—or advocates new norms—in arguing for new policy or practice. But the importance of norms to the campaigns is highly varied. Environmental advocates advance the principles of prior consultation and compensation of communities affected by infrastructure projects and have successfully won new norms for resettlement practice largely through advocacy at the World Bank.

Norms have proven less effective in antipoverty advocacy because internationally endorsed social and economic rights are not direct guides to practice. Growth-oriented economic strategies, which many NGOs criticize, are the centerpiece of the World Bank's stated antipoverty strategy, and the World Bank increasingly represents itself as first and foremost an antipoverty organization. Antipoverty advocates have appealed more successfully to an increasingly accepted professional norm, that popular "participation" (however weakly construed) is good practice in the development profession. Finally, opponents of structural adjustment have tried throughout the 1980s and 1990s to shore up an eroding norm—national sovereignty in economic policymaking—against the increasing strength of the norms embodied in the so-called Washington Consensus on liberal economic policy.

Environment and Infrastructure

In 1983 several U.S.-based environmental NGOs launched an effort to address environmental problems associated with World Bank lending. The campaign began with a series of critiques of specific dam or road construction projects, usually involving forced resettlement of communities (Rich 1994). NGOs such as Friends of the Earth, the Environmental Defense Fund, the Sierra Club, and the Natural Resources Defense Council had long histories of environmental lobbying in the United States. Working with overseas affiliates and with national and local environmentalists, they lobbied the U.S. Congress and met with WB staff to challenge "problem" projects and accelerate environmental reforms.[3]

Conservation of energy, protection of river basins, and preservation of tropical forests and biodiversity dominated the early agenda. But three related issues have equaled or even eclipsed these conservationist themes, and much of the campaigning now centers around involuntary resettlement of communities for dam projects; the protection of indigenous people's lands; and accountability and transparency at the World Bank.

Transnational networking grew as U.S.-based advocates formed alliances with local NGOs, unions, rural associations, and community organizations to protect livelihoods and lands from the effects of projects such as major dams, slum clearance, and power plants. The participants include federations of community organizations, often formed to resist a project, and national-level organizations. International support for campaigns against the Narmada River projects in western India, the Arun III Hydroelectric Project in Nepal, and a series of projects encouraging colonization in Rondônia, Brazil, brought the concerns of relatively small populations (relative to the intended "beneficiaries") to the forefront by exposing them to international discussion (Khagram, this volume; Keck 1998).

These networks had specific political objectives, usually to force cancellation of the World Bank loan or modification of the project. In this process, contacts were made which, while not requiring regular, systematic exchanges or becoming institutionalized, endure, evolve, and are periodically reactivated for a new round of advocacy.

The loose network that emerged from these project-focused advocacy efforts produced a campaign, the principal strategy of which was the "internationalization" of domestic policy issues—amplifying, interpreting, and legitimating local claims by appealing to international norms. Projects where local resource management has implications for global issues—loss of biodiversity or rainforest cover, production of greenhouse gases—have been susceptible to the argument that a global interest justifies new or larger roles for the World Bank. In other cases, appeal to international norms has reinforced a minority voice where indigenous peoples' land rights or the land rights of communities threatened by a major dam project are involved. By successfully forcing the WB to adopt safeguards that articulate these norms, the campaign also specifies and strengthens the norms themselves.

Beyond its successful assaults on problem projects and calls for environmental staffing, impact assessments, and consultations (LePrestre 1995), the environmental network has argued for greater transparency and accountability at the WB. After several years of lobbying, environmental advocates won a modest liberalization of WB information disclosure policy in 1993. Broader access to WB documents—especially limited information available during project planning—is intended by its advocates to facilitate informed participation by affected communities (World Bank 1993b, 1993c; Chamberlain and Hall 1995; Nelson 2001).

A second procedural reform, an independent inspection panel to hear citizen complaints against the World Bank, reinforces the accountability link. The inspection panel investigates claims by directly affected groups who charge that the World Bank's failure to implement its own policy or procedures has materially harmed them. The panel has received twenty-one appeals, carried out four full or partial investigations, and resulted in the modification of several projects and the cancellation of a planned loan to Nepal for a hydroelectric plant on the Arun River. The panel is explicitly limited to investigating violations of official WB policy; it cannot consider complaints that implicate the borrowing government or that appeal to broader international norms (Shihata 1994; Hunter and Udall 1994).[4]

These information and inspection reforms are examples of a second generation of NGO advocacy that emerged in the 1990s. Second-generation reforms go beyond amending projects or adopting new policy to creating mechanisms for expanded transparency, access, and accountability. By disseminating information and opening an inspection panel to NGOs and communities from the borrowing countries, the second-generation reforms could lessen the advantage of Washington-based advocates and broaden the direct participation of organizations of affected peoples. The differences in goals between first- and second-generation advocacy networks point to the interactive, responsive, and evolving nature of network strategies.

Both scholars and practitioners have cited this growing network as a leading example of the new, diverse, and international character of network advocacy (see, e.g., Wirth 1998; Keck 1998). This account stresses the importance of the networks in voicing views and interests of disenfranchised groups and in winning influence through the international arena. But the networks' methods, it should be noted, also represent an application and even a replication of quintessentially U.S. political culture to international debates. U.S.-based environmental NGOs have, arguably, led the network in a strategy of public relations, legislation, regulation, and now litigation (informally, through the World Bank's independent inspection panel) that draws strongly on their experience in U.S. environmental advocacy.

Poverty

Like most development aid donors, the World Bank states that all of its lending is intended, directly or indirectly, to alleviate poverty (Wolfensohn 1995; World Bank 1992b). Many NGOs have challenged the WB and other donors to allocate more resources to activities that directly improve poor people's welfare, expand their access to productive assets, and involve them as active participants.

NGO advocacy around poverty reduction in the 1970s and early 1980s was almost exclusively Northern-based. NGOs argued through the 1980s for greater poverty focus, more social sector lending, and public participation in project planning and implementation. The antipoverty network includes participants in the NGO Working Group on the World Bank, a 1993 Conference on World Hunger hosted by the World Bank, and NGO signatories to a statement appended to the World Bank's 1994 "Report of the Participation Learning Group." Active participants in the industrial countries have included Oxfam (Great Britain and United States), Bread for the World (United States), Church World Service (United States), Community Aid Abroad (Australia), CARE Canada, Christian Aid (United Kingdom), Save the Children Federation, World Vision International, and NOVIB (Netherlands).

Robert McNamara's presidency (1968–81) featured a new policy emphasis on poverty reduction and programmatic innovations, an emphasis that stimulated development NGOs' interest in the WB (Ayres 1983; Finnemore and Sikkink 1998). After the United States succeeded in mandating increased "poverty-targeted" lending at the Inter-American Development Bank in the late 1970s, the Washington-based NGO Bread for the World argued for and won a (weaker) stipulation for World Bank lending in 1982.[5]

During the 1980s, three developments changed the NGO antipoverty lobby. First, North-South NGO interaction became more frequent and intensive. The widely held ideal of North-South "partnership" in development assistance encouraged international NGO advocates to consult and make common cause with Southern colleagues (see also Brown Thompson and Donnelly in this volume for discussion of North-South issues in network advocacy).

Second, "participation" became established as a priority among development practitioners. Theorists and practitioners increasingly emphasized not "targeting the poor" but eliciting their initiative and participation in aid projects. "Popular participation" and "empowerment" spread from the vocabulary of NGOs and certain UN specialized agencies to virtually all development assistance agencies, including the World Bank (Stiefel and Wolfe 1994).

Third, NGO collaboration in World Bank–financed projects grew steadily during the 1980s and sharply after 1988. Such "operational collaboration" is the World Bank's preferred form of engagement with NGOs, especially where governments' capacity to implement projects is limited. In most cases, a single NGO, rather than an international-national partnership, is involved (predominately transnational NGOs in the early 1980s, with a trend toward local involvement since mid-decade). NGOs implement project components designed by government and WB officials; some projects give NGOs an earlier and more formative role, and many of these feature transnational NGO partnerships (Nelson 1995; Malena 2000).

In 1984 the WB agreed to form a standing NGO–World Bank Committee, the first official international venue for NGO input into World Bank development policy. With members from each of five major global regions, it is geographically the most balanced NGO forum and the closest approximation to an institutional base in any of the networks. But the committee was largely ineffective in the 1980s in winning change in practice.[6] Its most visible success came with the creation of a three-year "participation learning process," which documented and promoted participatory methods to WB staff and led to the adoption of a modest set of proposals in 1994 (World Bank 1994a).

The participation agenda has benefited from indirect support by other NGO campaigns. Indirectly, every public controversy over an infrastructure project sends the message that investments can be implemented more smoothly if affected communities are advised and consulted earlier. It is not surprising that the clearest and earliest operational directives (OD) to WB staff regarding participation were in the controversial project areas of infrastructure, involuntary resettlement, and indigenous peoples (OD 4.0 on dams, 4.20 on indigenous peoples, 4.30 on involuntary resettlement).

North-South NGO partnerships in antipoverty and participation advocacy have generally formed not in struggles over particular projects, but from cooperation in funding and implementing projects or in international meetings. Unlike the environmental campaign, which relies on critique of specific infrastructure projects, the poverty discussion began and remains largely at the level of global, bankwide policy and lending priorities, addressing issues related to the practice of microenterprise credit funding, health policy, and popular participation. The development NGOs active in the antipoverty network have had difficulty, for example, mobilizing local or international participants to monitor implementation of commitments to participatory strategies. The most systematic monitoring has involved a desk review of project documents by the Washington-based consortium of U.S. NGOs—InterAction (InterAction 1999).

Major development NGOs find it difficult to coordinate their desire to advocate for new policy and practice with their dominant organizational need to secure funding from major aid donors. Thus, development NGOs' discussions of participation with the WB have focused on procedural issues for NGOs implementing WB-financed projects: up-front project costs, procurement rules, and similar operational issues.[7] Project-level contact by development NGOs has been largely uncoordinated with advocacy campaigns. This discussion of participation as project methodology allows the WB to encourage participation on grounds of effectiveness, stressing economic results rather than promoting political values, and to draw civil society organizations, including NGOs, into the implementation of projects that many governments are increasingly unable to manage.

The World Bank, too, appears to struggle with the challenge of being the "new" bank of the Wolfensohn era: poverty focused, participatory, open. Its *World Development Report 2000,* drafted after extensive consultations with scholars, NGOs, and other external "stakeholders," fell under a cloud of controversy when its principal author, Cornell University economist Ravi Kanbur, resigned in June 2000, claiming editorial interference from within the World Bank and from the U.S. Treasury.[8]

The disagreement centered on the emphasis on asset distribution versus on growth as the central policy concern in understanding and reducing poverty. Oxfam Great Britain was quick to deplore the downgrading of the asset distribution approach, calling Kanbur's resignation "the ultimate victory for the Neanderthal forces within the World Bank."

Structural Adjustment

The World Bank began attaching explicit policy conditions to some loans in the 1980s. These "structural adjustment loans" gave the WB a vehicle to advance policy prescriptions it had long promoted in "policy dialogue" with borrower governments: reduced current accounts deficits, currency devaluation to promote exports, privatization of many government holdings, and reduced payrolls and expenditures.

Structural adjustment loans provoked opposition from community groups and NGOs such as Oxfam (United States and United Kingdom), the Development Group for Alternative Policies (Development GAP) (United States), Christian Aid (United Kingdom), NOVIB (Netherlands), and many others. NGOs have criticized specific effects of orthodox, neo-liberal restructuring plans on income distribution, public services, gender inequality, natural resource depletion, and food self-reliance (Development GAP 1993; Oxfam United Kingdom and Ireland 1994; Heredia and Purcell 1994). At the same time they have attacked the lack of broad national participation in economic policy decisions and linked the World Bank's adjustment lending with the inegalitarian and disempowering effects of "corporate globalization" (Bruno 2000).

International NGO cooperation on adjustment was ad hoc until 1996 and less sustained than on environmental and poverty issues. Despite extensive domestic debate and protest in many countries (Nelson 1989; Mosley, Harrigan, and Toye 1991), international NGO campaigning on adjustment was sporadic. The most active participants in international efforts are from a handful of countries, including Mexico, Nicaragua, Ecuador, the Philippines, India, Ghana, and South Africa. Network activity has largely centered around NGO gatherings coinciding with World Bank and IMF annual meetings, and UN-sponsored conferences such as the 1994 World Summit on Social Development.

Advocacy on economic policy, both antipoverty and structural adjustment, appears to have benefited less from transnational networking than have the environmental and human rights agendas. Cloaked in economic parlance and lacking vivid images of megadams, flooded villages, and threatened species, adjustment has never mobilized significant, sustained public or media attention until the antiglobalization protests at World Bank/IMF meetings in Washington, D.C. and Prague. International norms afforded effective political leverage in the mid-1980s, when UNICEF articulated the call for "Adjustment with a Human Face" and contributed to the World Bank's practice of funding special welfare and job-creation programs to mitigate the adjustment programs effects on "the vulnerable" (Zuckerman 1989). But the impact has been limited to these compensatory measures, and advocates have been unsuccessful in winning changes in the adjustment strategy or in reducing adjustment lending. In the absence of either legal/normative grounds or a compelling public constituency, international advocacy is less potent in moving the World Bank.

The adjustment network's strategy shifted in September 1995, when WB President James Wolfensohn met with some ten U.S.-based groups and subsequently accepted in principle their proposal for a joint WB–NGO review of selected experiences with adjustment.[9] NGO and civil society participation is coordinated by an international steering group and focuses on preparing in-country reviews of the adjustment experience in nine countries. The NGO participants aim to maximize domestic input by NGOs and organizations opposed to the adjustment strategies.

The Structural Adjustment Participatory Review Initiative (SAPRI) process, formally launched in July 1997, has secured agreement from eight governments (Bangladesh, Ecuador, El Salvador, Ghana, Hungary, Mali,

Uganda, and Zimbabwe) for national reviews. NGOs have begun NGO-only reviews (Citizen Assessments of Structural Adjustment, CASA) in four countries that are not participants: Brazil, Argentina, Mexico, and the Philippines. The international process is managed by an NGO secretariat at the Development GAP in Washington, and each national review is managed by a joint committee of government, national NGO, and World Bank participants. This institutional structure for a two-level process at the global and national levels is an innovation among NGO networks, a formal governing structure that could permit greater independence by local participants while maintaining international involvement and the support it offers.[10]

The adjustment campaign's call for domestic control over economic policy is contrary to the internationalizing strategy of the environmental campaign. Critics treat neo-liberal economic policy primarily as an artifact of the WB and the IMF and call for a return to national economic policy-making. Whatever the limitations of national political systems, it implicitly argues that citizen participation is more likely to be effective in the absence of the World Bank's overpowering financial and intellectual leverage.

The NGO critique of adjustment, whether focused on public sector job loss, reduced social benefits, export-oriented exchange rate policies, or the privatization of public and parastatal enterprises, has a common refrain: economic policy should be local politics, and effective citizen participation is being thwarted by the WB.[11] The extent of the World Bank's actual effect on national policy decisions varies widely (Mosley, Harrigan, and Toye 1991). But in many borrowing countries, WB influence over economic policy creates at least the perception that its opponents are effectively disenfranchised.

Claiming Legitimacy: Conflicting Bases

Seeking a role in a policymaking process dominated by states, NGOs have explicitly or implicitly asserted their legitimacy as participants. The issue is most problematic for international NGOs based in the industrialized countries: many have daily communication with WB staff, and have sought to assert their legitimacy as political actors in the World Bank's policymaking processes. (The broadening of Southern NGOs' direct roles, sometimes facilitated actively by Northern colleagues, is discussed in this chapter's concluding section.)

NGO documents in the 1980s and early 1990s make four broad claims to legitimacy on the part of transnational NGOs: *representation* of Southern views, *expertise,* a *domestic political constituency,* and *designation.* NGOs often invoke the four bases in combination and treat them as complementary. This section identifies and illustrates the claims; the third section analyzes a case in which legitimacy claims and the constituencies to which they refer have come into acute tension.

Representation and Partnership

International NGOs depend for their legitimacy at the World Bank on their ability to speak for affected communities. Through this relationship of partnership and representation, NGOs can claim to offer a unique contribution to the global forum: perspectives from people affected by policies and projects but normally excluded from global or national policymaking.

A 1994 Oxfam paper on structural adjustment in Latin America, for example, begins with the assertion that "Oxfam's work with community and grassroots organizations across the world gives it a privileged perspective from which to assess the impact of IMF and World Bank policies"; it cites "the experiences of many of its partner organisations across the continent—from shantytown dwellers in Lima, agricultural labourers in Chile, indigenous organisations in Colombia and Brazil, to peasants in Central America." These perspectives are invoked to counter official reports on the distributive effects of adjustment (Oxfam U.K. and Ireland 1994).

Expertise

Expertise has been an effective source of influence in certain aspects of the networks' work. NGOs working on poverty, social services, and participation have sometimes been sought out for expertise that the WB attributes to them in community development, participation, and the social sectors. Environmental NGOs' expertise on sectoral policy issues was an important asset in early stages of the campaign, but as the WB increased its own environmental staffing, outside expertise became less effective.

Commenting on the World Bank's 1994 *World Development Report* on health, the Save the Children Federation notes its "experience in working in the health sector in over 30 countries" and its research program on health sector sustainability (Save the Children Federation 1993). Within the global World Bank–NGO Committee, the WB has welcomed NGO input in participation, input presumably based in the NGOs' project experience. Comments from the same NGOs on the impact of adjustment—often citing and purporting to represent local organizations' views—are given much less credence.

The World Bank's participation in the Structural Adjustment Participatory Review Initiative (SAPRI) is seen by some NGOs as an indication of Wolfensohn's openness to a genuine exchange of views with NGOs. But the internal WB memo proposing the review focuses on the need to reconcile the sharply different *perceptions* of NGOs and the World Bank. At the beginning of the SAPRI process, the expected result of a review of NGOs' and the World Bank's different bodies of experience appears, for the World Bank, to be not so much a deeper understanding of the policies' effects as an accounting of how NGOs have arrived at these heterodox views (World Bank 1996).[12]

Domestic Political Constituency in the G-7 Countries

For U.S.-based NGOs, a strong domestic constituency has been a third basis for legitimacy. The World Bank's increasing preoccupation with U.S. congressional funding of its concessional lending window (International Development Association, or IDA) makes the promise of a progressive, internationalist constituency one the WB cannot ignore.

Since 1994, the "Fifty Years Is Enough" campaign in the United States has brought more grassroots political constituencies into work on World Bank issues. In addition to longtime NGO participants, the Fifty Years campaign includes student organizations, church-based bodies, and material aid and solidarity organizations focused on Central America. Advocacy features phone-in days and postcard campaigns to U.S. government and WB officials, and tap some of the same political currents mobilized by labor-environment-consumer opposition to NAFTA (Fifty Years Is Enough Campaign 1996).

U.S. environmental NGOs have the most plausible claim to a politically significant constituency, but mass expressions of public opinion were not a significant part of environmental NGOs' efforts to influence the World Bank until 2000. Spurred by the expanding grassroots involvement in Jubilee 2000 debt forgiveness efforts and the protests at the 1999 World Trade Organization's meetings in Seattle, the World Bank/IMF 2000 spring meetings in Washington became a venue for antiglobalization and antistructural adjustment public protests (Bruno 2000).

Designation

Legitimacy is sometimes conferred by an NGO's participation in an officially sanctioned committee or other meeting. The twenty-five NGO members of the NGO–World Bank committee, for example, use their status to gain access to WB officials. Other examples of official designation include the NGO committee on WB information policy, NGO participants in the advisory board for the new microenterprise lending facility (Consultative Group to Assist the Poor, CGAP), and NGO participation on the international steering committee of the SAPRI process. The WB generally gives less emphasis to such formal consultative status than do the UN specialized development agencies, preferring to encourage operational dialogue and cooperation.

"Expertise" and "representation" are not always easily distinguished. Major U.S.-based development NGOs, for example, often cite field experiences and reports by their country offices in making their case. But when they argue from their own information network (national or regional offices), not from any partnership understanding with local or national organizations, they clearly appeal to expertise and experience.

Other legitimacy claims can be intertwined as well. When the U.S. Catholic Conference of Bishops, for example, calls for expanded debt forgiveness, it is responding to appeals from African church leaders, to a long tradition in Catholic social teaching, and to the community development experience of U.S.-based Catholic agencies such as Catholic Relief Services, and it expresses the position of a major U.S. church constituency.

The Networks Summarized

The efforts of NGOs to influence the World Bank, while in agreement on broad themes for reform (greater popular participation, accountability, transparency) are far from homogeneous. Despite the increasing conceptual integration of the networks' agendas, direct planning, information sharing, and joint advocacy among them is only recent, and their agendas remain distinct. Poverty-alleviation advocates gave formal support but little effort to the information and inspection panel reforms initiated by environmental campaigns. Environmentalist critics have agreed with much of the critique of export-oriented economic strategies, but rarely enter extensively into the adjustment debate.[13] Some NGOs, North and South, participate in more than one of the networks, particularly the networks on antipoverty and adjustment. Advocates in each sector in the industrialized countries continue to organize their campaigns, information exchange, and constituency building along the lines of environment, development, and human rights.

The partnerships in each network have distinct patterns of origin. The networks' largely complementary agendas have not been substantially integrated, and they tend to make different claims to legitimacy in addressing the World Bank and its major shareholder governments. Finally, the calls for participation implicit in their advocacy are distinct and, at one level, contradictory: expanding the international role in national environmental planning versus reducing the international hand in macroeconomic policymaking. Table 7.1 summarizes some of these differences.

Managing Conflict within and among NGO Networks

Southern NGOs occasionally find themselves aligned with their governments against some of their Northern NGO colleagues, especially in debates

Table 7.1. Selected Characteristics of NGO Networks on Environment, Structural Adjustment, and Poverty.

Characteristic	Environmental	Adjustment	Antipoverty
Principal Agenda	Limit big dam projects; improve resettlement policy; more resource-efficient energy policy; greater accountability and transparency	Protect social services; promote food security; reduce use of policy conditionality; reduce lending for structural adjustment	Increasing lending that benefits poorest groups and social sector lending; social safety nets; participatory project methodologies
Coalition origins	National struggles over WB-financed projects; Washington-based "MDB campaign"	Country-specific campaigns in Mexico and Philippines; international meetings	Development project cooperation; international meetings
Focal organizations	Friends of the Earth; Environmental Defense Fund, Bank Information Center	Development GAP (U.S.), Oxfam, Christian Aid (U.K.), NOVIB (Netherlands)	CARE, Oxfam, Save the Children, Bread for the World (U.S.), InterAction
Norms	Major role: appeal to and strengthen norms regarding indigenous peoples' rights	Minor role: support norm of economic sovereignty against norm of neoliberal economics	Problematic: antipoverty norms are interpreted by economic theory. Participation promoted as a professional norm.
Legitimacy claims	Representation, U.S. constituency, expertise	Representation of Southern views	Expand local participation and influence on donors and governments in projects
Basic governance strategy	Expand international role in national policy; use WB to regulate borrower practice	Reduce international role in national macroeconomic policy	Expand local participation and influence on donors and governments in projects
Tactics	Lobby U.S. Treasury, Congress; information exchange with Southern NGOs; focus on projects; public opinion	Direct discussion with WB; joint review of adjustment projects began in 1997; national dialogue through SAPRI; public protests at 2000 WB spring meetings	Direct dialogue with WB; collaborate on projects with WB; lobby U.S. Congress

over World Bank funding. NGO critics of the WB have seen the triennial replenishments of IDA, the World Bank's concessional financing window for loans to the poorest countries, as an opportunity to exert leverage through governments over the WB. Because of the difficulty of securing U.S. congressional approval, recent replenishment agreements have made other donors' payment obligations contingent upon the United States completing its payments (World Bank 1992a). Thus, NGO strategies that involve the U.S. Congress or public opinion are especially controversial.

The sharp disagreements among NGOs over financing IDA have their roots in the issues of legitimacy, accountability, agenda setting, and representation in the networks. While the split is in part between the networks, the networks themselves are divided as well. Many Southern NGOs objected to attacks on IDA, but others, especially those that have worked to stop World Bank–financed projects, were among the principal attackers.

Several groups of NGOs, coordinated only loosely, sought to influence the funding and policy-setting process for IDA's tenth replenishment (IDA-10) in 1991–92.[14] A group of Washington-based development and environment groups, taking no position on funding, lobbied U.S. Treasury officials for changes in information policy, poverty and structural adjustment lending, and energy and water sector policies. More than forty U.S.-based NGO representatives signed on, and the Treasury did adopt provisions in the spirit of the NGOs' positions on water and energy sectors and information disclosure.[15]

Others, in the United States and India, initiated a second, contemporaneous effort. Reacting to protracted conflict over WB involvement in the Sardar Sarovar Dam project (see Khagram, this volume) some Indian, U.S., and other NGOs concluded that the WB was beyond reform and they announced their opposition to funding for IDA-10.

Seeking to marginalize their radical critics, WB officials invited six Southern NGO representatives, including four members of the NGO–World Bank Committee, to discuss policy issues with the IDA's governing board (IDA Deputies) during September deliberations on the replenishment (World Bank 1992b).[16] While commenting critically on WB policies, the NGO representatives called IDA funding essential for many countries and urged a full replenishment.

In October, the NGO Working Group on the World Bank endorsed IDA-10 in an open letter to then-President Lewis Preston. European and African members chided U.S.-based colleagues at their October meeting for proposing policy conditions to U.S. funding. These NGO statements of support were widely cited by the World Bank in an effort to show broad global NGO support for IDA.

In the end, Congress authorized funding for the U.S. contribution in one-year installments, with conditions attached that helped force the WB to adopt a new information disclosure policy and create an independent appeals panel.

The IDA-10 episode was both a high-water mark in NGO efforts to exert leverage over the World Bank and the most visible split among network participants (Udall 1994). Despite marked deference by many Northern NGO activists to African NGO concerns during the two years that followed, the NGOs' disagreements over IDA flared again at the October 1995 annual meetings of the WB and the IMF. Three prominent development NGOs (Oxfam International, the African NGO consortium FAVDO, and the U.S. consortium InterAction) spoke at a press conference with President Wolfensohn in support of continued funding of IDA (World Bank 1995, 10). Others were quick to object, and when their misgivings were reported in a news wire service story in October, Southern representatives in Washington for the annual meetings of the WB and the IMF were furious, and they expanded plans for advocacy efforts independent of the U.S. NGOs.[17]

The irregular divisions—neither strictly North-South nor environmentalist-developmental—follow from the selective nature of the network affiliations: partnerships are self-selecting, with organizations gravitating toward others with similar interests. NGOs whose primary interest is in protecting river basins (or villages in a particular river basin) form partnerships, as do those around promoting agro-forestry or providing social services. In the absence of a setting in which to debate the issues across network lines, they pursue their agendas until a collision of interests forces them to talk.

The very broad coalitions that formed to protest globalization at the Washington, D.C., World Bank/IMF meetings in April 2000 encountered similar splits. Oxfam and Greenpeace split with economic justice protesters when protesters called for the WB and IMF to be "shut down" (*New York Times,* 15 April 2000, A5).

The relative lack of exchange among the networks and the absence of a global forum or secretariat make it difficult to resolve such differences. Global NGO assemblies and parallel forums to the United Nations meetings on social development, the environment, population, and women brought many of the NGO participants together. But they have not led to discussions of strategic issues in the World Bank–related campaigns. Strategy meetings organized by the Bank Information Center in October 1995 and again in 1998 brought NGOs together expressly to discuss World Bank–related campaigns, but such gatherings are infrequent and have not been a venue for discussing controversial issues such as IDA funding.

NGO activists are not unaware of the problem. Among U.S.-based NGOs, the monthly meeting of the "Tuesday Group," once almost exclusively a meeting of environmental NGOs with U.S. government officials on multilateral development bank (MDB) issues, is now more widely attended by poverty- and human rights–focused NGOs. The NGO Working Group on the WB was until 1995 a global body without strong claims to representing NGO opinion beyond its own membership. The Working Group restructured itself in the mid-1990s, planning regional meetings to cultivate broader NGO participation and empowering those regional meetings to elect NGO participants in the global NGO forum.[18]

A Second Generation of NGO Networking at the World Bank

NGO networks have claimed a place among those who shape policy at international organizations. Their success, and the prominence that accompanies it, raises new and difficult questions for a second "generation" of NGO network advocacy. In a first generation of lobbying, NGOs gained the attention of the WB and its major shareholders. The strategies included confrontation over specific projects and collaboration in project implementation, and dialogue over issues such as participation. NGOs won results—projects altered, new policies adopted—particularly in issue areas with highly visible "problem projects," strong international sentiment (environment and infrastructure), and where the WB could adopt a cooperative posture (participation).

A second generation of network advocacy appears to have two distinctive characteristics. First, network advocates give greater attention to putting new policies into practice and to effecting systemic changes at the WB. More liberal information disclosure and the Independent Inspection Panel are the first successes in the second generation of advocacy, but even with relatively open leadership at the World Bank, this second phase of change in structure and practice is proving difficult. It requires broader monitoring (rather than exclusive focus on a few cases), which in turn demands greater, more sustained coordination between North and South.

Second, the three networks are at least temporarily being supported, challenged, and sometimes eclipsed by a vigorous antiglobalization movement. The antiglobalization advocates have less historic engagement with the WB as an institution and are less interested in the nuances of policy implementation than in vocally protesting the global economic trends they oppose and the institutions they associate with structural adjustment and trade liberalization. These relative newcomers to the WB campaigns gave the structural adjustment theme new prominence at the World Bank's 2000 spring meetings in Washington and mobilized U.S. students and union members to take action on international economic policy in unprecedented numbers.

These new strategies and actors reinforce the need for clarity about accountability, representation, and the changing political environment of NGO networks. Questions are raised about these topics here, in turn.

Accountability

Who has gained greater and more influential participation in international development policymaking? What accountability relationships have been built, strengthened, or weakened? International networks' campaigns have undoubtedly added to the ability of nonstate actors to influence some development policy decisions. Local NGOs in some borrowing countries have increased their access to national decision-making processes, sometimes with World Bank encouragement to their governments. Transnational NGOs have won expanded access and influence at the WB, and remain the networks' principal voices.

But at the same time that some local organizations have won gains in building accountability links to their own governments, most borrowers' accountability to the World Bank has been deepened. Policy conditionality under adjustment loans gave the WB a new means of influence, and new policy mandates in environmental and social fields expanded its influence over details of national policies and institutions. Especially with smaller and poorer borrowers, the urgent need for concessional credit strengthens the World Bank's bargaining position in enforcing this accountability.

The international NGO critique of the World Bank and the use of its leverage to affect national development priorities have reinforced and expanded the World Bank's influence, even while it created a measure of accountability by the WB to transnational NGOs. The campaigns' internationalizing strategy relies on a sequence of accountability links: government to World Bank, World Bank to transnational NGO, transnational NGO to local group. The figure below illustrates this accountability circuit.

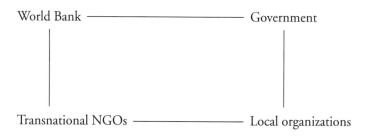

This indirect form of accountability has been effective in influencing government management of projects financed by the WB, especially in countries where government accountability directly to (most) citizens is weak. But the links are not well developed, nor are they institutionalized, and it is not a foregone conclusion that the circuitous international account-ability route promotes, rather than slows, efforts to build national account-ability mechanisms. The SAPRI process may suggest one solution: three-party discussions among NGOs, governments, and the WB, in which the World Bank's participation could be used to help open national dialogue.

Close observers of NGOs are suggesting other solutions, including codes of conduct and agreements regarding transparency and accountability by international NGOs. One proposal, published by the British Foreign Policy Centre, would create incentives for transnational NGOs to cooperate with such a code by requiring cooperation in order to gain access to NGO consultations at some international organizations (Edwards 2000).

Legitimacy and Representation

The networks' successes and increasing visibility in international policy dis-cussions create new demands—internal and external—for clarity about legiti-macy and representation. These demands are surfacing within the networks as well as from their critics, and they focus on how the networks do business, whom they are speaking for, and how they set their agendas and strategies. It is no longer sufficient to invoke the name *NGO*; governments and WB offi-cials are increasingly prepared to press NGO representatives on whose views they represent, what experience they draw on, and whether a larger con-stituency in fact supports their demands. Nor are Southern NGOs content to continue existing arrangements without question.

Critics of the NGO role have concentrated on the environmental and human rights agendas. An essay by two former WB and U.S. Treasury offi-cials, for example, criticizes "environmentalist critics" for overestimating the World Bank's influence, rejecting the possibility that governments can act democratically or in the interests of the poor, and ignoring governments' re-sponsibility for project problems by assigning blame to the World Bank (Sherk and Berg 1993).

Southern NGOs also challenge the roles of international NGO spokes-people. Several Southern networks have proposed establishing direct Washing-ton representation, and one, the African network FAVDO, has created such an office.[19] The eleven national Oxfam organizations have similarly created a Washington, D.C., Oxfam International office to advocate with the inter-national financial institutions and United Nations. Transnational NGO staff are often called to task for initiating lobbying campaigns, planning major meetings, and negotiating positions without extensive consultation with Southern colleagues. Of the three networks, only environmental NGOs have a systematic and well-equipped center for coordinating action and disseminating information: the Bank Information Center, based in Washington. None has a forum for making policy or strategy, or discussing or resolving differences, and many Washington-based NGO representatives devote considerable time and energy to floating proposals and positions among Southern colleagues.

Relating to Member Governments

Not surprisingly, many borrowing governments resent the expanding involvement of transnational networks in World Bank policy. They are wary of the increasing penetration of their societies by international NGO actors, and, increasingly, by World Bank staff and consultants determined to establish consultative relations with community groups and NGOs. Most governments seek to limit, oversee, or regulate such activity by foreign-based NGOs even when the activity is a community development or relief project. But NGOs have called for and won explicit requirements that WB staff consult with such groups in project planning and facilitate their involvement in any resettlement and compensation scheme, and World Bank financing for a project often carries with it an obligation to tolerate an international NGO presence.

Some governments also see networks' influence at the World Bank as usurping governments' sovereign prerogatives with respect to an international governmental organization. Resentment on this score is leveled particularly at the Washington-based NGOs that coordinate or speak for networks, and is intensified by the networks' emphasis on reforms that strengthen the World Bank in relation to borrowers. Many of the most successful NGO efforts have increased WB regulation or specification of borrower practices: environmental impact assessments for projects, required community consultation in certain circumstances, poverty assessments, and information disclosure are examples.

Finally, the NGO agenda is widely perceived by borrowing governments as essentially "foreign" in its inspiration. The strong association of the "sustainable development" slogan and agenda with Northern environmentalism has been characterized as an imposition of values without adequate regard for the poor countries' development imperative. One Southern executive director to the WB does "not like the involvement of single purpose [advocacy] NGOs. Their agenda is too one-sided. They lack regard for the presently very complex situation and suffering in the Third World today" (Bichsel 1994, 161–62). From the viewpoint of the borrowers' official representatives at the World Bank—the executive directors—the lobby on any particular project or policy appears dominated by Washington-based activists. One executive director complains: "It is not clear to whom [the Northern NGOs] are accountable. . . . Sometimes they provoke a response just because they have a loud voice and resources. Others who may be more representative may not be heard or have any influence at all" (161).

Encouraging Transnational Authority?

The internationalization of social movements and advocacy has advanced some NGO agendas in important ways. But the continued development of strong civil societies, able to shape national policy and build broad, effective participation in national politics, requires that significant responsibility, initiative, and real choice in national economic policy remain in the hands of national governments.

NGOs' success in internationalizing some domestic policy decisions contributes to a process that Robert Cox has called the "internationalization of government." Advocacy networks demand that the WB (and national governments) be more responsive and accountable to community organizations. But the effect of much of their advocacy—borrowing governments' increased accountability to the WB—may sometimes be in tension with this agenda.

The WB has assumed expanded authority not only in macroeconomic policy and the environment, but also in information disclosure and social sector policy. This internationalization of government is particularly present among the World Bank's poorer and smaller member governments. In many of these countries, the WB finds itself in a contradiction with several dimensions: how is it to enforce its environmental and economic policy priorities, maintain lending levels that meet its borrowers' balance-of-payments needs, and consult with NGO and community-based actors without completely undermining governments' own initiative and "ownership" of policies? How, to put it bluntly, can the World Bank retain substantial influence over significant aspects of national policy while "putting the government firmly back in the driver's seat" (World Bank 1998) of policymaking?

As the World Bank is forced to deal with this tension between directing policy and encouraging locally grounded initiative, NGOs will play a role. Effective NGO pressure, especially in environmental policy, is likely to continue to require the WB to prescribe and initiate processes such as National Environmental Action Plans and (broader) Country Assistance Strategies.

Will international NGO advocacy increase national accountability as it reinforces global standards for matters of global interest? The answer may depend in part on NGOs' and the World Bank's careful attention to the maintenance of real choice, initiative, and capacity for national polities and for that old-fashioned national institution, the state.

Notes

Research for this chapter was supported by a grant for research and writing by the Program for Peace and International Cooperation, John D. and Catherine T. MacArthur Foundation.

1. Campaigns on adjustment and on the environment have also lobbied the Inter-American Development Bank (IDB) and the Asian Development Bank (ADB); antipoverty lobbying has focused as well on the major bilateral aid donors. On the IDB and ADB, see Nelson 1997 and Quizon and Corrall 1995.

2. NGO networks have also been active on global change, debt (see Donnelly, this volume), and human rights (see Levinson 1992; Lawyers Committee for Human Rights 1993a).

3. Among other principal NGO participants are the Bank Information Center, the International Rivers Network, the National Wildlife Federation, the Center for International Environmental Law, Probe International (Canada), Greenpeace, *Urgewald* (Germany), and the International Institute for Environment and Development (UK).

4. For an updated account of the inspection panel, see Fox 2000. Borrowing governments' insistence that the panel's investigations not implicate governments was reinforced by a 1999 "clarification" of the panel's mandate (World Bank 1999).

5. The 1992 legislation encouraged but did not require the U.S. Treasury to press for such a poverty "targeting" benchmark.

6. Covey 1998 notes that among the NGOWG's limitations are its generalist character, its members' geographic diffusion, and, in its early years, a lack of cooperation with other NGO campaigns and networks.

7. Interaction with NGOs on the Bank's Project Cycle, 7–8 July 1994, meetings at the World Bank, record on file with the author.

8. "Development News: The World Bank's Daily Webzine," Thursday, 16 June 2000. Available at www.worldbank.org.

9. NGO participants included Center of Concern, Church World Service, Development GAP, Oxfam International, World Vision International, and the World Wildlife Fund.

10. See the World Bank's SAPRI Web site: www.worldbank.org/html/prddr/sapri/saprihp.htm. Information on CASA is found at the NGO secretariat's Web site: www.igc.org/dgap/saprin. The two-level structure does not resolve North-South or

other differences among the NGO participants, of course, but it does provide a governing structure for discussion and decision making.

11. Jordan 1996 observes that there are NGOs who call for a more positive, but not necessarily smaller, World Bank role.

12. The World Bank's report for the final SAPRI global forum, released in July 2001, emphasizes changes in the World Bank's thinking about structural adjustment during the late 1990s. The report suggests that the SAPRI process unearthed evidence that further supports the directions the WB has already taken (World Bank 2001).

13. For an exception, see Reed 1992.

14. This section draws heavily on the account of the IDA-10 negotiation in Nelson 1997.

15. Letter to George A. Folsom, Deputy Assistant Secretary, 16 April 1992, on file with the author.

16. NGO participants were Allan Kirton (Caribbean Council of Churches), Mazide N'Diaye (Senegal, FAVDO), Abdal Latif (Ethiopia, Inter-Africa Group), Shripad Dharmadikary (India, Narmada Bachao Andolan), Hugo Fernandez (Bolivia, Centro de Investigación y Promoción del Campesinado), and M. Iqbal Asaria (London, Third World Network).

17. Meeting of the NGO Working Group on the World Bank, Washington, D.C., October 1994, author's observations.

18. NGO Working Group on the World Bank 1998, unpublished paper on file with the author.

19. Atherton Martin (1993) proposed a joint Southern NGO representation to the World Bank in Washington.

8

Proclaiming Jubilee: The Debt and Structural Adjustment Network

Elizabeth A. Donnelly

Carmen Rodriguez heads the Catholic Charismatic Movement in a sprawling shantytown parish south of Lima, Peru. She and other lay leaders of her diocese prepared for the new millennium in a rather unusual way. In early 1999, having participated in Lenten workshops offering economic and theological perspectives on debt relief, they went door-to-door and gathered some ninety thousand signatures on an internationally circulated petition calling for a one-time cancellation of the unpayable debt of highly indebted poor countries by the end of the year 2000. Countrywide, more than 1,850,000 Peruvians signed the petition in just three months' time. Worldwide, seventeen million people from over 160 countries signed the petition, which was presented to G-7 leaders meeting in Cologne, Germany, in June 1999. The delegation presenting the petition signatures to German Chancellor Gerhard Schroeder, who accepted them in the name of the G-7 leaders, included such disparate figures as Archbishop Oscar Rodriguez Maradiaga of Tegucigalpa, Honduras, and Bono of the Irish rock group U2.

An extraordinary transnational coalition of churches, antipoverty NGOs, and other civil society organizations organized the petition as part of the Jubilee 2000 campaign. Invoking a biblical norm from the Book of Leviticus, the coalition urged the international community to mark the millennium by recognizing a period of "jubilee" in which debts are canceled and the freed-up resources are used to alleviate poverty. Of particular concern are thirty-six low-income countries and twelve middle-income countries the World Bank categorizes as "severely indebted" (World Bank 1998, 67).[1] Jubilee 2000 organizers, led by such groups as Christian Aid (U.K.),

Oxfam, EURODAD (the European Network on Debt and Development), and Catholic national episcopal conferences, relief agencies, and the Vatican, have argued that heavily indebted countries devote an inordinate portion of their national budgets to making interest payments on the debt, leaving too little available for desperately needed outlays for health, education, housing, and job creation.

The coalition has also protested the disproportionate burden placed on the poor by structural adjustment programs (SAPs) mandated by the International Monetary Fund and the World Bank in conjunction with debt rescheduling and reduction. Such programs have regularly featured national currency devaluations to enhance export earnings and discourage imports, the privatization of government-controlled industries and services (causing cuts in jobs and wages), and cuts in government budgets, which have typically slashed food subsidies and spending on health and education.

This chapter attempts to summarize and assess the network that has developed to urge private and public creditors to adopt policies in their treatment of debtor countries that would embody the following transnational norm: "Debt servicing cannot be met at the price of the asphyxiation of a country's economy, and no government can morally demand of its people privations incompatible with human dignity" (Pontifical Commission on Justice and Peace 1987, 601, citing Cardinal Roger Etchegaray). Accordingly, the network has targeted three categories of creditors: commercial banks, creditor governments organized in the "Paris Club," which governs the handling of official bilateral debt, and international financial institutions (IFIs: the International Monetary Fund, the World Bank, and the regional development banks) to which multilateral debt is owed.

NGOs and churches have been working on debt and structural adjustment issues since the late 1970s, with efforts at national, regional, and then transnational collaboration leading to a functioning transnational network by the late 1980s. The chapter will review why and how that network emerged and then evolved into a more integrated but still loosely affiliated coalition of groups in the mid- to late 1990s collaborating on the Jubilee 2000 campaign. The chapter will then assess what impact the network/coalition (hereafter "the network") has had, suggesting several factors accounting for its limited, yet measurable influence, and conclude with a brief discussion of questions the case raises for the transnational advocacy network research program. Until approximately three years ago, the network could be categorized as a relatively weak one when compared to those in other issue areas covered in this volume, the principal reason being the complex, technically difficult, and geographically diffuse nature of the issue addressed. Nevertheless, particularly with the rapid expansion and activism of the Jubilee 2000 campaign, the network's work has arguably led to limited debt reduction and review of the poverty impact of SAPs. One can also argue that an international norm has emerged, in that a critical mass of the creditor country governments in the late 1990s committed themselves verbally to substantial debt reduction tied to antipoverty social spending. Most notably, the network's intense letter-writing and lobbying campaign on Capitol Hill in 1999 and 2000 led to bipartisan support for a combined appropriation of $545 million toward the U.S. share of bilateral debt relief pledged and the freeing up of $2.65 billion in IMF resources to reduce the debts owed the IMF. While activists celebrated these victories, they also pointed out that the monies appropriated have been paltry given the pressing needs. By the end of 2000, they estimated that only twenty-two countries had had their annual debt service payments reduced, by an average of only 30 percent, and that sixteen of those twenty-two countries were still spending more on debt payments than on health care (Jubilee 2000 UK 2000). This limited success is attributable in part to the persistence of core activists and their increased sophistication in exchanging information and coordinating initiatives with partners in both creditor and debtor countries. Also, in the post–cold war period marked by a Republican-led U.S. Congress, network activists have had greater access to more sympathetic G-7 finance ministry and international financial institution staffs interested in maintaining, if not reforming, existing bilateral and multilateral concessional loan programs.

A further distinguishing feature of the network is the prominent role played by churches, religiously affiliated NGOs and foundations, and activists working for secular NGOs who had previously worked for church agencies. As indicated above, the Jubilee concept of periodic wholesale debt forgiveness has consistently undergirded much of the network's work and in the 1990s provided a vital frame and sense of urgency as Christians and non-Christians alike sought a way to celebrate the year 2000 with substantial progress against world poverty. Pope John Paul II has drawn the most sustained media attention to the debt problem by consistently highlighting its impact on the poor during his travels and meeting with creditor government and IFI officials. At his request, the Pontifical Commission on Justice and Peace (PCJP), the Vatican's think tank on international development questions, issued a lengthy statement in 1987 on the ethical dimensions of the crisis (Pontifical Commission on Justice and Peace 1987).[2] More recently, Jubilee 2000 activists have often quoted the pope's endorsement of debt cancellation in "Tertio Millennio Adveniente," his 1994 reflection on preparation for the millennium. Among the pope's 1999 meetings in which he raised the urgency of the issue were meetings with President Clinton in St. Louis and in Rome with a global delegation of Jubilee 2000 leaders.

In addition to the Vatican, national Catholic bishops conferences of various creditor and debtor countries, the World Council of Churches, and the bishops of the Anglican Communion meeting at Lambeth in July 1998 have all called for far more comprehensive debt reduction. Many of these churches have extensive institutional networks of parishes, social service and relief agencies, lobbying organizations, schools, and research centers active on the Jubilee 2000 campaign.

It is also argued that a radical/reformist cleavage has marked the network from its inception in the mid-1980s. Activists have consistently had sharp debates over which policies and strategies would accomplish the international norm sought, most basically along the lines of a wholesale condemnation of SAP conditionality and complete debt cancellation versus qualified acceptance of substantial debt reduction with reformed conditionality geared toward poverty alleviation. Nevertheless, the dominant tendency has been to seek common ground and maintain a steady critique of target institutions while acknowledging incremental improvements in policy.

Why and How the Network Emerges
Phase I: Late 1970s to 1984/85

From the late 1970s through the 1980s, the Third World debt crisis had focused attention on large, middle-income countries whose possible default on loans threatened the stability of the international financial system. The "Mexican Weekend" of August 1982, during which the Mexican government threatened to default on its international debt, was the watershed event triggering widespread public attention to the debt crisis; however, some of the first transnational expressions of concern about its impact on the poor came much earlier by way of missionaries working in debtor countries who would return to their countries of origin and urge churches and NGOs to take up the issue. Many activists had experienced firsthand the devastating effect of the crisis on their parishioners and friends in debtor country shantytowns, and had been deeply imbued with the injunction of Latin American liberation theology to examine and confront "sinful structures" that contribute to poverty.

It proved quite difficult in the early years of the crisis—even after August 1982—to convince organizations to take on the debt question. Although the case for urgent action had been made by several blue ribbon commissions (e.g., the Brandt Commission and Jimmy Carter's Presidential

Commission on World Hunger), groups had difficulty identifying legislative handles around which to mobilize grassroots membership. Also, the concern at the time, particularly between 1982 and 1985, was overwhelmingly middle-income-country debt owed to commercial banks. With the fear that default by any one of the major debtor countries could bring down the international financial system, even congressional critics of the banks were reluctant to press the latter on debt reduction. NGO efforts were thus sporadic and limited to the staging of protests at the joint IMF/World Bank meetings, visits to congressional offices to elicit support, and attempts at popular education through talks and newsletter briefings.

Phase II: 1984/85 to 1989/90

The next phase was characterized by increased NGO and church interest as (1) the enduring social impact of both debt and SAPs became more apparent; (2) U.S. and European-based commercial banks took action to defuse the crisis from their perspective by increasing their reserves and severely curtailing new lending to debtor countries; and (3) creditor-country legislators became more willing to take on the banks. National debt crisis networks were established to exchange information and coordinate efforts on the issue, and nascent efforts at international information exchange and policy coordination were attempted through conferences and mailings. Nevertheless, the end of the decade saw a temporary falloff in activism as a dominant impression among policymakers and the media that the issue had been sufficiently addressed coincided with personal and policy rifts in several of the networks and the departure of key activists to different jobs.

Phase III: 1990 to 1995

In the third phase, persistent efforts by key NGOs and individuals led to the revival of the U.S. and European networks under new names. While these networks continued to facilitate the exchange of information among organizations conducting their own campaigns, joint action became the norm as they strengthened ties to Latin American, Asian, and African groups.

Jo Marie Griesgraber of the Jesuit-sponsored Center of Concern helped organize a "Rethinking Bretton Woods" project, spurred by the then-upcoming fiftieth anniversary of the 1944 Bretton Woods Conference establishing the IMF and the World Bank. In the summer of 1993, representatives of many of the same long-active development and environmental groups met to establish the "Fifty Years Is Enough" campaign. Like the "Rethinking Bretton Woods" project, the groups desired far-reaching reform of the World Bank and the IMF: *process* reform (transparency and accountability), *policy* reform (with regard to debt and structural adjustment), and *project* reform (what kinds of projects are funded, who decides where funds go, and how local communities participate). While the two campaigns had some overlapping membership, the "Fifty Years Is Enough" coalition was more explicitly a grassroots movement. Thirty-three U.S. groups cosponsored its May 1994 press conference launching the campaign, and parallel campaigns were held in twelve other countries. Development GAP, which housed the campaign's secretariat and coordinated the steering committee of some twenty to twenty-five groups, reported in 1997 that the campaign represented some five hundred citizens' groups around the world, including labor and farm groups, with over 70 percent Southern representation.[3] The campaign was somewhat more radical and confrontational in style, language, and strategy than the "Rethinking Bretton Woods" group. Nevertheless, the divide was not a complete one as the two coalitions had some overlapping membership and the Fifty Years leadership began to have dialogue, as had those from Rethinking Bretton Woods, with officials of the World Bank, the IMF, and the Clinton administration.

In the spring of 1994, some of the religious NGOs active in the two campaigns felt the need to have an additional forum for groups working out of a faith perspective and thus formed the Religious Working Group on the World Bank and the IMF. Still active in 2000, they have exchanged information, coordinated prayer vigils at the annual joint World Bank/IMF meetings, developed materials for local church groups, and arranged meetings between IFI officials and denominational leaders and missionaries. In December 1995, many of the same secular and religious U.S.-based groups, led by Oxfam International, the Center of Concern, and the United States Catholic Conference (USCC), formed the Multilateral Debt Coalition. Oxfam International had opened a Washington office in January 1995 from which to coordinate its lobbying efforts on debt and other multilateral issues, thus reassuming a leading role on debt that had earlier been played by Oxfam UK.

In Europe, Dutch foundations and NGOs in 1990 decided to finance a newly named network—EURODAD (the European Network on Debt and Development), seeking funding from as many European groups as possible. While EURODAD's policy and management is determined by an international coordinating group (ICG) composed of one NGO from each of the sixteen European countries, by the mid-1990s approximately sixty other NGOs from Europe, the United States, Canada, and the South cooperated actively with the network (EURODAD 1994, 24). European member foundations and NGOs provided just over 60 percent of its funding, with the remainder financed by the European Community (EURODAD 1993, 5).[4] FONDAD (Forum on Debt and Development) Latin America played a co-ordinating role for that region, working out of its Quito secretariat. With no major U.S. NGO consistently working on the debt issue, EURODAD emerged in the early 1990s as the lead institution providing information for transnational efforts on the issue. By the mid-1990s, network leadership was shared by EURODAD, the U.S. coalitions described above, and Oxfam International.

The lead network in Asia has long been the Philippines Freedom from Debt Coalition (FDC), which represents over ninety organizations. In August 1993, the FDC brought together NGOs from countries throughout Asia to found the Asian Campaign on Debt and Structural Adjustment. As with the other regional networks, participating groups include those engaged in research, campaigning, and popular grassroots work (EURODAD 1993, 5).

The major gap in the debt network had long been sub-Saharan Africa. AFRODAD (the African Network and Forum on Debt and Development) was created in May 1994. Financed by European NGOs and church foundations, AFRODAD provided member groups and national coalitions in Zambia, Tanzania, Ethiopia, Uganda, and Mozambique with information and guidance on research and campaign methodology.[5]

In summary, most network activists in the early 1990s turned their attention from commercial banks and targeted creditor-country finance and foreign ministries, the IMF, and the World Bank on the issues of bilateral and multilateral debt and SAPs. This was because the poorest, most heavily indebted countries tend to owe the vast majority of their external debt to bilateral and multilateral creditors rather than commercial lenders. Systematic efforts were undertaken to strengthen regional and international coordination of network initiatives.

Phase IV: 1996 to Present

The campaign's latest phase has been the most global as NGOs, churches, and other civil society organizations increased collaboration to work on the Jubilee 2000 campaign. British groups, led by the overseas relief agencies of the Anglican and Catholic churches, launched the Jubilee 2000 U.K. campaign in 1996, with South African–born Ann Pettifor, a seasoned and astute political organizer, leading the staff. The U.K. network was the first to establish the campaign's goal of a one-time cancellation of the unpayable debts of the world's poorest countries by the end of the year 2000; some fifty-seven national Jubilee 2000 networks in other countries were subsequently formed.[6]

The Jubilee 2000 USA campaign, organized by leaders of the Religious Working Group and the Multilateral Debt Coalition, was officially launched at the time of the G-7 summit in Denver in June 1997. Funding was provided by many of the same Protestant churches and Catholic religious orders that had financed earlier debt network efforts. Many of the other national Jubilee 2000 campaigns were launched in 1998, with Northern campaigns often sponsoring and financing Southern affiliates. While most national campaigns, such as those in Canada, Guyana, Mexico, and Zambia, have been initiated and led by church-affiliated groups, others, such as those in Cote d'Ivoire and Uganda, are led by secular NGOs.[7]

In summary, then, with a pause in activism at the turn of the decade partially due to policy differences and the departure of key personnel, the debt network in the mid-1990s gradually became more global in scope. EURODAD and successive U.S. coalitions effectively replaced Oxfam U.K. in the early 1990s as the lead institutions supplying information to and co-ordinating strategy among network participants. With the 1995 establishment of an Oxfam International office in Washington, Oxfam regained its role as a network leader. The "Fifty Years Is Enough" campaign has pursued a somewhat distinct agenda, as will be seen below. In the late 1990s, both the launching of the Jubilee 2000 campaign and technological developments facilitating much more intensive information exchange by e-mail led to a very rapid expansion in the number of groups around the world that were collaborating, yet retaining autonomy in their work on debt.

Network Campaigns: Increasingly Transnational

Given the diversity of the network's target actors—the three categories of creditors described above—network members have engaged in a broad range of "venue shopping" similar to activists' efforts in other networks. To educate their constituencies, they have produced pamphlets, comic books, and fake issues of major newspapers. To pressure commercial banks to cancel outstanding debt owed them and to develop socially and environmentally sensitive lending criteria, they have sponsored shareholders' resolutions and campaigns to cut up bank-issued credit cards; they have also urged national and European Community legislators to hold hearings on the issue and apply pressure on the banks through regulatory reform. To convince their governments of the need to apply more lenient terms and/or to cancel official bilateral debt and, in the last several years, IFI multilateral debt, they have developed grassroots mobilization campaigns, pamphleted and lobbied legislators and finance ministry staffs, and held conferences and demonstrations during major international meetings, linking hands to form human chains around conference sites to symbolize the chains of debt. They have pursued similar strategies in an attempt to convince the IFIs and member governments of the need to modify or eliminate structural adjustment programs associated with debt rescheduling and reduction. The global campaign to gather signatures to present to the G-7 leaders meeting in Cologne, Germany, in June 1999 clearly represented the most extensive effort.

During the last decade, network activists have made more deliberate attempts at transnational collaboration. Even as creditor- and debtor-country groups began to collaborate regularly in the late 1980s and early to mid-1990s, Northern NGOs clearly led, although Southern NGOs by the mid-1990s had become more involved in the implementation phase of a project to review SAPs. This trend has continued in the current Jubilee 2000 campaign, with much more explicit North-South tensions.

It has also become increasingly routine in the last decade for civil society groups to interact with other sectors, contributing to a broader network of contestational communication, if not consensus on the issue. A regular pattern has developed of meetings between Jubilee 2000 groups and officials from creditor governments and IFIs, initiated by both sides. Academics have also played an increasing role in the network, most prominently Jeffrey Sachs, director of Harvard's Center for International Development. A longtime critic of the IMF, Sachs became an advisor to the Jubilee 2000 U.K. campaign in mid-1999. With well-publicized experience as an advisor to, among other countries, Bolivia, Poland, and Russia, Sachs has sufficient stature to have his editorials regularly published or covered in newspapers of record.

Multilateral Debt Reduction and the HIPC Initiative

The campaign to reduce the debt owed to multilateral financial institutions and creditor-country governments was initiated in late 1993 and continued as a main thrust of the Jubilee 2000 campaign. It has been characterized by a clear pattern of network-sponsored conferences, research and documentation, the drafting of joint platforms in advance of the G-7 summer summits and World Bank/IMF meetings, media and grassroots campaigns, and then the issuance of praise for incremental policy change and persistent calls for additional reform.

In December 1993, EURODAD organized a conference in The Hague to analyze the problem of those countries with significant percentages of their outstanding debt stock owed to the IMF and the World Bank. While WB and IMF officials had long insisted that they could not cancel any debt owed them on both legal and prudential grounds (e.g., such a move might affect the World Bank's AAA credit rating), network activists questioned the policy.

Following the 1994 publication of a EURODAD-financed major study of the issue, EURODAD and two of its member organizations drafted a platform of action. Over two hundred NGOs from around the world signed on to the platform, and European- and U.S.-based NGOs used the text to lobby governments and leading IMF and World Bank officials. Just prior to the July 1994 G-7 summit in Naples, conferences sponsored by EURODAD and the Swiss Coalition in Geneva and the Center of Concern in Washington produced similar, more detailed positions that were reflected in a network letter to the G-7 leaders meeting in Naples (EURODAD 1994, 5–6).

While there was little movement at Naples on multilateral debt, the network claimed small victories in 1994 when Sweden, Denmark, and Britain— three countries in which NGOs had waged major campaigns—became the first donor governments to raise the issue. Sweden and Denmark called for multilateral debt reduction at a July 1994 Consultative Group meeting chaired by the World Bank, and the British chancellor called for the sale of IMF gold to finance the reduction at the September Commonwealth Conference (EURODAD 1994, 6).

Transnational collaboration on multilateral debt continued in the form of a joint letter to the G-7 leaders meeting at the 1995 Halifax summit; it was signed by twenty-three U.S. groups and twenty-two other NGOs from around the world. The letter and an associated extensive letter-writing campaign arguably contributed to the G-7 Halifax request that the staffs of both the World Bank and the IMF study the issue. The two IFIs produced several successive draft proposals in the fall of 1995. Lead NGOs, most notably Oxfam International and EURODAD, issued and disseminated detailed critiques of these staff proposals,[8] and lobbied World Bank President James Wolfensohn and World Bank and IMF executive directors from creditor countries. At the 1996 Lyons summit, G-7 leaders announced their intention to seek comprehensive multilateral debt reduction for qualifying countries, and finally, at the fall 1996 WB/IMF meetings, the Heavily Indebted Poor Countries Initiative (HIPC) was announced. As the first comprehensive plan to reduce the bilateral and multilateral debt of qualifying countries, it featured among its complex terms the possibility of forgiveness of 80 percent (up from 67 percent) of such countries' bilateral debt. Lead NGOs again immediately responded with critiques of the initiative, which were disseminated throughout the global network.

Some activists in the "Fifty Years Is Enough" campaign strongly opposed network involvement in the multilateral debt reduction issue. Nevertheless, many members of the Fifty Years campaign, for example, members of the U.S. Religious Working Group on the World Bank and the IMF, remained active on the issue, vigorously recommending further reforms. As indicated in Nelson's chapter, leaders of the Fifty Years campaign approached Wolfensohn in June 1995 with their critique of SAP conditionality. Following the failure of the U.S. Congress to fund the World Bank's concessional loan program (IDA) and the widespread publicity surrounding the 1994 Fifty Years campaign, Wolfensohn sought dialogue with the bank's most vocal critics. The result was a plan for a joint World Bank–NGO Structural Adjustment Policy Review Initiative (SAPRI) (see Nelson, this volume).

Jubilee 2000

As indicated above, leading network activists welcomed the 1996 HIPC Initiative, but protested that the debt relief provided by it must be much deeper, broader, and faster. In its first three years only four of the forty countries qualifying for HIPC debt relief had advanced to a point in the review process where their debt had been actually reduced. The G-7 leaders meeting in Cologne in June 1999 agreed in principle to an "enhanced" HIPC initiative that would cancel an additional $45 billion of the bilateral and multilateral debt owed by the qualifying countries. This was to be added to the $55 billion already proposed through the Paris Club of bilateral creditors ($30 billion) and the HIPC Initiative ($25 billion).

The Cologne Initiative would also lower the level of debt that is considered "sustainable" under HIPC. Countries with debt above this level would also begin to receive debt relief after demonstrating compliance with IMF-mandated structural adjustment for three years, down from six years under HIPC. The G-7 leaders also directed the IMF and the World Bank to assist qualifying countries in drafting and implementing poverty reduction plans "for the effective targeting of savings derived from debt relief, together with increased transparency of budgetary procedures to protect social expenditure." The leaders also recommended, but did not require, that the IMF and World Bank consult civil society groups in the design and implementation of such programs. The two IFIs complied with the G-7 mandate by announcing at the September 1999 meeting that the institutions would implement a Poverty Reduction Strategy more explicitly tying debt relief to the funding of health and education, the provision of rural infrastructure, and job creation. To qualify for further HIPC debt reduction, a government must formulate a Poverty Reduction Strategy Paper (PRSP) based on widespread consultation with civil society groups.

While Jubilee 2000 leaders welcomed Cologne's explicit link between debt relief and poverty reduction, the call for civil society participation, and greater transparency of budgetary procedures, they nonetheless objected to several features of the plan. Network activists continue to raise these criticisms at present:

1. The amount of relief is still insufficient. Critics such as Sachs have charged that the economic indicators used to determine if a government is able to repay its debts are arbitrary and unrealistic, and that the IMF and the World Bank could afford far more extensive relief.[9]

2. Too few countries will receive relief. As indicated above, the Jubilee 2000 U.K. campaign pointed out that only twenty-two countries qualified for some reduction in debt service payments by the end of the year 2000. No additional debt relief was offered to lower-middle income and other poor countries that do not qualify as HIPCs but also have high debt-servicing requirements that impede government commitment to poverty reduction.

3. Under Cologne's Enhanced HIPC Initiative, the IMF and the World Bank yield *more* control over the debt-reduction process. Countries receiving debt relief must still undergo IMF-sponsored structural adjustment, which network critics have long charged exacerbates poverty and contributes to environmental degradation. Many Jubilee 2000 supporters are skeptical that civil society groups will be adequately consulted in IMF and World Bank programs for their countries as well as any poverty reduction programs, and question the *increased* IMF role in designing the latter, given its track record on sustainable development.

Before and since Cologne, campaign activists have worked on a variety of fronts, as did their network predecessors. Campaigners in some debtor countries, most notably Uganda, have engaged in dialogue and lobbying efforts with their own governments as well as with governments of countries considering the cancellation of bilateral debt to carve out a role for civil society groups in ensuring that monies saved are allocated to poverty reduction. In creditor countries some activists are working with finance ministries, legislatures, and IFI officials to draft and pass legislation for bilateral and multilateral debt reduction.

For example, members of the Jubilee 2000 USA's "Legislative Group" worked over the course of 1998 and 1999 with sympathetic members of Congress and their staffs to draft and have introduced H.R. 1095, "The Debt Relief for Poverty Reduction Act of 1999," which would have authorized monies for both bilateral and multilateral debt relief explicitly tied to poverty reduction. The group deliberately sought broad bipartisan support for the bill, mobilizing constituents—especially church groups—to lobby their representatives. Tensions within the global network did emerge concerning the legislation, as many Southern NGOs objected to any link between debt reduction and IFI-imposed conditionality. In January 1999,

Latin American Jubilee 2000 campaigners gathered in Honduras issued the Tegucigalpa Declaration, pointedly requesting that Northern groups not accept terms less favorable than those demanded by their Southern allies.

With the strength of the campaign, government and IFI officials in the late 1990s *initiated* more meetings with civil society groups. The U.S. campaign's Legislative Group, for example, met regularly with U.S. Treasury officials during 1999 and 2000 to work out differences on debt-reduction legislation. IMF and World Bank leaders committed their institutions to a comprehensive review of HIPC, including consultation with civil society groups. At a July 1999 seminar in Addis Ababa, Ethiopia, representatives of creditor and debtor governments, the IFIs, regional development banks, relevant UN agencies, and African and Northern NGOs met to examine practical ways to strengthen the link between debt relief and poverty reduction. Conference participants agreed that the IMF's Enhanced Structural Adjustment Facility should be revamped to strengthen its focus on poverty reduction. The same month, U.S. Treasury Secretary Lawrence Summers invited World Bank, IMF, and U.S. government officials to join NGOs and churches in a meeting to discuss the U.S. response; the civil society groups insisted that their Southern partners also be represented. In October 2000, President Clinton assembled a broad range of congressional, church, and NGO leaders in the White House West Wing to plot for achieving passage of that year's debt-reduction legislation (Beckmann 2000).

To summarize, network campaigns became increasingly global in scale in the late 1980s and early 1990s. Nevertheless, Northern NGOs continued to play the leading roles, often relying on their own organizations for information to use in campaigns. Third World activists have always strongly advocated debt relief, so the impetus for campaigns often came from debtor countries, although the tactical initiatives were designed in the North. The principal role of Southern NGOs through the mid-1990s was to endorse the initiatives of the North and lend them additional credibility. However, by the mid-1990s, several national and regional networks had also collaborated with Northern NGOs in initiating campaigns at the international level, the SAPRI project and PRSPs provided an opportunity for an increase in Southern participation, and Southern groups criticized Northerners assenting to IFI-imposed conditions to debt reduction. The network's political opportunity structure improved in the mid-1990s as politically moderate G-7 leaders and IFI officials expressed limited support for campaign demands; however, many campaigners still view such officials as targets rather than partners. A reformist/radical cleavage persisted, both among Northern groups and between North and South, driven by differences on goals and strategy and in personality. Nevertheless, some network members have bridged the divide, and efforts have been made to collaborate on initiatives such as the 1999 petition signature-gathering campaign.

Types of Impact

While it is difficult to assess the degree of impact that debt network members individually and collectively have had, this chapter argues that they have achieved limited success in several of the categories of influence that Keck and Sikkink suggest (1998, 20). This case study also suggests two additional categories of influence: (1) grassroots education/network expansion—the extent to which the network's actions contributed to grassroots understanding of the issue and the broadening of the network itself; and (2) "reverse lobbying during policy formation"—the extent to which major policymakers seek the support of network members in the correct or mistaken belief that the latter have influence on other key policymakers or, more broadly, on their membership, voters, and/or public opinion.

Grassroots Education/Network Building

Particularly on complex, technical issues that are both far afield from the everyday experience of Northern constituencies and insufficiently covered in the mainstream media, grassroots education and network expansion are essential components of a network's impact. However, as in the cases of the other categories of influence, such change is hard to measure. Quantitative indicators, such as numbers of participants at conferences and demonstrations and numbers of subscribers to network publications, provide an initial indication. As of 2000, over twenty-four million people had signed the Jubilee 2000 petition to the G-7 leadership.

As the earlier discussion reveals, activists created and expanded diverse networks in all parts of the globe and engaged in far-reaching efforts to educate publics on these issues. Most recently, the rapid expansion of e-mail and the Internet has greatly facilitated information exchange and educational efforts, as leading organizations such as the U.K. and U.S. Jubilee 2000 campaigns have developed detailed, regularly updated Web sites. With musicians such as Bono actively participating in the network, these Web sites are listed as links by sites such as NetAID, making the issue much more accessible to young people around the world.

Issue Attention/Agenda Setting

Given that the debt crisis was not a particularly salient issue in U.S. or European politics after the mid-1980s, NGOs and churches have played a crucial role in insisting that it be addressed. Most recently, the global network's initiatives pressing for multilateral debt reduction, continued criticism of the HIPC Initiative, and review of SAP conditionality most clearly put topics on the agenda that no one else in creditor countries would have raised. These issues would simply not have been on the agenda had it not been for the work of these diverse networks.

It could be argued that successive U.S. networks have been most successful at engaging policymakers' interest through direct contacts with them. Since the mid-1980s they have supported and worked with members of Congress already interested in the topic, and began in the early 1990s to lobby Treasury, State Department, and IFI officials directly, supported by letter-writing campaigns. Officials are customarily reluctant to admit that outside actors actually helped to shape their agenda, however.[10] Nevertheless, a pattern of intersectoral dialogue has become much more routine. Many Jubilee 2000 campaigners have been more deliberate in seeking bipartisan support in renewing their efforts at legislative change. During the earlier phases European network members had relatively more success than did their U.S. counterparts at generating media attention and affecting the policy agenda, though the latter have been more effective on HIPC and Jubilee 2000.

Reverse Lobbying During Policy Formation

In studying a case of network activism on an issue, one can look for evidence that major policymakers sought network members' support in the belief that the latter had access to, and therefore influence on, either voters or, more narrowly, other key policymakers. It may be that this category of influence applies only to a small number of potential network participants who possess either: (1) widely recognized (though not necessarily uncontested) moral authority (e.g., the Catholic hierarchy or Nobel Peace Prize winners); (2) technical expertise on the issue (e.g., Nobel laureates, other scientists with broad media recognition or, in this case, UNICEF and perhaps Oxfam); or (3) political clout due to a large membership base (e.g., the NRA or the larger environmental NGOs). The point is to identify those members of the network, if any, who are the *objects* as well as the subjects of lobbying and campaigning.

In the debt case, at least two major U.S. players whom the U.S. Catholic bishops consulted during the drafting of their 1989 statement on the debt crisis's moral dimensions sought the bishops' support with the stated (if not actual) belief that the bishops could influence other key actors. Democratic Senator Bill Bradley of New Jersey, one of the most outspoken members of Congress on the debt crisis, indicated that he had agreed to meet with the bishops at the January 1989 meeting of the USCC's Committee on International Policy (CIP) (two months before the Brady Plan for debt reduction was announced) because, "I was actually lobbying the USCC in the hopes it could influence the Bush White House—to use the access they had to effect a change in policy, having been unsuccessful since '83 with Reagan."[11] David Mulford, undersecretary of the treasury in the first Bush administration, told those gathered at the June 1989 USCC CIP meeting that he had agreed to meet with them because of their contacts with leading (Catholic) money center bank officials. He vigorously urged the bishops to get the bankers to do their part promptly in the Brady Plan debt-reduction package then being negotiated with Mexico.[12] In both cases, as political scientist Timothy Byrnes concluded in the case of the 1976 presidential candidates vis-à-vis Catholic voters, they "overestimated the political influence, either direct or indirect, that the hierarchy could exert" (1991, 71).

In addition to the Catholic hierarchy, one could make limited claims that some of the less powerful creditor governments sought out Oxfam for information and advice (the second category),[13] and that Wolfensohn agreed to talk with some of the World Bank's toughest critics in the case of "Fifty Years Is Enough." Most recently, as indicated above, U.S. Treasury officials and IFI officials sought meetings with leading NGOs and church groups active in Jubilee 2000 in the belief that they had made inroads with recalcitrant Republican legislators. Several U.S. Jubilee 2000 activists suggested that Treasury Secretary Summers's newfound interest in legislative action in 1999 (after several years of tepid response by midlevel Treasury officials) was prompted by his surprise that two leading House Republicans (Jim Leach and Spencer Bachus) challenged him at the June 1999 House Banking Committee hearings, asking why the administration had not done more on debt reduction.

Influence on Formal Commitments Made by Creditors

As outlined above, NGOs' persistent lobbying efforts helped to account for Swedish, Danish, and British verbal commitments to the need for multilateral debt reduction in mid-1994. The network then collaborated with the Non-Aligned Movement and the G-7, which had adopted positions similar to that of the network, in lobbying and conducting media work on the issue. While the G-7 leaders meeting at the 1995 Halifax summit did not endorse significant debt reduction, they did recognize the problem of multilateral debt as a "substantial" one for many of the poorest countries and promised to encourage the Bretton Woods institutions "to develop a comprehensive approach to assist countries with multilateral debt problems, through the flexible implementation of existing instruments and new mechanisms when necessary."[14] Network members assert that their efforts, which included demonstrations, prayer vigils, and meetings with IFI officials, are a necessary but not sufficient explanation for the WB and IMF staff proposals issued in the fall of 1995 and the G-7's verbal commitment to multilateral debt reduction at the 1996 Lyon summit.[15]

As for the case of commercial banks, the New York–based Interfaith Center on Corporate Responsibility (ICCR) filed shareholder resolutions throughout the 1980s with most of the nine major U.S. money-center banks that would require them to pursue debt reduction and enact socially responsible future lending criteria. Only one such initiative proved successful: in 1991 the Bank of America agreed to a code governing its future lending to low-income countries after repeated lobbying by several Catholic religious orders that are ICCR members. The code lists factors that will routinely be considered in prospective credit decisions, ranging from the likely impact of such lending on the environment to that likely on the political system, public health, and living standards.[16] ICCR, however, has not been an active member of the successive Washington-oriented U.S. debt networks, though network members have been aware of ICCR initiatives.

NGOs in several European countries have proven more successful vis-à-vis commercial banks than their U.S. counterparts, and their cases lie somewhere between obtaining formal commitments and causing actual policy change. Dutch and Belgian NGOs mounted sustained campaigns urging those countries' largest banks to write off the debt owed them by the poorest countries. They succeeded in arranging meetings on the subject with leading bankers and finance and development ministry officials. In 1991, after more than one hundred Dutch activists holding shares in the largest Dutch bank, ABN AMRO, challenged the bank's board at the annual shareholders meeting, the bank's leadership made a commitment to match any official debt reduction for the poorest countries agreed to in the Paris Club. Continued NGO pressure on the bank to act on its commitment led to the institution of debt reduction at the end of 1992; however, actual debt reduction—several million dollars—has been "quite disappointing."[17] In the Belgian case, the agreement between banks and NGOs was worked out in 1993 and the debt network spent several years awaiting its implementation. The Belgian Minister for Development Cooperation and then-President of the EU Development Council also made a commitment to the NGOs in 1993 to work with EU governments and commercial banks to reduce the commercial debt of sub-Saharan African countries (12 percent of their total debt but 40 percent of debt service) in a way similar to the Belgian agreement but again, little change resulted (EURODAD 1993, 8). The international network contributed to these national initiatives by way of EURODAD's Working Team on Commercial Debt, in which NGOs from Germany, France, the Netherlands, Luxembourg, Belgian, Switzerland, and the U.K. meet regularly to exchange information and plan common initiatives.

As argued above, lobbying by North and South representatives of the "Fifty Years Is Enough" campaign and other critics of SAP conditionality is a necessary but not sufficient explanation of the World Bank leadership's verbal commitment to SAPRI. The global Jubilee 2000 campaign clearly contributed to: (1) the G-7 call at Cologne for the revision and deepening of the HIPC Initiative and more extensive bilateral debt relief linked to poverty reduction; (2) President Clinton's September 1999 announcement that the United States would cancel 100 percent of the bilateral debt owed it by HIPC countries, and his intention to seek $970 million over four years in funding from the U.S. Congress; and (3) the Treasury Department's subsequent negotiation with the more skeptical Republican leadership to fund debt relief.

In summary, earlier network members succeeded in extracting verbal commitments to policy reform and debt reduction from several commercial banks and European governments, with limited actual effect. The more recent and more global campaigns on multilateral debt reduction, SAP review, and Jubilee 2000 have contributed to commitments by G-7 and IFI leaders, but the jury is still out on the implementation phase of the expanded HIPC and SAPRI initiatives.

Influence on Policy Change in "Target Actors"

Actions taken by network members and, in more recent years, the network itself, are necessary but not sufficient explanations for limited policy change by Dutch and Belgian commercial banks (described above), the Swiss and U.S. governments vis-à-vis bilateral debt (1989–92), Paris Club countries with regard to bilateral debt (1988–94), the HIPC Initiative (1996), and its expansion at Cologne (1999).

Swiss and U.S. Bilateral Debt Reduction

Following a widely publicized NGO campaign of popular education and lobbying, the Swiss government in 1991 established the Swiss Debt Reduction Facility (SDRF) with an endowment of Sfr 500 million (U.S. $350 million). Its major feature is the repurchase of officially guaranteed export credit debt from Swiss suppliers and banks; potential beneficiaries include all low-income countries and several lower-middle-income country recipients of Swiss official development assistance. By 1992, 95 percent of the outstanding export credit debt owed by twenty-two low- and lower-middle-income countries was bought back at an average price of 18 percent of face value (EURODAD 1992, 19). Following negotiations with debtor country governments, the Swiss have used these funds to establish counterpart funds in local currency, the proceeds of which are used for development projects at the discretion of local committees, which in some cases include representatives of NGOs and multilateral development agencies.[18]

As for U.S. bilateral debt reduction, in July 1989 Bush announced the administration's intent to cancel approximately $1 billion of the bilateral debt owed by sixteen sub-Saharan African countries, just prior to the Paris G-7 summit. By December 1993, total bilateral debt reduction under the Bush administration, for nineteen sub-Saharan African countries, eleven Latin American countries, and Bangladesh, had reached $3.585 billion. Network member Bread for the World claimed to have contributed to the reduction of $2.71 billion of this total.[19] It would be more of a stretch to argue that NGO pressure contributed to Bush's decision to implement the enabling legislation.

Paris Club Terms Governing Bilateral Debt Reduction

The 1986 Oxfam U.K. media campaign decrying the scandal that African debt repayments to Britain exceeded aid monies and follow-up efforts by the British Debt Crisis Network (DCN) helped to account for the April 1987 declaration by Thatcher's Chancellor Nigel Lawson that the British government favored cancellation of two-thirds of the principal of bilateral debt owed by the poorest debtor countries and longer terms at lower interest rates to repay the remaining debt. As evidence of the initial campaign's influence, Oxfam's Development Policy Advisor John Clark cited the begrudging comments made to him by Peter Mountfield, who was then undersecretary of the British Finance Ministry: "Your campaign was well-placed and shameless."[20]

These so-called "Trinidad Terms" were resisted by several of the other G-7 governments, most notably the United States, Japan, and West Germany, and less generous terms were agreed upon in December 1988. NGOs and church groups protested that these latter "Toronto Terms" were insufficient and their 1990 campaign helped to explain the British government's ensuing call for better terms for the poorest countries. The early 1990s saw successively more generous terms announced. While more interviews with policymakers would be required to prove that persistent network education, media, and advocacy work contributed to these reforms, posing the counterfactual would seem to indicate that the network's efforts were a necessary factor.[21]

The 1996 HIPC Initiative

As argued above, the move to reduce the *multilateral* debt of qualifying countries constituted actual policy change in that this category of debt was previously considered off-limits. One senior World Bank official who specializes in debt issues said, "I don't want to say it was the NGOs that forced us to change, but NGOs played a major role." He observed, "There were some NGOs that became very involved in the details of the [HIPC] process," having a beneficial effect on the initiative by their mastery of details. He added that they had a say "by being able to make forceful arguments" to the donor nation governments.[22]

The Cologne Initiative and U.S. Funding

Similarly, persistent network criticism of the HIPC Initiative is a necessary but not sufficient explanation for the Cologne Initiative and U.S. government approval in 1999 and 2000 of funding for both bilateral and multilateral debt relief. In November 1999 the U.S. Congress passed legislation appropriating $110 million for U.S. bilateral debt relief explicitly tied to poverty reduction. Also, in a deal negotiated between U.S. Treasury officials and Republican congressional leaders, the IMF would be permitted to revalue part of its gold stock to finance reduction of HIPC-country debt owed to the IMF. The revaluation of approximately thirteen million ounces of gold would generate some $2.1 billion in profit; the interest would go toward debt relief.[23] Again, the following year, despite heavy opposition to increased expenditure on foreign aid, the network's lobbying blitz led Congress to appropriate $435 million for bilateral debt relief and approve the release of $550 million from IMF gold sales to finance additional debt reduction. Several network activists quoted Treasury officials' acknowledgment of the network's impact. The IMF gold revaluation, for example, would have been highly unlikely without the persistent, technically detailed, and well-publicized calls for such a move by Jeffrey Sachs and other Jubilee 2000 campaigners. Also, Republican members of Congress such as Spencer Bachus of Alabama reported that lobbying efforts by church groups from their districts convinced them to cosponsor debt-relief legislation (Beckmann 2000).

Factors Accounting for Earlier Relative Lack of Influence and More Recent Success

Throughout the network's history, several factors have inhibited its ability to influence debt and structural adjustment policies. These factors may be divided into three categories: characteristics of (1) the issue area, (2) the target actors, and (3) the network itself. In the case of all but one of the factors, changes are observable in the late 1990s that help account for the recent relative success of the network.

Issue Area

A network is arguably less likely to have influence on complex, technical international issues with few *apparent* implications for prospective Northern audiences. The problem of Third World debt has simply been one far removed from the experience of the overwhelming majority of creditor country populations. Earlier network members found it difficult to frame the issue in a way that was compelling, familiar, and intelligible to creditor-country audiences.

Nevertheless, in the last few years, Jubilee 2000 activists have successfully promoted resolution of this complex problem as what can only be termed a "millennium imperative." They have made progress in garnering the support of legislators who usually oppose foreign aid spending by expanding the frame of the moral demands of Jubilee year justice to apply to contemporary North-South relations, linking debt to the AIDS crisis overwhelming sub-Saharan Africa, and the desperate need to free up funds for health and education. They also injected a sense of urgency into the campaign by repeatedly insisting on the 2000 year-end deadline.

U.S. activists interviewed in the early to mid-1990s pointed out how difficult it was to both keep up with developments and educate interested groups and individuals when dealing with an issue affecting perhaps one hundred countries. Several raised the contrasting case of NAFTA, in which they could focus on forging links with just Mexican and Canadian NGOs. Key U.S. and European activists said they had better results when they provided concrete illustrations of the social impact of the debt crisis and failed SAP policies in individual countries such as Peru, the Philippines, Zambia, and Uganda.

However, with the Jubilee 2000 campaign, in a point related to the first factor, the widely held perception that substantial bilateral and multilateral debt reduction would significantly contribute to poverty alleviation in a broad range of countries has made the campaign a worthy form of celebrating the millennium.

Activists also found it difficult (more so in the United States than in Europe) to generate interest in a topic that is both severely undercovered by the media and portrayed as having been resolved. *The Financial Times* of London is the only major newspaper of record to have featured regular coverage of debt and adjustment throughout the 1990s.

Activists in the Jubilee 2000 campaign have made a much more concerted effort than their predecessors to get media coverage of their position(s). The *New York Times* explicitly endorsed much of the network's criticism of the Cologne Initiative in a 4 October 1999 lead editorial and profiled the network's disappointment with the lack of progress at the 2000 Okinawa summit. As argued above, the contributions of high-profile figures such as Pope John Paul II, Bono, and Jeffrey Sachs have drawn additional media attention.

Target Actors: Insulation/Few Legislative Handles

It could be argued that transnational networks are less likely to have influence on issues over which the executive branch exercises predominant authority and few legislative means are available to influence policy decisions of the executive branch, international organizations, and other key nonstate actors. In the case of Third World debt, the policy process has been fairly well-insulated in finance ministries, international financial institutions, and major money-center banks.

Network members had few direct means by which to affect the behavior of the IFIs and the money-center commercial banks. In the case of the former, as indicated in Paul Nelson's chapter, they could attach language to the periodic authorizations for IDA and even less frequent IMF quota increases. Affecting the behavior of the major commercial banks was even more difficult and technical, for example, changing tax treatment of the banks' loan loss reserves in order to induce them to write off more outstanding debt. U.S. NGOs in particular found that this was not the stuff of intelligible extensive grassroots campaigns.

Only with the multilateral debt reduction and SAP review campaigns has network cultivation of finance ministry and IFI officials begun to bear fruit. Neo-Social Democratic administrations in the United States, Great Britain, and Germany in the late 1990s created new political opportunities for G-7 action. In the case of H.R. 1095, it was again the network's cultivation of legislative supporters—this time bipartisan—that made the difference.

Network Characteristics: Reformist-Radical Cleavage

Throughout the history of the network, tensions have persisted on several enduring questions: whether the network should accept partial debt reduction or insist on cancellation (this includes the question of what constitutes "unpayable debt"); how many countries should be covered (just HIPCs or also large "middle-income countries" like Peru and Brazil); whether legislation is a worthwhile strategy; whether to accept debt reduction tied to revised conditionality tied to poverty alleviation or insist on no conditionality; and whether accepting limited legislation would undercut further efforts. Many NGOs in the international network, including EURODAD and Oxfam International, favor delinking debt relief from the dominant IMF and WB structural adjustment model, but are more willing to accept interim incremental policy reform, such as conditioned debt reduction. More radical members believed that the debt was illegitimate and had already been repaid; they therefore opposed any debt swaps (be they for equity, the environment, or development) or any moves toward conditioned debt reduction that continued external control over debtor country economic policy. Other members, who often shared many of the radicals' views, labeled the former group as "purists," complaining that their positions effectively isolated them from the policy debate. Many who favor some sort of positive conditionality on debt relief expressed the view that UN agencies such as UNDP, UNICEF, and the World Health Organization should play a greater role—and the IMF a much reduced one—in the design of that conditionality.[24]

It appears that in both the United States and Europe, groups more accepting of incremental policy change have prevailed in the last two phases of international networking, and radicals are now among those engaged in intersectoral dialogues they previously eschewed. As Marie Dennis of the Maryknoll Justice and Peace office put it, "There has been some concern in the movement about the institutions breaking us up into 'good' NGOs you could talk to and confrontational ones that you couldn't. We've tried to be clear; while we have different styles, we agree on an agenda as much as possible."[25]

Network Characteristics: Understaffed and Underfinanced

Earlier groups active on the debt issue tended to be small organizations lacking extensive membership bases (with the exception of Bread for the World in the United States and several of the groups in "Fifty Years Is Enough"), with small staffs often covering several issues with very limited funds. Oxfam International, with its larger budget, research arm, and relationship to regional Oxfams, was a notable exception. The Jubilee 2000 campaign has spurred a profound expansion of the network, particularly with the active participation of extensive networks of institutions affiliated with the Catholic and mainline Protestant churches. While many of these churches have begun to fund more systematic work on debt, including efforts to strengthen North-South collaboration, many activists interviewed reported that they are still overworked with insufficient resources.

One problem is that many of the staff people in Southern NGOs are so overcommitted that they are not able to participate fully in network activities. One of the Jubilee 2000 campaign's principal goals has been to fund and strengthen the capacity of debtor country civil society groups to document the impact of the debt overhang and SAPs on the poor, to collaborate with responsive governments in the design of poverty action plans associated with debt reduction, and to monitor their implementation. The expansion of the Internet, network Web sites, and e-mail has greatly facilitated this work.

Conclusion

The enduring problems of external indebtedness and the disproportionate burden borne by the poorest in countries undergoing SAPs have posed considerable challenges to NGOs and churches working toward their alleviation. As in the cases of other advocacy networks, the issue area is multifaceted, technically complex, and difficult to organize around, but perhaps more so than in the cases of human rights, women, and the environment.

Efforts at network building were shown to have begun in the mid-1980s at the instigation of religious and secular NGOs whose staff had had considerable grassroots experience in debtor countries. While policy and personal differences somewhat hampered early collaboration and successful campaigns were organized by groups that could rely on their own information rather than that of Southern NGOs, nascent attempts at transnational information exchange did enhance the U.S. and European network's educational work.

The emerging *global* network, primarily but not solely under the leadership of EURODAD and then Oxfam International in conjunction with successive U.S. NGO and church networks, increasingly mobilized national networks in creditor and debtor countries to endorse, publicize, and advocate major joint initiatives, such as those on multilateral debt reduction and SAP review. Facilitated by network Web sites and e-mail exchange, the Jubilee 2000 campaign has developed into a much broader network of civil society groups increasingly interacting with government and IFI officials.

The debt network has been most successful at grassroots education/ network expansion and issue attention/agenda setting. Most significantly, the network placed the issues of bilateral and multilateral debt relief linked to poverty reduction and civil society participation and SAP reconsideration on the agendas of creditor and debtor governments and the IFIs. The Catholic Church hierarchy had limited impact in the third category, reverse lobbying during policy formation, but the church as a whole has not formally signed on as a member of specific campaigns such as Jubilee 2000, even though many Catholic religious orders and affiliated NGOs have. Oxfam

International, "Fifty Years Is Enough" leaders, and leaders of national Jubilee 2000 campaigns have also had limited impact in this category.

Network actions helped to account for verbal commitments made by several European commercial banks and creditor country governments to debt reduction, as well as actual policy change by several of the commercial banks, and the Swiss, U.S., and Paris Club governments vis-à-vis bilateral and multilateral debt reduction. Jubilee 2000 activists were able to garner some bipartisan support for debt relief funding by pointing to the relatively small cost of initiatives that could significantly improve the lives of several hundred million of the world's poorest people. Nevertheless, debt reduction to date has represented a tiny percentage of the most heavily indebted countries' outstanding debt stock (see World Bank 2000, 169–73, and individual country debt tables).

Issues raised by the case for the network research program include: (1) the degree to which lead organizations (in this case, successively, Oxfam-U.K., EURODAD, Oxfam International, and Jubilee 2000 U.K.) enhance cooperation among network members and increase the network's efficacy—or provoke resentment; (2) the extent to which leading Northern members are themselves active transnationally, thus not requiring Southern NGOs' informational input; (3) the comprehensiveness of the network (the extent to which significant nonstate actors active on the issue remain outside the network—in this case UNICEF in the earlier years); (4) categories of influence (the addition of grassroots education/network building and reverse lobbying during policy formation); and (5) the extent to which rifts between reform-oriented and radical groups inhibit network cohesion and efficacy.

Notes

An earlier version of this chapter was presented at the Latin American Studies Association XIX International Congress, Washington, D.C., 29 September 1995. I am grateful for the time and insights provided by all those whom I interviewed, and I am particularly indebted to Marie Dennis, Jo Marie Griesgraber, Paul Nelson, and Kathryn Sikkink for their comments on earlier drafts.

1. Countries whose GNP per capita is less than $785 are defined as low income. The severely indebted "middle-income" countries include Bolivia and Peru.

2. Due to the Vatican's permanent observer status at the United Nations, it was able to have the Venezuelan government introduce the 1987 statement as a UN document; it was thus translated into the UN's six official languages and distributed to all member governments.

3. Doug Hellinger, director, Development GAP, interview by author, 3 June 1997.

4. See also www.oneworld.org/eurodad.

5. Fax from Opa Kapijimpanga, AFRODAD coordinator, 4 September 1995; EURODAD, *1994 Annual Report*, 2.

6. See www.jubilee2000uk.org/wwcol2.html.

7. A brief description of each Jubilee 2000 coalition is available at www. jubilee2000uk.org/wwcol2.html (15 October 1999).

8. C.f., Oxfam International 1996.

9. *New York Times,* 11 June 1999.

10. At the time of my most extensive interviews (1992–93), at least ten policy-makers (including several leading officials at the IMF) mentioned UNICEF as the sole outside organization to influence them. UNICEF has not been a consistently active participant in the debt network, however, though its officials sponsored and participated in several European conferences on the subject.

11. Senator Bill Bradley, interview by author, Washington, D.C., 13 May 1993.

12. Martin McLaughlin's typed notes from the meeting, USCC files. Also, Thomas Trebat, interview by author, New York, 18 November 1993.

13. Veena Siddharth, economic and social advocacy officer, Oxfam International, interview by author, 5 June 1997.

14. "G-7 Economic Communique Text," Halifax, Nova Scotia, 16 June 1995, 6.

15. C.f., Oxfam International 1996.

16. Bank of America 1991. Also interview by author with Paul Dorfmann, executive vice president, executive officer for credit policy, Bank of America, 7 June 1992.

17. Ted van Hees, coordinator, EURODAD, phone interview by author, 1 September 1995.

18. Swiss Coalition of Development Organizations, *Swiss Coalition News* 1 (June 1994): 2–4; 2 (September 1994): 8; 3 (March 1995): 5; 4 (May 1995): 7.

19. "BFW Wins $2.7 Billion in Third World Debt Relief," *Bread for the World Newsletter* 4, no. 5 (June 1992): 1–2. A BFW staff member and sympathetic con-gressional staffers wrote the enabling legislation.

20. Cited by John Clark during interview by author, Washington, D.C., July 1992. See also Clark 1987.

21. Cf. Matthew Martin, "Official Bilateral Debt: New Directions for Action," EURODAD 1994.

22. "Policy Change for World Bank," *The Christian Century* 113, no. 32 (6 November 1996): 1065.

23. John Burgess, "Deal Will Allow IMF to Fund Debt Relief," http:// washingtonpost.com/wp-srv/WPlate/1999-11/17/2041-111799-idx.html.

24. C.f. the September 1999 Meeting on Alternative Approaches to Debt Relief, http://www.jubilee2000uk.org/news/usa2709.html (4 October 1999).

25. Marie Dennis, phone interview by author, 21 May 1996.

9

NGOs, Transnational Networks, International Donor Agencies, and the Prospects for Democratic Governance in Indonesia

James V. Riker

On 21 May 1998, the people of Indonesia found themselves in the midst of a political change that had seemed unattainable only a short time before. President Suharto, a former general who had ruled Indonesia with impunity for thirty-two years, abruptly resigned and handed over authority to his vice president, B. J. Habibie. Just sixteen months later, Abdurrahman Wahid, an Islamic cleric and NGO advocate committed to pluralism and democracy, was elected president in late October 1999. In the process, the world witnessed a decisive shift toward democratic governance in Indonesia. The significance of this shift is remarkable for three reasons. First, it represents a break away from over forty years of authoritarian government to a pluralistic, democratic government in Indonesia. Second, it gives renewed hope to citizens and NGO leaders who are actively making demands to reform and democratize Indonesia's institutions and political system. Finally, as economic and political reforms proceed, Indonesia is now embarked on reconfiguring relations between state and society and reshaping the bases for democratic governance.

How do we understand the factors that led to this definitive shift toward democratic governance in Indonesia? This chapter examines how NGOs and various transnational actors have influenced the structuring of development politics vis-à-vis the state and assesses the rise of civil society in contemporary Indonesia. The chapter emphasizes the importance of the transnational dimension for political change by examining how NGOs, transnational networks, and international development agencies have strengthened civil society and reshaped the discourse about sustainable development and democracy in Indonesia. First, NGOs throughout Southeast

Asia have attempted in varying degrees to redefine the roles and boundaries of civil society and to pressure their governments to reorient development policies toward more just, equitable, and ecologically sustainable outcomes in India, Indonesia, Malaysia, the Philippines, and Thailand.[1] Second, transnational networks of NGOs from the North and South have emerged to address pressing development and political issues, including the environment, human rights, and democratic governance. The chapter highlights the case of the International NGO Forum on Indonesian Development (INFID), a transnational network of NGOs that lobbied international development agencies and Indonesia's Suharto government to address pressing development and political issues. Third, international donor agencies have sought to promote sustainable development and to foster democratic practices and governance by providing aid and technical assistance to receptive elements within civil society in Southeast Asia. Thus, this analysis examines the strategies that NGOs have employed to strengthen civil society vis-à-vis the state; explores the linkages among NGOs, transnational networks, and international donor agencies; and assesses the prospects for fostering democratic governance in Indonesia.

Forming Transnational Networks and Coalitions: The Basis for a New Politics?

On an unprecedented scale, NGOs around the globe and across national boundaries are building new horizontal links and political alliances to monitor human rights, corporate business practices, and major development projects, as well as environmental and labor practices. In the process, NGOs have become a visible political force in a number of transnational arenas. The formation of transnational issue networks by NGOs and other international actors in the areas of the environment, human rights, and international development policy has presented a new mode for international politics (Keck and Sikkink 1995, 1998; Smith, Chatfield, and Pagnucco 1997; Sikkink 1993a; Woods 1993). Citizens are no longer depending on their governments alone to take the initiative or to provide full and accurate information about the issues and decisions that affect their lives. NGOs have protested major hydroelectric dam projects, mounting campaigns that have reached beyond the grassroots to national and transnational arenas.[2] Where Asian governments have not been responsive to criticisms of these projects, NGOs have bypassed the state and lobbied the World Bank and other international donors to reconsider their funding of these projects.[3] The combined advocacy efforts of NGOs in the developing world and citizen groups in the West prompted the World Bank to reexamine and reorient some of its development policies and programs, especially in the area of the environment and the bank's support for dam and resettlement projects (Rich 1994). Asian NGOs have come together to challenge the Asia Pacific Economic Cooperation (APEC) forum (Pacific Asia Resource Center 1995; "People's Forum on APEC 1996" 1996), as well as to advocate an alternative vision for Asian society under the rubric of the "General Assembly of the People's Plan for the 21st Century" (Kothari 1996; Ichiyo 1996). While NGOs in Asia appear to be gaining greater voice in transnational arenas, difficult questions remain for NGOs throughout the developing world and their constituencies as they confront the challenge of linking up with global agendas that are largely set in the West (Fowler 1992). The key issue facing NGOs in the developing world as they adopt global agendas is how to maintain their autonomy and identity while simultaneously collaborating and building effective alliances with other actors.

These forays into the transnational political arena have prompted much discussion about the rise of transnational activism from above and below to challenge developments within the global political economy and to influence the bases of global governance. The emergence of transnational activism linking North and South has challenged traditional state-based notions of North-South relations (Ekins 1992; Wignaraja 1993; Marchand 1994; Smith, Chatfied, and Pagnucco 1997; Fisher 1998), while raising fundamental questions about the role of global institutions such as Bretton Woods (Kothari, Pratap, and Visvanathan 1994; Rich 1994). A growing number of scholars suggest that this concerted political action by nonstate actors across state boundaries provides the basis for constituting a new emerging global civil society (Brecher, Childs, and Cutler 1993; Lipschutz 1992; MacDonald 1994; Wapner 1994; Kothari 1996; Smith, Chatfield, and Pagnucco 1997; Keck and Sikkink 1998).

Redefining Civil Society in the Global Political Economy: The Case of Indonesia

The prolific growth of indigenous nongovernmental organizations (NGOs) in Indonesia's authoritarian political order during the 1980s has made them a key institutional actor in its development politics. There is a growing presence of Indonesian NGOs throughout the country.[4] Since the mid-1980s, Indonesian NGOs have undertaken environmental, legal, and economic and social development activities to broaden the role of citizens and strengthen their voice within civil society (Lev 1987; Eldridge 1989a, 1989b, 1995; Budiman 1990; Soetrisno 1991; Riker 1994/1995). The growing prominence of Indonesian environmental NGOs in the late 1980s enabled them to critique the government's development plans not only in the environmental and development arenas, but also in the areas of human rights and political reform (Aditjondro 1990c). Environmental NGOs coming together under the banner of sustainable development have spearheaded a nascent social and political movement for alternative development and political liberalization in Indonesia (Riker 1994/1995). Indonesian NGOs have initiated an ongoing debate about the nature of development policy, the role of the state, the participation of NGOs and the public in the development process, and the prospects for democratic forms of governance within Indonesia's political order (Sanit 1991a, 1991b).[5] In the process, an alternative development agenda and democratic discourse have emerged that extend beyond the national level to include transnational actors and forums.

The great majority of Indonesian NGOs working at the provincial, district, or local levels are primarily engaged in promoting development from below. Through their various social and economic development activities, these NGOs seek to improve the capacities of local peoples, organizations, and communities to solve their own problems (Eldridge 1989a, 1989b, 1995; Riker 1994/1995). In addition, a fair number of NGOs based at the provincial and national levels have principally sought to promote institutional pluralism and the strengthening of groups within civil society on a wide scale. Accordingly, the strategies that Indonesian NGOs have employed to increase political space for their operations have varied.[6]

As NGOs' developmental role in Indonesian society became more readily accepted by the Suharto government in the late 1980s, the basis for NGOs' development approaches, organizational forms, and strategies evolved to reflect the changing dynamics of political space in specific contexts. To counter the Suharto government's actions to restrict their activities, a number of Indonesian NGOs have taken steps to expand their political space at various levels. These strategies have included: promoting effective development activities and community organizations; cultivating alliances with supportive elements in the government; selectively cooperating with the government on development activities; forming federations and networks of NGOs at the provincial, regional, and national levels; and developing links to international donors, international NGOs and agencies, and other elements in civil society and the press.

During the late 1980s and early 1990s, a symbiotic relationship was developing between NGOs and the Indonesian press. A number of favorable editorials emerged that recognized the positive role and contributions NGOs had made to the nation's development. At the same time, NGOs targeted high-profile development issues, such as environmental pollution from the Indorayon pulp and paper mill, land disputes, the Kedung Ombo dam project in Central Java, and the proposed Muria nuclear power plant, providing information and framing the issues for the press. The press would seize the issue and highlight the controversies involved. In the process, NGOs became more sophisticated in preparing press releases, holding press conferences, attending important meetings and events, and providing rebuttals to official government viewpoints. An articulate alternative voice to the government emerged within civil society, and the skillful use of the media assisted NGOs in drawing attention to their agenda for sustainable development and democracy.

Since the mid-1980s, Indonesia's national networks of NGOs have taken an increasingly active and visible role in challenging the Suharto government's policies. The networks are loosely structured and provide a forum for discussion among a wide range of NGOs, from small to large, and enable advocacy-oriented NGOs to raise important issues collectively. During this period, various Indonesian NGOs also came together with international environmental groups to organize international campaigns against the transmigration program (INGI 1988), the Kedung Ombo Dam (Aditjondro 1990a), the Scott Paper project (Vatikiotis and Schwarz 1989; Smith 1992; Riker 1994/1995; Cleary 1995), and Indonesia's tropical forestry management (Smith 1992). NGOs' high-profile advocacy efforts in the transnational political arena have not gone unnoticed within Indonesia. As an editorial in the *Indonesia Times,* 14 June 1993, noted:

> The signs are out and clear that national non-governmental organizations or NGOs are, by invitation, beginning to take their crusade to the international arena in radical fashion.

The International NGO Forum on Indonesian Development (INFID)

At the international level, Indonesian NGOs have forged alliances with a transnational network of NGOs that consists of Asian NGOs and networks as well as NGOs from the West, especially from those countries that provide Indonesia with development aid. The International NGO Forum on Indonesia Development (INFID) was initiated by several leading Indonesian NGOs and the Dutch organization NOVIB in the spring of 1985 and has met on an annual basis prior to the meeting of Indonesia's international donor aid consortium.[7] INFID's two primary objectives have been to "strengthen people's participation in development" and to "direct its advocacy" toward the international donor agency consortium by producing an annual aide memoire that critically evaluates Indonesia's development performance (INGI 1986). Specifically, INFID has targeted its efforts on the eighteen bilateral and ten multilateral donor agencies that make up the Inter-Governmental Group on Indonesia (IGGI), which was responsible for providing foreign assistance to Indonesia from 1967 to 1992, and subsequently the Consultative Group on Indonesia (CGI), which has been convened annually by the World Bank since July 1992.

INFID is a transnational network of nongovernmental organizations that have come together on the basis of shared principled ideas (see Sikkink 1993a; Keck and Sikkink 1998). INFID has explicitly sought to use the discursive power of international norms as a basis for transnational political action (Keck and Sikkink 1998). Since 1985, INFID's role has evolved to the point where it acts as watchdog over the New Order government's development policies, providing an annual critique of government programs and highlighting major themes for debate. Each INFID meeting has produced an aide memoire listing areas of concern for both the government and donors. It is an indigenous (Indonesian NGO) answer to the annual World Bank country report that is prepared for the donor consortium. By August 1989, cabinet officials in the Suharto government were rebuking INFID for criticizing Indonesia's development record in international forums (Vatikiotis 1989; Riker 1994/1995).[8] By April 1992, the Minister of Home Affairs was calling for INFID to cease its operations. In just seven years since its inception, this transnational network influenced and redefined debates within Indonesian society, challenged the government on its development priorities and prompted rebukes, and gained access to the World Bank and other international donor agencies that provided aid to Indonesia.[9]

Under what conditions did INFID emerge? Within Indonesia's authoritarian political order, Indonesian NGOs were experiencing considerable difficulty gaining sufficient domestic political space for their activities to address development and democracy issues. Indonesian NGOs had little influence on the Suharto government and were finding the political arena at the national level closed to debate. The INFID network was formed to address this disjuncture by shifting the locus of contestation to a new political arena at the transnational level. A small group of Indonesian NGOs in conjunction with the Dutch aid organization NOVIB came together to form the fledgling network in 1985 as a means to exert greater influence on Indonesia's development policies. Abdul Hakim Garuda Nusantara, former director of Indonesia's Legal Aid Institute (YLBHI) and a member of INFID's board, argued that given the authoritarian context limiting Indonesian NGOs' domestic action, "the only alternative is policy advocacy" at both the national and international levels.[10] Initially many Indonesian NGOs were extremely hesitant to link themselves formally to other groups internationally or to INFID itself. The concern was that unless they did so, they would not command sufficient influence to affect the development and democracy discourses within Indonesia. INFID sought to strengthen Indonesian NGOs' voice by making links to leading NGOs in the West working on similar issues. INFID sought to promote the formation of shared values and goals among Indonesian and non-Indonesian organizations involved in its informal and loosely knit network. This process has involved regular exchanges of information for advocacy purposes through annual meetings, daily communications (via e-mail and faxes), and joint communiqués.

During the late 1980s, INFID built transnational linkages or political alliances in support of sustainable development, human rights, and democratic governance in Indonesia. Since its founding in 1985, the network has grown to include over seventy-five Indonesian and international organizations representing fifteen countries. A wide range of foreign NGOs from Asia, Australia, Europe, Japan, and the United States have come together with Indonesian NGOs to participate in its meetings.[11] By providing foreign NGOs with information and a forum to mobilize joint action on development issues, INFID has highlighted and emphasized Indonesia's development record within donor countries.[12] For example, following the INFID meeting in Tokyo in March 1992, the Japan NGO Network on Indonesia (JANNI) was founded to inform the Japanese public about the impacts of Japanese aid and business practices in Indonesia, to network with Indonesian and other NGOs, and to lobby the Japanese government and multilateral institutions (such as the Asian Development Bank and the World Bank) to support sustainable development, the protection of human rights, and democratization in Indonesia (INFID 1993b). In the process, INFID has identified supportive partners among international NGOs and, to a lesser extent, the international donor community.

INFID placed collective pressure on the Suharto government and international donor agencies for public accountability by submitting its aide memoire to the IGGI, the World Bank, and other multilateral and bilateral donors. INFID's aide memoires have sought to employ "moral leverage" by commenting critically on Indonesia's development policies and priorities; by questioning the merits of specific government development projects in Indonesia supported by international donor agencies such as the transmigration program and the Kedung Ombo Dam project; by raising concerns about the protection of human rights and the government's detention of students, its repression of demonstrations, and its restrictions on trade unions; by proposing that the government adopt antimonopoly and antitrust laws, and a small business act; by questioning the role of the military; by advocating fair and open elections of local representatives; and by arguing for the democratization of international development aid to Indonesia.[13] These same concerns for full disclosure, accountability, and transparency in international aid have been picked up and echoed more broadly in the Indonesian press. Given the high visibility of these issues, representatives of INFID have engaged in "symbolic politics" by gaining audiences with Indonesia's international donor consortium, the World Bank, and certain donor governments, to the chagrin of the Suharto government.[14]

Finally, INFID has actively engaged in a process of political learning that draws on similar advocacy efforts from the local to the global levels. Agus Rumansara, former executive director of INFID's Jakarta Secretariat, notes that its large network of Indonesian and foreign NGOs has provided "an educational opportunity for advocacy. Where we are learning by doing, political learning is occurring."[15] This is an ongoing, inductive approach where INFID constantly tests the boundaries of political space and interprets the government's response. This process of political learning has not occurred solely within Indonesia. NGO leaders have traveled to Japan, South Korea, Malaysia, the Philippines, Thailand, and elsewhere to build linkages with NGOs in these countries and to learn about their development approaches and political strategies vis-à-vis the state. The exposure to a new political context has provided fresh insights and new possibilities for NGO strategies regarding policy advocacy.

Challenges Limiting Indonesian NGOs' Democratic Potential

Despite its attempts to forge links outside Indonesia, within Indonesia's NGO community the INFID network has often been perceived as an elite-based group of national-level NGOs seeking political visibility abroad. Concerns have been voiced by NGOs both inside and outside the network that INFID lacks a broad-based domestic constituency representative of the NGO community within Indonesia.[16] Some analysts suggest that many of the Indonesian NGOs involved in INFID seek only to become power brokers in the decision-making process, and do not intend to empower citizens to represent themselves. One observer from the donor community based in Jakarta noted that INFID and its high-profile Indonesian NGOs have engaged in "very little discussion about the institutions through which the democratic process should occur. The emphasis has been on high-level lobbying, not on changing decision-making structures within society."[17] Thus, considerable challenges face INFID in its efforts to mobilize elements within civil society.

The Role of International Donor Agencies in Promoting Democratization

International donor agencies have pursued their various agendas of good governance and political liberalization in two distinct ways in the developing world. First, international donor agencies have developed special assistance programs to promote institutional and political reform and to support a wide range of activities that strengthen democratic practices and institutions within the state and civil society (Goldman 1988; Algappa 1994; Carothers 1999). This has included bilateral agencies such as the United States Agency for International Development (USAID), through its Democratic Pluralism Initiative (DPI);[18] multilateral agencies, such as the World Bank, that have sought to promote "good governance"; and nonstate agencies, such as foreign private and political foundations, trade unions, religious organizations, and development assistance organizations that have sought to promote democratic practices in a number of spheres (see Nelson, this volume). International donor agencies have sought to promote democratic practices and governance in Indonesia by providing aid and technical assistance to receptive elements within the state and also civil society.

Second, in a number of settings in the developing world, international donor agencies have sought to apply direct pressure on governments to adopt democratic reforms through various forms of political conditionality. Seeing donors as potential allies for democratic governance, indigenous NGOs have lobbied the donors to exert greater leverage over nondemocratic governments through informal persuasion or donor-imposed conditionality. The case of INFID demonstrates how transnational networks have engaged international donor agencies to gain adherence to international norms for human rights, environmental sustainability, and democracy in Indonesia.

Growing Recognition of NGOs by Donors

Indonesian NGOs' international linkages to donor countries and international development agencies have provided considerable legitimacy for their activities and served as a safeguard against government attempts to take action against groups. Initially in the mid-1970s, Indonesian NGOs' links to the international donor community were limited to being recipients of donors' assistance. But as the larger and better-known Indonesian NGOs have developed their expertise and received both national and international recognition for their accomplishments, international agencies have called on NGOs to serve not only as project providers, but also as consultants engaged in project assessment and evaluation and even policy analysis. Increasingly international donor agencies have directed their aid to domestic-level NGOs, especially to those in Indonesia involved in environmental and human rights issues that are engaged in policy advocacy.[19]

A growing number of officials and diplomats from donor countries have met with leading Indonesian NGOs either in Indonesia or in their host country.[20] Some of these visits have taken on a high profile in the press, depending on the stature of the visitor. For instance, Dutch Minister of Development Cooperation Jan Pronk, as chairman of the IGGI, met with INFIGHT, a Jakarta-based human rights group, and other NGO representatives on his visit to Indonesia in May 1991. The decision to meet with NGOs was unprecedented and caused considerable consternation within government circles.

Indonesian NGOs, at the same time, lobbied the donors to put pressure on Suharto's New Order government for various reforms. As Buyung Nasution, former head of the Legal Aid Institute (LBH), noted:

> It is obviously important to . . . maintain strong international ties. The New Order regime does pay some heed to world opinion, and is open to pressure from that source. (1994, 120)

INFID's appeals found a sympathetic ear within the donor community in just four short years. By the late 1980s, IGGI, the donor consortium for Indonesia chaired by the Dutch Minister of Development Cooperation, began to give greater scrutiny to Indonesia's development performance by focusing its annual meetings on the prominent themes of alleviating poverty, development with equity, and democratic governance in Indonesia.

The Growing Challenge of Indonesia's NGOs

Indonesia's NGOs put pressure on the Suharto government not only from below (i.e., at the domestic level), but also from above (i.e., at the regional and international levels). By building alliances with and mobilizing support among groups in Asia, the United States, Europe, Japan, and the international press, Indonesian NGOs raised important questions about the direction of development in Indonesia. The political legitimacy and leverage gained through transnational alliances increased the political space for NGOs within Indonesia to comment not only on development issues, but on political liberalization and democracy. Consequently, Indonesia's NGOs became a considerable political force both at home and abroad, one with which the Suharto government had to contend.[21]

Attempts to Undercut INFID's International Linkages

The Suharto government responded to the growing strength of the INFID network by seeking to undercut Indonesian NGOs' international linkages.

In March 1991, the government of Indonesia threatened to withhold visas and exit permits for NGO officials who were planning to attend the seventh annual INFID meeting in Washington, D.C. A blacklist was revealed and some members of the NGO delegation were threatened with the prospect of not being granted exit permits, until the government acquiesced at the last minute. In March 1992, the government of Indonesia adopted new regulations banning the reentry of any Indonesian citizen who spoke critically of the government while abroad. The timing of this legislation appeared to be more than coincidental, as it was adopted just three weeks before the eighth INFID meeting was scheduled to be held in Japan. Because the Japanese government was the largest provider of Indonesia's development assistance, the Indonesian government was duly concerned that such an international forum would prompt donor agencies to reduce the overall level of support and impose political conditions on future development aid. On 25 March 1992, the Suharto government announced its decision to suspend its meeting with the IGGI, the donor aid consortium for Indonesia. Six days later, the government of Indonesia ordered Dutch government officials to leave the country.

While the government's reaction can be partly attributed to Indonesian sensitivities about the 1991 East Timor massacre, after which the Dutch, Canadian, and Danish governments suspended aid to Indonesia, the Suharto government also sought to limit further scrutiny of its development and human rights record. This decision was a significant political act, as Indonesia received U.S. $4.75 billion in aid for fiscal year 1991/1992. The Suharto government asked the World Bank to reconstitute a new donor aid consortium—now known as the Consultative Group on Indonesia (CGI)—having made its point that it expected donors not to question Indonesia's politics and development priorities.

In addition to severing its aid relationship with the Dutch government, the Suharto government took steps against Indonesian NGOs.[22] On 28 April 1992, the government of Indonesia banned all NGOs from receiving aid from the Netherlands (Schwarz 1992). This action led to the estimated loss of about $15 million in aid to Indonesian NGOs, accounting for nearly 80 percent of funding for leading human rights NGOs, such as the Indonesian Legal Aid Institute (YLBHI) and the Institute for the Defense of Human Rights (LPHAM) (van Tuijl 1993; Algappa 1994). The Suharto government's decision to severe its links to the Netherlands-led donor consortium in late March 1992 led to the cutting of Dutch aid for Indonesian NGOs as well, especially among some of the more outspoken groups involved in INFID (Riker 1994/1995). Moreover, the minister of home affairs,

Rudini, stated that with the dissolution of the IGGI, INFID was no longer needed or relevant and should cease to exist. INFID responded that it would continue its transnational advocacy as long as the issues of sustainable development, social justice, democracy, and people's participation in Indonesia's development remained salient.

The dissolution of the IGGI prompted leading NGO officials to reflect critically on their accomplishments and failures, and to reassess their political strategy vis-à-vis the Suharto government. The leadership of INFID was forced to reconsider their methods of advocacy and lobbying tactics, as well as to redefine the organization's structure and purpose. At that time, there was recognition within and outside INFID's circle that its strategies would have to change if it was to maintain its influence on Indonesia's development priorities. A chief concern was that INFID's capacity to conduct research and do policy analysis should be improved. Many NGO leaders felt that INFID needed to provide the hard data to counter the government's position on specific development issues and to propose alternative projects and policies;[23] they also felt that its policy studies and recommendations should be made more concrete and directed to specific audiences, such as the World Bank, the Department of Home Affairs (Depdagri), and the National Development Planning Agency (Bappenas). Agus Rumansara, the former executive director of INFID in Jakarta, readily admitted that INFID "is just one alternative for widening political space, but we need others as well."[24] The high visibility of INFID and the risks of being associated with its activities posed a problem for its ongoing effectiveness: "The prevailing security mindset limits participation (of other NGOs) and our access to information, and thus the potential expertise for INFID."[25] This dynamic limited the range of organizational resources on which INFID could draw for joint research and policy advocacy. Other Indonesian NGO leaders contend that though much had been accomplished, the Suharto government's response to INFID left NGOs, as a broader social movement, in potential disarray. As one environmental NGO leader notes: "We blew some chances as a movement due to a lack of clarity and leadership within our own ranks."[26] The key concern was that Indonesian NGOs had no clear end goal, which led to considerable differences over strategy and tactics, especially about advocacy efforts taken at the national and international levels. Moreover, Indonesian NGOs' primary constituency should not be themselves but Indonesian citizens, where "NGOs must be accountable to the people."[27]

Following the severing of aid, INFID took a "low profile" over the next year to avoid further antagonizing the Suharto government. Though the name of the organization was formally changed to the International NGO

Forum on Indonesian Development (INFID) in November 1992, its basic mandate remained essentially unchanged (INGI 1992; INFID 1993a). INFID acts as an advocate for "democratization, protection of human rights and a more people-oriented and sustainable development in Indonesia" (INFID 1993b). After several abortive attempts to reconvene its annual meeting over a two-year period,[28] INFID met in Paris in April 1994 to reaffirm its commitment to political reform and democratization in Indonesia: "INFID believes that the Indonesian government should implement principles of good government equitably and unequivocally throughout the country" (INFID 1994a).

Attempts to Silence Transnational Debate and Advocacy

The Suharto government sought to stifle debate about its development and human rights record in a number of international forums. In some instances, the Suharto government infringed upon the rights of private citizens and NGO leaders attempting to participate in international meetings.[29] One case dramatizes the lengths that the Suharto government pursued to silence debate in international forums. In mid-May 1994, the Indonesian government strongly urged the Philippine government to stop the the Asia Pacific Conference on East Timor in Manila, which involved human rights groups from fifteen countries.[30] The request prompted Philippine President Fidel Ramos initially to respond that his government was not at liberty to intervene due to constitutional guarantees of freedom of speech and assembly.[31] Viewing the conference as an affront to its sovereignty, the Suharto government exerted considerable direct and indirect political pressure on the Philippine government to cancel the conference.[32] Claiming that the participation of East Timorese in exile and foreign human rights leaders in the conference would be "inimical to the national interest," President Ramos finally relented to Indonesian pressure by issuing an executive order banning all non-Filipinos from attending the event (*New York Times*, 24 May 1994). When pressed to explain his decision, Ramos frankly spelled out the stark terms of political conditionality that the Suharto government had presented him, stating: "What was at stake here? Some fifteen billion pesos (U.S. $700 million) worth of investments, projects, enterprises and agreed partnerships or consortiums" (*New York Times*, 11 June 1994). Ramos's decision made it clear that democratic principles only applied to Filipino citizens, and that the nation's interest was best served by protecting its ongoing economic relations with the Indonesian government, thus silencing broader debate on the East Timor issue. This case underscores the difficulties that human rights NGOs face in seeking to find arenas for transnational debate of politically sensitive issues in civil society, especially given the response of authoritarian regimes in Southeast Asia.[33]

A Crackdown on Indonesia's NGO Movement?

By spring 1994, signs emerged that Indonesia's high-profile NGOs posed enough of a threat to the Suharto government to prompt a stern warning. Brigadier General Agum Gumelar, who served as chief of the army's elite force, Kopassus, charged that certain NGOs were using such issues as "democratization, political openness, environmental protection, and human rights" to challenge the legitimacy of government and the armed forces in national and international forums.[34] He openly questioned the more political NGOs' motives and allegiance to the Indonesian government, saying:

> We know many NGOs have become vocal, both at home and overseas, on human rights and environmental issues in their efforts to discredit the government and ABRI [the armed forces]. They are also against the constitution and *Pancasila*. (*Jakarta Post*, 14 April 1994)

He argued that "Western-educated liberal-minded intellectuals who constantly demand political and economic reforms" constitute a threat to the political system. "They focus on labor and land conflicts to attack the government. Such movements, if not controlled, will worsen the social, political and economic conditions."[35] Rumblings in the military again prompted greater government scrutiny of some of Indonesia's high-profile NGOs.

In mid-July 1994, the Suharto government announced that it was preparing a Presidential Decree (*Keputusan Presiden* or *Keppres*) to regulate the formation, funding, operations, and dissolution of all Indonesian NGOs. While the new government regulations were not officially released at the time, they stipulated that any NGO could be banned if it was found to be "undermining the authority [of the state] and/or discrediting the government . . . hindering the implementation of national development" or engaged in "other activity that upsets political stability and security" (cited in Cohen 1994, 33). Any new organizations and the staff of existing Indonesian NGOs would now be required to get clearance and approval for their activities from the police, military, and national intelligence. In response, six leading NGOs lodged a formal request to meet with the Minister of Home Affairs to discuss the terms of this decree (*Kompas* 19 July 1994; INFID 1994b). The Minister of Home Affairs Yogie SM acknowledged in a meeting before district officials in Ambon that "[a]t this moment a planned Presidential Decree is in the process of being composed concerning the guidance of social organizations *(lembaga kemasyarakatan)*, under which

[NGOs] will be included."[36] This action was only another in a long line of government attempts designed to regulate and repress independent-minded NGOs in civil society (Riker 1994/1995; Eldridge 1995).

The new regulations spawned a new battleground between the Suharto government and NGOs. About forty NGOs participating in a regional NGO forum in Central Java issued a joint statement rejecting the regulations, arguing that they would abrogate the basic rights already guaranteed under the Indonesian constitution (LSM se-Jawa Tengah 1994). The Suharto government responded with increased harassment of NGOs. The government canceled or disrupted several NGO meetings in Jakarta and throughout Java in late August and September 1994 where NGOs were meeting to discuss their response to the new guidelines. Buyung Nasution, head of Indonesia's Legal Aid Institute at the time, characterized the political situation in stark terms:

> The current situation is grim, and it is getting worse. Systematic state harassment and persecution of community activists and the country's more than one thousand voluntary non-governmental organizations (NGOs) show no signs of abating. Any meeting that may be construed as political must have a permit, and even then there is no guarantee against arbitrary arrests and beatings if the authorities turn out to be displeased with the character of the gathering. (1994, 116)

Through its new decree and intensified harassment of NGOs, the Suharto government made clear its intent to clamp down on those NGO elements that continued to push the boundaries of acceptable conduct within Indonesia's political order.

International Openings for Spurring Transnational and Domestic Action

While the prospects for political liberalization and democratic reform within Indonesia were quite bleak at the time, the openness of international opportunity structures offered transnational networks the possibilities for gaining greater political space for domestic action. For example, as the Suharto government sought to be a leading player in the proposed Asia Pacific Economic Cooperation (APEC) trade grouping within an increasingly interconnected global economy, it faced a challenge from a growing number of actors both within Indonesia and abroad. Increasing demands emerged for continued economic as well as political reforms, especially as it concerned the rights of labor, the issue of trade, and an unfettered press. Two weeks prior to the APEC summit in Indonesia in November 1994, Winston Lord, U.S. assistant secretary of state for East Asian and Pacific affairs, made clear the dilemmas facing the Indonesian government, especially concerning its relations with the United States:

> Suharto wants a big victory for his hosting [APEC], and we're supporting him all the way. There are, of course, problems on the human rights side in Indonesia. We have a very good relationship with Indonesia on many fronts, but we also have a frank dialogue on some of the problems, and we're going to have to pursue a balancing act. We very much hope that the Indonesians in their own self-interest will take liberalizing measures in their society, whether it's treatment of the press or East Timor or journalists or NGOs or labor issues, both as an end in itself, but also to create a positive atmosphere for the APEC meetings and allow Indonesia, which has had remarkable growth and has done so well and is so hopeful in so many other ways, to show its best face. (Lord 1994)

Working in conjunction with Indonesian NGOs, international human rights groups such as Amnesty International and Human Rights Watch publicized and protested the bans on three of Indonesia's leading news magazines in late June 1994, the detaining of leading academics and labor activists, the harassment of NGOs, and the continued violence in East Timor. Western governments and donor agencies were under increasing pressure at home to express their displeasure with this wave of government repression.

Most important, Indonesia's Minister of Defense Edi Sudrajat acknowledged that Indonesian NGOs' links to donor countries had led to significant international pressures on Indonesia. Due to Indonesian NGOs' sustained advocacy as part of larger transnational networks, the Suharto government was under greater scrutiny to adhere to international standards for human rights and democratization while also being subjected to international trade conditionalities. Sudrajat readily noted that the scope and impact of NGOs' activities had reached beyond Indonesia's borders, saying, "Just like multinational corporations, Indonesian NGOs are now involved in international politics as well as domestic politics" (*Kompas* 30 September 1994). Foreign governments and international donor agencies increasingly recognized the legitimacy of Indonesian NGOs' advocacy on human rights and development policy. In July 1996, U.S. Secretary of State Warren Christopher met with the Indonesian Human Rights Commission, stressing the need for continued support and assistance for NGOs' efforts to address human rights concerns within the country. Moreover, Christopher reaffirmed the United States' support for political pluralism and liberalization in Indonesia (Christopher 1996).

At the domestic level, a number of advocacy-oriented Indonesian NGOs organized in anticipation of the 1997 parliamentary elections. Like their counterparts in the Philippines, Thailand, and Bangladesh, these Indonesian NGOs formally announced the formation of an independent organization, known as *Komite Independen Pemantau Pemilu* (KIPP) (Independent Committee to Monitor the Elections), in mid-March 1996 to monitor the elections (*Media Indonesia* 19 February 1996; *Kompas* 16 March 1996, 27 March 1996). A coalition of thirty NGOs formed the Indonesian People's Council to rally support for the political reform efforts of Megawati Sukarnoputri, the daughter of Indonesia's first president Sukarno, after the Suharto government successfully ousted her as head of the Indonesian Democracy Party (PDI) in June 1996 (Cohen 1996). Military-supported thugs raided the PDI's party headquarters to expel Megawati's supporters in late July 1996, sparking a major riot in Jakarta (Schwarz 1997). While the government intensified efforts to squash any signs of dissent in Indonesia prior to the May 1997 elections,[37] NGOs and social activists worked together to dramatize to the world the need for increased international pressure on the Suharto government for its human rights, labor, and environmental records (Unny et al. 1996; Jones 1997). As Indonesia became increasingly subject to economic and political liberalizing forces from abroad, one Indonesian analyst noted: "There is an increasingly persuasive argument that the key to a democratic future for Indonesia is the empowerment of civil society" (Jemadu 1997). In the process, Indonesian NGOs brought international scrutiny, in varying degrees, to bear on Indonesia's economic and political order.

Economic Crisis and the Transition to Democracy

The Asian economic crisis of 1997–98 that started in Thailand and then spread to Indonesia provided the major shock that tested the Suharto government. A destabilized currency and the collapse of financial markets greatly challenged the Suharto government's capacity to manage and resolve the crisis. After registering over a decade of sustained growth, the Indonesian economy hemorrhaged and ultimately contracted. Indonesia's per capita gross domestic product (GDP) declined by 16.2 percent from mid-1997 to mid-1998 (Emmerson 2000, 96). Nearly half of Indonesia's 210 million people faced food insecurity and poverty. To stem this severe economic crisis, the Suharto government eventually signed three successive agreements with the International Monetary Fund (IMF) that contained over a hundred specific provisions for reforming the economy in exchange for a $43 billion bailout package in loans. The impact of the Asian financial crisis in Indonesia coupled with an ineffective government response eroded people's confidence in the Suharto government.

By early 1998, transnational and domestic social and political forces had come together to build a growing social movement advocating for democratic governance in Indonesia. This situation led to increased political mobilization and cooperation among university students, NGOs, and leading opposition elements within and outside the government. INFID, representing over a hundred Indonesian and foreign NGOs, issued a communiqué appealing for urgent reform of the Indonesian political system on 7 May in Bonn, Germany (INFID 1998, 1). Signaling to international donor agencies that the moment was propitious for political change in Indonesia, INFID argued that "NGOs, working together with the international community, have a vital role to play in helping Indonesia through the transition toward a new, democratic system. . . . We seek the cooperation of donor governments and international financial institutions to bring that new system about" (INFID 1998, 4). Several major donor governments, including the United States, strongly urged the Suharto government to uphold human rights and pursue democratic reforms.

During the spring of 1998, thousands of students organized peaceful demonstrations at over eighty universities calling for political reform and for President Suharto to step down (Jones 1998). What had started as campus-based demonstrations culminated in sustained public protests throughout the country by early May. In the capital city of Jakarta, students were emboldened to take to the streets in active displays of "people power," demanding *reformasi* or political reform. Despite government attempts to silence news accounts of these events, independent journalists, NGO activists, and students used the Internet to inform and mobilize growing public opposition to the Suharto government (Eng 1998, 20–21). The pivotal event occurred when government troops shot and killed four students taking part in a peaceful demonstration at Trisakti University on 12 May, sparking widespread riots throughout Jakarta that led to over 1,200 deaths and left many areas of the city in ruin (Emmerson 1999, 296; Schwarz and Paris 1999). Seeking political change, thousands of students peacefully took over the national parliament building on 19 May (Cohen 1998). Key ministers within the government, most of them longtime loyalists, privately and publicly urged President Suharto to step down. On 21 May 1998, the unexpected happened—President Suharto resigned after thirty-two years of authoritarian rule and his protégé, Vice President B. J. Habibie, assumed power!

Shortly after taking office, President Habibie enacted various political reforms to strengthen the rule of law, to remove controls on the press, and to prosecute government corruption. Most important, Habibie promised to hold democratic elections within a year. In June 1999, Indonesia held its first democratic parliamentary elections since 1955. Indonesian NGOs played a critical role in advocating changes in electoral laws and monitoring the elections. Some NGOs accused the Habibie government of vote buying, intimidation, and tampering with the ballots, putting them both at odds and raising fundamental concerns about the prospects for democratic governance taking root in Indonesia. A number of international donor agencies and governments provided support, training, and international observers to promote a free and fair election process.

The election saw forty-eight parties contest seats for Indonesia's parliament, with only five parties gaining solid support. Megawati Sukarnoputri, representing the Struggle for Indonesian Democracy Party (PDI-P), received the greatest support with 33 percent of the vote. The ruling party, Golkar, finished second with 22 percent of the vote. The Nation's Revival Party (PKB) led by Abdurrahman Wahid, an Islamic cleric and leader of Nahdlatul Ulama, a Muslim social organization with 30 million members, received 12 percent of the vote. The United Development Party (PPP), the traditional Islamic group, gained 10 percent. The National Mandate Party (PAN), led by Amien Rais, took just 7 percent of the vote (Emmerson 1999, 347). The election results found the three leading opposition parties working together to take control of parliament from the ruling party of Golkar in anticipation of the meeting of the People's Consultative Assembly (MPR) to select the president five months later.

On 20 October 1999, Abdurrahman Wahid was unexpectedly elected Indonesia's president by an unusual coalition of conservative Muslim, military, and Golkar supporters in parliament over Megawati Sukarnoputri. Despite the coalition's concerns about her administrative and leadership experience and the prospects of a woman leader, Wahid championed Megawati's election as vice president the following day. Wahid brought strong credentials to the presidency as a progressive Islamic religious leader and NGO advocate with a deep commitment to human rights, pluralism, and democracy. He had long been identified as a leading independent voice for the opposition outside the government during the Suharto era.[38] Wahid recognized the critical role that Indonesian NGOs play as effective advocates for reform and democracy. He chose a few NGO leaders for posts in his National Unity Cabinet and others served in the new parliament and People's Consultative Assembly (MPR) (Munir 2000, 5).

The Wahid government faced the daunting challenges of stabilizing and reinvigorating the economy; overcoming Suharto's authoritarian legacy, which permeated the bureaucracy and other political institutions; resolving ethnic violence and various movements for self-determination across the country; and reducing the military's dominant role in order to build and consolidate democratic governance in Indonesia. The enormity of these challenges, combined with internal power struggles within Wahid's coalition government and a strengthened parliament, slowed progress and dampened public expectations on all fronts. Facing the threat of a vote of no-confidence from the People's Consultative Assembly in August 2000, President Wahid apologized to members of parliament for the poor performance of his government. President Wahid named a new streamlined cabinet in late August 2000, which included several people who were former leaders or had close ties to leading prodemocracy NGOs in Indonesia.[39] Despite these changes, Wahid's ineffective leadership in stabilizing the economy and resolving political conflicts across Indonesia, coupled with his antagonistic relationships with parliamentary leaders, ultimately doomed his presidency. In late July 2001, the People's Consultative Assembly voted to remove Abdurrahman Wahid from office and to appoint Megawati Sukarnoputri, the daughter of Indonesia's first President Sukarno, as its first woman president.

President Megawati Sukarnoputri inherits formidable challenges and faces an uncertain future. Whether or not her government can successfully navigate the myriad of Indonesian's economic and political problems will largely determine whether the country will achieve progress in building "the political institutions necessary to construct a real democracy" (INFID 1998, 5). Due to lingering political disputes about the legitimacy of Wahid's removal and to concerns about the balance of power between Indonesia's combined presidential and parliamentary systems, five leading Indonesian NGOs called for a special commission to reform Indonesia's constitution in August 2001. Megawati and various political parties have also echoed the need to explore constitutional reforms to allow for the direct election of the president and to ensure that Indonesia's political institutions foster effective and accountable democratic governance at both the national and provincial levels.

As Indonesia comes to grips with these challenges, Indonesia's NGOs will continue to be an important force in redefining politics and shaping the transition to democracy. Indonesian NGOs have brought critical political issues about the structure of civil society and power relations within it to the fore. Due to their strategic articulation of issues and mobilization of support at home and abroad through transnational networks, Indonesian NGOs have established themselves as advocates for democratic change in Indonesia's political order. These transnational networks and international donor agencies have an important stake and roles to play in assuring a successful transition to a stable democracy. To the extent that their advocacy efforts toward the state and international donors have efficacy, Indonesian NGOs will continue to influence debates within civil society and the possibilities for real political reform and democratic governance within Indonesia.

Notes

1. The growing role of NGOs in strengthening civil society is not limited to Southeast Asia, but is increasingly recognized in Latin America as well as in contemporary Africa (Fisher 1993; Shaw 1995; Ndegwa 1996).

2. Noteworthy cases in Asia include the Narmada Dam project in India, the Kedung Ombo Dam in Indonesia, the Bakun Dam in Malaysia, the Arun III Dam in Nepal, and the Pak Mun Dam in Thailand (Riker 1995; McCully 1995; see also Khagram and Kothari, this volume).

3. In the case of the Narmada Dam project, Indian NGOs forged linkages to groups in key donor countries. For instance, intensive lobbying by Japanese environmental groups in conjunction with international NGO coordination and pressure led the Japanese government to withdraw its funding for the Narmada Dam project in May 1990 (Rich 1994; see also Khagram and Kothari, this volume).

4. The exact number of indigenous NGOs operating in Indonesia is not clear. Over seven thousand NGOs had registered with the Ministry of Home Affairs by mid-1990, and over twelve thousand were estimated to exist by mid-1994 (*Kedaulatan Rakyat,* 11 July 1990; *Kompas,* 6 August 1994). Buyung Nasution estimates that over one thousand NGOs are actively engaged in development, environmental protection, and human rights activities in Indonesia (1994, 116).

5. See also Nelson, this volume, for a discussion of emerging norms of good governance and popular participation.

6. The aims and purposes of Indonesian NGOs vary depending on the sphere, sector(s), level of operation, orientation to the state, and type of political role that they adopt. While it is difficult to generalize, nearly all independent NGOs in Indonesia seek sufficient political space to carry out either their social and economic development activities and/or their political development activities in strengthening civil society. These two distinct roles highlight NGOs' different purposes and motivations and the diversity of approaches that NGOs have employed to realize their aims.

7. The organization has changed its name several times over this period. Initially known as the Inter-NGO Conference on IGGI Matters, this network became the International NGO Forum on Indonesia (INGI) in 1988 and was changed to the International NGO Forum on Indonesian Development (INFID) in November 1992. For the sake of simplicity, the organization is referred to as INFID here.

8. A non-Indonesian representative of INFID appeared before the U.S. Congressional Human Rights Caucus in 1989 to discuss the case of the forced resettlement of villagers under the World Bank–supported Kedung Ombo Dam project (Eldridge 1995).

9. In his historical review of INFID, Dan Lev notes that its political impact is a remarkable development for a loosely knit network "of relatively small organizations with little tangible economic or political clout" (1993, 20).

10. Abdul Hakim Garuda Nusantara, interview by author, 30 May 1991.

11. Some of the foreign NGOs that attended INGI meetings include: the Asian NGO Coalition for Agrarian Reform and Rural Development (ANGOC, Philippines), the Asian Cultural Forum on Development (ACFOD, Thailand), the Australian Council for Overseas Aid (ACFOA, which is a council of ninety NGOs), Christian Aid (United Kingdom), the Development Group on Alternative Policies (D-Gap, United States), the Environmental Defense Fund (EDF, United States), the Environmental Policy Institute (United States), the Natural Resources Defense Council (NRDC, United States), the National Wildlife Federation (United States), Friedrich Ebert Stiftung (FES, Germany), Friedrich Naumann Stiftung (FNS, Germany), HIVOS (Netherlands), ICCO (Netherlands), and the International Confederation of Free Trade Unions (ICFTU, Belgium).

12. Meetings have been held in The Hague, Bonn, Brussels, Washington D.C., Tokyo, Paris, and Australia. Participation and attendance for these meetings is on an invitation-only basis, issued by a steering committee composed of Indonesian and (non-Indonesian) international NGO leaders. The proceedings are closed to the media, but aide memoires are circulated to the press and submitted to the government (Eldridge 1995).

13. Specifically, INFID has argued for the full participation of citizens in the decision making, planning, and implementation of donor-aided projects and programs, and for full access to information regarding the development plans and projects of international donor agencies, as well as the Indonesian government (INFID 1994a, 1998).

14. In June 1990, the Dutch minister of development cooperation, Jan Pronk, in his capacity as chairman of the IGGI, extended an invitation to INFID to attend its annual meeting in The Hague. Because of the high political visibility and the prospect of little opportunity to address the donor delegation, leading NGO officials decided not to attend the meeting (Jan Pronk, interview by author, 6 June 1990; *Kompas,* 12 June 1990). However, INFID participated in meetings with World Bank officials in Washington in 1991 and the Japanese government in 1992 to make known its concerns about Indonesia's development record (Lev 1993, 19).

15. Agus Rumansara, interview by author, 23 May 1992.

16. An overwhelming number of INFID's Indonesian NGO participants are based in Jakarta or the main island of Java.

17. Gordon R. Hein of the Asia Foundation, Jakarta, interview by author, 24 May 1991.

18. Because of the growing visibility of NGOs, USAID and the U.S. State

Department are now monitoring NGO activities and positions on a wide range of issues, including the environment, human rights, labor practices, and democracy.

19. In August 1994, the U.S. Senate approved an allocation of $500,000 to be shared equally by Indonesian human rights and environmental NGOs. USAID has provided direct support to Indonesian NGOs since the early 1980s, targeting $1.7 million for human rights NGOs such as the Legal Aid Institute and other groups during 1994 (Holloway 1994).

20. For instance, U.S. officials publicly voiced their support for Indonesian NGOs on several occasions during the 1990s. Hilary Rodham Clinton met with Indonesian NGOs during her travels to attend the meeting of the Asia-Pacific Economic Cooperation (APEC) forum in November 1994. In April 1995, John Shattuck, U.S. assistant secretary of state for democracy, human rights, and labor, made a special point of meeting with representatives of development, human rights, and environmental NGOs and labor unions during his visit to Indonesia. U.S. Secretary of State Warren Christopher expressed his support for Indonesian NGOs' efforts to protect human rights in July 1996. In March 1999, U.S. Secretary of State Madeleine Albright stressed the importance of strengthening civil society and citizens groups in assuring a fair and open process in Indonesia's parlimentary elections in June 1999 (Albright 1999).

21. One possible sign of this growing NGO influence was that the Suharto government was particularly sensitive to Indonesian NGOs expressing critical perspectives on human rights and environmental concerns abroad. Indonesian embassy and consular offices were instructed to monitor the statements of NGO leaders abroad and to issue official statements to counter the NGOs' positions.

22. After the East Timor massacre in November 1991, the Suharto government consistently sought to challenge the more politically outspoken NGOs' legitimacy by questioning their patriotism. These Indonesian NGOs have frequently been put in the position of being persona non grata in the eyes of both the government and the press. Indonesian Vice President Try Sutrisno characterized these groups as being unpatriotic, especially in their reaction to the East Timor massacre. INFID specifically addressed the East Timor issue by stating that it "deplored" the killings and calling for an independent investigation of the event (Uhlin 1993, 536).

23. Indonesian NGOs were hard-pressed to compete with the mobilization of knowledge, economic resources, and authority wielded by the Suharto government, which retained a monopoly on these resources and often presumed that its pursuit of large-scale development projects was a necessity. The case of the Kedung Ombo Dam and the debate over the proposed Muria Nuclear Power Plant in Central Java are just two examples (Aditjondro 1990a).

24. Rumansara interview.

25. Ibid.

26. Emmy Hafild, interview by author, 23 May 1993.

27. Ibid.

28. Attempts to meet in Jakarta were canceled due to difficulties in securing a permit for a meeting and the Suharto government's denial of visas for some INFID members from abroad.

29. In late April 1994, five Indonesian NGO officials who were returning from the ninth conference of the International NGO Forum on Indonesia (INFID) held in Paris had their baggage searched and documents from the conference seized by government authorities at the Jakarta airport (*Suara Pembaruan,* 30 April 1990). INGI officials had previously submitted a set of the documents from the conference to the government via Indonesia's ambassador to France (YLBHI 1994).

30. The Indonesian government sought to characterize this conference as being a one-sided event organized by a few, small disaffected groups not representative of the wider world community. Mr. Nugroho Wisnumurti, Indonesia's representative to the United Nations, contended that "the so-called 'human rights conference' is part of a political campaign waged by a small group of East Timorese in exile, with the helping hands of a small group of leftist Filipinos" (*New York Times,* 8 June 1994). In fact, twelve human rights groups from several countries (including a Japanese NGO) sponsored this international conference and invited pro-Indonesian East Timorese to participate in the meeting (*Jakarta Post,* 28 May 1994; *Asahi Shimbun,* 14 May 1994).

31. Referring obliquely to the Philippines' adherence to democratic principles, President Ramos stated: "[W]e hope [Indonesia] will understand that with our Constitution we cannot stop the activities of a private sector organization like this" (*Asahi Shimbun,* 14 May 1994).

32. The Indonesian government stressed through diplomatic channels that on-going relations would be unduly affected if the conference proceeded. Adding weight to its appeal, the Indonesian government threatened to pull out as host for "peace talks between the Philippine Government and Muslim separatist rebels," canceled its participation in a Filipino trade fair, and threatened to cancel "$300 million in contracts it has with the Philippines" (*New York Times,* 24 May 1994; 31 May 1994). Yuwono Sudarsono, a leading political scientist at the University of Indonesia with close ties to the Indonesian government, suggested that the Indonesian government was seriously considering organizing its own event about the Moro National Liberation Front in the Philippines, saying that "if the Philippines goes ahead with the seminar, Islamic NGOs in Indonesia and Malaysia would hold seminars about the Muslim Moro problem in the Southern Philippines" (*DeTik,* 25–31 May 1994).

33. Indonesia's lobbying efforts have not been limited to the Philippines. The government of Thailand, in consultation with Indonesian officials, sought to block a

human rights conference involving activists and NGOs from Indonesia in July 1994 (Robinson 1994).

34. Gumelar's statement was made just one week prior to two major events involving Indonesian NGOs' advocacy efforts abroad: the 1994 annual INFID meeting in Paris, and a meeting with the European Parliament to discuss the proposal for a boycott on importing tropical woods from unsustainable timber producers.

35. This echoes Brown Thompson's (this volume) analysis of how authoritarian states respond to the discourse of human rights. Accounts in the national press at the time highlighted local land, labor, and environmental controversies. In many instances, leading Indonesian environmental and human rights NGOs were portrayed as advocates for the affected groups and communities.

36. He went on to state, however, that NGOs "are a societal strength that we very much need as a partner in carrying out the functions of administration, development, and guidance of the people" (KBRI 1994).

37. For instance, NGO pro-democracy organizers were forced by the Intelligence Unit of the Central Jakarta Resort police to cancel a one-day seminar on the topic of open and free general elections in May 1997. While the Suharto government had issued a permit for the meeting, the police claimed that the seminar organizers had not complied with the government's regulation requiring at least a seven-day advance notice for any meeting (LPHAM 1997; *Kompas* 14 March 1997).

38. In addition to serving as head of the grassroots Islamic social organization Nadhlatul Ulama for fifteen years, Wahid served as president of the organization Forum Demokrasi (Fordem), or the Democratic Forum, which was formed in April 1991 to stimulate dialogues about the issues of political openness and freedom in Indonesia. The Suharto government, seeing the apparent allusion to Vaclav Havel's Democratic Forum in Czechoslovakia, asked the local variant's leadership to "change its name to something 'less provocative' and [said] it should not act as an opposition force" (*Economist* 20 April 1991, 33).

39. For instance, Indonesian scholar Arief Budiman suggests President Wahid might have first met Rizal Ramli, his coordinating minister of economy, finance, and industry, at an NGO forum sponsored by INFID (2000).

10

Restructuring the Global Politics of Development: The Case of India's Narmada Valley Dams

Sanjeev Khagram

Planned to generate thousands of megawatts of power, irrigate millions of hectares of land, and provide drinking water to hundreds of chronically drought-prone villages, India's Narmada Valley Dam Projects are a promise for plenty to proponents. If completed, they would likely constitute the largest river-basin scheme in the world.

The Narmada Projects are also expected to submerge thousands of villages, displace millions of mostly peasants and "adivasis," and destroy hundreds of thousands of hectares of forest lands. Opponents thus charge that they would result in the greatest planned social and environmental tragedy in Indian history.[1]

The development initiative that invokes such conflictual positions was long in the making. After more than three decades of controversy-ridden investigations and planning, Indian authorities finally formulated the current Narmada Projects in 1978. The gargantuan scale of the river-basin scheme ultimately designed—involving 3,000 "small dams" and approximately 165 "big dams"—drew the immediate interest of the World Bank.[2] The World Bank commenced its formal support in 1980, at first for the 455-foot-tall Sardar Sarovar major dam, the centerpiece of the broader Narmada scheme. This quickly attracted further backing from the United Nations Development Program, Japan, and other foreign bilateral donors. At the time, proponents confidently asserted completion of the Sardar Sarovar Project (SSP) in less than a decade.

But more than fifteen years later, in a dramatic turn of events, the SSP was still not built and the entire scheme for the Narmada Valley was imperiled. Japan and other foreign donors were compelled to withdraw their support due to a transnational campaign waged by local peoples and domestic activists with the support of nongovernmental organizations (NGOs) from across India and all over the world. Under severe pressure, the World Bank finally acquiesced in 1991 to an independent review of the SSP—the first ever since its establishment. The review team produced a highly critical report, resulting in major reforms within the World Bank.

Besieged by opponents at home and losing credibility abroad, domestic authorities grudgingly announced in 1993 that India would forego hundreds of millions of dollars of World Bank funding. India's Supreme Court dealt another blow in 1995 when it ruled a halt on implementation for the foreseeable future, a decision based partially on a domestic review of the SSP.

Why were historically weak and marginalized groups able to prevent far more powerful interests and organizations from completing the SSP? What does the trajectory of the broader Narmada Projects demonstrate about the changing dynamics of big dam building in India and around the world? What are the more general implications of the changing dynamics around big dams for restructuring the global politics of development?

In this chapter I argue that the campaigns of two overlapping transnational coalitions, constituted primarily by NGOs from across India and all over the world, were critical to altering the trajectory of the Narmada Projects from the early 1980s on. These transnational coalitions were empowered by, and further contributed to, the spread of international norms on the protection of indigenous peoples, human rights, and environmental preservation.[3] The institutionalization of these norms into the procedures and structures of both states and international organizations offered new political opportunities for these transnational coalitions to leverage in their campaigns.

But the success of these transnational coalitions was strongly conditioned by the existence of a sustained grassroots social movement and the political opportunities presented by India's democratic regime. Linkages to organized domestic mobilization provided powerful sources of information, strategy, and legitimacy to those NGOs lobbying at the national and international levels. India's democratic regime facilitated access to domestic decision-making institutions and the ability of domestic groups to act with less fear of, and at least with the right to legally contest, physical repression.

The case of India's Narmada Projects is not an isolated one. Rather, it is part of a historical trend of mounting transnational contestation over big dam building across the Third World in countries ranging from Brazil and Thailand to Uganda. In recent years, conflicts over the construction of big dams have grown into intense national policy debates in several developing countries. At the international level, these projects have been at the center of heated campaigns to substantially reform states and international organizations. The transnational struggles around the SSP have been significant not only for altering development policies and practices in India, but also those of international organizations such as the World Bank (Khagram 1999).

The stalling of the SSP and the changing dynamics around big dams across the Third World have manifold implications for the restructuring of world politics. First, they demonstrate that novel transnational coalitions and networks consisting of historically weak NGOs and social movements have increasingly been able to challenge the interests of more powerful states, intergovernmental organizations, multinational corporations, and domestic elite classes.

Second, progressively institutionalized international norms on indigenous peoples, human rights, and the environment, among others, have empowered and legitimated these novel transnational actors in their political activities from the local to the international levels. The dialectical interaction between these transnational coalitions and international norms in the issue area of big dams has contributed to the reconstitution of global development policies and practices.

In order to substantiate these claims. I first examine an episode of failed domestic opposition to the SSP and the formation and impact of the first transnational campaign to reform the resettlement aspects of the project. While this first transnational "reform" coalition depended heavily on extant international norms on indigenous peoples and human rights, the second transnational campaign that superseded it was further bolstered by the global spread and international institutionalization of norms on the environment and sustainable development.

I then analyze the emergence and effectiveness of the second transnational coalition, which opposed any further construction of the SSP and the Narmada Dam Projects more broadly. It did so by integrating normative concerns for tribal peoples, human rights, and the environment into a broader critique of big dam building. The success of this transnational anti-dam campaign, even more so than its predecessor, depended not only on the political opportunities provided by these international norms, but also on the existence of sustained grassroots resistance in the context of India's democratic regime. I conclude by discussing some theoretical tensions and practical problems with respect to the dialectic interaction between transnational agency and international norms in restructuring the global politics of development.

Failure of Grassroots Resistance and Success of the First Transnational Coalition

The Sardar Sarovar Project was the centerpiece in the broader development scheme to harness the river resources of the Narmada Valley in western India. The initial grassroots mobilization against the SSP began on 19 August 1978. This was less than one week after an Indian Inter-State Water Disputes Tribunal ruled in favor of the massive development scheme, which involved the construction of over three thousand dam projects (Government of India 1978). As a front page story in the *Times of India* noted, "Cutting across party lines, reactions to the Narmada Tribunal award continue to be sharp. . . . A massive rally was organized by the 'Save Nimar Committee' in protest against the award." Nimar was a region in the state of Madhya Pradesh, which was to be submerged if the SSP was constructed to the Tribunal's proposed height of 455 feet.[4]

This purely domestic resistance based in the riparian state of Madhya Pradesh involved a series of massive demonstrations and protests against the Tribunal's order to build the SSP. On 28 August, opposition party members created "virtual pandemonium in the Vidhan Sabha," or state legislature, of Madhya Pradesh, pressing the governing Janata Party of the state to take a stand against the Tribunal's decision. At the same time, "outside the assembly, hundreds of demonstrators from Nimar, the area which would be affected by the award, courted arrest under the all-party banner of the Nimar Bachao Sangarsh Samiti," or "Save Nimar Action Committee" (*Times of India* 30 August 1978).

Unsatisfied with the slow response of state officials to their demands, local opponents responded with an even larger protest ten days later. During this protest, a massive procession of the Save Nimar Action Committee marched through Bhopal, the capital of Madhya Pradesh. After forcing entry into the Vidhan Sabha with the use of elephants and horses, the protesters were teargassed and lathi charged by state police.[5] The police detained over 1,000 people and jailed a reported 365 individuals, including Dr. Shankar Dayal Sharma (a future president of India), V. C. Shukla (a future federal minister of water resources), and Arjun Singh (a future chief minister of Madhya Pradesh) (*The Statesman* and *Times of India* 8 September 1978).

This initial grassroots mobilization ultimately failed to halt the momentum building behind the SSP in India. The ruling Janata Party of Madhya Pradesh was eventually compelled by the grassroots resistance within its borders to petition the tribunal to lower the proposed height of the dam to 436 feet to prevent submergence of the Nimar area. The tribunal refused to amend its ruling, however, stating that India's 1956 Inter-State Water Disputes Act prohibited the tribunal from readjudicating its decision once it had been promulgated.

The villagers from the Nimar region withdrew their overt protests, believing that the Congress(I) Party would represent their opposition to the SSP after being elected to govern the state of Madhya Pradesh. Partially as a consequence of the Janata Party's inability to secure a reversal from the tribunal on the height of the dam, the Congress(I) Party won the state elections in 1980, and Arjun Singh—who as a key opposition leader had been extremely critical of the project—became chief minister. Local people were shocked, however, when Arjun Singh then signed a memorandum of understanding with Chief Minister Madhavasingh Solanki of Gujarat—also a Congress(I) Party member—to "implement the decision of the Narmada Water Disputes Tribunal" with respect to the SSP as long as "both the states of Gujarat and Madhya Pradesh agree to explore the possibility of reducing the distress of the displaced persons as much as possible" (8 August 1981).

Moreover, foreign support for Gujarat to begin implementing the SSP emerged during this period of the grassroots resistance in Madhya Pradesh. In November 1979, the government of Gujarat hosted the first mission from the World Bank, which was keen to support the project. The bank's mission recommended that a high level Narmada Planning Group be established and that domestic and foreign consultants be hired to conduct further investigations. The bank helped secure ten million dollars from the United Nations Development Program to finance these activities.

All but a few of the studies and activities, conducted between 1979 and 1983, focused on technical and economic aspects of the SSP, despite the fact that international norms on indigenous peoples and involuntary resettlement had emerged by the early 1980s as critical issues on the global development agenda. The World Bank, for example, had issued a statement on involuntary resettlement in February 1980 that stated: "[T]he Bank's general policy is to help the borrower to ensure that after a reasonable transition period, the displaced people regain at least their previous standard of living" (World Bank 1980). This operational statement was updated two years later with a specific focus on indigenous peoples: "As a general policy, the Bank will not assist development projects that knowingly involve encroachment on traditional territories being used or occupied by tribal people, unless adequate safeguards are provided" (World Bank 1982).

But practice did not follow policy norms at the time. The World Bank agreed to support the SSP even though the government of Gujarat had issued a resolution on 11 June 1979 specifying that only landholders with legal land titles were entitled compensation from displacement (Government of Gujarat 1979). This meant ruin for most of the adavasi families to be displaced because they rarely held legal land titles. The 1979 resolution, moreover, undermined the more expansive policy for those to be displaced in Madhya Pradesh and Maharashtra from the SSP in the tribunal 1978 ruling. Finally, the World Bank's own resettlement expert Michael Cernea documented that, "[d]uring 1982–83, four Bank missions, two each for preappraisal and appraisal were mounted, but none of them appraised the resettlement component" (1986).

The first grassroots resistance to the project in Gujarat supported by domestic nongovernmental organizations was launched in March 1983, nearly three years after the protests in Madhya Pradesh had quieted down. The mobilization was instigated by the first episode of displacement in Gujarat without compensation.[6] In addition to supporting their protests and demonstrations, local NGOs such as the Rajpipla Social Services Society and Chutra Yuva Sangharsh Vahini assisted the Gujarat villagers by documenting their landholdings, publicizing the issue of forced displacement in the Indian press, and lobbying domestic and World Bank officials to ameliorate the conditions faced by the oustees.

A letter from one of the local NGOs to the World Bank subsequently sparked the first round of transnationally allied lobbying that focused on reforming the resettlement aspects of the SSP. Dr. Anil Patel of the Gujarat-based Arch Vahini sent a note to the World Bank in August 1983, detailing the resettlement problems on the ground. The World Bank had grown more apprehensive because it had already sent three letters on the issue of resettlement based on its own norms and guidelines in July 1983 without a response from Indian authorities. Receiving the letter from Patel confirmed the World Bank's suspicions. The World Bank then contracted Dr. Thayer Scudder—an expert on resettlement issues—to lead an appraisal mission to India in September 1983. Scudder returned with a highly critical report, echoing much of what Anil Patel of Arch Vahini had written months earlier (see Scudder 1983).

Continued domestic mobilization in India, in conjunction with increased monitoring of the World Bank by foreign supporters, produced some initial changes in domestic resettlement policy over the next six months. The World Bank's growing concern with resettlement issues was due primarily to a mounting transnational campaign led by Washington-based NGOs to reform international development agencies. This multilateral campaign exposed the World Bank's failure to adhere to its own operational guidelines, that is, its own norms, in many of the World Bank's projects, such as Polynoreste in Brazil and Transmigration in Indonesia (see Rich 1994; see also Nelson, this volume). The SSP eventually became the central focal point in this overlapping campaign.

Simultaneously, the grassroots struggle to reform government resettlement policies in India grew stronger. A massive march involving potentially displaced people from the states of Gujarat and Maharashtra occurred on 8 March 1984. The protesters demanded that all families to be displaced receive five acres of compensation and that the tribunal's resettlement policy for Maharashtra and Madhya Pradesh be adopted by Gujarat. This was followed by further nonviolent actions, including the submission of writ petitions in the Gujarat High Court and Supreme Court of India (see Narmada Control Authority 1984). As a result of the initial round of pressure "from above" via the World Bank and "from below" at the grassroots, Gujarat authorities produced a first outline resettlement plan in April 1984.

But Indian authorities and World Bank officials soon faced increased pressure from a rapidly growing transnational coalition of NGOs linked directly to the grassroots resistance in Gujarat that was dedicated to reforming the resettlement aspects of the SSP. The local Gujarat-based NGO Arch Vahini was being funded at the time by Oxfam, a transnational NGO headquartered in the United Kingdom. By the early 1980s Oxfam had established a new international policy unit to conduct advocacy campaigns to reform the policies and practices of bilateral and multilateral donors. John Clark, head of the new unit at Oxfam, believed that a campaign to reform the resettlement and tribal impacts of the SSP would make a broader impact internationally, particularly with respect to the practices of the World Bank.

The first transnational coalition was built around the link between Oxfam U.K. and Arch Vahini in Gujarat. Based on the consent and information given to him by Anil Patel, John Clark quickly sent correspondence to the World Bank stating Oxfam's apprehensions with respect to the resettlement component of the SSP. At the same time Oxfam enlisted the support of NGOs working on similar issues from around the world. The first transnational reform coalition quickly expanded and soon included local community groups, domestic NGOs located outside the Narmada Valley, and transnational NGOs.

The initial lobbying of this transnational coalition, working with and through supportive intermediaries such as Thayer Scudder (resettlement consultant to the World Bank) and Tim Lancaster (the United Kingdom's executive director to the World Bank), generated increasingly progressive resettlement policies and activities. First, the World Bank hired Scudder again in August 1984 to lead a postappraisal mission focusing on the resettlement component of the SSP. Scudder met local villagers and activists during this field visit, stating: "Tell me whatever you want, give me in writing whatever you need (with respect to resettlement and tribal rights) because there is going to be a loan agreement with the World Bank and all the governments in India, and I am going to write that part of the agreement."[7] He prepared an aide memoire to the World Bank shortly after returning from his trip in which he reiterated that "[i]n order to comply with Bank/IDA policy, the Government of India, the Narmada Control Authority and states concerned would be required to provide at negotiation an overall detailed plan for the resettlement and rehabilitation of oustees."[8]

By the time of the negotiations for the SSP credit and loan agreements between the World Bank staff and Indian officials in late 1984 and early 1985, the transnational lobbying efforts began to more directly utilize international norms to legitimate their cause. Survival International, an international NGO dedicated to protecting the rights of tribal/indigenous peoples around the world, sent a letter to the World Bank and the International Labour Organization (ILO) stating its concerns about the SSP. Survival International argued that the resettlement program "besides being inhumane and liable to result in serious physical and social problems for the tribals involved, is also illegal" because it violated ILO Convention 107 (of which India was a signatory), which acknowledges both the right of tribal populations to the lands that they traditionally occupy, and to the provision of equal land in the exceptional instance they be removed from their traditional lands.[9] This was the first time that the government of India's potential violation of the norms on the protection of tribal peoples embodied in ILO Convention 107 was invoked in the transnational campaigns, but it would not be the last.

The transnational coalition also continued to utilize its links to like-minded institutional insiders to lobby for resettlement reform. Thayer Scudder sent correspondence to Ronald P. Brigish of the World Bank on 24 January 1985 to pass on the worries of Gujarat-based NGOs about the failure of Indian government officials to move ahead with proper resettlement measures. Tim Lancaster, armed with similar information he had received via Oxfam and Survival International from Gujarat-based NGOs, then strongly criticized the resettlement component of the SSP credit and loan agreements at the executive directors' meeting held in early March 1985 in Washington, D.C.

As a result, the World Bank's board of executive directors included the explicit condition that Indian authorities execute a resettlement plan consistent with international norms and the World Bank's own policies in the loan and credit agreements of $450 million for the SSP. The World Bank's proposed resettlement program was based on the tribunal's orders of 1978 and 1979. It further required Indian authorities to release forest lands for resettlement and, if this was not possible, to offer alternative means of livelihood to ensure that all displaced peoples would "improve or at least regain the standard of living they were enjoying prior to their displacement" (World Bank 1985). In addition, those individuals that depended on encroached lands would be given land for the land they had been cultivating, even if they did not have legal land titles.

Despite these proposed reforms, the pressure on the World Bank and thus on Indian authorities from the transnational campaign intensified. Less than two weeks after the credit and loan agreements were signed, Survival International again expressed concern about ensuring compensation for tribals relocated by the dam project, and sent copies of the letter to the British, Japanese, West German, American, and Indian executive directors of the World Bank.[10]

The letter further stated that, based on the information that Survival International had received from its partner organizations in India, Gujarat officials were ignoring the legal agreements signed with the World Bank. The World Bank, in turn, prodded Indian authorities more firmly. This resulted in the passage of a Gujarat government resolution entitling encroachers to a minimum of three acres of land as compensation for displacement (Government of Gujarat, Irrigation Department 1985).

On the other hand, while the government of Gujarat partially accommodated the World Bank's conditions to implement a more comprehensive resettlement policy on the international front, domestically it pushed construction forward and denied the rights of encroachers to replacement lands. The Gujarat government clearly stated that encroachers were on the land illegally and would not be given land compensation in the proceedings of a first Supreme Court case in 1985. The Indian courts came to play a critical role in the campaigns to monitor and pressure domestic authorities vis-à-vis the SSP. They also provided means by which various civil liberties and human rights abuses perpetrated by proponents of the projects were reviewed and punished. In fact, without the relatively autonomous functioning of the courts in India's democratic system, the transnational campaigns would likely have been much less able to stall the SSP.[11]

The information exchange among the members of the transnational coalition proved critical in exposing the duplicity of Indian authorities during this period. As Dr. Anil Patel of Arch Vahini remembered:

In May 1985, the World Bank agreement was signed and in it there was a clause that oustees would regain the previous standard of living from which it was understood that encroachers would be given land. By then, we knew that the Gujarat officials were up to mischief and they were just going to throw these people out. We were desperate to get a copy of the loan agreement but the government would not give it to us. So we went to the Supreme Court in 1985 where they stated that encroachers were on the land illegally and therefore had no rights. Scudder had told us that they were to be included but the rest of the World Bank would take no cognizance of us because we were not an elected authority. So we sent our affidavits to John Clark of Oxfam, U.K. and he would write letters to U.K. Executive Director, Tim Lancaster, and he raised a stink at the Board of Executive Directors. Lancaster wanted to know what was in the World Bank loan agreement and he wrote letters giving information to Oxfam and Survival International, which were sent to us sometime in 1986. I was shocked. In those days, the Gujarat government was just lying to the Supreme Court. Even John Clark couldn't understand the double game Gujarat was playing—agreeing to give encroachers' land to the World Bank while denying their rights in the Supreme Court.[12]

Under mounting pressure from Oxfam and the other NGOs, the World Bank once again reminded Gujarat authorities of their obligations to the resettlement conditions of the credit and loan agreements. Once again, the government of Gujarat conceded by passing another resolution that offered a choice of lands to displaced peoples with land titles (Government of Gujarat, Narmada Development Department 1985).

But criticism grew because the policy revisions still excluded encroachers and the lands offered were primarily of poor quality. In December 1985, the first monitoring and evaluation report on resettlement required by the World Bank was completed by a local university in Gujarat. It acknowledged that serious problems existed with the relocation effort, particularly with respect to a basic lack of information. Simultaneously, the domestic NGOs continued to press their case in the Supreme Court, which in turn ordered that a displaced person must "be provided either alternative land of equal quality but not exceeding three acres in area and, if that is not possible, then alternative employment where he would be assured a minimum wage" (Order in the Writ Petition (C) No. 7715, 4 February 1986). As a result, the government of Gujarat passed another resolution increasing the loan subsidy for oustees.

Domestic Indian and World Bank officials were now facing pressure from multiple sources and a wide variety of channels. For example, groups such as the International Federation of Plantation, Agricultural, and Allied Workers along with Survival International petitioned the ILO's Committee of Experts to investigate possible violations of ILO Convention 107 on the protection of indigenous peoples. The Committee of Experts reviewed the case and warned the World Bank and the government of India to follow the norms of the convention. Both the World Bank and Indian authorities responded by acknowledging their commitment to the convention and to ensuring that a proper resettlement package would be offered to all tribal peoples (ILO Committee of Experts 1986, 258–60).

Motivated by the continued criticism internationally, worried about growing evidence from its own monitoring efforts, and aware of broadening opposition domestically within India, the World Bank sent its largest ever resettlement mission to the Narmada Valley in April 1987. The leaders of the World Bank's first biannual supervision mission of the SSP submitted a highly critical report of the resettlement situation in mid-1986 (see Morse and Berger 1992, 127). Tensions in the region were on the rise as there were now signs of organized grassroots mobilization not only in Gujarat, but in the states of Maharashtra and Madhya Pradesh as well. India's Ministry of Environment and Forests, moreover, had only given a conditional clearance to the SSP, partially because of the low likelihood of adequate resettlement. The World Bank mission of 1987 confirmed the lack of compliance with international norms. Indian authorities were given ten months to remedy this failure or risk losing the remainder of loans and credits for the project.[13]

Caught between the determined and sustained resistance of local groups and the increased vigilance of the World Bank, which was responding to the persistent lobbying efforts of the first transnational reform coalition, the government of Gujarat grudgingly passed more significant policy revisions. The first resolution affirmed a five-acre minimum land compensation for landed individuals. Two weeks later, on 14 December and 17 December, a number of other resolutions were passed. The final resolution in the series— and by far the most unexpected—completely liberalized the government's resettlement policy by offering the same package to all those who might lose land, not just those cultivating unauthorized lands (Government of Gujarat, Narmada Development Department 1987).

The initial transnational coalition to reform the resettlement aspects of the SSP had thus won an unprecedented victory after nearly five years of mobilization and lobbying from the local to the international levels. While attempts at independent domestic resistance failed to make a sustained impact on Indian authorities, the balance of power between the proponents and the critics of the projects began to shift once links were formed with transnational human rights and indigenous peoples' organizations. The existence of extant international norms and procedures on tribal peoples and resettlement such as ILO Convention 107 and those promulgated at the World Bank in the early 1980s was critical to the empowerment of this transnational reform coalition. Finally India's democratic political opportunity structures, in particular the ability of citizens to organize themselves, to form linkages internally and externally, to gain access to information and an open press, and to pressure and hold authorities accountable (especially through the courts), facilitated some success by this first campaign.

But despite the victory that had been won, a rift soon emerged between those groups who took a "no implementation of resettlement, no dam" position and those who progressively took a more unequivocally "anti-dam stand." While the former groups, such as Arch Vahini and Anand Niketan Ashram, began to cooperate with project authorities on implementation of the reformed resettlement policies, other groups, such as the Narmada Dharangrast Samiti in Maharashtra and Kalpavriksh in Delhi, demanded that a complete and comprehensive reevaluation of the SSP into the context of the broader Narmada scheme be completed before any further construction occurred. The latter groups integrated a number of critiques into their opposition: that the resettlement reforms would not be implemented, that the projects would cause irreparable environmental damage, and that the project's costs were underestimated while its benefits were overestimated. They thus launched an even more massive multilevel, transnational campaign against the SSP as the centerpiece of the broader Narmada schemes, saying that it was symbolic of a destructive development model that had to be stopped (see Kalpavriksh 1988).

International Environmental Norms and the Second Transnational Campaign

An inter-state tribunal conducted proceedings on dam building in the Narmada Valley between 1969 and 1979, as mentioned previously. Even though the tribunal was not asked and did not explicitly take up the issue of the environment, many of the decisions it made "were triggering mechanisms for almost all environmental impacts," which would subsequently become a central axis of the conflicts over the Narmada Projects (Morse and Berger 1992, 220). During those ten years, dramatic changes had begun to occur in terms of international norms on the environment and sustainable development. In particular, by the 1980s, procedures and organizational structures institutionalizing environmental norms had been adopted at the international level and in numerous countries around the world (see Khagram 1999).

Simultaneously, there was a tremendous growth in NGOs and social movements working domestically, internationally, and transnationally on issues of environment and development, and a gradual integration of these with extant concerns for tribal peoples and human rights. This transformation prepared the context in which a second transnational coalition emerged to contest the Narmada Projects. While building on, and to some extant overlapping with the first transnational reform campaign, this second transnational coalition was dedicated to halting all further construction on the SSP, and thus undermining the broader Narmada scheme of which it was the centerpiece.

Formal institutional changes within the Indian state with respect to the environment occurred partially as a result of the internationalization of norms in this issue area during the 1970s.[14] In India, the process of integrating environmental factors into development policy had begun in preparation for the UN Conference on the Human Environment with the fourth Five-Year Plan (1969–74), which was completed in 1970. In the plan, Indian authorities formally stated for the first time that "planning for harmonious development . . . is possible only on the basis of a comprehensive appraisal of environmental issues," although no concrete changes in actual development practices or state institutions were proposed consistent with this principle at the time (Government of India 1970).

It was only after the international legitimation provided by the Human Environment Conference that Indian authorities actually translated these novel environmental principles into institutional structures. They first established the National Committee on Environmental Planning and Coordination (NCEPC) within the prestigious Department of Science and Technology in 1974 to serve as an advisory body on environmental issues facing the country. Chaired by Prime Minister Indira Gandhi herself—who personally attended the Human Environment Conference—the NCEPC established various task forces to deal with issues such as identifying environmental problems, carrying out investigations, and integrating general environmental concerns into specific development programs and projects. Prior to these reforms, few Indian leaders were interested in environmental issues and self-conscious civil society mobilization in this area was just emerging.[15]

The creation of additional domestic environmental institutions followed quickly. In 1976, India's parliament transferred forests from the State List to the Concurrent List (shared federal/state authority). By 1977, based on recommendations from the NCEPC, Prime Minister Indira Gandhi issued a directive that environmental impact assessments be completed by federal agencies for all medium and major irrigation projects—most of which included dams. This trend culminated in 1980 when, based on the recommendations of the high-level, federal-government-appointed committee on India's environment, the prime minister created a federal-level Department of Environment and Parliament passed the Forest Conservation Act (Government of India 1980; see, for example, Angarwal 1982). This federal environmental department was subsequently upgraded in status to the Ministry of Environment and Forests in 1985.

The trajectory of the Narmada Projects would not have been so significantly altered without these institutional changes in the Indian state. The SSP, for example, had to acquire environmental and forest clearances—the expanded version of the environmental impact assessment that had been mandated in 1977—from the Department of Environment. The 1980 Forest Conservation Act imposed restrictions on diverting (reserved) forest areas for other uses, such as reservoirs created by dams. Before its enactment Gujarat had established two resettlement sites for those to be displaced by clearing forest areas, a practice that would have continued unhindered had the Forest Conservation Act not come into effect and a federal environment agency not been created to implement it.

At the international level, during the same time period and by the time it had become involved with the Narmada Projects, the World Bank had also incorporated a number of environmental procedures and structures into its institutional framework. In preparation for the Human Environment Conference, then-President Robert McNamara appointed an advisor to create an environment and health unit at the World Bank, primarily to conduct research on these issues. The following year an Office of Environmental Affairs was established. Based on the investigations and recommendations of this unit, the bank subsequently amended its project appraisal procedures "to caution against the selection of projects that might have excessive social and environmental costs," and "loan officers were given special responsibility to ensure that all issues related to socio-culturally relevant institutions and the protection of the environment were properly considered" (Morse and Berger 1992, 217–20, with quotes on 218).

By 1984, one year before signing the loan and credit agreements for the SSP, the World Bank had issued its most comprehensive statement ever on environmental guidelines in operational manual statement (OMS) 2.36. The new code called for the inclusion of environmental factors from the earliest stages of project formulation. It prohibited the World Bank from supporting initiatives that would result in irreversible environmental damage, infringe upon any international environmental agreement the recipient country had adopted, or displace people without satisfactory mitigation measures (see Muldoon 1986, 152). When the World Bank was reorganized into four regional divisions in 1987, an environmental unit was mandated for each. In the process, the Office of Environmental and Scientific Affairs was transformed into the Environmental Department.

These changes in the World Bank's procedures and structures were motivated, in large part, by the lobbying of NGOs (see Fox and Brown 1998). A former director of the Environmental Department stated that NGOs "were undoubtedly instrumental in bringing about the changes that were initiated" at the World Bank during the 1970s and 1980s (see Piddington 1992, 217). While actual practices were much slower to change than formal procedures and structures, these reforms also expanded the political opportunities available to NGOs to pressure and monitor the World Bank. The second transnational coalition around the SSP successfully exploited these new points of leverage.

Environmental issues were no longer absent from discussions of the Narmada Projects less than five years from the time of the Tribunal's award. As a consequence, in early 1983 the government of Gujarat state hired the Maharaja Sayajirao (M.S.) University of Baroda to coordinate a benchmark report on the environmental aspects of the SSP, both for the federal environmental clearance it needed within India and to satisfy the World Bank requirements. Based on this report and information from the master plan for development of the Narmada Valley that Gujarat had submitted to the tribunal, the SSP was referred for clearance to India's Department of Environment approximately six months later.

The institutionalization of international environmental norms had partially begun to alter practices, but the studies and reports conducted at the time were so crudely prepared that they provided easy targets for domestic critics. A team of Delhi University students from the Hindu Nature Club and Kalpavriksh, a Delhi-based environmental NGO, was the first independent group to complete a holistic study of environmental and social impacts. Based primarily on a fifty-day research trip they had undertaken in July and August 1983, they suggested that the government-authorized M.S. University report had numerous problems and that "much of the information in the study derives from Government sources rather than from fresh empirical studies."

This independent NGO report identified several environmental issues that needed further research, such as geological impacts, the impact on flora and fauna, and the treatment of catchment area forests, among others

(Kalpavriksh 1983, 8). Citing Thayer Scudder's 1983 World Bank prefeasibility report on resettlement, and based on their own research, the authors further argued that "it is a callous mistake to let officials from the Irrigation and Revenue Department (of the GOG [Government of Gujarat]) handle resettlement." It concluded that "without a total understanding of the cultural ethos and psychological makeup of the tribal and the peasant, rehabilitation is bound to be a failure"; thus, the SSP should not be built (Kalpavriksh 1983, 30–31).

The report contributed to the strengthening of the first transnational "resettlement" campaign and sowed the seeds for the eventual emergence of the second transnational "anti-dam" coalition (Goldsmith and Hildyard 1986). The report was distributed to various NGOs such as Arch Vahini in India and Oxfam and Survival International in England. But the environmental critique was not incorporated into the activities of the first transnational coalition constituted by these NGOs and their allied groups.

The combination of this environmental critique and the increasing involvement of India's federal environmental agency with the Narmada Projects did produce, on the other hand, a major hurdle in the path of SSP proponents between 1984 and 1987. Based on its own recently established guidelines and the Kalpavriksh report, the Ministry of the Environment refused to grant environmental clearances for the SSP during this period, despite the fact that the World Bank approved $450 million in project funding in 1985. Had this federal agency not been established primarily as a result of the internationalization of environmental norms, this set of political dynamics around the project would likely not have occurred.

The fact that the Ministry of Environment had become a major bottleneck within the Indian state preventing work on the SSP convinced many villagers and activists working in the Narmada Valley to take up environmental issues more directly. Medha Patkar, later leader of the Narmada Bachao Andolan or Save the Narmada Movement, recounted that in the struggle against the project, environmental issues "were soon firmly rooted in the notion that environmentally sustainable resource use and control by local peoples, and the prevention against the encroachment on those resources by outsiders, was fundamental to our vision of participatory, socially just and equitable development."[16]

The second transnational coalition that coalesced to halt construction on the SSP was also linked more directly to organized grassroots mobilization than the one that preceded it. From the summer of 1988 onward, a multilevel campaign came into full swing. By September of that year, major demonstrations were launched all over India by the villagers and a coalition of domestic NGOs that supported the grassroots struggle against the project. As Vijay Paranjpye, an Indian economist who conducted an independent cost-benefit analysis of the project, reported:

> In a desperate attempt to stem the agitation, the government resorted to violence and assaulted eight activists. They also arrested 4000 tribals who were among the 6000 persons who converged on Waghadia after a three-day-long march. This triggered off a dharna in Bombay, a relay hunger strike in Madhya Pradesh and meetings of intellectuals and concerned citizens to express their solidarity with the oustees' cause throughout India. (1990, 29–30)

The combination of continued grassroots mobilizing, cases filed by NGOs in the Indian courts against the human rights abuses perpetrated by domestic authorities, and the pressure of transnational NGOs via the World Bank, however, eventually compelled the Gujarat government to withdraw the Official Secrets Act, under which it had unleashed a reign of repression.[17]

The "Narmada Bachao Andolan," which linked most of the villages and domestic NGOs of the Narmada Valley in a broader social movement, was formally established during the spring and summer of 1989. This massive organizational effort culminated in the Harsud Rally of 28 September 1989. As activist Shripad Dharmadikary later recounted, "[M]ore than three hundred NGOs and sixty thousand people came from all over the country, perhaps the largest rally on this issue ever held in India."[18] The sankap, or resolve, taken was *Vikas chahiye, vinash nahin!* or "We want development, not destruction." Sympathetic observers identified the rally with the "coming of age of the Indian environmental movement" (Kothari 1991).

The transnational campaign against the SSP had also intensified at the international level during this same period of time. The Environmental Defense Fund had taken a leadership position after one of its campaigners, Bruce Rich, had met Medha Patkar in the Narmada Valley in 1986. After that meeting, a series of activities against the World Bank's involvement in the SSP was initiated by the fund, other foreign NGOs, and the domestic movement.[19] As part of the broader transnational campaign to reform international development agencies, Rich and other Washington-based activists lobbied extensively at the World Bank, and convinced the senior vice president, Moeen Qureshi, to lead a high-level mission to investigate the project in autumn 1988. After returning and holding further meetings with World Bank management and Washington-based NGOs, Qureshi threatened Indian authorities with suspension of World Bank support unless a comprehensive plan including "prompt identification of suitable lands for resettlement, careful preparation of rehabilitation options for landless peoples and designs for development or relocation sites," was formulated.[20]

Washington-based NGOs also pursued the environmental critique of the project via the United States House of Representatives' Subcommittee on Natural Resources, Agricultural Research, and the Environment. They convinced chairman James Scheurer to organize a special oversight hearing to investigate the World Bank's support for the SSP. Testimonies were delivered by three Indian activists, including Medha Patkar, less than one month after the Harsud Rally had been held in India. Peter Miller and Lori Udall of the Environmental Defense Fund also spoke at the hearings. The overwhelming evidence presented on the negative social and environmental impacts persuaded a number of representatives to ask for a suspension of World Bank support (U.S. House 1989).

The congressional hearings provided a catalyst for the formation of the Narmada International Action Committee. Key members of the committee included Kalpavriksh and the Save the Narmada Movement (India), the Rainforest Information Center (Australia), Survival International (England), Action for World Solidarity (Germany), the Environmental Defense Fund and International Rivers Network (United States), Probe International (Canada), and Friends of Earth (Japan). Friends of Earth—Japan hosted the committee's first International Narmada Symposium in April 1990 in Tokyo. The lobbying conducted through the conference and associated meetings held by representatives of the transnational coalition with Japanese officials ultimately resulted in the withdrawal of Japanese assistance from India for the SSP (Udall 1995, 212).

Back in India, the domestic mobilization had intensified further after the Harsud Rally of 1989 but was unsuccessful in achieving its primary goal: an independent and comprehensive reappraisal. The domestic movement continued to organize rallies, investigate the project and potential alternatives, and spread its message to the wider Indian and international publics through the press, newsletters, and letter-writing campaigns. The next major event occurred on 6 and 7 March 1990 when ten thousand people blocked the Bombay Agra highway, which passes through the Narmada Valley, for twenty-eight hours. Medha Patkar and a number of other activists participated in a fast in Bombay to highlight opposition. Unsatisfied with the responses of state-level authorities, hundreds of members of the Save the Narmada Movement protested for four days in front of the prime minister's residence.

Undeterred, domestic authorities continued to move ahead with the project. The domestic movement responded with a *Jan Vikas Sangarsh Yatra*, or "March of the Struggle for People's Development," in December 1990.[21] Thousands of villagers, activists, and supporters walked for six days through the Narmada Valley from Madhya Pradesh toward the dam site in Gujarat. The Gujarat government, on the other hand, had organized a pro-dam rally and a police barricade at the border to prevent the marchers from getting to their destination. In turn, Medha Patkar and four others went on an indefinite fast to demand once again a comprehensive reappraisal of the project.

The World Bank received information about the march and the standoff from the transnational coalition members, who were in constant communication via fax and e-mail with their domestic Indian counterparts. As the activists grew weaker from the fast and transnationally linked NGOs continued their lobbying efforts, the World Bank finally acquiesced to the demand for an independent review.

After state authorities failed to forcibly remove the fasters in a massive police raid on the protesters' camp, federal authorities in Delhi announced that a comprehensive domestic review of the projects would be conducted. The fast was called off on the twenty-second day and the protesters triumphantly returned to their villages in the Narmada Valley proclaiming *Hamare gaon me hamare raj,* or "Our rule in our villages."

The second transnational coalition continued to ratchet up the pressure after the successful march and fast. Representatives of the domestic movement traveled through Europe on a tour organized by European NGOs to increase pressure on the World Bank to fulfill its promise of an independent review.[22] NGOs around the world lobbied the World Bank via their executive directors on the matter. On 17 June 1991, ex-UNDP Director Bradford Morse and Canadian human rights attorney Thomas Berger were appointed to chair the review—the first ever such body in the World Bank's history.

Representatives from the Narmada International Action Committee met with Morse and Berger to ensure that all the social and environmental effects of the projects would be reviewed. Given the fact that environmental issues had not been considered by the Inter-State Water Disputes Tribunal or by the World Bank, their inclusion in the independent review's mandate demonstrates the remarkable change that had taken place in international development norms during the 1980s (Morse and Berger 1992).

The independent review team headed by Morse and Berger did not commence its investigations until September 1991. In the meantime, domestic authorities continued with dam construction and a number of villages faced potential submergence. In desperation, authorities attempted to forcibly relocate villagers and arrested hundreds of people who refused to resettle. Domestic NGOs such as the Peoples Union for Civil Rights and transnational NGOs such as Amnesty International documented the human rights violations perpetrated by Indian authorities.[23] A number of additional cases petitioning the Indian courts to punish violations of India's constitutionally guaranteed democratic rights were filed. Finally, the movement in the Narmada Valley took the vow of *doobenge par hatenge nahin,* or "We will drown but move we will not." This *jal samarpan* tactic, the ultimate protest against the project of "suicide by drowning," was not implemented that year but the domestic movement remained committed to it.[24]

The independent review team was deluged with information on the project from pro-dam actors as well as from the transnational coalition during its ten-month-long investigations. Morse and Berger ultimately concluded in favor of the opponents, saying that the World Bank should "step back" from the project due to its negative social and environmental effects. Noting that the opposition had ripened into hostility, the report stated that implementation would be impossible except as a result of "unacceptable means."

The review summed up with the following findings, demonstrating the critical import of international human rights and environmental norms to their deliberations:

> We have found it difficult to separate our assessment of resettlement and rehabilitation and environmental protection from a consideration of the Sardar Sarovar Projects as a whole. The issues of human and environmental impact bear on virtually every aspect of large-scale development projects. Ecological realities must be acknowledged, and unless a project can be carried out in accordance with existing norms of human rights norms espoused and endorsed by the Bank and many borrower countries the project ought not to proceed. . . . The Bank must ensure that in projects it decides to support the principles giving priority to resettlement and environmental protection are faithfully observed. This is the only basis for truly sustainable development. (Morse and Berger 1992, 357–58)

This integration of human rights and environmental concerns was remarkably similar to the arguments formulated in the Hindu Nature Club/ Kalpavriksh Report of 1984.

The World Bank and Indian officials attempted to downplay the severity of the independent review's recommendations. They quickly negotiated an agreement in which domestic authorities were given a six-month period to meet a series of conditions on environmental protection and resettlement. The Narmada International Action Committee published an open letter to the World Bank in the *Financial Times* (1992) criticizing the World Bank's duplicity and calling for a suspension of the SSP. The letter was signed by 250 NGOs from thirty-seven countries. As the six-month deadline grew closer, the transnational coalition continued to lobby feverishly against the project. The Indian executive director to the World Bank finally announced on 26 March 1993 that India would voluntarily forego further World Bank funding and support for the project (see Roychowdhury and Jacob 1993, 57).

By nearly unanimous agreement, the transnationally allied opposition to the SSP produced the most visible change in the policies and practices of the World Bank. The World Bank's own Operation Evaluations Department acknowledged this fact in 1995: "The Narmada Projects have had far-reaching influence on the Bank's understanding of the difficulties of achieving lasting development, on its approaches to portfolio management, and on its openness to dialogue on policies and projects" (Operation Evaluations Department 1995, 7). In terms of resettlement, the World Bank's policy revisions led to few improvements in practice until the 1990s, by which time the Narmada debacle had generated increased awareness (see Fox 1998).

And, according to Robert Wade:

> [A]round 1992 and 1993 the more comprehensive ideas of the "environ-ment management" paradigm began to take hold at senior management and operational levels. The conversion came partly from love and partly from fear. Narmada was the fear factor. By the early 1990s staff through-out the Bank were aware of the NGOs' antiBank campaign. As a division chief in the Africa region put it, Narmada had become "a four-letter word." . . . [M]anagers in other parts of the Bank reinforced their signals that environment and resettlement should not be ignored or fudged. (1997, 685–86)

A new information disclosure policy and an inspection panel instituted to assess violations of policies with respect to large-scale development proj-ects were also largely a response to the Morse Report's conclusions (World Bank 1993b, 1993c; see also Shihata 1994, especially 9–13; Udall 1998). The second transnational coalition had clearly achieved a huge victory both domestically and at the international level with the removal of the World Bank's support for the SSP, not to mention other Narmada dams.

Nevertheless, the domestic movement continued to organize against the project, focusing on the comprehensive review that had been promised by Indian officials at the time of the "Long March." A domestic Indian review group was established in June 1993, less than three months after the World Bank's withdrawal. India's democratic institutions thus offered domestic op-ponents a range of political opportunities that would not have existed in an authoritarian regime. The domestic movement and allied Indian NGOs pressured Indian authorities to stop project implementation during the review via demonstrations, the media, face-to-face lobbying, and a series of petitions filed in the Indian courts.

But between June and December of that year, even after the World Bank had pulled out and while the domestic review was underway, construction continued (see Government of India 1994). The movement reissued the pledge to drown rather than be displaced while at the same time filing two petitions in the Indian Supreme Court. The first demanded that project implementation be stayed until the report of the domestic review, which had been completed in April 1994, was made public. The second demanded that the SSP be halted completely because it was in violation of the fundamental human rights of the peoples to be displaced, because the social and environmental costs were too high relative to the expected benefits, and because it was financially and economically unviable.[25]

Once the World Bank and other foreign supporters of the project were no longer involved, the combination of the Supreme Court hearings, the investigations of the domestic review group that was ordered to produce a further report by the Supreme Court, and the continued grassroots mobilization by the domestic movement and allied NGOs stalled implementation of the SSP (see Government of India 1995). India's Supreme Court found that the fundamental rights of the persons to be displaced under Indian's democratic constitution had been violated as well as that Indian law and international agreements on various environmental issues had not been fulfilled by project authorities. Despite the repeated pleas made by Indian state and federal authorities, the Supreme Court ordered a halt on construction until these social and environmental issues were resolved.

Implications and Lessons

The success of the two campaigns around the SSP vividly demonstrates the potential power of transnational agency and international norms in restructuring the global politics of development. The first transnational coalition was successful in altering the resettlement aspects by linking the lobbying efforts of domestic and transnational NGOs to evolving international norms on resettlement and indigenous peoples. The second transnational coalition was ultimately successful in stalling implementation by linking an even more organized and sustained domestic social movement with transnationally allied lobbying efforts to an even wider and deeper set of international norms on indigenous peoples, resettlement, human rights, and the environment broadly construed.

The impact of the dialectical interactions between transnational organizing and international norms in both campaigns depended on the existence of grassroots opposition in the context of a relatively democratic regime
in India. Domestic social mobilization dramatically increased the costs (both
political and economic) of forging ahead with the project faced by Indian officials and foreign donors. It also added to the legitimacy of the lobbying activities of members of the transnational coalitions who were not to be directly affected by the SSP. India's democratic regime offered a set of political
opportunity structures that gave domestic groups the right to organize and
mobilize, the ability to forge coalitions with like-minded foreign actors and
access large quantities of information, a relatively free press, decision-making
authorities, and a legal system in which the courts could be petitioned to
hold domestic state and nonstate actors accountable to Indian and international norms, procedures, and laws (see Khagram 1999, chaps. 2–4).

The political opportunity structures available to the coalitions were also
altered by the gradual institutionalization of transnational norms at both the
international and domestic levels. In the case of India's SSP, the creation of
environmental procedures and structures at the World Bank and in India,
for example, clearly opened up avenues of contestation for the members of
the transnational coalitions that would not have existed otherwise. In addition, NGOs were able to collaborate with sympathetic "insiders" who were
positioned in these newly adopted organizational structures.

Related comparative research on the dynamics of big dam building suggests that the domestic factors of social mobilization and democratic political opportunity structures are critical in conditioning the impact of transnational organizing and supportive international norms (see Khagram 1999,
chap. 5). Further research will be required to examine whether these domestic variables are important in other issue areas. A hypothesis that seems war-
ranted, given the findings from the other chapters in this volume, is that the
presence of social mobilization and democracy is likely to contribute to the
impact of transnational collective action in the issue area of sustainable development. These factors may also be important in campaigns that involve
broader human rights concerns, such as in the areas of labor, gender justice,
and minority rights, an avenue of research that could more systematically
link scholarship and practice on transnational collective action with that on
domestic social movements.

In conclusion, at least three practical lessons can be teased out from the
analysis presented in this chapter. First, combining and coordinating the full
range of strategies, from grassroots protests to elite lobbying, in the widest
possible range of institutional contexts, from the local to the international

levels, can greatly contribute to the success of transnational campaigning. Second, it is clear that not only transnational linkages within a single issue area but also transnationalized, cross-issue linkages can significantly increase the power and effectiveness of collective action. Lastly, the value of integrating different types of international norms—such as human rights with environmental conservation—more systematically into broader visions or worldviews can facilitate and further empower these types of transnational, cross-issue area coalitions and networks. Indeed, the construction, internationalization, and deepening of these holistic normative frames may be critical to the future formation of powerful transnational social movements from transnational coalitions and networks.

Notes

1. Adivasis, or tribal peoples, are nearly analagous terms for what in many countries are called indigenous peoples. Adivasis constitute approximately one-tenth of India's population.

2. I include both "large" and the even more massive "major" dams in the category of "big dams." According to instructions from the International Commission on Large Dams, domestic dam agencies can report dams over 15 meters and those of 1,015 meters if they meet other technical requirements as "large dams." "Major dams" meet one or more of the following requirements: heights of over 150 meters, volume greater than 15 million cubic meters, reservoir storage of more than 25 cubic kilometers, and/or electricity generation of more than 1000 megawatts. See ICOLD 1988 and Mermel 1995.

3. For a related discussion of the emergence of these norms, see Nelson, this volume.

4. The Narmada is the only major river in India that remains virtually un-dammed today. At close to 1,300 kilometers, it is the longest river in central India, as well as the longest west-flowing and the fifth-longest river overall on the South Asian peninsula. It passes through three major states in western India: Madhya Pradesh, Gujarat, and Maharashtra. However, until 1960, much of Gujarat and Maharashtra were part of what was then known as Bombay State.

5. Lathis are police batons used by Indian police.

6. Some villages were commandeered when the construction colony for the SSP was established in the 1960s.

7. Dr. Anil Patel of Arch Vahini, interview by author, Baroda, Gujarat, 5 February 1996. My translation from Hindi.

8. Thayer Scudder, "Aide Memoire on the Relocation Component in Connection with the Sardar Sarovar (Narmada) Project," 21 August 1984.

9. Letter from Robin Hansbury Tenison, president of Survival International, to Ronald P. Brigish of the World Bank, 28 January 1985.

10. Letter from Robin Hansbury Tenison, president of Survival International, to C. L. Robless, chief of the India division in the South Asia Programs Department of the World Bank, 23 May 1985.

11. Advocate Girish Patel, interview by author, Ahmedabad, Gujarat, India, 14 March 1993.

12. Dr. Anil Patel, interview.

13. Letter from World Bank director to government of India on resettlement and rehabilitation issues, 1 July 1987, and letter from World Bank director to government of India expressing concern about failure to provide agreed-upon two hectares of land with threat of suspension, 2 November 1987.

14. A sharp division over the orientation of the new agenda between First- and Third-World countries did emerge at the conference. As Akhileshwar Pahtak correctly notes, "The globalisation of environmental considerations by the late sixties shifted the environmental agenda from the concerns of pollution in the developed countries to natural resources degradation in the developing countries" (1994, 32). See also Gupta 1998.

15. Local discourses on nature and the environment have long histories in India and are not being discounted here. However, the point is that these local discourses did not primarily produce structural changes in the Indian state during the 1970s; rather, globally constructed environmentalism did.

16. Medha Patkar, interview by author, Narmada River Valley in Madhya Pradesh, India, 26 January 1996.

17. Girish Patel, interview.

18. Shripad Dharmadikary, interview by author, Baroda, Gujarat, India, 3 February 1996.

19. Medha Patkar, interview.

20. Moeen Quereshi, vice president of operations at the World Bank, letter to Arjun Singh, chief minister of Madhya Pradesh, 28 November 1988.

21. The following account is based on numerous articles, interviews, and a video on the march.

22. Shripad Dharmadikary, interview.

23. Reports on human rights abuses included Wold 1992 and Lawyers Committee for Human Rights 1993b.

24. Medha Patkar, interview by author, Narmada River Valley, Madhya Pradesh, India, 2 February 1996.

25. *In the Supreme Court of India: Writ Petition (Civil) No. 319 of 1994, Narmada Bachao Andolan versus The Union of India*, 1994.

11

Globalization, Global Alliances, and the Narmada Movement

Smitu Kothari

The past decade has witnessed several significant regional and global efforts to build horizontal linkages that transcend national boundaries. Prior to this, most earlier nongovernmental efforts were focused on building international solidarity (e.g., the Socialist International, the various Communist Internationals, or the forums of the working class), were based on single issues (e.g., the women's movement), or were regional (e.g., the solidarity efforts against imperialist intervention at home in many of the countries of Central and South America).

This recent past has seen the evolution of very different transborder alliances—from hesitant efforts seeking small concessions from dominant and dominating institutions, to initiatives that challenge global power interests, current patterns of economic development, and cultural control. This brief note will concern itself primarily with the latter two since that is the evolving thinking with the Narmada Bachao Andolan (NBA, the Movement to Save the Narmada) (see also Khagram this volume).[1] Of course, global alliances like the ones that have been built around the struggles for justice in the Narmada Valley are still at a nascent stage since any significant challenge to dominant structures and the building of *countervailing* power requires a political coherence that movements, groups, and party activists (the world over) still lack. But, it is clear from recent analysis and action in and around the Narmada movements, as well as the other cases in this volume, that the challenge is being increasingly recognized and the strategies of resistance and of articulating and building alternatives is actively on (Kothari 1995; Patkar and Kothari 1995; "Fifty Years of Bretton Woods Institutions: Enough" 1994; Kothari 2000a; Alvarez, Escobar, and Escobar 1998).

Before specifically discussing the Narmada experience, it is critical to situate it in the larger context of globalization. It is also important to outline some issues that still seem to be neglected in the process of creating better coordination among and between emerging global alliances seeking to transform the dominant economic and political systems.

The Wider Context

Much of the alliance building around the Narmada issue has attempted to make the donor governments, transnational corporations seeking to invest in projects on the Narmada River, and the World Bank accountable to international norms and to the international human rights regime. In the case of the World Bank, it is also to its own policies, which on paper have evolved in directions that are much closer to social movement concerns than before (see Nelson, this volume). However, recent thinking in the movement—which is not equally shared by all constituents of the alliance and thus, consequently, raises several crucial issues—recognizes that the World Bank and other Bretton Woods institutions, as powerful as they are, are still only the more visible symbols of a power configuration that is firmly embedded in the contemporary structures of corporate capitalism. The gulf between the extent of morality and responsibility that these institutions overtly display and what is actually internalized is therefore a function of this basic structural reality. There is, therefore, a growing belief that critiques and campaigns must evolve and strengthen strategies that challenge the structures themselves. In fact, at the moment, even if the World Bank were forced to shut down, in the absence of other structural changes in the global economic order, another similar institution (or institutions) would take its place.

These institutions are aligned in more or less the same way as the current configuration of economic (and military) power, with the G-7 nations (*and* the interests that they represent) dominating the hierarchy. Very few individuals involved in building horizontal linkages of citizens' initiatives and people's movements address the deeper systemic and structural issues. This is partly because so much energy is expended in the local space, in "fire fighting," and in ensuring that some of the changes accepted by dominant institutions after an intense period of campaigning and advocacy actually get implemented. But partly it is also because the deeper questions are harder to deal with; they confront very fundamental aspects of our own lives and challenge us in turn by exposing our institutional and personal weaknesses. This is not to minimize the significance of efforts to hold those in power accountable. Each effort and each step forward helps create democratic space where the potential to nurture political struggle is strengthened (Kothari 2002). The other challenge that those in the process of building these alliances must face is that while there is a committed base and ample idealism within each participating movement or group, most efforts are still dispersed, fragmented, and scattered. Take for example the resistance in India against Cargill or Monsanto (hybrid and transgenic seeds), Union Carbide (the Bhopal tragedy), and the Sardar Sarovar Project. Not only is there very little coordination between groups and movements involved in the opposition to the specific corporations and the dam project, there is little sustained work in responding to the larger political threat that the current patterns of globalization are posing. (And most groups now realize that strengthening the local alone is a necessary but insufficient condition for resisting the global.) This lack of political consolidation presents a major challenge to domestic and transnational networks since the forces of national and transnational capital are increasingly demonstrating significant coherence and consistency in their policies and practice.

Many efforts to challenge the forces of transnational capital have met with criticism from within India. It is argued that focusing on global institutions that have an adverse impact on India detracts from the more basic task of mobilizing within the country and of holding the Indian state accountable to its social and constitutional obligations as well as its obligations to the United Nations charter and instruments to which it is a signatory. Additionally, the argument states that these critiques detract us from the task of compelling the state to become an agency of controlling (or regulating) both global capital and other destabilizing or disrupting political interests. While much of this analysis is true, it can be argued that the time has come to pursue both strategies—the national and the global—with better coordination and transparency.

Can this coordinated action across movements and concerned groups take place without radicalizing political parties or participating in electoral politics? In most countries, both in the Third World and the First World, groups have found the process of sensitizing political parties an enormously difficult one. In countries that have a functioning electoral system, this limitation inevitably inhibits the creation of public debate. The lack of response from parties is not just because their caste-class affiliations obstruct or constrain a focused response to the threats—after all, many Third World societies still have active socialist and Marxist parties. Granted, however, that with the end of the cold war, any political strategy adopted by a political party has to contend with an even more aggressive capitalist enterprise and consequently, the task of convincing constituencies of the importance of an alternative vision is all the more difficult. Precisely because of this political dynamic, the need for a deeper debate within parties regarding the dangers of predatory capital (both global and national and the tactical and strategic alliances between the two) and the adverse implications of greater dependency on undemocratic, secretive, and unjust global institutions like the World Bank and the IMF continue to be urgent.

Equally, an overwhelming proportion of the poor and the oppressed as well as the victims of the development process are not organized and, in many ways, continue to depend on a patronizing political and economic establishment that can no longer deliver even the crumbs of the past. Similarly, the middle classes, both in the Third World and the First World, are still largely oblivious not just to the role of the World Bank and the IMF in imposing a new hegemonic order, but to the real conditions, contexts, and roots of poverty, ecological degradation, and social injustice found within and across states.

Unfortunately, most Third World nation-states have been usurped by their ruling elites. A significant proportion of their bureaucratic, political, and military elites are almost no better than agents and carriers of elites in the First World. This criticism might seem too strong, but if we look at the evidence (despite occasional "hard lines" that are taken by Third World leaders), we can witness a growing affinity between elites across the world and a consequent distancing from the base of their own societies, as well as from the struggles for social justice. This process clearly reflects a decline in nationalistic idealism, which continues to survive in a few scattered groups and continues to have a persistent appeal for a significant proportion of the masses in the country who have, however, been confused and oppressed by obscure economic discourses and the rhetoric of progress and prosperity.

This task acquires more seriousness particularly since international economic institutions and national governments are becoming far more sophisticated in "dealing" with criticism and dissent. The large sums of donor money available for NGOs, the cooptation and "management" of dissenting or alternative language (one of the best examples is the concept of "sustainable development," for within the present patterns of economic growth, sustainable development will remain an oxymoron, a contradiction in terms), as well as the possibilities for lucrative contracts and consultancies have effectively muffled and divided dissenting voices. Too much of active dissent is coopted, contained, or derailed; as a result, the roots of present political and economic control remain largely unaddressed. It is only recently that a renewed mobilization within and across borders is becoming evident, and looking at its growth and the resulting nervousness among ruling elites and the dominant structures of governance, it is obvious that this countervailing process is clearly beginning to take root. As it does, it will have to draw on the learning of the past and innovate new strategies and tactics of transnational engagement. This interplay and contestation will be one of the many crucial developments in the political and cultural landscape of the globe.[2]

This landscape will also witness significant changes in political theory and action as global production, the mobility of global capital and finance, and the creation of megacorporations contest and even attempt to smother nationally bound labor-capital relations. The role of the state in transforming relations, as well as its reconceptualization as capital seeks to use it for its ends and international and transnational democratic forces pressure the state to democratize itself will also increasingly occupy political and social consciousness and action. At the moment, however, in the name of good governance,[3] the dominant logic is that the state must embrace market-friendly policies, ensure a stable climate for global investment, and implement massive programs of infrastructure development that facilitates free play to the neoliberal agenda.

All this—the changing face of dominant processes of globalization; the unity of ruling elites; the fragmentation and dispersal of popular movements; the lack of strategies to sensitize the political parties, the poor, and the middle classes; the consequent decline of radical politics; the emerging mobilization and transnational alliances; and the innovation and creativity that is emerging in the debates and actions of those involved in building and strengthening transnational linkages—all these form the backdrop to understanding the building of the global alliance for justice and human rights in the Narmada Valley.

A Brief History of the Alliance

During the mid-1980s, when the Narmada movement was gradually expanding its mass base and picking up momentum, the predominant strategy was to seek reforms from the state and central governments. It was believed that most issues could be resolved through a process of dialogue. Every avenue of pursuing this was explored and it gradually became evident that as far as the governments were concerned, the gap between rhetoric and practice was continuing to grow. A wide range of nonviolent strategies were adopted and the country's intelligentsia and political opinion makers, as well as other democratic movements in the country, were mobilized. This resulted in generating significant countervailing pressure that compelled successive chief ministers and prime ministers to meet with movement leaders. Assurances to resolve outstanding problems were secured from these political leaders. These meetings, however, resulted only in unfulfilled expectations.

It was during this time that several World Bank missions visited the valley. The mobilization of those who were to be displaced by the dam had created enough public awareness that the World Bank could not easily disregard the organized voices of those who faced displacement and other issues of social and environmental impacts. Nevertheless, even the World Bank was unsuccessful *and* unwilling to make its disbursements conditional on a demonstrated commitment by the various governments to implement policies that had evolved over the past two decades.

Additionally, the Japanese government was evaluating its involvement in the project. The realization among Narmada Bachao Andolan (NBA) activists that the local and national campaign would have to extend itself beyond the national boundaries created intense debate within the movement. Should movement representatives go abroad to pressure the World Bank or could this be done from within? Since there was no discussion of an alliance then, should a relationship be forged with organizations based in the United States, Europe, and Japan?[4] What should the basis of such a relationship be, particularly since there were significant economic, cultural, and social differences? Who should represent the movement? How should that representation be defined?

The first testimonies before subcommittees of the U.S. Congress were organized by the Washington-based Environmental Defense Fund (EDF). One of the main leaders of the movement, Medha Patkar (see Khagram for a broader discussion of the creative role played by Patkar), and myself were among the first to make presentations on the adverse social and environmental implications of World Bank funding and the need for the U.S. government to exercise its influence within the World Bank to make it more socially and environmentally responsible in the context of the Sardar Sarovar Project.

Gradually, EDF, as well as a wide range of U.S.-based organizations, testified before Congress and used a complex set of advocacy strategies to pressure the World Bank. In Japan, Friends of the Earth (Japan) launched a major campaign, initially organizing two public hearings. Japanese academics, activists, and press correspondents made site visits in India. Most of them reported on the grave consequences of the project and on the vast gaps between promise and performance on the part of the governments and dam-building authorities. A media campaign, coupled with pressures on key members of the Japanese Diet (parliament) and relevant central ministries, created a public embarrassment for the government. In Europe, activist groups were meeting their parliamentarians and pressuring their respective executive directors in the World Bank. By 1991, 60 percent of Swedish and 80 percent of Finnish parliamentarians had signed a memorandum to the president of the World Bank seeking a review of the SSP.

A series of unprecedented responses ensued. The Japanese government announced that it was withdrawing its commitment to provide loans to the SSP. The World Bank reluctantly announced that it was setting up, for the first time in its history, an independent review committee under the chairpersonship of Bradford Morse, who had recently stepped down as an administrator of UNDP. Their report, *Sardar Sarovar: Report of the Independent Review,* was a path-breaking document that called on the World Bank "to step back" (Morse and Berger 1992). However, the World Bank did not heed this recommendation and issued a note called "The Next Steps." The collective pressure from the alliance was stepped up, including full-page advertisements in major newspapers signed by over eight hundred organizations from all over the world calling on the president of the World Bank to withdraw funding. In less than six months, the Indian government and the World Bank, recognizing that the Next Steps could not be satisfactorily implemented, decided on a face-saving decision—that the World Bank should be asked to withdraw from the project. It was one of the first times that the World Bank was compelled to withdraw from such a prestigious project that it had defended so vociferously and for so long.

It needs to be stressed here that much of this would not have been possible without the successful mass mobilization in the Narmada Valley. Estimates of the number of people in the movement range from 70 to 80 percent of those to be affected by the project (approximately 150,000 people in over two hundred villages in the three states of Madhya Pradesh, Maharashtra, and Gujarat).

By this time the global alliance had extended itself to other parts of Europe and the rest of the world. Newer strategies had to be planned to respond more rapidly to the growing human rights violations in the valley. One initiative that took shape in 1993 was the formation of an International Panel on Human Rights, which has regularly sent a representative from the international human rights community to spend between a week and a fortnight to report, from the point of view of established human rights convention and covenants, the violations taking place. One of the most difficult tasks for communities affected by the processes of globalization has been to make the representative institutions accountable to the international human rights regime. The World Bank and the IMF, even though they were formed under the UN, continue to be diffident in respecting established standards.

In fact, many within these institutions see the norms as a hindrance to the successful implementation of their structural adjustment programs and other institutional changes that seek to create a viable global marketplace.

The alliance has gone on to challenge the involvement of corporations and financiers in other projects in the Narmada Valley.[5] Many of the partnerships that have been forged in the process of the alliance building have led to solidarities on issues beyond the struggle against a cluster of dams.

One of the most dramatic achievements of the movement in the Narmada Valley has been its central influence in the formation and direction of the World Commission on Dams (WCD). An innovative institutional innovation on a contemporary controversy, the WCD is a pioneering step in defining the structure of institutions of global governance that would mediate contentious global or regional issues in the future. The years since it was formed in 1998 have witnessed some of the best coordinated global efforts by social movements and people's organizations to make inputs before a group of commissioners who represent the entire spectrum of "stakeholders"— from leaders of anti-dam movements and indigenous peoples to senior representatives of financial institutions and corporations. Other stakeholders have also made crucial submissions, but the sustained and coordinated efforts by transboundary networks of dam-affected communities, support groups, and the extended global alliances have had a dramatic influence in highlighting the comprehensive adverse impacts of large dams, as well as in democratizing the work of the commission itself. A comprehensive independent assessment of the WCD locates the commission historically, critically maps the process, and looks at the lessons this process has for future commissions, multistakeholder processes, and transnational alliances.[6]

Numerous questions have been raised in this process of building the alliance. Debates on governance and development policy within India have increasingly focused on the need to transform the very structures of power. In a class- and caste-based society, processes of economic globalization inevitably compound the loss of control of local communities over their resources and their lives, which may exacerbate conditions of social unrest and conflict or lead to the growth of insecurity among cultural and political identities. Without this control, transforming the dominant processes of policymaking—national and globally—is an almost impossible task. (This underscores, as do the other chapters in this volume, the need to attend simultaneously to both domestic and international processes when evaluating or responding to transnational networks.) Additionally, to what extent can global alliances transit from seeking concessions from international institu-

tions and national governments to concentrating on issues of social and ecological justice in both the First and Third Worlds?

Global Alliances: Some Challenges

Like the NBA, more and more groups and movements from the Third
World now feel that solidarities need to be created not just by expressions of
compassion, but in a climate of collective and individual self-introspection
and change. Relationships should be marked not by a patronizing attitude,
but by a spirit of fellowship. This is more difficult than it sounds because
even among alliance members there are significant class and privilege differences. Collectively molding an authentic alternative vision is an enormously
arduous task. In fact, it is a much greater challenge for those in the First
World, who will have to fight greater personal battles, than for elites in our
milieu. Additionally, for them there is a further need to be rooted authenti-
cally within their own societies, as indeed we need to root ourselves in ours.
In fact, participation in global initiatives needs to move beyond the better
known, more visible, primarily elite activists.

All this calls for urgent political consolidation. Given the growing stir-
ring for justice and democracy all over the world, one of the biggest challenges for individual struggles and for nascent global alliances is to convert
sentiment, anger, and assertion against dominant institutions into effective
and sustained political strategies. It also calls for a rethinking of rigid ideological orientations and greater humility in the task of building a broad
democratic front that does not imply the submergence of plural institutional
identities. The collective task of politicizing diverse constituencies—in both
the North and the South—is now as urgent as ever.

It also presents challenges for a new vision of universalism—a universalism that does not impinge on smaller identities and pluralistic structures and
which, in turn, is not impeded by the struggles of the same. Stated differently, the challenge is how to build international solidarities and links toward a
holistic, universalistic worldview that does not impede the cultural flowering
of diverse identities—a process that not only reverses the cultural aggression
and hegemonic thrust of dominant institutions, but strengthens the fabric
of pluralism, diversity, and justice.

Notes

This essay presents some brief reflections based on a long-term involvement in the
Movement to Save the Narmada (Narmada Bachao Andolan-NBA). Since complete
objectivity is in any case a contradiction in terms, I will only say that while the task
of writing about a popular struggle that I am involved in requires some distancing

from the "subject," I cannot avoid the deeper levels of "subjectivity" that run through the paper. There will also, obviously, be differences between how I "read" the Andolan's history, how it would like the history to be presented, and how different participants in the Andolan understand it.

1. The NBA, while rooted in the Narmada River Valley, is a national alliance of organizations jointly campaigning for justice in the valley. It was set up in 1988 to initially seek comprehensive rehabilitation for those displaced by the Sardar Sarovar Project (SSP) in west-central India. By August 1990, the NBA, recognizing the inability of the state and central governments to provide rehabilitation, decided to oppose the building of the project.

2. This is not to say that the defense of economic and cultural globalization is universal among global elites. There are powerful currents in almost all Third World societies and several First World ones that resist the logic and hegemony of globalization and seek to protect both fundamentalist and progressive traditions. What is important, however, is that the potential and role of domestic social and political forces (as they challenge the forces of capital) and the influence of these nationally bound struggles on the nature of transnational alliances and linkages should not be underestimated. Conversely also, transnational alliances often strengthen local social movements by providing a wider arena to pursue advocacy and political strategies that contribute to the democratization of society. There are two crucial lessons: one, the central need for transnational alliances to be rooted in local movements with the active participation of local communities; and two, the profound demand for a major restructuring of contemporary democratic institutions, from the local to the global.

3. One of the more eloquent prescriptive documents that propagates this worldview is the World Bank's World Development Report of 1997, which centers on the role of the state in an era of economic globalization.

4. Movement activists supporting the need to go beyond national boundaries believed that alliances with European and Japanese groups were crucial since the governments of these countries were members of the World Bank and sent influential citizens as their executive directors to the World Bank headquarters in Washington, D.C.

5. In late 1999 and early 2000, the existing alliance was reactivated and new actors were brought in as the state of Madhya Pradesh went ahead with its decision to build another dam in the Narmada Valley at Maheshwar. A U.S.-based corporation, Ogden, and German state guarantees to German corporate investments in the project were challenged. The German government was also compelled by an alliance of local and German NGOs to constitute an independent commission. The commission's report left little doubt about the apathy of local corporate partners and government officials to the plight of those to be displaced. It also documented the almost

total opposition by local communities to the project. After some delays, the German government decided to withdraw its promised guarantees. Similarly, in the United States, a comprehensive campaign against Ogden has forced another independent investigation, eventually compelling even Ogden to withdraw from the project. See www.narmada.org for details of this process.

6. For details of the commission's work, see World Commission on Dams 2000. Also see their Web site, www.dams.org. For a comprehensive report of the process, the lessons, and the limitations of the commission's work, see Dubash et al., 2001. This report and related material are also available at www.wcdassessment.org.

Part IV
Organizing Labor

12

Marx and Engels: The Prototypical Transnational Actors

August Nimtz

About a half year before his death in 1895, Frederick Engels, then seventy-four, described his busy schedule, which included a reading regimen:

> I have to follow the movement in five large and a lot of small countries and the U.S. America. For that purpose I receive 3 German, 2 English, 1 Italian *dailies* and from Jan. 1, the Vienna daily, 7 in all. Of *weeklies* I receive 2 from Germany, 7 Austria, 1 France, 3 America (2 English, 1 German), 2 Italian, and 1 each in Polish, Bulgarian, Spanish and Bohemian, three of which in languages I am still gradually acquiring. (Engels, Lafargue, and Lafargue 1963, 347)

The "movement" that Engels had to follow was the very one that he and his partner, Karl Marx, who had died more than a decade earlier, had helped to bring into existence—the first transnational movement of workers. The many requests for advice that poured into his study in London from workers and workers' organizations around the world—one of the reasons he needed to be informed—registered the enormous progress they had made. Its origins could be traced directly to the International Working Men's Association (IWMA), the First International, the short-lived but highly influential body that Marx led from 1864 to 1872. What the IWMA achieved and laid the basis for in its aftermath—independent, working-class political action—could in turn be traced to the seeds that Marx and Engels had planted two decades earlier.

Precursors to the First International
Toward Proletarian Internationalism

The historian Eric Hobsbawm points out that in the wake of the French Revolution, all revolutionary movements displayed a degree of consciousness. Its "most formidable legacy . . . was the set of models and patterns of political upheaval which it established for the general use of rebels anywhere . . . to turn unrest into revolution, and above all to link all of Europe in a single movement . . . of subversion" (1962, 140–41). Of particular importance for our purposes was a "strong tradition of internationalism," especially after the 1830 revolution in France; "[a]ttempts to set up international revolutionary bodies," says Hobsbawm, "never ceased" (160). An "accidental" but important factor, he notes, that contributed to internationalism was the exile condition. Owing to political repression—"blockage in the domestic society"(see Khagram, Riker, and Sikkink, this volume)—most militants were forced to flee their home countries to seek refuge in places that were relatively more open, such as London, Geneva, and Zurich, and, depending on the political circumstances, Paris and Brussels. While exile politics could be extremely contentious, these refuges were often the venues in which activists of different nationalities first came to meet and work with one another. "A common fate and a common ideal bound these expatriates and travelers together," says Hobsbawm (161). The politicization of the young Marx and Engels revealed that they too were the products of this legacy.

Informed by the "materialist conception of history" and the thesis of "revolutionary practice," i.e., active involvement in "real" struggles, the Marx and Engels partnership, established in 1844, sought to link up with Europe's small but growing proletarian movement. They were led in this direction by their theoretical conclusion that a "really open" society (see Khagram, Riker, and Sikkink, this volume), or what they called "true democracy," necessitated the end of class society, a "social revolution"; only the proletariat, they argued, had the interest and capacity to lead such a transformation.

With Engels, Marx traveled to England in 1845 to get his first glimpse of what was then the world's most advanced proletariat. Because of Engels's prior transnational activism, they were able to make contact not only with the English movement, but also with revolutionary German workers in exile. On the basis of these contacts, they took the initiative to forge what was perhaps the first transnational advocacy network of democrats, the London-based Society of Fraternal Democrats, established, in its own words, "to succour the militant democracy of every country"(Marx and Engels 1975–95, 6: 384).[1] It sought, as its declaration of principles stated, to overcome the "national prejudices" that divided the "working classes" (Cole and Filson 1951, 402–3). Although the organization effectively came to an end after a few years, these initial efforts constituted the first transnational organizing for the Marx and Engels team and laid the basis for much of their subsequent work.

Back on the continent and in exile, this time in Brussels, Marx and Engels immediately took steps to capitalize on their new contacts. They established "a new system of propaganda"—the Communist Correspondence Societies (hereafter CCC) (Draper 1985, 22). Taking their name from the ventures of Thomas Paine—testimony to the influence of his own transnational activism on subsequent generations—and the Jacobins, the CCCs, with their center in Brussels, sought to institute the exchange of letters among various socialists and communists on the continent and in England.

The CCCs were intended to be a network through which self-styled socialists and communists in different countries would begin to talk with one another in a systematic way. Their conception of the committees' modus operandi (38: 38–39) revealed some of the most basic assumptions that would always inform Marx and Engels's practice—the necessity to strive for proletarian internationalism by overcoming national particularism and the value of discussion as a basis for revolutionary political action. The formation of the CCCs testified to another distinguishing feature of the Marx and Engels team from the very outset—a recognition that it was necessary to organize to make ideas influential. While they were certainly not the first radicals who, in the aftermath of the French Revolution, tried to propagate their ideas, they were among the few who put in the necessary time and organizational effort.

In an important letter about procedures for the CCCs, Marx and Engels made a number of recommendations and proposals that would forever be part of their political and organizational arsenal. Three of these are particularly pertinent. First, they advised that "regular meetings" should be held so that through discussion communists could "clear up things among themselves." Second, there should be "monthly contributions" from members. This reflected their general view that communist organizations should be self-financing, particularly when it came to the publication of communist literature.[2] Lastly, they objected to "authors" being subsidized by CCCs. Although they did not explain why, it is safe to assume that it had to do with their principled opposition to an elite strata of "educators" within a communist organization. One might suspect, also, that Marx and Engels were especially sensitive to any appearance of privileges for "authors," given the kind of class baiting they had been subjected to on occasion. In a world in which educational opportunities were quite limited—the vast majority of workers were not in a position to become writers—it was necessary to take steps to avoid any possible charge of class privilege.

The League of Communists and the 1848 Revolution

The CCCs' real success was that they laid the basis, owing to the contacts, for the first Marxist party, the League of Communists, established in 1847. One of those contacts was with the largely German exile proletarian group, the League of the Just. Like virtually every revolutionary party after 1815, the league's modus operandi was conspiratorial. Its own roots went back to Babeuf's Conspiracy of Equals in 1796 and Auguste Blanqui's Society of Seasons—the prototypes of conspiratorial organizing.[3] Convinced of Marx and Engels's views, the leadership of the league invited them in 1847 to join their organization (that they were recruited by the workers is of utmost significance given later suggestions that Marx and Engels imposed themselves on the workers' movement). They agreed provided the league abandon its conspiratorial tradition and adopt a new program they would help to formulate. By the end of the year a new organization was born, the League of Communists (LC). A few months later, in February 1848, Marx had completed, on the basis of Engels's drafts, its new program, the *Manifesto of the Communist Party.*

The adoption of the *Manifesto* by the LC revealed an important difference between it and the CCC. The former was a much more politically homogenous body. In this manner, the CCC rather than the LC anticipated more the First International, as will be seen later. The *Manifesto* codified Marx and Engels's basic views, such as the relationship between the democratic and the socialist revolutions; that is, the former was the prerequisite for the latter, which was in turn dependent on workers taking political power. It is infused throughout with proletarian internationalism.[4] Whereas the League of the Just's motto had been "All Men Are Brothers" (the same for the Society of Fraternal Democrats), the LC at Marx and Engels's urging adopted "Working men of all countries, unite!"

In deeds as well as words, the LC was clearly an international organization. Shortly after its founding congress in December 1847, at which delegates from five countries were present, it sent emissaries to "Lapland in Sweden and Wisconsin in the U.S." to set up new branches. While its orientation was generally toward German workers, wherever they resided, its members were expected to participate in their country's broader democratic movement. Thus, Marx and Engels continued their own activism in the broadbased Brussels Democratic Association. This was the setting, at a time when England had just repealed the Corn Laws, that Marx put forward for the workers' movement his views on an issue that would bedevil many a transnational labor activist at the end of the twentieth century—the matter of free trade versus protectionism (see Kidder, this volume).

Hardly before the ink was dry on the *Manifesto,* Marx and Engels were forced to apply and concretize their views on the basis of what they liked to call the real movement, in this case the revolutionary upheavals that swept Europe between February 1848 and the middle of 1851. Of all the lessons they distilled in the aftermath of the upheavals, that of independent, working-class, political action would be the most crucial for their later activities in the First International. Also, their expectation that the revolutionary process would be transnational was verified by the 1848–51 upsurge. As the reality of the German revolution clarified the democratic limitations of its bourgeoisie and middle class, Marx concluded that its fate would be linked to the successful outcome of a worldwide revolutionary process that combined national liberation with antifeudal and anticapitalist struggles "waged in Canada as in Italy, in East Indies as in Prussia, in Africa as on the Danube" (8: 215).

The International Working Men's Association

The more than decade-long lull in the class struggle following the defeat of the 1848 revolutions forced Marx and Engels to cut back on their political activism and concentrate on what they called the scientific work—researching and writing for what would eventually be *Capital* and other projects. Yet from their headquarters, in London and Manchester, respectively, they maintained their international links, especially with close contacts in the United States and Switzerland who were refugees of the German revolution. They also researched and wrote extensively on international developments. It was at this time that Marx acquired a following in the United States owing to his articles not only in the German press there, but more importantly in the *New York Daily Tribune.* With Engels's invaluable assistance, through frequent visits and correspondence that averaged a letter every other day, they both deepened their global view in this period. Without these international ties and interests—in essence, a transnational advocacy network—they would not have been able to seize the initiative when presented with new political opportunities.

The Formation of the First International

Early in 1863 Marx wrote to Engels that "the ERA OF REVOLUTION has now FAIRLY OPENED IN EUROPE once more" (41: 453).[5] The basis for Marx's conclusion was the peasant uprising in Poland that year. However, even before that event other signs had appeared on the political horizon that gave cause for optimism. At the beginning of 1860, Marx declared, and Engels concurred, "that the most momentous thing happening in the world today is the slave movement—on the one hand, in America, started by the death of Brown, and in Russia, on the other" (41: 4, 7). Marx was referring to the abortive rebellion of the abolitionist John Brown at Harpers Ferry, Virginia, a few months earlier, which in turn had stimulated at least one slave uprising in its aftermath. As for Russia, its "slaves," i.e., serfs, had also been on the march for emancipation as he had noted the previous year. A year later, in a move to preempt a revolt from below, the Czar abolished serfdom. Of enormous significance was that the Russian movement was coinciding with the one in the United States. Precisely because they viewed the class struggle from an international perspective they gave more weight to the conjuncture of struggles in various countries than to isolated ones. The fight against slavery and other precapitalist modes of exploitation was obviously key in labor's struggle against capital.

The U.S. Civil War was one of the immediate factors that gave rise to the First International. It politicized Europe's proletariat and brought Marx and Engels back into active politics. They sought through their writings to win the English and German proletariat to the Northern cause. Since British capitalists, led by the textile barons, campaigned to get their government to intervene on behalf of the Confederacy—the most important source of cotton for their mills—it was crucial that supporters of the Union cause organize an anti-interventionist movement in Europe. It was in Britain that this effort was most successful. Interestingly, this occurred only after Lincoln issued his Emancipation Proclamation in 1862. According to trade union leader George Howell, "[O]nce it became clear that slavery was the issue the workers rallied to the North with almost singular unanimity" (Collins and Abramsky 1965, 21).[6]

In addition to reporting on this campaign through his articles, Marx helped organize in March 1863 the largest of several English trade union–sponsored meetings in solidarity with the North (Draper 1985, 116). The anti-interventionist sentiment and movement, Marx felt, were decisive in preventing the British government from coming to the Confederacy's defense.

Effective opposition on the part of English workers to their government's threat of intervention on behalf of the Confederacy taught them that they could indeed have an impact on ruling-class foreign policies, provided they organized themselves. It was exactly this sentiment, which was echoed to varying degrees by workers on the continent, along with an increasing recognition that effective strike activity required the coordination of Europe's trade unions—in order to avoid workers from one country being employed as strikebreakers in another country—that led to the formation of the International Working Men's Association (IWMA) at an international meeting in London in September 1864. Originally called to support the Polish and Italian struggles for self-determination, the gathering registered the internationalism of Europe's working classes. Because Marx possessed a party nucleus with a definite program, one of whose planks was proletarian internationalism, he quickly emerged as the body's guiding force. He would also be able to leverage his standing in the German workers' movement to advance his perspective in the IWMA, as well as to do the same in the former by drawing on his influence in the latter—the interaction between domestic and international opportunity structures (see Khagram, Riker, and Sikkink, this volume).

Program and Organization

Right from the beginning, Marx placed his stamp on the organization. Its basic programmatic positions, which he wrote with the approval of the General Council (GC), the IWMA's executive committee, were consistent with the political conclusions he and Engels had drawn from their 1848 experiences. Thus, the *Inaugural Address* and *Rules* were based on the two fundamental points that he (at the outset) and Engels (after September 1870) incessantly strove to make a reality—independent, working-class, political action and the necessity for workers to take political power. Among the disparate forces that composed the GC, there were those—especially the English trade union officials and the anarchists of varying stripes—who opposed, in deed if not always in word, these positions.

Unlike the League of Communists, which was not only a politically homogenous body but a centralized one as well, the IWMA in Marx's view was best served by a more inclusive set of principles and a more flexible structure. Programmatically, it adopted what might be called his and Engels's minimum program, the two above-noted fundamental points. Any workers' organization in any country that supported the "protection, advancement, and complete emancipation of the working classes"—the first of the *Rules*—was eligible to join.

In 1871, Engels wrote "the moment the Association were to become a sect," that is, espouse the views of only one current, even the communist one that he and Marx belonged to, "it would be finished. Our power lies in the liberality with which the first rule is interpreted, namely that all men who are admitted aim for the complete emancipation of the working classes" (44:

163). This was the basis for his and Marx's growing differences with the anarchists within the organization led by Mikhail Bakunin. The problem, he continued, was that they wanted to make their program, some of which he agreed with, the condition for membership. "But to put all those things into our programme would mean alienating an enormous number of our members, and dividing rather than uniting the European proletariat" (44: 163). The long-term goal was one of theoretical homogeneity, but to require it at that moment, given the reality of the differences between working classes of various countries as well as within them, would have been counterproductive. Only through discussions and debates and working together could such a common perspective emerge. In this regard it should be noted that Marx often emphasized that the IWMA was "the militant organization of the working classes," that is, a society for action and not simply for discussion.

The IWMA's organizational principles were, in general, patterned on those of English trade unions. The GC, based in London, served as the executive of the IWMA, whose authority, as Marx once described, was mainly "moral." National sections were permitted to organize themselves in any manner as long as it did not conflict with the shared principles of the *Rules*. In instances of such violations the GC could bar membership to a section. Delegated congresses, which occurred almost every year, amended rules and adopted new programmatic positions for the association and decided on appeals of GC decisions. In both the GC and congresses, decisions were passed with a simple majority rule. The GC was responsible for calling, organizing, and drafting policy positions for the congresses. While national sections had the right to be represented on the GC, the latter had the final authority on its membership. Lastly, while it is true that the increase in the "moral authority" of the GC led over time to an increase in its effective powers resulting in a relatively more centralized association, the IWMA retained, at Marx's insistence, its organizational flexibility. What the history of the organization reveals is that if the Society of Fraternal Democrats had been a transnational advocacy network, the IWMA strove under Marx's leadership to be a transnational social movement (see Khagram, Riker, and Sikkink, this volume, for the distinction).

Marx as Political Organizer

Marx was deadly serious about his injunction in the preamble to the *Rules* that "the emancipation of the working classes must be conquered by the working classes themselves." If there was one lesson from 1848, surely it had been that the proletariat should entertain no illusions about the petite bourgeoisie, let alone the bourgeoisie. To address that concern Marx initiated organizational and rule changes that placed severe limits on middle-class participation in the leadership of the IWMA.

When a prominent lawyer who had collaborated with the IWMA sought a seat on the GC in 1865, Marx convinced other members that his request should be rejected on the basis of the class interests that he represented. "I believe him an honest and sincere man; at the same time, he is nothing and can be nothing save a Bourgeois politician. . . . We cannot become *le piedestal* for small parliamentary ambitions. . . . [Otherwise] others of his class will follow, and our efforts, till now successful at freeing the English working class movement from all middle class or aristocratic patronage, will have been in vain" (42: 92–93). Hence, very early in the IWMA's existence Marx opposed any efforts to make the International into an electoral conduit for, certainly, the petite bourgeoisie and the bourgeoisie itself.

Marx also demanded that GC members be active in building the organization by forming branches and signing up new members; they could themselves be barred from the GC if they didn't pay their dues to get their membership cards. This was clearly another way of preventing "honorary" membership and discouraging opportunists with parliamentary ambitions who were not prepared to be activists in the body. Such organizational norms, the prohibition of paper membership and the expectation that leaders had to be activists, were, of course, consistent with Marx's long-held position that only through active involvement in the real movement could the leader or "educator"—to recall the *Theses on Feuerbach*—be "educated." He himself was intimately involved in every organizational detail including the signing and issuance of membership cards, the close monitoring of association documents and finances—at times advancing his own limited funds to keep it afloat—and, not unexpectedly, drawing up the agendas and draft policy statements for congresses. Marx's insistence on this mode of functioning cast him in the role of the GC's disciplinarian.

A major debate broke out in the first year of the IWMA's existence about the place of "literary men," i.e., intellectuals, in its leadership, that is, individuals who were clearly not workers but who contributed to the organization's advancement. Obviously, this had implications for Marx and Engels, who on occasion described their role in the workers' movement as that of "literary representatives of the proletariat" (see, for example, 20: 81). While the details of this dispute cannot be explored here, suffice it to say that it was resolved through a vote at the IWMA's first congress, at Geneva in 1866. Henri Tolain, the Proudhonist leader of the French section of the International, moved that sections be required to select only "hand-workers" for delegates to a congress. The main opposition to the motion came from the

British trade union leaders, one of whom argued that were it not for some of the nonmanual worker members of the GC, the IWMA "would not have struck so deep a root in Britain. Among those members I will mention one only, Citizen Marx [who was not in attendance], who has devoted all his life to the triumph of the working classes."

The ringing endorsement that Marx was given at Geneva testified to the enormous influence he exercised in the IWMA by the time of its first congress. Even six months after the organization's founding Marx could accurately tell Engels that "I am IN FACT the HEAD of it" (21: 130). He was not far off the mark when he wrote to a close contact in Germany, Ludwig Kugelmann, shortly after the Geneva congress eighteen months later, "I am in fact having to run the whole Association myself" (42: 328). With such influence, Marx had to be careful how he wielded it. "*Fortiter in re, suaviter in modo* [strong in deed and smooth in style]" as he once put it, was indeed his modus operandi. While, for example, he did not attend the Geneva congress he was instrumental in directing it by writing the main document for its discussions, "Instructions for the Delegates of the Provisional General Council—The Different Questions," and having his closest contacts lead the gathering in his absence (42: 314–15). Sensitive, also, to the potential of class baiting, he declined the post of GC president, which was offered to him in the aftermath of Geneva. The GC minutes record that Marx "thought himself incapacitated because he was a head worker and not a hand worker" (20: 412).[7]

As the administrative and political center of the IWMA, Marx was most vigilant about bookkeeping matters, especially the preservation of the organization's documents, such as correspondence, and GC and congress minutes. The IWMA is one of the best documented social movements of the nineteenth century exactly because of the extant records for which Marx and Engels were mainly responsible. From a communist perspective—the necessity of drawing the lessons of the class struggle—such documentation was essential.

An essential trait of Marx's modus operandi was to combine daily organizational activism in the most detailed way—what today would be called "licking the stamps" or doing the "s—t work"—with theoretical leadership: the quintessential example of a nongovernmental sector actor (Khagram, Riker, and Sikkink, this volume). The effectiveness of the latter, in fact, was enhanced by that of the former; it made Marx a more credible leader. Marx epitomized the middle-class thinker who subordinated his life to the revolutionary cause of the proletariat. Being a doer as well as a thinker had the added advantage of rendering class baiting ineffective. This model of revolutionary leadership, the theoretician-activist, was unique in the annals of the revolutionary process—the realization of Marx's *Theses on Feuerbach*. Though much briefer in existence than the IWMA, the German revolution had well prepared him for such a role. What was new this time was that Marx was a theoretician-activist among forces with far more political weight than what existed in the Rhineland in 1848–49.

The International In Action

Strike Support Work

Since trade union issues had been one of the reasons for the IWMA's formation, it was not coincidental that the activity it most consistently engaged in was international strike solidarity; this solidarity was the basis for its popularity and growth among workers. The strike wave that rocked the European continent from 1867 to 1869—spurred on by the recession that had commenced the previous year—put the organization on the political map. Of particular importance was its assistance, coordinated through the GC, to the Paris bronze workers lockout in 1867, the Geneva building trades strike in 1868, and the bloody Charleroi, Belgium, coal miners confrontation, also in 1868. All three struggles were victorious to varying degrees due in part to the kind of national and international solidarity that the GC, working with IWMA affiliates in various countries, was able to generate on their behalf. The IWMA was thus seen by increasing layers of workers, not only in Europe but elsewhere, as an effective fighting force and it was continuously called upon to provide strike assistance.

A unique contribution made by the Marx party—as his and Engels's closest political contacts were usually called—via the GC and IWMA affiliates, was the codification and dissemination of the lessons of these struggles for workers. In what was probably a first in the history of the workers' movement, a pamphlet on the struggle of the Geneva building trade workers was written and published by a long-time contact. The inexpensive brochure—the proceeds from its sales were used for strike support work—assured that the story of the strike would get into the hands of workers. The pamphlet was in turn publicized in what became in 1868 the first history of the IWMA, Wilhelm Eichoff's *The International Working Men's Association: Its Establishment, Organisation, Political and Social Activity, and Growth*. Eichoff, a close Marx and Engels contact and an IWMA activist in Berlin, wrote this short work (originally in German) with the assistance of Marx and largely under his direction; Marx, who apparently wrote part of it, also did the final editing (21: 517–18). About a third of the sixty-page pamphlet is devoted exclusively to the three above-mentioned strikes. Containing also what were then all the official documents of the International, the work became an effective recruitment tool for the organization. Only by documenting for workers the experiences of their movement, which is what both pieces of literature did, would it be possible to generalize the lessons of the class struggle—the necessary step in the proletariat's quest for political power.

Under Marx's leadership the IWMA became the de facto worldwide strike center, dispensing information and solidarity assistance in a way that had never been done and setting a precedent to be built upon. The IWMA's reputation as an effective source of solidarity for workers' struggles brought affiliation requests from as far as New Zealand, India, and Argentina. Not surprisingly, the activities of the IWMA earned for it the animosity of governments in Europe who self-servingly viewed the insurgent labor movements in their countries as under the direction of "decrees sent from London"; the result was the first international campaign in red-baiting and persecution of trade union activists.[8]

One significant aspect of Marx's leadership in the IWMA was his systematic attention to the inclusion of women in the workers' movement in general and in the International in particular. From the very beginning Marx was the most conscious of all the GC members in putting the issue of women on the agenda. To do so meant having to oppose the Proudhonist current in the International, especially its French section, which was "resolutely hostile to women working" and the "participation of women in industry" (Thomas 1971, 411).[9]

The IWMA as a Social and Political Movement

As much attention as Marx gave to the IWMA's strike support work, it soon became clear that he viewed its mission more broadly. For its first congress in Geneva in 1866 he drafted the proposals to be discussed there, called "Instructions to the Delegates," one of which was entitled "Limitation of the Working Day." It was crucial to limit the working day—the specific proposal was for eight hours—in order "to restore the health and physical energies of the working class, that is, the great body of every nation, as well as to secure them the possibility of intellectual development, sociable intercourse, social and political action" (20: 187). Thus, the beginning of the international campaign to institute a norm that continues to have profound significance for all working people—the eight-hour workday.

The most well-known "Instruction" was "Trade Unions, Their Past, Present and Future." While trade unions were crucial in what he called the "guerilla fights" between capital and labor, he criticized them because they "kept too much aloof from general social and political movements"—the problem that would be called in Russian revolutionary circles four decades later, "economism." That, however, they had recently become active in England for the fight to extend the suffrage was a positive sign. This anticipated, in fact, what they would have to do in the "Future."

> Apart from their original purposes, they must now learn to act deliberately as organising centres of the working class in the broad interest of its *complete emancipation.* They must aid every social and political movement tending in that direction. Considering themselves and acting as the champions and representatives of the whole working class, they cannot fail to enlist the non-society men [i.e., nonorganized] into their ranks. They must look carefully after the interests of the worst paid trades, such as the agricultural labourers, rendered powerless by exceptional circumstances. They must convince the world at large that their efforts, far from being narrow and selfish, aim at the emancipation of the downtrodden millions. (20: 192)

This charge to the trade union movement was the most concrete elaboration Marx had ever made on his oft-quoted passage from the *Manifesto:* "The proletarian movement is the self-conscious, independent movement of the immense majority in the interest of the immense majority." The essential concern was how to get the proletariat and its class organizations to think and act socially beyond its own immediate economic interests. In the context of the Russian Revolution, this would be one of the central themes in Lenin's famous polemic, *What Is to Be Done?* Marx's call anticipated the direction in which he would increasingly take the International.[10] To employ the language of the first chapter of this volume, Marx's efforts were consciously "directed at changing understandings and interpretations of actors," specifically, workers.

Within six months of the IWMA's formation, the GC, with Marx's enthusiastic support, helped bring into existence the Reform League, the working-class organization that played a key role in pressuring parliament to enact the 1867 Reform Act, which extended the suffrage to almost half of Britain's male heads of households (Smith 1966, 236).[11] At his urging, the GC had agreed that its members in the league would only support the demand of universal male suffrage. His perspective, however, was not implemented, which explains in part the limited outcome of the 1867 act.

In Defense of National Self-Determination

The right of oppressed nations to self-determination had been a long-held view of Marx and Engels. Within a year and a half of the IWMA's birth,

Engels made an especially important programmatic contribution in a series of letters, which were published in the IWMA's journal in 1866 as "What Have the Working Classes to Do with Poland?" (20: 152–61). Written at Marx's behest, their purpose, largely successful, was to strengthen the fight against the Proudhonist objection to the International's support for Polish self-determination. Contrary to the Proudhonist view that political action in general and support to national liberation movements in particular should not concern the International, Engels argued that the proletariat did indeed have an interest in what happened in Poland.

Engels's articles provided the theoretical and programmatic basis for the defense of Irish self-determination when it was posed a year later. The Irish struggle first attracted the GC's attention in 1867, when a group of Irish nationalists belonging to the conspiratorial Fenian society were arrested after carrying out an armed attack to free their incarcerated comrades. A broad-based movement emerged to protest the scheduled execution of those who had been charged with the murder of a policeman in the attack. Within the GC and the milieus in which it functioned, Marx, as he told Engels, "sought by every means at my disposal to incite the English workers to demonstrate in favour of FENIANISM" (42: 460). Most GC members, at a special meeting attended by the press, voiced strong support for the right of the Irish nationalists to employ armed struggle and vehemently condemned the judgment against them. Marx wrote the GC's appeal to the British Home Secretary to halt the executions, but to no avail. For Marx there were actually two issues at stake: "(1) The attitude of the British government on the Irish question; (2) The attitude of the English working class towards the Irish" (General Council of the First International 1963–68, 3: 176–77). Cognizant of the GC's British trade union contingent's history of "cringing to" or "flirting with" (as Marx and Engels respectively characterized it) the recently installed liberal prime minister William Gladstone, Marx, as part of his overall goal of independent, working-class political action, consciously sought to drive a wedge between the former and the latter. Hence, in a debate that ranged over three consecutive meetings, Marx took every opportunity to expose and denounce the hypocrisy of Gladstone's liberalism on Ireland and proposed a resolution to that effect.

The last paragraph of this resolution, which was unanimously approved, required that it be distributed to all IWMA sections in order to be publicized as widely as possible. For Marx, the denunciation of the British government's policies was intended to be an expression of the IWMA's solidarity with the Irish movement, which would hopefully gain a hearing for the organization among the Irish proletariat. Within a month of the publication of the GC's resolution, this policy bore fruit as inquiries were made from Ireland that led to the establishment of the first Irish section of the IWMA.

Marx and Engels were convinced that political collaboration between the English and Irish sections of the IWMA should not be to the disadvantage of the latter. Thus, when the British trade union leader and GC member, John Hales, sought to subordinate the Irish branches of the IWMA to the umbrella British section in 1872, on the grounds that the branches undermined the "fundamental principle of the Association [which] was to destroy all semblance of the nationalist doctrine," Engels, who was now on the GC, voiced and successfully mounted opposition. His reply reflected the essence of the Marx and Engels team's position on the national question vis-à-vis proletarian internationalism.

> The Irish formed a distinct nationality of their own, and the fact that [they] used the English language could not deprive them of their rights [to have their own branches]. . . . There was the fact of seven centuries of English conquest and oppression of Ireland, and so long as that oppression existed, it would be an insult to Irish working men to ask them to submit to a British Federal Council. . . . [Hales's motion] was asking the conquered people to forget their nationality and submit to their conquerors. It was not Internationalism, but simply prating submission . . . true Internationalism must necessarily be based upon a distinct national organisation, and they [the Irish branches] were under the necessity to state in the preamble of their rules that their first and most pressing duty as Irishmen was to establish their own national independence. (General Council of the First International 1963–68, 3: 197–98)

It is simply disingenuous, then, to suggest, as has been done ad nauseam, that Marx and Engels were principled opponents of nationalism. Thus, an important organizational principle—the right of distinct nationalities to have their own sections—was established for international workers' organizations.

Antiwar Work

As it became increasingly clear in the first half of 1870 that France and Germany would go to war—the Franco-Prussian War from July to September of that year—Marx led the International in an antiwar campaign. This was largely a propaganda effort since he harbored no illusions that the workers' movement, certainly at that stage, could prevent such a war.[12] Antiwar work, in the name of proletarian internationalism, had been one of the activities of the IWMA since its inception. Marx's *Inaugural Address,* until then the organization's most widely distributed document, contributed much to this effort.

Once the war began the GC asked Marx to write a statement on its be-half known later as the *First Address of the General Council of the International Working Men's Association on the Franco-Prussian War*. This address, along with a *Second Address* that was issued in September, constitute Marx's most important foreign policy statements for the International. The first address called attention to the IWMA's record opposing war, the antiwar stances and activities of its affiliates in France and Germany, and the ex-change of fraternal messages between French and German workers. The lat-ter was "unparalleled in the history of the past."

While only a few aspects of the *First Address* were significantly distinct from the positions of other antiwar forces in England, what distinguished the IWMA was the international campaign that Marx led to publicize its stance and to win others to it. In addition to having two thousand copies printed and distributed in English and another thirty thousand in French and German, the GC was successful in having it reprinted in part or in full in newspapers in London and the British provinces, as well as in Geneva, Zurich, Vienna, Augsburg, and New York. A conscious effort was made to get it into the hands of not only opinion makers like Thomas Huxley and John Stuart Mill—the latter was reported to be "highly pleased with the address"—but also to organizations and trade unions that the IWMA may or may not have had ties with. The *Address* even found its way, favorably, into a speech by an American statesman, the very influential reconstruction senator Charles Sumner (General Council of the First International 1963–68, 4: 87).

The war also witnessed, perhaps a first in the history of warfare, coordi-nated antiwar actions on the part of the working populations of the belliger-ent countries. Again, the International, largely under Marx's direction, was responsible for this. The anti-interventionist movement in Britain during the U.S. Civil War, which helped to bring the IWMA into existence, had served, certainly, as an important precedent for such activities.[13]

The *Second Address* accurately anticipated that Bonaparte's defeat would lead to a revolutionary situation in France for which he counseled restraint on the part of its workers. Coupled with similar advice to the French affili-ates of the IWMA, Marx worked feverishly to put pressure on the Gladstone government to recognize the new French republic that emerged in the wake of the defeat and not to give into pressures from the British oligarchy to in-tervene in the conflict on behalf of Bismarck and his king, William I, a rela-tive of Queen Victoria. Although the International was never successful in getting the Gladstone government to recognize the republic, its noninter-vention campaign played no small part in Britain's official neutrality toward

the Franco-Prussian events—a most concrete example of transnational organizational effectiveness (see Khagram, Riker, and Sikkink, this volume).

The Paris Commune

The Marx and Engels team's counsel of revolutionary restraint notwithstanding, on 18 March 1871 the working masses of Paris took the initiative.
More specifically, the National Guard in Paris, a civic militia composed
mainly of workers, revolted against the conservative bourgeois republican
government at Versailles after it had tried to disarm the guard. Ten days later,
following elections that the Central Committee of the National Guard had
called for, a new government, or Commune, was proclaimed for Paris.

In spite of their warnings against premature revolution making, Marx
and Engels quickly threw themselves into the defense of the Commune. One
of the immediate tasks was to counter the slanders in the bourgeois press,
like the *London Times,* which said the war and uprising had provoked a split
between the German and French sections of the International. To this end,
Marx, on behalf of the GC, wrote numerous letters to the editors of newspapers in Germany, France, and England, of which a number were actually
published.

Marx's most important and enduring contribution to the Communards
came in the immediate aftermath of their demise with the publication in
mid-June of *The Civil War in France.* The address that Marx wrote for the
GC, written in the heat of the Commune's final days, was as much a defense
of the Communards as a political analysis. As a GC document it also, like
two of the most important Marx party political statements—the *Manifesto*
and the *Inaugural Address*—had to take into account the political tendencies
within the organization in whose name it was issued. Yet Marx's unswerving
support for the Communards made life increasingly uncomfortable for the
British trade union officials on the GC. Their class collaborationist posture,
looking for approval from the liberal Gladstone government—the origins of
the labor-liberal coalition—soon led to their departure from the body.

Along with key figures in the House of Commons, trade union bodies
in London, Manchester, and Birmingham were sent copies of the *Civil War.*
As Marx told the GC, "[I]t was necessary now to circulate the address as
widely as possible among the working class" (General Council of the First
International 1963–68, 4: 225). Near the top of the handbill for the second
edition was written, "THIS OUGHT TO BE READ BY EVERY BRITISH WORK-
MAN)." The original run of a thousand copies was soon followed by another
two thousand, as well as a German edition that Engels prepared. "It ran

through three editions in two months, sold 8,000 copies in the second edition and was translated into most European languages" (McLellan 1973, 400). No other work by Marx was read so widely and so quickly. Nothing he published in the remaining twelve years of his life surpassed its importance.

Ruling-class attacks—including even one from the pope[14]—on the International in the aftermath of the Commune had an unintended consequence. They did more to publicize the organization and its de facto leader than anything else had until then. For working-class fighters and progressives in whatever corner of the globe who had been inspired by the Parisian insurgents, the calumnious campaign simply raised the International's prestige in their eyes. Requests for affiliation with the International began to pour in from the most far-flung cities in the world. Whether it was workers in Calcutta,[15] New Orleans, San Francisco, Buenos Aires, or Copenhagen, or a group of journalists in Washington, D.C., who "were determined that the International should exert an active influence upon American politics" (General Council of the First International 1963–68, 4: 241), or the great American abolitionist Wendell Phillips, the requests reflected the undeniable fact that at that historical moment the International was viewed by friend and foe alike as the foremost transnational defender of the producing classes. Once it was revealed that Marx was the author of the *Civil War,* he, too, was propelled into the public spotlight in a way he had never been before. The reporters who flocked to his home for interviews were in part responsible for making him, if not a worldwide household name, recognizable, certainly, among the most politically conscious everywhere. The campaign to defend the Communards seems to have been successful, then, at the level of issue attention/agenda setting and discursive change (see Khagram, Riker, and Sikkink, this volume, for details).

The London Conference: Resolution IX

The need for organizational regrouping in the wake of the ruling class offensive against the IWMA resulted in a special leadership meeting in London in September 1871. During its deliberations, Marx and Engels waged a concerted campaign to have the association take an unequivocal position in support of independent working-class political action. The abstentionist line of Bakunin's anarchist wing, Engels argued, however revolutionary it might sound, "would push [workers] into the arms of bourgeois politics" (22: 417–18, and 44: 258–59, respectively). Political action, he continued, was a necessity for workers because it "prepares . . . [and] gives the workers the education for revolution." To avoid the deadly trap of "bourgeois politics," the "workers' party must be constituted not as the tail of some bourgeois party, but as an independent party with its own objective, its own politics." Hence, workers not only had an inherent interest in defending basic democratic rights, but were obligated to do so since their existence gave them the space to further their own class interests. "The political freedoms . . . these are our weapons—should we fold our arms and abstain if they seek to take them away from us" (22: 417–18)?

Against the strong opposition of the Bakuninists, they won a majority of the delegates to this perspective. Authorized to draw up the resolutions agreed to at the conference, Marx and Engels presented to the GC a month later the now famous resolution "IX. Political Action of the Working Class," which incorporated the majority position in the debate. As well as a reaffirmation, the resolution elaborated on the two key tenets in the IWMA's "Inaugural Address" and "Rules": "[A]gainst [the] collective power of the propertied classes the working class cannot act, as a class, except by constituting itself into a political party, distinct from, and opposed to, all old parties formed by the propertied classes . . . indispensable in order to insure the triumph of the social Revolution and its ultimate end—the abolition of classes" (22: 427). A year later a far more representative meeting in The Hague—sixty-four delegates from fifteen countries—effectively the International's last congress, ratified this perspective.

The historic significance of the decisions taken at London and The Hague is that they constitute, as a result of Marx and Engels's interventions, the first explicit international call for what would eventually be Europe's mass working-class political parties. The origin, in other words, of the norm—to employ the language of this volume—that workers in each country should have their own political party, can be traced to these meetings. While much would need to be done to implement the resolutions, they nevertheless gave those forces who were predisposed to move in this direction the authority, i.e., the prestige of the International, to go forth boldly.

Lastly, the victory Marx and Engels won at London provoked the Bakuninists, who had long maneuvered to undermine Marx's leadership, to openly carry out a split operation. In successfully challenging the operation Marx and Engels provided many lessons, which they consciously documented, about democratic functioning and the handling of political differences in the workers' movement—issues that would trip up many a twentieth-century would-be revolutionary.[16] The fight, nevertheless, took its toll on the organization and, combined with the ruling-class attacks, it became clear to Marx and Engels a year after The Hague congress that the first workers' international organization was moribund.

The International's Legacy

With the authorization of The Hague Congress, Marx and Engels immediately codified and publicized its decisions. Their goal, of course, was not only to promote independent, working-class political action, especially in countries where there had been IWMA sections, but also to stymie the class collaborationist and Bakuninist perspectives. Therefore, maintaining the programmatic integrity of The Hague was essential. It was for this reason that Engels in 1889 put on the back burner for about a half year the completion of Marx's two unpublished volumes of *Capital* (Marx had died in 1883).

At the time of Marx's death, the number of workers' parties had increased significantly. Virtually every European country, with the glaring exception of the country with the largest proletariat, Britain, had such a party, though at varying stages of development. Understandably, there was growing agitation to resurrect another international. Although Engels was not convinced that the time was ripe—"such events," he said in 1882, "are already taking shape in Russia where the avant-garde of the revolution will be going into battle . . . and then the moment . . . for . . . the establishment of an *official,* formal International" (46: 198)—he felt compelled to enter the fray in order to defend what had been achieved at The Hague. Rather than launch a new organization he suggested that the various national parties function as a transnational network and focus on specific campaigns. The success of one of these campaigns—internationally coordinated demonstrations for the eight-hour work day on the first of May—played a key role in the establishment of what eventually became the Socialist or Second International, the body that directly nurtured Europe's mass working-class parties.

Engels, especially after Marx's death, spent innumerable hours counseling Marx party members and supporters in Germany, France, Britain, Russia, Austria, Spain, Italy, Belgium, Denmark, Norway, and the United States on how to implement the decisions of The Hague. Filling in for Marx, his was the address that class-conscious workers anywhere in the world wrote to for advice to this end. Even Britain, the last major European country to form a workers' party, benefited, if indirectly, from his activities, specifically, his counsel to Marx's youngest daughter, Eleanor. Her leadership in the labor upsurge that took place in London's East End in the early 1890s played no small role in the formation of what eventually became the Labour Party.[17]

Two years before his death Engels was feted in Zurich at the International Socialist Workers' Congress—the immediate forerunner to the Second International—attended by more than four hundred delegates of socialist organizations and workers' parties from eighteen countries. He accepted the accolades in the name of his deceased partner. "Marx is dead, but were he still alive there would be not one man in Europe or America who could look back with such justified pride over his life's work" (27: 404). For Engels this proved, as he and Marx had argued, that the end of the First International after The Hague was a sign not of weakness, but strength. "The proletariat in the various countries was left to organise itself in its own forms. This happened, and the International is now much stronger than before" (27: 404–5).

In what is still the most authoritative treatment of the IWMA, Henry Collins and Chimen Abromsky write: "Despite its comparatively short life, that organisation changed the history of the world. . . . The International was the first working-class organisation to make a decisive impact on European politics. If it helped actively in shaping and moulding the early labour organisations in Europe, this was largely the achievement of one man—Karl Marx" (1965, v). It was not for want that Engels, at his partner's funeral, said that the "crowning effort" of Marx's activities was "the creation of the International Working Men's Association of which he was the acknowledged leader from 1864 to 1872" (24: 464). Marx's leadership, in other words, both politically and organizationally was indispensable for the International's success. Precisely because of the conclusions he and Engels had reached two decades earlier, that is, owing to the globalization of capital "workingmen have no fatherland" and that proletarian internationalism is labor's only defense in the face of its adversary, Marx had long expected, and was therefore prepared to respond to, the new transnational orientation in the labor movement prompted by the "Age of Capital." Thus, Marx and Engels's political program, that is, the theoretical conclusions they reached as early as 1844; the lessons learned from their baptism of fire in the 1848 upheavals, specifically, the need for independent, working-class political action; the party nucleus or advocacy network that they kept intact during the decade-long lull in the class struggle after 1852; and his daily activism all explain why Marx could be so effective in leading the International.

Marx and Engels's achievements take on even wider significance. In their well-received work on the institutionalization of what Marx and Engels would have termed bourgeois democracy in the advanced capitalist countries of today, Rueschemeyer, Stephens, and Stephens argue that "it was the growth [in the latter half of the nineteenth century] of the working class and its capacity for self-organization that was most critical for the final breakthrough of democracy" (1992, 141). If this is true—the case they make is most convincing—then it must be said that that their legacy is far broader than is usually thought. As I have argued elsewhere (see Nimtz 1999 and

2000), no two individuals contributed more to this breakthrough than Marx and Engels precisely because no two individuals did more to promote the "self-organization" of the working class. With the IWMA as its organizational and political center, the international democratic movement, based on, at Marx's insistence, the "self-organization" of the working class, was successfully revived after the long lull of reaction throughout Europe following the defeat of the 1848–49 revolutions. If ever, then, there were a case to be made for the impact of transnational organizing on public policy—the extension of democracy—it must surely be the example of the IWMA. The democratic movement it helped to consolidate, whose modern roots can be traced to the same two historical seisms that gave rise to the transnational activities of Marx and Engels, the Industrial Revolution and the French Revolution, continues to exercise a powerful influence on humanity into the twenty-first century.

The literature on transnational social movements and networks tends to suggest that these are relatively recent phenomena. The activities of Marx and Engels easily dispel, certainly for labor at least, such notions. The interesting issue is why so little of this history is known today. The answer to that question, unfortunately, cannot be addressed here. Suffice it to say that with the rise and consolidation of Stalinism by the end of the 1920s the continuity between the perspectives and activities of Marx and Engels and the vast majority of revolutionaries who followed in their stead had been broken. The succor that Stalinism gave, wittingly and unwittingly, to cold war proponents both in governments and labor movements everywhere has yet to be fully analyzed. The consequences, nevertheless, were tragically dear for the revolutionary process as a whole and for transnational labor organizing in particular.

Notes

1. Hereafter, citations from the *Collected Works* will be designated by the volume (as 6, for example) and then the page(s).

2. About a month before writing the letter, Marx complained of his difficult personal financial straits and his limited options for getting money. "No doubt there are sundry bourgeois in Cologne who would probably advance me the money for a definite period. But some time ago these people adopted a line that in principle is diametrically opposed to my own, and hence I should not care to be beholden to them in any way" (38: 43). At the personal level, Marx, quite early, therefore, avoided financial arrangements that might be potentially compromising for his politics. A self-financed communist movement was the way to avoid such a problem at the organizational level.

3. See Corcoran 1983, particularly, the Blanquist "Oath of Membership into the Société des Saisons" (34–35).

4. Engels' draft, *Principles of Communism,* written in the catechistic style popular in workers' circles, was in one respect more explicit. To the question, "Will it be possible for this revolution to take place in one country alone?" the answer was an emphatic "[N]o. . . . The communist revolution will . . . be no merely national one. . . . It is a worldwide revolution" (6: 351–52).

5. In Marx and Engels's *Collected Works,* small caps indicate the original was in English.

6. Royden Harrison, in his very useful essay, "British Labour and American Slavery" (1965), argues persuasively that it was rank-and-file proletarian support for the Northern cause that was decisive, since significant elements of the trade union leadership and its newspapers were either sympathetic to the Confederacy or non-supportive of the North.

7. For the record, it might be noted that in 1862 Marx, who, in an effort to "prevent myself and my family from actually being relegated to the streets," tried to get a job as a clerk for the railroad—which might have qualified him for a "manual worker"—but was denied owing to his unintelligible handwriting (41: 435–36).

8. On the details of government harassment and the persecution of IWMA activists and affiliates, see Eichoff's aforementioned report (21: 517–18) and Marx's reports to the Basel and Hague congresses in 1869 and 1872, respectively (21: 68–82 and 23: 219–27).

9. Proudhon's own views on women were notorious as exemplified by his "famous dictum that woman is either housewife or courtesan," as quoted in Hunt 1971 (431).

10. In the aftermath of the Paris Commune and its defense, which exposed the limitations of the British trade union officialdom, Marx and Engels were especially critical of the English trade unions: "The trade unions . . . are an aristocratic minority—the poor workers cannot belong to them. . . . [They] can do nothing by themselves—they will remain a minority—they have no power over the mass of proletarians"(22: 614).

11. On the Reform League's impact, see Smith 1966 (126–33, 229).

12. Two years earlier when the issue was raised at the Brussels congress, he wrote that "the working class is not yet sufficiently organised to throw any decisive weight onto the scales. . . . [The main thing was that the congress] in the name of the working class [loudly declare its opposition to war] . . . and those who instigate war" (43: 94).

13. Possibly another precedent was the antiwar activity of students in France, Germany, and Italy on the eve of the Austro-Prussian War in 1866. Specifically, they issued appeals to each other as well as workers in the belligerent countries to oppose

the war drives of their governments. The GC issued an appeal in solidarity with their effort that was drafted by Paul Lafargue. For details, see Lessner 1907 (36–38) and Marx and Engels (20: 421–25).

14. For details of the pope's opinion of the International, see General Council of the First International 1963–68, 2: 242.

15. Regarding the request from Calcutta, the GC secretary, according to the minutes of 15 August 1871, "was instructed . . . also to urge the necessity of enrolling natives in the Association" (General Council of the First International 1963–68, 2: 258), the GC, thus, making clear that the new affiliate was not to be an exclusively expatriate body.

16. Marx and Engels's 130-page report for the GC, which includes the relevant documents, is still the best account of the fight with Bakunin's operation (see 23: 454–580).

17. See Tsuzuki 1967, chapters 8 and 11, for details on Eleanor's involvement and Engels's assistance and its contribution to the formation of the Independent Labour Party in 1893.

13

Networks in Transnational Labor Organizing

Thalia G. Kidder

In the past twenty years, workers and their allies have developed new forms of transnational labor organizing. In the context of increasing economic globalization, some labor activists have strengthened their contacts with allies across borders to expand and defend labor rights. I have noted three characteristics that appear to distinguish recent organizing from that of prior periods. Many activities have been organized and funded outside of union institutions. Conferences and periodicals often focus on nonfinancial issues and even noncontract issues, such as empowerment, union democracy, or feminist consciousness. The new linkages among labor activists tend to take the form of transnational advocacy networks, although there are also examples of transnational coalitions around certain labor rights issues.

Since transnational labor organizing goes back at least 150 years, the main "emergence" research question is not "Why does transnational organizing exist?" but rather "Why have some of these linkages changed form?" Practitioners also ask how—under what conditions—do these networks emerge and grow? Furthermore, are these new forms of organizing effective in achieving their goals? What are the goals, what are networks doing well, and what are the shortcomings? I aim to connect the theoretical inquiry with the practical and strategic questions being raised by network participants and unions with transnational organizing.

As August Nimtz's chapter demonstrates, workers organizing transnationally is not a new phenomenon. Since the 1920s workers' organizations have formed worldwide confederations, the International Trade Secretariat (ITS) and the International Workers of the World (IWW). In North America, many international unions have memberships in both the United States and Canada. However, since the 1970s many new transnational linkages between workers have been created.

In the 1980s and early 1990s an explosion of conferences, networks, newsletters, actions, and organizing campaigns connected workers across borders. Some of these have been organized through unions, and many by coalitions and groups outside of the union institutions. Some have focused on a particular union, work site, or contract issue, and many have linked work-site issues with issues of community, racism, gender, democracy, human rights, militarism, health, or the environment. The boundaries of transnational labor networks are now blurred, overlapping with other movements and networks.

The case studies in this paper show many common characteristics of the new networks, three of which differentiate "new" transnational labor networks (TLNs) from historical international union activity. First, new TLNs often have conveners that are not connected to unions, or are coalitions that go beyond unions, even though they include many union actors. This research demonstrates that issues are complex and the combined strength of various movements is perceived as necessary or advantageous to address these. Funding mostly comes from sources other than unions, including foundations, churches, and academic institutions.

Second, new TLNs place much emphasis on nonfinancial issues. Many of the early labor activists of the First International discussed by Nimtz also emphasize nonfinancial issues like independent, working-class political action and proletarian internationalism. Likewise, some goals and objectives of current transnational labor organizing may not be related to worker-corporation contract issues at all, but may focus more on individual or local goals. Workers have created spaces to discuss issues from workers' perspectives, rather than focusing on institutional (union) goals. The networks often seek to empower, raise consciousness, or promote changes in norms and policies of union institutions or governments. In this way network participants may be said to have shared beliefs or principles, as compared to a shared strategy or goal (Keck and Sikkink 1995). For this reason, many of the TLNs fit more closely the volume's definition of a transnational network than a coalition or transnational social movement.

Third, new TLNs are intentionally organized in network form, rather than as hierarchical organizations. Together these characteristics are notable in many workers' transnational efforts, though they are not intended to be definitive about all transnational labor organizing.

Why and under what conditions are these "new" transnational labor networks emerging? There are two significant parts to this question: first, why do workers organize transnationally, and second, why in networks? These questions allow several approaches to the study. On the local level, why is it that groups including workers decide to cross borders to meet other workers? How does it happen? On an international level, what are the reasons for creating linkages outside of international union structures? Does it have to do with the unions or the structures or other factors? Lastly, how do the networks work? What is it that they do well, and in what ways are they less effective? Have these forms developed because they do the work at hand "better," or are there incongruities between forms and goals? In sum, although I consider questions of effectiveness, I am mostly concerned with the emergence of TLNs.

To approach these questions, I outline several major campaigns and networks in North American and European transnational labor organizing from the past twenty years. These examples include work done by international trade secretariats and union institutions, which offers comparisons with network organizing. I also explore the histories of three networks of women workers in the United States and Mexico, networking that has been taken up by women workers in the Caribbean basin in recent years. The descriptions cover the international contacts that were first made, the actors involved (including funders), the objectives, the activities, and the problems and obstacles encountered. These case studies provide a perspective from individuals and local groups.

The women's networks seem to highlight certain new organizing approaches and issues. These networks are not unique, nor did the practices and principles necessarily originate in women's networks. Nevertheless, when I compare interviews and materials of these (predominantly) women's networks with those of other transnational labor networks, and with the work of international institutions, there are significant differences. Women's networks emphasize testimonials and exchanges that integrate personal, community, and work-site experiences, rather than discussing the work realm in isolation. These networks are motivated to empower participants, seeking to build long-term solidarity by constructing new collective identities. As a result, organizers focus on a longer time frame for change and thus for evaluating network "success." These examples encourage organizers and policymakers to consider changes in strategy and practice in transnational labor organizing.

Globalization and Labor Rights

Why do workers organize transnationally? And why in networks? This section looks at the theories developed by academic researchers, beginning with transnational organizing. Charles Tilly argues that globalization undermines the power of states to enforce labor rights, and that workers must invent new transnational strategies if they are to protect and expand their rights. In particular, "collective action at an international scale" is needed to reduce the loss of labor rights. Transnational labor networking is one new strategy for international collective action. Tilly is pessimistic, however, about potential international collective action because he sees organized labor everywhere in retreat (1995). I offer a somewhat more optimistic view here, in part by identifying innovative transnational networks that are happening outside or on the edges of labor unions.

The North American Free Trade Agreement and other trade agreements lessen the ability of governments to set or enforce standards within their states. Transnational organizing around labor rights is often a reactive response to this weakening of existing protections that workers have acquired within their states. Increased transnational movement of firms in the Americas and the NAFTA process moved many activists into the international arena. Activists understood that global economic processes constrained governments and meant that solutions could no longer be sought solely at the domestic level (Ayres 1997).

Despite the powerful impetus to organize transnationally to retain or regain labor rights, labor movements have often been less successful than other domestic groups in taking advantage of transnational opportunity structures. For example, well-organized European labor movements have been less effective in operating at the European level than other social movements have been (Imig and Tarrow 1999). Another author argues that on a global scale, transnational labor organizing has not kept pace with other forms of international organizing (Boswell and Stevis 1997). There are many barriers to effective transnational labor organizing.

On the other hand, transnational corporations and trade agreements are not always disadvantageous to unions. They can bring workers into closer contact and present new arenas for transnational labor organizing, if leaders take advantage of these opportunities (Jane 1998). Strong domestic organizing, together with high levels of international support, appear to be effective in getting labor's demands met, as the following case studies affirm. Heather Williams's study of organizing on the U.S.-Mexican border found that "campaigns that involved moderate to high levels of trans-border cooperation are the most likely to achieve positive results" and that "institutional forms (such as stockholder resolutions) were most effective when coupled with direct pressure" (1997, 19–20). One of the most successful campaigns discussed here—the campaign of Coca-Cola workers in Guatemala—involved just this sort of tenacious domestic organizing with far-flung international pressures, both institutional and in the form of boycotts.

Second, why do some workers organize networks? In academic research, labor organizations have been studied as both political networks/social movements and as economic organizations seeking to maximize total (or average) material returns to participants. Economic organization theory helps us clarify differences between union institutions and labor networks. Walter Powell discusses networks in economic organization and distinguishes them from markets and hierarchical firms. He characterizes networks as forms of exchange where actors "possess qualities that are not easily measured, and the relations are long-term and recurrent," where "entangling of obligation and reputation" makes actions of parties interdependent, "but there is no common ownership or legal framework" (1990, 301).

Powell proposes that each organizational form has its strengths. "Markets offer choice, flexibility and opportunity," he says, but the price mechanism oversimplifies information and "markets are a poor device for learning and the transfer of technological know-how" (298). Hierarchies are appropriate for mass production and distribution, for reliability of producing uniform units and quality in high-speed situations. Administrative rules and authority are efficient in these situations. In the context of union organizing, one could argue that if the "product" offered is a fairly uniform contract and/or mass political mobilization for elections, then large hierarchical organizations have been most appropriate. Yet networks would be more appropriate for distributing complex, idiosyncratic information, strategies, and know-how, which flow (too) slowly through hierarchies and for which there is no market.

Powell describes networks as flexible and "lighter on their feet." Actors are dependent on intangible resources held by other parties, and therefore assume mutual gains, "forgo[ing] the right to pursue their own interests at the expense of others" (303). Reciprocity, interdependence, and indebtedness tie parties to the network over the long term and create incentives for learning and innovation. Networks not only disseminate but interpret information rapidly. Network forms of organization would seem consistent with Rosenau's description of recent "turbulence" in the international realm, and with the more complex, diverse information needed in issue campaigns beyond the work site and national borders.

Examples of Transnational Labor Organizing in Europe and the Americas

Transnationals Information Exchange (TIE)

The Transnationals Information Exchange was founded in 1978 by labor researchers and organizations working in solidarity with revolutionary movements in Third World countries. In the quarterly *TIE Bulletin* of September

1983, TIE proposed to be an international forum for those concerned with the growth of transnational corporate power and to promote the "development of internationalist strategies in the labour movement." The objectives were to strengthen "contacts between workers" and to discuss issues from the perspective of workers' own experiences. TIE Europe's bulletin reported that conferences "certainly had a primary concern with short-term issues—closures, redundancies, wages etc.," yet looked for "democratization within the labor movement" and a "clearer future vision . . . an alternative to the degradations and injustices of market forces."

The TIE focused on worker empowerment. Workers needed new networks to integrate information and views of other movements in order to grapple with complex problems. An "alternative view" included "a move away from fighting on terms dictated by the management . . . to extend the scope of collective bargaining . . . to include the aspirations and interests of other social groups, not just those working in the industry . . . broad coalitions are required." In TIE meetings, issues were raised about biotechnology and World Bank programs in connection with the cocoa workers' issues, about the wisdom of world transportation systems so heavily dependent on cars, and about women's family and work dilemmas as well as pay discrimination.[1]

Snow, Rochford, Worden, and Benford's concept of "frame alignment processes" is helpful in understanding the activities of the TIE. The authors argue that participation does not simply occur as the result of the existence of a problem or grievance, nor do individuals participate at a uniform level after making a single rational decision (e.g., to join). Rather participation arises and fluctuates from changing interpretations of problems (Snow et al. 1986, 464). The authors identify four frame alignment processes, including "frame bridging" and "extension" between groups and their issues, and "frame amplification" to include new issues and interests. Most relevant to these cases is the concept of "frame transformation." Frame transformation means changing meanings and understandings of specific issues or one's worldview (465). As confirmed by the cases in this research, organizations may need to "adjust frames" when under attack, when in coalitions, or to reverse declining participation.

In TIE a primary motivation for workers networking was globalized production, so after 1986 TIE moved to focus on the production chain and the production process in each sector. As a staff memo noted, it was a "very attractive and useful approach for unionists to understand themselves in a world chain. [It] brought local work into international context." In 1986, the network publication, *GM Voice*, states,

We demystify false management claims about workers' performance in other countries. In all these [strike support] cases, the existence of personal contacts was essential. . . . It is only in GM's interest to keep the idea alive that there is just a *technical* and *economic* relation between its workers in different countries. And it is this notion which has to be replaced by another one which recognises the *social* relationships between *colleagues* (and not competitors, as GM would like us to believe).

In this passage, the "frame transformation" for workers is clear, as is the significance of having a common employer.

In the early 1980s TIE held one to two conferences a year, first with autoworkers and communications workers and later with workers in agribusiness and agricultural chemicals. Common employers linked workers across borders and networks were set up by company. By the late 1980s TIE was holding more than a half dozen major conferences annually, including ones on the links between "cocoa and chocolate" production, and rubber and tire workers.[2]

The participants in the TIE network were also unusual, as were the sponsors. As compared to the union officials commonly selected to go to international labor meetings, TIE's conference participants were often activist rank-and-file members, local union leaders as well as workers outside of unions, labor researchers, and representatives of religious and environmental organizations. In meetings of the International Trade Secretariat or the World Congress of the International Confederation of Free Trade Unions (ICFTU), participants have been almost exclusively officials from affiliate unions. U.S. union representatives to the conferences have often promoted mostly a conservative agenda. Recently, some U.S. international unions, including the Amalgamated Clothing and Textile Workers Union (ACTWU), have begun to "send more progressive people to the typical international meetings" and thus to work to challenge "historical suspicions about what we're looking to do."[3]

Networks like TIE were formed because of workers' desire to be involved, and also because funding was available. Transnational organizing is expensive, so access to funds and external organizations was an important condition. The sponsors of TIE's work included the World Council of Churches, elected officials, and academics, as well as union organizations. The Council of Churches had existing transnational operations on which to build the new network as well as money. TIE was initially based in Europe, though after 1990 regional offices were established in the United States, Brazil, Malaysia, and Russia. Lists of resources and periodicals in the TIE quarterly bulletin demonstrate the extent of transnational networks around labor in the early 1980s, especially those outside of institutional union structures.[4]

TIE's work had its problems and conflicts. Initially, participants recognized two in particular: researchers dominated the network and they needed independent funding. Later debates were focused on the lack of adequate follow-up, "too many countries" being involved in conferences, and the diverging issues faced by the First and Third World participants. TIE began to organize conferences regionally, and to create "South-South" conferences, where Third World workers could focus on common issues. In effect, this network was not immune to some of the "asymmetries" of power and participation that it attempted to overcome. Funding and follow-up problems, and First World–Third World or professional–workers dynamics are recurrent themes in several descriptions below.

Guatemalan Coca-Cola Workers Organize

The Guatemala City workers of Coca-Cola began their struggle for recognition of their union, STEGAC, in the late 1970s under the repressive conditions of a military dictatorship. The workers' organizing efforts faced violence from the military and thugs hired by the company, as well as opposition by corrupt company unions. When death threats forced a key union leader and STEGAC's lawyers into exile, the campaign found international support. This is a good example of how repression can serve as a "push factor" in the formation of transnational networks. In Costa Rica these Guatemalan labor activists met with churches, human rights groups, and trade unions (Gatehouse and Reyes 1987, 13). By 1976, these connections involved the Interfaith Center on Corporate Responsibility (ICCR), a central U.S. actor in corporate responsibility campaigns. In 1977 ICCR organized churches and religious orders owning shares in Coca-Cola to use a shareholder resolution to force an investigation of the Guatemalan situation by the Coca-Cola Atlanta headquarters. An ICCR delegation went to Guatemala City in 1978 to meet with the franchise owner and STEGAC and pressured Coca-Cola for a "code of conduct for labor relations" in contracts for franchisees (14–15). The ICCR was a "network convener" outside unions and made connections with other social movements. ICCR's work was also based on principles—corporate responsibility—more than on direct self-interest.

A second major transitional actor in the Coca-Cola campaign was the International Trade Secretariat (ITS) representing food-sector workers, the International Union of Food, Agricultural, Hotel, Restaurant, Catering, Tobacco, and Allied Workers' Association (IUF). The IUF general secretary,

Dan Gallin, first went to Guatemala as a member of Amnesty International's first fact-finding mission to Guatemala in August 1979. Afterward, Dan Gallin called for all ITSs to support a boycott of tourism to Guatemala, which led to the cancellation of German tours. Coca-Cola argued that the Guatemalan operation was an independent franchise that leased its recipe and trademark, but said that Coke did not have control over its labor practices. The IUF claimed that Coca-Cola should take responsibility for actions of independent bottlers and began plans for an international boycott of Coke (Gatehouse and Reyes 1987, 17). Leaders in exile, IUF secretary Gallin, and ICCR appear centrally in the creation of the network. Some parts of the network worked together on the international boycott of Coke and a tourist boycott of Guatemala, coordinating shared tactics. In this sense, this network converted into a coalition.

In 1980 many solidarity actions in support of the Coca-Cola campaign were carried out all over the globe.[5] The ability of large international unions to mobilize large numbers of people and resources was important in the campaign. I question whether a network alone could have accomplished such extensive mobilization so rapidly. In the words of Dan Gallin, "the measurable economic effect of these actions was very small, [yet] in almost every case they led to wide discussion of events in Guatemala . . . and image problems for Coke" (Gatehouse and Reyes 1987, 19). By July, tripartite negotiations were being held between Coca-Cola Atlanta and the IUF. In brief, they negotiated a new ownership for the bottling plant, including a Mexican manager and capital from Coca-Cola Atlanta.

After the March 1982 military coup by Ríos-Montt, repression and genocide escalated in Guatemala; another coup in August 1983 brought especially heavy repression against trade unions. The STEGAC Coke workers seemed relatively immune, apparently protected by their international support. By February 1985 a new owner took over the bottling plant; of 460 original workers, more than 300 were reemployed, and $250,000 was distributed in back pay to laid-off workers.

The strength of the local campaign was fundamental to its successes. Gatehouse and Reyes report on "the extraordinary discipline of STEGAC's members and its leadership . . . the permanent presence of the STEGAC executive committee [in the plant occupation], and the daily routine of maintenance, assemblies, education and leisure activity." In addition, they say that with many international delegations, "the leaders did not take the floor, but let the rank and file speak for themselves." An update on the union in 1987 reported continued rank-and-file strength, bolstered by "chorus groups, union education classes and English courses" (Gatehouse and Reyes 1987,

34–36). STEGAC's work stands out in two ways: first, members represented themselves in transnational settings and were empowered to participate. Second, the union's organizing addressed non–work site issues and needs.

The transnational campaign with the Guatemalan workers of Coca-Cola raises important questions. Why did a large campaign form around this issue, rather than around other cases of flagrant violations of workers' rights? Also, the Coca-Cola campaign coalition appears to be a mix of an international trade secretariat's organizing and a TLN as defined here—could the "mix" be a factor in the campaign's effectiveness? I propose two reasons that the struggle gained international prominence. First, the product—Coke—is so universal that organizers could make a direct connection between the workers' struggle and most people's daily lives. In addition, there are Coca-Cola workers in most countries, with a symbolic "common employer." Second, the campaign changed perceptions of who is responsible for labor rights violations. For example, the campaign successfully established an international debate around the idea that a parent company has responsibility for the actions of its subsidiaries, in this case the bottlers contracting to use Coca-Cola's trademark and syrup. In addition, the campaign held the Guatemalan government, and by extension, the foreign governments donating aid to Guatemala responsible for (not stopping) the human rights abuses of the bottling company against its workers. These claims, skillfully used by organizers, meant that more and more parties internationally perceived themselves as having self-interest in the results of a work-site struggle in a foreign country. This was true on both sides: transnational corporations pressured Coca-Cola not to agree to the above claims, which might become unfavorable precedents. An article in *Business Week* criticized Coca-Cola Atlanta: "A cardinal rule of labor relations for multi-national corporations has always been to prevent unions from gaining enough power to negotiate on a multinational basis" (Gatehouse and Reyes 1987, 21). To return to theory, network organizers won a series of "frame transformation" battles.

Organizing against NAFTA and GATT: A New Role for Farmers

Farmers' groups spearheaded anti-GATT organizing in the 1980s and were active in efforts around NAFTA, movements that involved many organizations, unions, and workers' associations. Mark Ritchie of the Institute for Agriculture and Trade Policy (IATP) says coalition building began at the local level and then expanded to the national and international levels. First organizations grew by defending family farms in Minnesota and in Canada, and black and white farmers organized together in the southeastern United

States. A summit on the family farm crisis was organized in the Canadian Parliament building, with participants from fifty countries.[6] In December 1990, thirty thousand farmers and others demonstrated at the GATT negotiations in Brussels, including farmers from North America, Japan, Korea, Africa, and Latin America (Brecher and Costello 1991). IATP was one "convener." IATP had external resources and helped support farmers who wanted to make international connections. In addition, some farmers' networking was built on contacts previously made by people working on other issues, specifically the solidarity movements with Central America in the United States and Canada and the environmental movement. "Crossboundary organizing—not necessarily borders—is a fuel for our movements," says Ritchie. "If we have respect for each other we can build a movement out of all of our common interests."

The early 1990s was a time of tremendous growth in North American transnational labor networks. The NAFTA debates built participation in existing cross-border organizations and spawned new ones. For labor activists, working on NAFTA meant encouraging others to mobilize around a "noncontract" issue. The campaign needed knowledge from various social sectors and required leaders to reinterpret this information to make it locally relevant for various groups. Unions joined with other organizations in coalition. A 1992 directory of organizations in Canada, Mexico, and the United States entitled *Cross-Border Links* identified twelve networks for "Fair Trade."[7]

Why did farmers cross borders and work transnationally? Farmers were able to connect macro-level policies to common issues in communities in many countries. Ritchie believes there are "still lots of problems that still need solving at home," however with GATT "we had to work together." The "corporations were running to an international level to gut the power of national laws," he says, and farmers had to work internationally "to make possible the world you want here at home."

It has often been debated whether organized farmers are a union, an interest group, or a sector of society. As in the other two cases, international meetings were important for individual farmers to redefine their understanding of themselves as workers with a collective demand of corporate "employers." In their new worldview they recognized, first, that agricultural inputs, production, and food-processing industries are monopolized by a few giant transnational corporations. Since the farmers' means of production, sale prices, and product distribution are often controlled by one company, farmers become little different than workers, even if they still own their land.

Union and fair trade periodicals were filled with news about trinational conferences and tours by maquiladora workers from the U.S.-Mexico border, and by teachers, telecommunications workers, autoworkers, and electronics workers. Annual national union conventions invariably invited international labor representatives to speak, institutionalizing transnationalism in union rhetoric and activities.

NAFTA was passed by national governments, with a surprisingly vigorous debate in the U.S. Congress. In this instance, the TLN was not effective in either mobilizing sufficient participation or in transforming the dominant discourse to reflect the claims and ideas of the TLN. Labor and environmental activists opposed to NAFTA did contribute to the government's decision to adopt two side agreements to NAFTA, one on the environment, and one on labor (The North American Agreement of Labor Cooperation), but these agreements are considered relatively weak. Activists evaluating the campaign point out that by focusing on Congress, fewer grassroots groups participated and nonlegislative issues important to many participants were ignored. Second, anti-NAFTA activists promoted different, even contradictory arguments—the "framing" of the issue was not consistent. Some unions spoke of protectionism and national sovereignty; others used a discourse of transnationalism and the collective identity of workers.

What is significant about the three cases of transnational labor organizing discussed above: the TIE, the Coca-Cola workers, and the farmers organizing against NAFTA and GATT? The cases demonstrate the importance of the experience of collective action for reinterpreting situations defined as unjust into a series of demands. Activists and members need also to develop the expectation that collective action can help meet those demands. Klandermans holds that "episodes of collective action" are crucial for the construction of these expectations. Through collective action, participants with certain socialized collective identities may have "their view of the world change[d] dramatically. They acquire new collective identities as participants in collective action" (1992, 93).

Individuals who start out believing they have the most in common with people from their country or with employees of a certain company may construct new expectations about common interests when they have the opportunity to meet and work with foreigners or other unions' members.

This suggests that protest mobilization is encouraged both by the creation and promotion of new ideas or worldviews and by *participation in episodes of collective action.* I propose that transnational meetings change participants' expectations about collective action, about the behavior of other, previously unknown, individuals, and about the effectiveness of one's own contribution. Furthermore, the meetings form these expectations more readily than written texts or statistical portrayals of injustices.

Case Studies: Women Workers' Transnational Networking in North America

My initial interest in the transnational networks of women workers was to understand why women workers organize transnationally and why the organizational form is networks. Later, I began to focus on the objectives of women's networks and their effectiveness. Through personal interviews and with a local perspective, I have been able to understand in more depth the mechanisms of change in individuals and organizations and how identities and worldviews are transformed. In fact, these networks' stated objectives tend to emphasize personal and group frame transformation—empowerment—rather than specific contract, legal, or legislative victories. These networks focus on a longer time frame for change and for evaluating their work.[8]

Some activists affirm that a motivation for these networks was to integrate information from social movements and unions. Others perceived the union response to workers' concerns as inadequate, thus the networks were an effort to amplify claims by transnational work directed at the state or existing unions. A salient aspect of these networks is that organizers use "exchanges of experiences" or "testimonials" as the mechanism to motivate participation and to empower. This contrasts with other NAFTA organizing, which has used more statistics, comparisons of laws or contract language, and projections of jobs or funding gained or lost as a means of motivating participation.

Mujer a Mujer—Woman to Woman

Mujer a Mujer, which began in the mid-1980s, describes itself as "a volunteer group of U.S. women in Mexico and Texas working to link key processes of women's organizing on both sides of the border." Mujer a Mujer organized "exchanges of experiences" with Mexican and North American women, facilitated coalition building between women's groups, and arranged tours of representatives for Mexican women's organizations visiting the United States and Canada. Through 1993 Mujer a Mujer published *Correspondencia,* a bilingual quarterly newsletter reporting on developments in women's organizing.

Informally organized exchanges motivated formation of the volunteer collective.[9] In 1984 one of the founders, Elaine Burns, invited women from the Mexican urban popular movement CONAMUP to meet with the urban women's organization in Little Rock, Arkansas, where she worked. CONAMUP women then invited U.S. women for a return tour to their conference in Mexico. A general women's exchange followed in 1985, involving women from many states organizing labor and community groups, fighting domestic violence, and providing women's health services. The volunteer collective of U.S. women formed soon after. Mujer a Mujer's history confirms a pattern in these networks that middle-class women establish the first transnational contacts.

Mujer a Mujer's union-sector networking intensified over the next years, especially with the independent "September Nineteenth" garment workers' union.[10] In 1987, Mujer a Mujer helped arrange for travel and translation for women workers of September Nineteenth to participate in the Labor Notes conference in Detroit. In 1988, *Correspondencia* (summer/fall) reported that workers had toured Texas and California and had gone to conferences in the Philippines and Austria. The September Nineteenth union hosted a delegation of U.S. rank-and-file union women who stayed in the Mexican women's houses and held a press conference to support September Nineteenth in their struggle with the U.S-based Roberts company. In November 1989 Mujer a Mujer organized the "First International Union Women's Exchange of Experiences" in Mexico City, with fifty participants from Guatemala, Korea, Mexico, the border, and the United States, including ILGWU textile workers from Los Angeles and Asian clothing workers from San Francisco organized by the Asian Women Workers Association (AIWA).

Responding to concerns about economic integration, in 1990 Mujer a Mujer began ongoing long-term "Global Strategies Schools" with Mexican women union leaders. In February 1992 Mujer a Mujer helped organized the Tri-national Conference of Women Workers on Continental Integration (Sinclair 1992, 165). Mujer a Mujer was involved in the Regional Workshops of Women Maquila Workers held in December 1992 and July 1993.

Mujer a Mujer's organizing had five objectives, as expressed in interviews and the *Correspondencia* newsletters: (1) activists aimed to make "connections" between women's projects and between Mexicanas and Latinas in order to break down the barriers of national borders; (2) they worked to create transnational solidarity for women's organizing; (3) they provided material support for Mexican women's organizing; (4) they developed women's organizing skills and their long-term vision; and (5) they supported union democratization and the empowerment of women.

Mujer a Mujer has encountered many obstacles as an organization, and as a facilitator of women workers' networking. Issues of First World–Third World relations were especially difficult. As Mary McGinn recalls, "In 1989–90 we decided we needed to stop being a gringa organization—to include Mexican/Chicana women in our connecting work and in the collective." This meant raising money to pay staff, rather than relying on U.S. women volunteering in Mujer a Mujer while earning dollars in translating and reporting jobs. The first Chicana woman to join had criticisms of the work patterns and expectations of the U.S. women, which seemed exclusive. Racial prejudices caused conflicts in a union women's exchange. A Mexican woman's stereotype of U.S. company owners was "they're all Jews," which provoked Jewish participants from Chicago to want to educate the Mexican women about the history of Jewish women organizing in the garment industry. Some Chicana women in the United States expressed reluctance to meet with Mexican women who might laugh at their Spanish.

Funding and resources to maintain networks were a perennial problem, a dilemma that seems to be heightened by the looser network form of organization. McGinn and Smith evaluated their work:

> We had no good system of follow-up with the people we met [on tours]. Only *Correspondencia*—and that wasn't the union connection. It was painful just to get letters in English and Spanish and make copies . . . or to get a thank you letter out. [Before e-mail] we had to go by bus to Laredo to make phone calls and send mailings. . . . There had been complaints about our U.S. tours. Because of self-funding we had to set up academic conferences to get honoraria and too little time was left to meet with other union women.

Nevertheless, there were many successes. The September Nineteenth union won their case against the U.S. company after the international meeting, although the decision wasn't attributed to international pressure. Tours usually netted one to two thousand for the September Nineteenth union and office machines and funds were donated.

Most important, women found new understandings and support for their visions, an objective that these networks appear to meet consistently. *Correspondencia* (June 1989) stated that September Nineteenth leaders felt "strongly connected with ACTWU and ILGWU members, with common interests in organizing and commitment to unionism free from hierarchical control" Leaders reported that they discussed "how to overcome the personal and power boss-worker relationship" and "sexual harassment and family control that limits women's participation." Mexican women supported U.S. women's struggles against unions not hiring Asian/Latino organizers, and resistance to organizing the undocumented, both of which are unusual and significant examples of solidarity from South to North.

Tennessee Industrial Renewal Network (TIRN)

In June 1989 a conference was organized on deindustrialization in Tennessee. The organizers were the Highlander Center, ACTWU, and others with funding from a Ford Foundation grant. The conference participants later established TIRN after the first connections were made between grassroots women workers' groups and unions involved in transnational work.[11] In Morristown, Tennessee, a small industrial center, the General Electric plant had laid off hundreds of workers after a failed union campaign in 1988; the subassembly part of the plant had gone to Nogales, Mexico. When workers with ten years seniority found themselves in lines at temporary agencies, they formed an organization called Citizens Against Temporary Services, or CATS. They marched through town, contacted legislators, and, after a local newspaper report, were invited to the first TIRN conference.[12]

Also at the conference was Norm Harper from the UAW in Buffalo, New York. Harper showed slides of the Matamoros windshield-wiper plant he had visited after the Buffalo plant where he worked closed. Women of the Morristown CATS group also watched the movie *Global Assembly Line* in one workshop. TIRN included committees on plant closings, contingent work, and alternative forms of ownership.

The new understandings gained from these various sources of information motivated women to participate. Fran Ansley, a founder of TIRN, described TIRN meetings with workers:

> With them and other people—providing information was support. You were providing information to people whose lives had been turned upside down. People felt it was their own fault somehow, and it was disorienting. And in that situation, when women find out there's a pattern going on . . . it's a huge resource that we're bringing in. We could attract people to us because we had this thing we could give them which was this feeling that they might be able to get a grasp on what was happening.

Susan Williams, also a founder of TIRN, said the meetings gave workers a chance to share their experiences:

> For people who have worked in factories and been treated like they don't have brains, the experience of talking to other people, and realizing what they know is important and they can share it with others—people *like* that. We didn't know what to do, so we all learned together. . . . We bring people together with the idea that there's something we can do.

Information made sense of local events by changing parts of people's worldview, which is consistent with theories about "frame transformation." The plant closing committee developed a manual about closings and worked on issues of state retraining programs.

The first cross-border connections were made by Fran Ansley at a National Lawyers Guild conference. The Guild's Toxics Committee had invited

Ed Krueger of the American Friends Service Committee's (AFSC) border project to talk about pollution in the maquiladoras. Ansley negotiated with Krueger to bring a delegation to the border. She was motivated to organize the delegation because of her understanding of the tranformative experiences of the Highlander Center in the early civil rights movement. The Highlander Center had been a rare racially integrated living space. Ansley recalled,

> As someone said, [it was a] place where you could watch people changing in front of your eyes. . . . So I thought if you could bring people to the border there would be that kind of experiential change—that you wouldn't be able to figure out what it was—but something profound would happen.

There was resistance to the idea of spending time and money on a trip to the border. Susan Williams remembered, "I thought: why would we do that—unless it was long term? Because I have questions about international work when you just *go* . . . and then what happens?" In February 1991 TIRN brought two maquiladora organizers to Tennessee on tour, in part so that the nine Tennessee delegation members could talk to Mexicans before their trip in July 1991. Funding came from a grant for the Fund for Labor Relations Studies, ACTWU, and the Peace Development Fund.

On the border TIRN met with the Coalition for Justice in the Maquiladoras, the AFSC, and the Comité Fronterizo de Obreras (Border Committee of Women Workers). Back in Tennessee, TIRN and ACTWU used a slide show of the trip for education about deindustrialization, the maquiladoras, and eventually NAFTA. TIRN raised five hundred dollars toward a vehicle for the maquila organizers. Staff and leaders of TIRN went to transnational network meetings in Philadelphia (AFSC) and Matamoros (Mexico-U.S. Diálogos).

There were problems following up with people contacted on the border. "The woman who had been our primary contact left," recalled Ansley. "Language has been a huge problem because we've not had consistently a fluent Spanish speaker." In addition, she said, "It was hard to raise money, and the border organizations didn't have the infrastructure for what we wanted to do—we had unrealistic expectations." Williams added that "tensions arose in planning meetings—whether it should just be NGO types or not." While many human rights groups were there, she said, "there were people right in the community who hadn't been invited."

Network participants continued to debate the merits of transnational and local organizing. As Susan Williams commented,

There were some reactions like "there are plenty of poor people here at home." A few people on the trip, nervous about the direction and the politics of TIRN, tended to fall back on the "children, the little children," as if we felt "sorry for these little people." But most people came from a different point of view.

In favor of transnational exchanges, Shirley Reinhardt described in her testimony to the 1991 NAFTA consultation hearings in Atlanta, "the change in my attitude . . . and things I have learned" from networking and from her experiences. Since being laid off she no longer looked down on her neighbors on food stamps. She remembered the colonias of Mexico:

> To me [the colonias were] living proof that corporations have no bottom line of their own . . . [they] were willing to treat workers and communities as expendable . . . it is hurting not only Mexicans, it is a direct threat to the standard of living of American workers. I blame corporations. I blame the government too. . . . Any trade deal we reach with Mexico should start with a commitment to a healthy development pattern for both countries.

TIRN was involved in the Fair Trade Campaign, and in 1993 hosted a Tennessee tour of Victor Quiroga from the Frente Autonomo de Trabajadores (FAT) and Hassan Yusef from Canada. In 1993 funding came in from the Kellogg Foundation for a second trip to the border, organized in August 1994. This time participants were selected whose employers had plants in Juarez and El Paso. The delegation spent time with farm workers, La Mujer Obrera (a women workers' center in El Paso), and the Border Rights Coalition, which works on immigration issues.

Susan Williams evaluated the trip:

> (Again) we were a novelty because we were workers. People were excited about us. Most of the groups [visiting the border] were religious groups, Congress people. What we accomplished remains to be seen when we come back. That's how I think you judge this work.

TIRN is an example of local coalition organizing leading to cross-border networking. Activists interviewed also emphasized the importance of "episodes of collective action" to motivate people to participate and to change their views of themselves, others, and institutions (frame transformation). Funding was more available through connections with the foundation community, and middle-class transnational contacts were important in initiating the network. The network gathered information, and interpreted and used it strategically to mobilize and empower workers.

Factor X (Tijuana, Baja California)

Factor X is a Mexican organization of feminist women who have been work-ing with women maquila workers since 1990.[13] The group includes many women who have worked on women's health issues, human rights and immi-gration, racism, and union organizing. Factor X began working in the colo-nias as part of a commitment to working on health and education with poor women. Involvement in the networks of maquila organizing was a logical next step, as most women in the colonias work in the maquilas and reproduc-tive health issues often stem from the workplace. Contacts were made inside the factories through a friend working on literacy education. Unions exist in Tijuana factories, but many are known for company collaboration, secret meetings, and nonresponsiveness to workers' concerns on noncontract issues.

The first cross-border connections of Factor X were to get political sup-port from the U.S. women's health network—WomanCare—around police repression of an abortion clinic in Mexico City. Factor X followed up with letters to U.S. women's health clinics, especially looking to connect with Chicana/Latina women working in them. The primary motivation for trans-national connections was information, and it was only later that financial support became an issue and a goal. Eventually Factor X received funds from a women's church group that came on tour to the border. In addition, the American Friends Service Committee facilitated a one-day tour of four hundred autoworkers attending a convention in San Diego, where an im-promptu collection raised $1,200 to fund organizing activities.[14]

Factor X women, including maquila workers, attended the Jane Addams Conference in Chicago in November 1992, where they learned about Hull House work with women workers in the last century. They connected with Mujeres Latinas en Accion, who also have a "house" and work with women workers. I note that "women workers' houses," a model of organizing exist-ing in both North and Latin America, pay attention to work site, communi-ty, and personal realms of life, promoting economic, political, and cultural claims. "Women workers' houses" is a significantly different approach from institutional union organizing models. The "houses" strategy appears to be more effective in mobilizing participation. In "houses," collective action is promoted on many fronts, aiming to change personal and group views and expectations by integrating exchanges of experiences on all levels.

Factor X has conducted workshops on "women's identity" and on the connections between feminism and community work. Factor X was in-volved in the Regional Workshops of Women Maquila Workers, held in July 1993 and in March 1994. Through popular education, women mapped their work sites for health hazards and discussed the reproductive health problems experienced by many maquila workers. Factor X has been a member of the "Border Commission" (Comision Fronteriza), a network including community, labor, and other organizations.

In 1993 Factor X became involved with two solidarity campaigns for maquila workers: first, for workers laid off after rains and flooding closed factories and demolished homes, and second, for workers of Plasticos Baja California organizing an independent union. Factor X worked with a Solidarity Committee in San Diego, also part of the Border Commission. Carmen Valadez considered the solidarity effort mostly one-way: the San Diego group raised money through mailings in the United States and deposited funds into a bank account from which Plasticos Baja California organizers were paid. The San Diego group conducted a media campaign leading to articles in major national newspapers. Lack of communication and First World–Third World dynamics exacerbated problems with the unidirectional efforts. According to Mexican members, the San Diego activists controlled text for fundraising letters and information on finances. As Valadez recalled:

> As [the San Diego members] brought the money, they felt that we in Mexico should discuss with them how we were going to organize ourselves, and do the campaign. We said, "No, the workers already have their vision and plan, and that's that!" It wasn't their money, other unionists had donated it—through them—to us. . . . We also didn't like how they described the work in the fundraising letter—a paternalistic, rather than a solidarity vision . . . but they didn't change it.[15]

San Diego activists had criticisms of the Mexicans' organizing, and eventually the network dissolved. The Baja California organizing drive was lost after intimidation by company and company union observers at the not-secret balloting. The gains from the campaign were primarily the consciousness raising of the workers and of the U.S. public through the extensive coverage in the press. In addition, as Valadez affirmed, "the workers weren't fired, and the leaders [who had been fired] were paid back wages." As with the Coca-Cola workers in Guatemala, transnational activity appears to have provided immunity to the "normal repression" experienced by other area workers whose struggle had not been part of a transnational network.

Caribbean Workers' Organizing and the Central American Network of Women in Solidarity with the Maquila Workers[16]

Organizing in assembly-for-export plants in the Caribbean and Central America was strong by the early 1980s, a dozen years after the first Free Trade

Zones (FTZ) were established. In the 1990s, however, these "maquiladora" plants expanded rapidly, totaling an estimated 400,000 workers (65 percent women) and the organizing of women workers paralleled this growth.[17] Campaigns integrated work by nongovernmental organizations, women's community groups, labor organizations, international donor agencies, and solidarity groups in the global North, working on a range of community, health, antiviolence, and work-site issues.

Pioneering campaigns were conducted in the Dominican Republic, including such diverse actors as the Coordinator of Cibao Women (CMC) in 1981, Las Zoneras Working Women Team, The Center for Research for Feminine Action (CIPAF) in 1980, the United Workers Confederation (CTU) in 1991 and Fenatrazona (union federation). Nationally, the organizations worked to change public opinion, challenging uncritical valuations of FTZ plants in the national economy. In 1996 these organizations initiated the "Employment, Yes, but with Dignity" campaign. Internationally, the campaign targeted multinational companies with a "code of conduct," in coordination with the Clean Clothes campaign in Europe, funding agencies such as Oxfam Great Britain and workers' organizations in Bangladesh. In the global North, campaign publicity and volunteer speakers worked to change consumers' choices about clothing purchases ("Was your sweatshirt made in a sweatshop?"). Achievements included a 1998 announcement by the Dominican Republic Association of Free Zone Enterprises of improvements in working conditions, including day-care facilities and health-care units, gains that would be uncommon in union-company negotiations. The Levi Strauss company asked Oxfam GB and CIPAF to help broker agreements on working conditions with subcontractors in the Dominican Republic and other countries.[18]

In the mid-1990s exchanges were held between Caribbean and Central American women workers' organizations, often funded by European and North American development agencies. These meetings and workshops often recognized the limitations of the male-dominated traditional unions in addressing "new" issues of women workers in the maquilas. In particular, women workers often faced sexual harassment, demands by employers to prove sterility, and the dismissal of pregnant women. These regional connections were based on strong local organizing and have been institutionalized in the Central American Network of Women in Solidarity with the Maquila Workers.

For example, in Honduras, the Collective of Honduran Women (CODEMUH), initiated in 1990 by professional women in conjunction with maquila workers in Tegucigalpa and Choloma, achieved significant results over the decade. Similar to organizations of Mexican women, CODEMUH's objectives integrated personal, community, and work-site concerns: women's rights and an end to violence against women, self-esteem, community organization, and workers' rights and working conditions. In Nicaragua, the women's movement María Elena Cuadra (MEC) has worked since 1990 on women workers' issues in the maquila, as well as on community and housing issues. CODEMUH and MEC have developed multi-faceted campaigns, drawing on skills of advocacy, public education, and labor organizing. In Honduras, CODEMUH's radio and television spots and lobbying with the labor ministry targeted the role of state institutions, as well as the employers. Since 1998 there has been a 50 percent increase in decisions favorable to workers from complaints filed, and reductions in the number of pregnant workers fired. The labor minister held meetings with organized workers and is now monitoring firings and layoffs in FTZ companies.[19]

In 1997, with Central American organizations of maquila workers, MEC furthered the "Employment Yes, but with Dignity" campaign. The network has successfully campaigned internationally for a "code of ethics" to be signed by FTZ plant companies. The network has also campaigned to monitor implementation of the code.[20] In 2000 CIPAF began coordinating the development of a common strategy for advocacy work on "codes of conduct" in the greater Caribbean region.[21] Transnational work on the code of conduct is understood to be a crucial step in improving the lives of maquila workers, so that highly mobile FTZ companies cannot play workers and governments off each other, threatening job losses if labor's rights are enforced or improved. Furthermore, as in North America, transnational networking has allowed organizations of women workers to share information, strategies, and innovative ways of organizing.[22]

Conclusion

Why and under what conditions are these "new" transnational labor networks emerging? The themes and trends of the networks discussed fall roughly into four areas. First, workers organize transnationally because of common transnational corporation employers and a common issue—the globalization of production and its consequences for worker participation and representation. In the cases of the TIE, the Coca-Cola, and the farmers' campaigns, the cross-national linkage of workers was aided by the perception that a common employer existed. Furthermore, initiatives between governments for economic integration encourage transnational labor organizing. The transnational nature of capital, in other words, demands a transnational response from labor.

Second, some networks are formed between union actors and other so-cial movements when issues are complex and movements need to combine their strengths to be effective. Other networks are initiated outside of unions because of problems within unions. Participants' concerns include member representation in transnational arenas, addressing noncontract issues impor-tant to the membership, and attention to membership empowerment. As noted in the case studies, workers seek spaces to discuss issues from their own perspectives, as workers and as members of families, rather than from the perspective of institutional (union) goals. Networks may work trans-nationally to amplify claims to put pressure on union institutions to change policies or practices.

Third, individual or group conveners outside of unions, foundations, and existing transnational linkages of other social movements all seem to play a significant role in the emergence of TLNs. The middle class in many cases seems to have played a particularly important role in making the trans-national connections. Like Mujer a Mujer and TIRN, Factor X's trans-national connections originate from personal contacts made by nonworkers. The worker-to-worker connection also happened after contacts were made on issues not specifically related to contracts—community organizing, toxics, and health. Furthermore, leadership in exile may further transnational orga-nizing, contrary to the intentions of governments or corporations whose human rights violations cause cross-border flight, as in the case of STEGAC and the Coca-Cola workers. Finally, affiliation with powerful international religious organizations—the WCC in the case of the TIE and the ICCR for the Coca-Cola workers—is another common factor important for the emer-gence and consolidation of the transnational linkages. These cases suggest that networks forming around *principled* issues, such as corporate responsi-bility, may be aided by the *moral* (as well as financial) support of religious or-ganization, since they often carry moral weight and authority.

Fourth, new organizing is done in networks because of the capability of networks to integrate and interpret new information, and to transfer knowl-edge and "know-how" between interdependent actors. Networks seem to be particularly effective at empowering people, transforming their views and identities (frames), and encouraging member participation. Networks seem to do less well at maintaining communication between large numbers of members and coordinating financial resources, which hierarchical organiza-tions may do better. There may be pressure to form such new organizations to increase effectiveness for rapid mobilization of numbers and resources. I propose that the effective transnational campaigns tend to skillfully combine the strengths of both networks and hierarchical organizations.

The new TLNs have new ways of encouraging participation. Organizers focus on personal contacts and other forms of collective action crucial for the social construction of collective identity and protest. Women workers' networks have emphasized testimonials and "exchanges of experiences." These networks focus on a longer time frame for change and for the evaluation of their work. They emphasize "mutual solidarity," perhaps because the participants are women who share "common ground" and "common issues." Nevertheless, networks continue to struggle with power dynamics—between professionals and middle-class participants and workers, and between First and Third World actors. More analysis and experience will be necessary to understand what conditions and elements of new transnational labor networks constitute better or more effective organizing.

Notes

1. See, respectively, Report on the September 1988 Meeting on Pesticides and Cocoa Production (7–8); IV Conference of Auto Workers, February 1989 Report (9); January 1990 GM Workers Meeting (4); and *GM Workers Voice* 1, no. 3.

2. Conference participants came most often from the following countries: the United Kingdom, West Germany, France, the United States, Belgium, Spain (auto components), the Netherlands (communications, chocolate, auto), Switzerland, Italy, Canada, Japan, Brazil (auto, rubber, and cocoa), South Africa (Mercedes), Argentina (auto), Mexico (auto), Ivory Coast (Cargill, cocoa), Ghana (cocoa), Malaysia and Indonesia (cocoa, rubber).

3. Richard Metcalf, ACTWU, interview by author, 31 October 1994.

4. The TIE bulletin lists include the following: Australia Workers Links, a group developing contacts between workers in Australia and Asia; Brazil Network (founded in 1986), which aims to link trade unions and other movements in Britain and Brazil by offering information, contacts, and interpreting services; *Labor Notes,* published in Detroit, reports on progressive union activities in the United States and elsewhere; IDOC Documentation Centre in Rome; and Comisiones Oreras in Spain.

5. These actions included the following: workers' industrial actions in Finland, New Zealand, and Sweden; students removing Coke from cafeteria sales in the United States and Europe; funds raised for STEGAC families of workers killed; Canadian Labor Congress pressure to stop Canadian aid to Guatemala; protests by Histradut, an Israeli labor federation, against arms sales to Guatemala; and UAW pressure on Congress against U.S. military aid to Guatemala (Gatehouse and Reyes 1987, 18).

6. Information on IATP and farmers' organizing, where not otherwise noted, comes from a talk by Mark Ritchie to a MacArthur Scholars' workshop on 28 October 1994.

7. The Action Canada Network lists thirty-six member organizations includ-

ing seventeen unions. The Red Mexicana de Acción Frente al Laibre Comercio (RMALC) lists forty-two member organizations, including twenty-six unions. The Coalition for Justice in the Maquiladoras (CJM-US) lists forty-seven organizations, of which ten are labor organizations. The Federation for Industrial Retention and Renewal (FIRR-US) lists twenty-eight community-based organizations, of which about half are specifically workers' organizations.

8. Information for the case studies comes primarily from interviews between the author and one, or at the most two, members of the network. Some written documentation was also studied. Most likely, others would have differing interpretations of events. Interviews were conducted at the "Beyond NAFTA" conference in Madison in October 1994.

9. General information about Mujer a Mujer comes from the author's association with the organization since 1988, and from an interview with Mujer a Mujer members Mary McGinn and Erika Smith, 7 October 1994.

10. El Sindicato National de Trabajadores de la Industria de la Costura, 19 de Septiembre. The union took its name from the day of the Mexico City earthquake, when garment workers trapped in a factory died.

11. Information and quotes about TIRN, where not otherwise noted, come from an interview by the author with Susan Williams and Fran Ansley, 8 October 1994, at the Beyond NAFTA conference.

12. Information about CATS comes from "Testimony of Ms. Shirley Reinhardt," presented at Hearings on NAFTA, Thursday, 29 August 1991, Atlanta, Georgia, available through Labor Notes.

13. The name comes from X, the female chromosome.

14. Information, where not otherwise noted, comes from the author's interview with Carmen Valadez, Factor X board member, 8 October 1994 at the Beyond NAFTA conference in Madison, Wisconsin.

15. My translation.

16. Red Contreamericana de Mujeres en Solidaridad con las Trabajadores de la Maquila. The information in this section comes from material published by the organizations described, as well as from internal reports of Oxfam Great Britain.

17. Harold Brown, Oxfam Great Britain, interview by author, Santo Domingo, August 2000.

18. Ibid.

19. Sonia Cano, Oxfam in Honduras, interview by author, and Adolfo Castrillo, Nicaragua, interview by author, August 2000.

20. CODEMUH report to Oxfam Great Britain.

21. CIPAF report to Oxfam Great Britain (2000).

22. Oxfam Great Britain report evaluating American organizing of maquila workers (2000).

14

A Practitioner's Perspective

Mark Ritchie

Both the rich historical window opened by August Nimtz and the practical contemporary analysis by Thalia Kidder stir strong emotions in practitioners like myself. The trials, tribulations, and triumphs they both so eloquently detail have the elements of the same human drama that I have experienced in my own cross-border organizing over the last twenty-five years.

First, there are the many positive personal benefits. My first cross-border organizing experience was with the Nestlé boycott in the late 1970s, one of the largest and most important global political campaigns of the century. This campaign was aimed at forcing Nestlé to stop their dangerous practice of aggressively marketing artificial infant formula in regions of the world and to families who could not afford it or did not have the refrigeration needed to prevent contamination. UNICEF estimated that as many as one million babies died each year as a result of these practices by Nestlé and the other formula companies.

As one of the cofounders and national leaders of this boycott in the United States, I gained an amazing amount of strength, hope, and sheer energy from the information sharing, strategizing, and collaborative work that we developed with colleagues from the nearly one hundred countries where there were organizations working to stop Nestlé's deadly marketing practices. I know from my own experience that cross-border organizing can empower you by taking you out of your "daily grind" and lifting you into a new perspective.

A second benefit of cross-border organizing, nicely described by both authors, is the political clarity (and therefore power) that comes from integrating differing perspectives from all over the planet. I know from my own experience in the global trade movement that the intense debates that take place are not all "peace and harmony"—especially when the subjects are the core debates in global economic organizing, like human and worker rights or environmental protection. As both articles describe, all cross-border organizing will be, by definition, based on differing interests and circumstances. For example, there are important North-South debates (as is a constant theme in the case studies discussed in this volume by Karen Brown Thompson, Paul Nelson, and Thalia Kidder) that have to be understood as beyond "national" interests. Many of these debates are, in fact, centered in class or economic interest. Let me give a couple examples.

In the early stages of the effort to convince Congress to reject the North American Free Trade Agreement (NAFTA), most of the literature and rhetoric of this campaign focused almost exclusively on domestic issues, such as the threat to family farmers, jobs, and environmental laws in the United States. I was organizing on this issue as part of the National Family Farm Coalition, one of the founding members of the national Fair Trade Campaign. As a result of several meetings with key farm, labor, and environmental leaders from all three countries (Mexico, Canada, and the United States) the demands being made by the key groups from the United States changed dramatically. At the same time, groups began to change even the language they were using in their campaigns to reflect perspectives newly learned from the other countries. For example, while many groups had been focusing on organizing around anticipated negative effects in their own national context, as a result of these trinational meetings many of these groups began to shift their focus (and rhetoric) toward the potential negative impacts in all three countries.

Another example comes from my experience in the Nestlé boycott. In the beginning, our focus was mostly on the dangers of artificial formula feeding in poor communities in the Third World. A number of colleagues from Third World countries soon began to point out that infant formula is just as dangerous to babies in poor communities in the United States as it is for poor people in Africa or Asia. This insight helped those of us working in the United States to see that we needed to address this issue in our own backyard. There is an element of "global reality checking" that takes place in the context of cross-border organizing that is nearly impossible to achieve any other way.

Third, there is the human element of friendship and commonality when people gather across borders. When farmers from different countries gather, their conversations quickly move to their crops, their animals, the weather, and, most important, prices. I have been present when autoworkers from the United States and Mexico have met for the first time to explore mutual support and political strategy. Official topics like corporate account-ability strategies are tackled, but so are questions about families, health care, and housing.

Beyond the personal growth elements, these last two chapters in the vol-ume capture another key aspect—the way in which cross-border organizing techniques are dramatically affected by new methods and modes of travel and communications. Steam engines turned into trains and steamships, which turned into airplanes. Mail was joined by the telegraph, then the phone, then radio and television. The latest revolution, led by computers, the Internet, and the World Wide Web, has brought about an explosion in global communications technology, revolutionizing cross-border organizing.

The recent defeat of the Organization for Economic Cooperation and Development's (OECD) proposed Multilateral Agreement on Investment (MAI) is an excellent example of the importance of technology in trans-national organizing. This treaty was discussed and then negotiated for near-ly a decade in virtual secrecy. With the advent of the Internet, all of this changed. When the first tiny bit of information was leaked from the OECD, it was instantaneously broadcast around the world via the World Wide Web. In the hands of savvy analysts, strategists, and communicators, this small amount of information was pieced together with other scraps of information to create fully informed descriptions of what they were up to at OECD.

This information was rebroadcast all over, eventually being converted into fuel for a full-blown global campaign. A brief review of how the MAI campaign took shape is a useful way to see the power of the new technologies.

First, the leaked original documents were scanned and put on the Internet and sent globally via fax, along with independent general analysis. This made it a global issue. Next, specialists began writing analysis about the potential impact of this proposal on the areas of work they were familiar with, such as agriculture, climate change, or poverty alleviation. These, too, hit the Internet, eliminating the need for tens of thousands of people from around the planet to duplicate this effort. Activists and policymakers con-cerned with family farm issues from Canada to Uganda all got excellent, usable information very rapidly. They could study the analyses of the impact of the proposal on other countries and then quickly do their own analysis in response to their local situation.

This turned out to be the key factor for mobilizing local NGOs and elected officials. Once people studied the MAI proposal, many became ac-tive in efforts to convince their governments to kill the agreement. It was in this area that the Internet played its most important role. In the past a politician who received a letter of concern from a constituent would write a letter to some official at the agency of concern and wait for an answer. That answer might or might not come soon, it might or might not be truthful, and it might or might not answer the question.

With the Internet, this has changed in key ways. Let's look at the global campaign to stop the MAI to illustrate the context of these changes:

1. Politicians and citizens alike can use the Web to go look at the original documents. Since most of the major economic institutions, such as the WTO, have previously operated virtually in secret, this flow of information is empowering. Many local city councils and county government officials were convinced to go on the Web and read the actual text of the proposed MAI agreement. Once they saw the sweeping new powers granted to investors at the expense of local communities, many were easily convinced to take strong action.

2. An e-mail can be sent by a politician (or the media) to a bureaucrat with the expectation of fast and accurate answers soon—really soon. This happened over and over in the MAI campaign when local elected officials sent many e-mail messages to both OECD and officials in national governments, challenging them to defend this treaty.

3. The Internet makes it possible to let the world's people know how their politicians are answering questions overseas. For example, when a U.S. politician would use totally opposite arguments in front of different groups, it was possible to prove it thanks to the powerful archiving tools available on the Internet.

4. Answers given by politicians and agencies can be posted on the Internet so everyone with a computer and Web access can hear about key information right away. At the same time, we all have to keep in mind the growing digital divide (both between and within countries) and the new cross-border organizing campaigns like the one to stop the MAI. In this context, it is important to act on ideas that can close this great divide.

5. Boastful speeches by politicians back at home can now be monitored. It is great to show the consumers and leaders in Europe and elsewhere that politicians promising one thing to other nationals are often promising quite the opposite to their own constituents. In the campaign to stop the MAI, for example, the speeches that politicians would make at the OECD itself, which is in Paris and fairly cloistered, were nearly 100 percent opposite of what they would say back in their

home countries. The Internet made it possible to show this to citizens without a great expense.

6. Minor and major victories can really keep a movement going via the Internet. In the stop the MAI campaign, we were able to use the passage of an anti-MAI resolution by the Seattle City Council. This was extraordinarily good news that was instantly circulated globally. I have heard many times from organizers how important that small victory was to their overall optimism and resolve. At the same time, excellent Web work contributed to the defeated mentality and ultimate capitulation by the OECD staff and leadership. In the MAI fight, for example, a key turning point was when OECD staff went on the Web and found a thousand sites opposing MAI and none in favor.

At the end of the day, the value of cross-border organizing has to be measured by what it contributes both to the individuals engaged and to the eventual success of the campaign—that sense of identity transformation captured by Thalia Kidder and Karen Brown Thompson, as well as Sanjeev Khagram. While these chapters begin to explore these questions, they leave much of this to future activists in future campaigns to write—as Nimtz did with Marx and Engels. However, this volume convincingly offers an important contribution to understanding past efforts, efforts that provide a benchmark for how we may evaluate the future.

Part V
Conclusions

15

Restructuring World Politics: The Limits and Asymmetries of Soft Power

Kathryn Sikkink

This book is part of a burgeoning literature that argues that norms are becoming increasingly consequential in international relations and international organizations and that transnational nongovernmental actors are
key instigators and promoters of new norms. The first chapter discussed the
major themes of this volume. This final chapter begins a preliminary exploration of issues that have received less attention: questions of "soft" or informal power, representation, democracy, deliberation, and accountability
within transnational social movements. If, as we argue, transnational social
movements and networks are increasingly permanent features of international life, scholars and activists need to grapple more thoughtfully with
the dilemmas that the presence and power of these nontraditional actors
pose. We believe that international NGOs and transnational networks,
coalitions, and movements enhance deliberation and representation in international institutions by providing voices and ideas that were previously absent. At the same time, NGOs and networks need to address their own
asymmetries and questions of accountability and transparency, so they can
enhance their internal democracy while helping to democratize international institutions.

Restructuring World Politics

International relations scholars have long argued that international outcomes are fundamentally influenced by the structure of world politics. Because there is no formal world government, realists characterize this structure as "anarchic," and derive predictions about the behavior of states from

this anarchic structure. All the chapters in this volume are premised on a different view of the structure of world politics as some form of "international society," in which states conceive of themselves as bound by a common set of rules and norms.[1]

In this view, the attributes of anarchy (the absence of world government) or hegemony by a single great power are attenuated by a parallel structure of common rules and norms. John Ruggie has suggested one way to think about this kind of international structure is as one where a particular power structure is wedded to a particular structure of "social purpose" (1982). Alex Wendt has made a similar argument, referring to this structure of social purpose as the "international distribution of ideas" (1999). Ruggie argues that knowing the power structure helps us understand the *form* of international order, but not its *content*. Thus we have two potential sources of regime change that can happen independently of one another—power shifts (the decline of a hegemon, for example) or norm change (Ruggie 1982). When we see social purpose (or norms and discourses) as a codeterminant of international structure, and if social purpose does not always derive from power, it becomes theoretically and empirically important to consider how these new international norm structures of social purpose are constructed, maintained, and transformed.

We suggest that transnational advocacy groups can help initiate processes of norm shift. Because we speak of a structure of world politics—a fusion of a particular structure of power and purpose—and because nonstate actors are crucial for the creation of new norms and discourses, we can speak of these actors as engaged in a process of *restructuring world politics.* Transnational advocacy groups contribute to restructuring world politics by altering the norm structure of global governance.

Since the end of the cold war, we find that there is considerable variation in norm structures or "distributions of ideas" across issue areas, and across different world regions. Some issue areas in some regions are indeed characterized by hegemonic norm structures, where others are in a state of high norm contestation. This variation across issue area and region suggests that the structure of global power in and of itself is insufficiently nuanced to provide full explanations for global stability and change, and only by adding an understanding of norm structures can we map more effectively the structure of the global system.

In some cases, the norm structure follows from the power structure. Such is the case with the powerful norm structure in favor of economic liberalization and free trade, which is a reflection of the interests of the most powerful states in the international system. Other norms discussed here offer greater challenges to the power structure, and are in some tension with it. Norms against big dams, in favor of debt relief, or calling for more democratic participation in the decision making of international financial institutions run counter to the perceived interests of powerful economic and political actors, and yet they are changing discourses at the margins, and in some cases leading to significant policy change. We understand that those movements calling for norms that challenge powerful economic and political interests will face great barriers, but ultimately, interests are not completely given, but are interpreted, and the norm structure is part of what helps states (and firms) interpret their interests.

Norm consensus can provide more stability in the international system than would seem likely from looking at the lack of formal world government. So, for example, human rights discourses were marginal discourses in the period from the mid-1950s to the mid-1970s, subordinated to the bipolar discourses of both communism and anticommunism. Since the end of the cold war, human rights and democracy norms have "cascaded" and become dominant in some regions, especially in Europe and the Americas. In other regions, human rights and democracy norms are still contested, as debates over "Asian values" illustrate. But the strength of democracy norms in Indonesia, as discussed in the chapter by James Riker, shows that even in regions where democracy norms are contested, they are making powerful inroads.

Other norms we examine here are also contested. Women's rights, environmental norms, and norms about labor rights, while commanding considerable support in some regions, are still in conflict with powerful opposing discourses. Other norms are in distinctly minority positions, but are gathering adherents and shaping discursive terrains at the margins. The discourse over debt forgiveness, discussed by Elizabeth Donnelly, is an example of such a minority position that has gained significant support in recent years.

The Nature of Soft Power

This capacity of nonstate actors to contribute to restructuring world politics by altering the norm structure is similar to what Keohane and Nye have called "soft power" (1998) or what Dryzek (1999) and Habermas (1986) have called "communicative power." These forms of power rely on the persuasiveness of information or communication. Ann Florini also uses this notion of soft power to convey how third sector actors use their moral authority and credible information to shape the terms of the debate (2000). But the term "soft power" suggests weak or superficial power. Although transnational networks do not have the traditional attributes of power—money and military might—the power to shape the agenda, or to shape the very manner in which issues are perceived and debated, can be a deep and substantial exercise of power (Lukes 1974). Dryzek suggests that communicative power is increasingly important in a world of reflexive modernity, and particularly in the international realm. Dryzek provides an interesting metaphor that may illustrate how soft or communicative power works. He argues that formal institutions and rules are like institutional hardware, while discourses constitute institutional software. Just as we have discovered in the world of computers that software may exercise a more powerful influence than hardware, it is possible that in the world of international relations, discourses and norms can play an equally important role. In particular, Dryzek argues that in the international system, where hardware is not well developed, international software becomes more important (1999).

Traditional international relations theory has been less interested in this discursive software because it has assumed that those states with hard power will also exercise soft power over norms and discourses. Many analysts of global civil society also argue that it is not autonomous from the hard power of states, either because NGOs are dependent on the desire of governments and IGOs to work with them, and are thus more constrained by state agendas, or because transnational advocacy is situated in the policy environment of global neoliberalism and expresses middle-class sensibilities from industrial countries (Pasha and Blaney 1998; Görg and Hirsch 1998). Frequently, powerful states continue to exercise both hard power and soft power simultaneously, but increasingly transnational advocacy groups also have significant degrees of autonomous soft or communicative power on some issues. If this is the case, it is necessary to explore more explicitly how this power is exercised.

First, soft power does not always depend on formal attributes. Many nongovernmental actors are not formal actors within international organizations (some have "consultative status" with the UN, but most don't), and yet they exercise soft power within these organizations. We can say that this influence is "hidden"—not in the sense of being illicit or secret, but rather in the sense of being informal or behind the scenes. One of the leading interpretations of NGOs in the UN states that in the UN, "by definition, nongovernmental organizations have no standing in this realm," and yet, as former secretary general Boutros Boutros Ghali recognizes in the forward to the same volume, nongovernmental organizations "are now considered full participants in international life," and are "a basic form of popular participation and representation in the present day world" (Weiss and Gordenker 1996, 18, 7). This presents a paradox between the unquestioning acceptance of the importance of NGOs in international life, and the meager formal recognition of and provisions for their influence in international institutions and international relations theory. In this sense, transnational social movements and NGOs engage in informal and unexpected exercises of power and influence. Even NGOs with formal consultative status often carry out roles above and beyond the roles envisioned for NGOs with such status.

Because of the divergence between the formal framework for NGO influence and the actual extent of that influence, many NGO actors and some states have argued for a more transparent form of civil society influence in international institutions. The Commission on Global Governance has proposed an Assembly of the People parallel to the General Assembly, an Annual Forum of Civil Society to precede each session of the General Assembly, and a right of petition by citizens to the UN (Schweitz 1995, 416). None of these more ambitious proposals has been seriously discussed, and it seems likely that NGO influence will continue to be exercised in a behind-the-scenes fashion for years to come. Nevertheless, some international organizations are attempting to design mechanisms to incorporate nonstate actors more formally into international deliberations, such as the World Bank's standing NGO-World Bank Committee, which Paul Nelson describes in his chapter.

In addition to having consultative status, an additional and powerful means of nongovernmental influence was achieved through the innovation of parallel NGO conferences to global conferences (see Clark, Friedman, and Hochstetler 1998). Many more NGOs were accredited to attend UN global conferences than those that had consultative status, and the global conferences gave them unprecedented opportunities for organizing, media attention, and lobbying. Karen Brown Thompson discusses the particularly effective use that the international women's movement has made of official UN conferences to draw attention to issues and generate new norms. NGOs have also used unofficial parallel conferences, such as the NGO gatherings held at the time of the World Bank and IMF annual meetings, to network and publicize their causes (see Nelson and Donnelly this volume; Clark, Friedman, and Hochstetler 1998). Once again, we see a circular pattern of influence: NGOs pressured for global parallel conferences, and the conferences in turn encouraging the formation of new NGOs and new networks of NGOs. The recent intense wave of global conferencing is now over, however, curtailed by budget constraints, exhaustion, and the beliefs of some states that NGOs exerted excessive influence (Florini 2000).

But how do transnational advocacy groups exercise soft power? Communicative power is exercised by proposing, questioning, criticizing, and publicizing (Dryzek 1999). This may take the form of information politics, symbolic politics, accountability politics, or leverage politics (Keck and

Sikkink 1998). It may be relatively dull reports, or lively street protests, or private meetings, but in all cases, the stress is on changing discourses and practices. By creating new issues and placing them on international and national agendas, providing crucial information to actors, and most importantly by creating and publicizing new norms and discourses, transnational advocacy groups help restructure world politics. Each of the movements described in this volume was able to help shape a new norm, or modify an existing one, to influence the global norms structure to some degree. As institutional software, these discourses and norms shape the way people think and make sense of their world. In some cases, these discourses indeed constitute actors—as carriers of rights, victims of globalization, or protagonists in global struggles.

These new norms and discourses don't enter an empty international stage, but rather interact in an already existing terrain of norms and discourses. It is more difficult to pinpoint the "global norm structure" at any particular point, nor do we know exactly what makes particular norms attractive at particular historical moments. But such methodological and theoretical difficulties should not dissuade scholars from examining these issues, for without attention to global norm structures and power structures, we will not understand the contours of the current global order or the possibilities for systems change.

Asymmetries and Power within Networks

In addition to exercising informal power within international institutions, transnational networks themselves are permeated by informal or hidden power. Although networks are horizontal, reciprocal, and voluntary, they also have internal asymmetries that raise important questions about their representativity.

First, although most NGOs stress democracy and democratization, many are not themselves internally democratic. This is not necessarily due to a lack of commitment to democracy, but rather because it is not always clear who should participate in decision making about leadership and policies— should NGOs be run by their staff, their boards, their volunteers, their members, those who provide funds, or those on whose behalf they organize? As groups become more accountable to one group—funders, for example— it is possible that they will become less accountable to another (Shaw 2000). How might such systems of representation and accountability be set up? Organizing systems of representation in dispersed transnational networks is an even more daunting task, since networks are informal and horizontal by nature, and involve primarily the exchange of information.

As we stress in chapter 2, the great bulk of NGOs originate and are still based in the developed world. Both in terms of the composition of membership and the location of their international secretariats, there has been a shift over the last forty years in INGOs toward more geographical dispersion, but INGOs based in Europe and North America still dominate.

These asymmetries within networks are connected in turn to the kinds of influence that networks exercise within international institutions. We would expect the more powerful NGOs with the greatest resources to be the most likely to have access to and wield influence in international organizations. This is partly because NGOs based in the North are more likely to be linked to First World states, which are usually most influential in international organizations. So these NGOs exercise influence directly in international institutions and indirectly through powerful states. Yet a recent survey of 150 human rights NGOs revealed that groups based in the South are equally likely to have contact with intergovernmental organizations (IOs) as groups based in the North, though they have contact with somewhat different sets of IOs; Southern groups, for example, had more contact with UNICEF and the UN Development Programme, and Northern groups had more contact with the Human Rights Centre in Geneva. Likewise, there was no substantial difference between Northern and Southern NGOs in the rates of participation in global conferences (Smith, Pagnucco, and Lopez 1998). Although contact alone does not tell us about levels of influence, this suggests that Southern NGOs have more of a presence in international institutions than might be expected, given differences in resources.

Even those NGOs based in the developing world often depend on funding from foundations located in the wealthy countries, or from Western governments. Many NGOs are not large membership organizations that depend on donations from members to sustain themselves, but are rather small advocacy groups without a large membership base. These groups often depend on grants from foundations or governments to sustain their work.[2] In many cases, foreign funding constitutes more than 90 percent of operating budgets of such NGOs (Uvin 2000, citing James 1990). Almost half of international human rights funding provided by U.S. foundations from 1973 to 1993, for example, was provided by a single foundation—the Ford Foundation (Keck and Sikkink 1998; see also Bell 1971). Governments provide increasingly important funding for NGOs. The nonprofit sector in OECD countries receives a greater share of funding from governments than from private giving (Salamon and Anheier 1996).

Foreign funding is both a lifeblood and a major source of asymmetries of power within transnational networks. Because of the dominance of northern NGOs and foundations, the asymmetries within transnational networks have often been framed in North/South terms. This may be a useful starting place or shorthand for some of the internal divisions within transnational networks, but it does not capture fully the complexity of such divisions and asymmetries. A study of the role of NGOs in global conferences found that Northern and Southern NGOs often had more in common with each other than they did with their own governments (Clark, Friedman, and Hochstetler 1998). Some activists have characterized Northern foundations and NGOs as primarily interested in individual political and civil rights, while Southern NGOs are interested in collective and economic, social, and cultural rights, arguing that this individualist bias reflects a Western capitalist ethos. The recent survey of human rights NGOs found that groups based in the global South were more likely to work on social, economic, and cultural rights and the right to development than groups in the North, but that many groups in both the South and North reported that they worked to promote civil and political rights *and* economic, social, and cultural rights (Smith, Pagnucco, and Lopez 1998).

The asymmetries within transnational networks are not only driven by the political/structural logic of North-South differences, but also by an organizational logic inherent in the nature of the often struggling NGOs, informal networks, and the large foundations and governments that fund them. Because many NGOs compete for limited resources from a handful of foundations, the priorities of a few key individuals within large foundations can shape the programmatic priorities of many NGOs. This competition for funding can block possibilities for useful collaboration between NGOs, since each NGO must profile itself as exercising leadership and producing innovative new programs and solid results in order to position itself for future funding. Finally, in the development area, NGOs may depend for funding on the very governments or international organizations they monitor, thus influencing their independence. Paul Nelson, for example, notes that major development NGOs "find it difficult to coordinate their desire to advocate for new policy and practice at the World Bank with their dominant organizational need to secure funding from the World Bank and other major donors."

Foundations, by the very nature of the enterprise, have a bias toward larger, more bureaucratized NGOs. A small struggling NGO may not have the expertise to write a grant proposal to attract funding from large foundations. Should it receive such a grant, it may not have the "absorptive capacity" to use such a grant fruitfully without distorting the growth and development of the organization. Further, it may not have the bureaucratic routines to provide satisfactory accounting of the grant in final reports to foundations. This can lead to a hierarchy among domestic NGOs in the developing countries, where a small handful of NGOs that have better contacts with the foundation world receive the initial grants that allow them to put into place the infrastructure they need to attract further funding, while other NGOs are effectively marginalized, not so much because of their programmatic stance, but because of their lack of bureaucratic capacity. The result has been a highly skewed nonprofit sector, where a handful of larger INGOs have budgets that dwarf not only all other NGOs, but in some cases are actually larger than the budgets of some international agencies (Uvin 2000).

Foundations have tackled this challenge in part by specialization, with some smaller foundations and church-based groups focusing on seed grants to smaller groups, or pass-through foundations, such as the Global Fund for Women, which itself seeks grants from large foundations and then distributes many smaller grants to NGOs in the developing world.

Perhaps even more important are issues of innovation, or what might be more negatively called faddishness, in the foundation and NGO world. Foundations and governments believe it is important to innovate in their patterns of funding. Certain issues become the fad, and every foundation must have "its own" project to fund. While this faddishness has a positive side—it is a source of innovation and renovation in the foundation and NGO world—it also has a negative side, as other promising projects are left behind. Foundations argue that after a certain number of years of funding, NGOs should begin to be able to sustain themselves financially, and yet in many developing countries with little tradition of charitable giving, such expectations may be unrealistic.

Networks, transnational coalitions, and movements are full of internal divisions and conflicts. Although networks may present a harmonious front to the external world, they often experience deep internal divisions. August Nimtz's chapter on the First International clarifies that this historical workers' movement was as divided as its modern counterparts and often along the same lines, as issues of class, gender, language, ideology, and personality led to internal struggles.

Modern movements and networks experience these same divisions. It is interesting to note, however, that internal divisions within transnational movements or networks do not necessarily undermine effectiveness. Paul Nelson argues that the debate over the World Bank's IDA tenth replenishment was "both a high-water mark in NGO efforts to exert leverage over the World Bank, and the most visible split among network participants." Karen Brown Thompson notes the divisions, disagreements, and asymmetries within the transnational movement for women's human rights, and yet notes the rapid pace at which global norms have changed in response to transnational activism in spite of disagreements among activists. Although it is not clear why internal divisions do not hamper effectiveness in all cases, it is possible that divisions enhance publicity, and that publicity is essential to effectiveness. Another explanation may be that internal divisions often lead transnational actors to modify their strategies to attempt to contain conflict. For example, Nelson argues that in the case of the IDA replenishment debate, internal conflict led Northern NGOs to exhibit more deference to African NGO concerns.

Internal network divisions may also derive from the very norms that networks advocate. Many norms have both empowering and exclusionary effects. Although the chapters in the book have tended to focus on the empowering effect of international norms, most also point to the "silences," exclusions, or paradoxical effects of some international advocacy. In his chapter on the World Bank, Paul Nelson points out that, ironically, the international NGO critique of the bank, and the use of its leverage to affect national development priorities, have contributed to the reinforcement and expansion of the bank's influence, something that not all activists think is a good thing.

Likewise, Brown Thompson reminds us that the movement for women's human rights increased the attention paid to the problem of violence against women at the same time that it legitimated the increased intervention of the state in the life of the family to help prevent and punish such violence. Brown Thompson points out that this tension between empowerment and exclusion is also expressed in divisions, disagreements, and asymmetries within the transnational movement. In the case of women's groups, for example, the choice to focus on human rights discourse and norms had the effect of privileging those groups with a more legal approach, and of privileging lawyers within the movement, because international human rights is a highly legalized terrain in which to negotiate. Other women's groups have argued that the focus on violence as bodily harm against women has marginalized issues of economic inequality between men and women that may be at the root of much physical violence.

Some transnational advocacy recommends an increasingly prominent place for international institutions and organizations in processes of global governance. As students of the European Union have come to recognize, however, all transfer of activities to higher levels beyond the state could contribute to a democratic "deficit" where decisions are taken out of the hands of more accountable and representative groups and put into the hands of less representative international bureaucrats. While increasing the influence of transnational advocacy groups within these institutions could help counteract this democratic deficit (Shaw 2000), it might also indirectly strengthen these very institutions. Perhaps in response to this concern, the latest wave of transnational organizing on international institutions—the campaigns against the WTO, IMF, and World Bank—has advocated taking power out of the hands of these institutions, as the chapters by Elizabeth Donnelly and Paul Nelson show.

Representation, Accountability, and Deliberation

What are the implications for the influence of NGOs and transnational networks and coalitions as they try to enhance transnational democracy? This involves two separate questions—to what degree do transnational networks enhance democracy in international institutions, and how democratic are transnational NGOs, networks, and coalitions themselves (see also Brysk 1994)? All the chapters here suggest that networks are far from perfectly representative. Many citizens and issues are not represented and representation goes disproportionately to those with organization and resources. How important and possible is internal democracy for transnational movements and networks? Some students of domestic social movements suggest that internal democracy is not that important as long as movements are effective in achieving the goals desired by the membership (Perrow 1970, as cited in Klandermans 1997; Baehr 1996).

But for many of the organizations studied here, democracy has become a "master-frame," and thus it is difficult for them to ignore questions of internal democracy without affecting their overall legitimacy.[3] Repressive governments, faced with criticism from transnational NGOs, have gone on the counterattack, asking whom NGOs represent and what right they have to criticize a sovereign government.

But representativeness is not the only issue involved when evaluating the internal democracy of networks and their impact on global democracy. Democratic theories stressing deliberation as a crucial attribute of democratic legitimacy would ask if networks bring diverse viewpoints into international debates, especially the viewpoints of people subject to international governance. Dryzek has argued that networks are indeed "the most appropriate institutional expression of a dispersed capacity to engage in deliberation" (1999, 48).

But it may not be useful to frame the debate in terms of deliberation instead of representation. Many mechanisms to enhance representation within transnational networks or international institutions will simultaneously enhance deliberation. Networks that are imperfectly representative may still contribute to increased international deliberation. But increasingly representative networks will most likely lead to increased deliberation. Where the conflict may arise is between increased deliberation/representativeness and effectiveness, in terms of influencing short-term policy. Efforts to enhance representation and deliberation will slow down networks and make it more difficult for them to respond quickly to global problems and crises. Likewise, efforts to enhance deliberation are likely to expand the agendas of all networks. The more viewpoints taken into account, the less likely a network will be able to keep a narrow focus on a small set of issues.

International NGOs claim to speak on behalf of affected communities and thus bring into international institutions perspectives from people affected by international policies and projects, but normally excluded from global or national policy making. This is one of the dynamics that Sanjeev Khagram describes in his chapter on big dams. The voices of one million mostly poor and "tribal" peoples in India who were to be displaced by the Narmada Dam found expression in a transnational movement that has transformed big dam building in the Third World. Yet Khagram argues that transnational movements are more likely to be effective in influencing domestic policies in democracies because these regimes offer greater opportunities to organize. In this sense, transnational actors may be less effective in enhancing representation of the groups most in need of it—those already suffering under authoritarian rule.

Paul Nelson argues that NGOs often base their legitimacy on their claim to represent "Southern" views, or a domestic political constituency. NGOs' claims to representativity may be based on images of networks, NGOs, and social movements as the autonomous spokespeople of civil society. But in many cases, this vision of autonomous social movements or NGOs is misleading, and the connections between NGOs and states is far closer than the name NGO would suggest. A list of new acronyms has emerged to account for this range of autonomy within the NGO sector: GONGOs (government-organized NGOs), DONGOs (donor-organized NGOs), and QUANGOs (quasi-NGOs) (Weiss and Gordenker 1996).

One reason coalitions and networks are effective is because they have acquired "moral authority" as a power resource that gives them influence beyond their limited material capacities (Hall 1997). Historically, religious authorities have been the main holders of moral authority. While religion and religious fundamentalism continue to be extremely important sources of collective identities in the late twentieth century (Castells 1997), religious authorities are no longer the principal holders of moral authority in transnational arenas because they are not able to bridge the religious differences present there. In a few of our cases, religious authorities and groups continue to play a significant role. The Catholic bishops have been one of the few groups exercising influential moral authority within the IMF, and the Catholic Church in Chile played a fundamental role in mobilizing transnational action on human rights. In most cases, however, the secular transnational coalitions and networks themselves attempt (and sometimes succeed) in invoking moral authority to support their efforts to create, promote, and implement new norms.

How is it possible for relatively weak actors like transnational networks to acquire this kind of moral authority and influence? Sometimes it is because the networks themselves and the norms and discourses they promote provide a physical and conceptual meeting ground for diverse groups to negotiate the meaning of their joint enterprise. Networks are communicative structures that, at their best, permit such negotiation to occur (Dryzek 1999; Keck and Sikkink 1998). Scholars have long understood that collective legitimation has become one of the major functions of international organizations (Claude 1966). What is less well understood is that nonstate actors like NGOs may play important roles in helping provide information or pressure for these collective legitimation exercises within international institutions.

To be effective in questioning the legitimacy of states, however, NGOs or networks may also have to prove their own legitimacy, which is frequently called into question by states. To sustain their claim to moral authority, however, movements and networks need to appear to have some of the following attributes:

1. *Impartiality or independence.* These networks and movements must be perceived as not self-interested. That is, they need to be seen as not personally interested in acquiring political or economic power, or as too linked to government or industry. It is exactly because these groups are neither political parties nor interest groups in the classic sense of the word, or representing the political or economic interests of a particular group, that they acquire moral authority. Yet it is also a balancing act for networks, since they need access to governments to be effective in advocating policy change (Baehr 1996) and contacts with the wealthy and politically powerful to fund their activities and push through their programs. At times, certain groups have symbolically demonstrated this impartiality by self-limiting their sources of funding. At one point, for example, Amnesty International prohibited its branches from accepting any money from governments or corporations.

But few INGOs and networks meet this ideal of pristine autonomy, nor is this fixation with autonomy useful in helping us understand the phenomena of transnational activism. What may be more useful is to specify the characteristic forms in which nongovernmental actors relate to other actors. One definition of network used in this volume includes some individuals within governments and intergovernmental organizations who share the principled ideas and discourse of the network. The case studies suggest that in many cases, governments, IOs, and NGOs are becoming even more enmeshed than we have previously thought. In Riker's chapter on Indonesia, for example, he describes how states fund many NGOs directly or indirectly through their foreign aid budgets, how multilateral organizations maintain constant liaisons with NGOs, and how international agencies call on NGOs to act as consultants to provide project assessments, evaluation, and policy analysis. Daniel Thomas also raises this issue in his chapter on the Helsinki movement. In the case of the United States, a senior U.S. diplomat and head of the Ford Foundation actually helped create the main U.S. NGO to monitor the Helsinki agreements—Helsinki Watch. Access to public funding is essential for many NGOs, which underscores the continued dependence of the nonprofit sector on the state (see Uvin 2000).

2. *Veracity and reliability.* Moral authority in this realm is also the result of the quality of the information that NGOs and social movements provide. This has been particularly important in human rights reporting, and Hawkins calls attention to "monitoring" as the primary tactic of human rights NGOs. But reliability is also important in other issues. Because the authority of these organizations is so linked to the power of information and the images they project, they are harmed by any suggestion that their information is less than accurate. Thus the larger NGOs have significant research staffs, and are careful about the links they establish with domestic NGOs, attempting to choose those with the best reputations for research.

3. *Representiveness.* Social movements have authority because they claim to speak for the weak, the repressed, the underrepresented. Thus, human rights organizations claim to represent the voices of repressed individuals in other countries who may not be free to speak for themselves. This is the most complicated link because the authority of networks is undermined when groups that networks claim to represent question or criticize their work. Some forms of internal democracy are necessary to sustain this claim to representativity, as well as to the attributes of authenticity discussed above.

4. *Accountability and Transparency.* Finally, transnational advocacy groups have moral authority to the degree that they are also perceived as accountable. One of the main requisites of accountability is transparency, since it is difficult to hold groups accountable without detailed and accurate

information about their activities and composition. Many INGOs and transnational networks do not yet have in place transparency practices and policies, or mechanisms for accountability. Some scholars argue that accountability will eventually take place in the marketplace of ideas. Because "all civil society advocacy stands or falls on the persuasiveness of its information," groups with bad or misleading information will eventually be discredited, and will lose funding and members (Florini 2000, 236).

INGOs will need to continue to address issues of their own accountability and representativity. These are not easy issues, but there are two possible models: an interest group model and a professionalization model. If NGOs see themselves as international interest groups, they can turn to an interest group model of representation, which includes dues, membership, and voting procedures for leadership. Amnesty International comes closest to this model. As a first step, NGOs need to be more self-conscious and transparent about decision-making processes within the organization and efforts at accountability and representation between NGOs and their global constituency.

If NGOs want to stress their role as social change professionals, they may need to think about mechanisms that other professions use to ensure accountability (such as doctors, lawyers, accountants, or even ministers). These mechanisms include credentialing, monitoring the behavior of members, and setting standards for professional behavior. Both of these models are somewhat troubling, because they may mean more bureaucratized professional organizations, which could undermine what is unique about NGOs—their flexibility to respond rapidly, their gadfly quality, and the informality of the global networks.

It is possible that there are other models for enhancing accountability, and these need to be identified and experimented with if networks are going to maintain their claim to moral authority. Because the NGO world is so diverse, it is an ideal place for such experimentation, and such experimentation is itself a valuable exercise in democracy. It is very likely that there is no single model of either representation or accountability, but rather diverse strategies appropriate for organizations of different sizes and purposes.

Conclusions

When measured against ideal visions of representation, democracy, deliberation, accountability, and autonomy, most transnational NGOs and networks fall short. Yet the appropriate standard against which to measure the representativity of NGOs is against the existing degree of democracy in international institutions and in international governance. International institutions are extremely imperfectly representative. The doctrine of state sovereignty has led to the one-state, one-vote rule in many international organizations, which creates formal political equality between microstates with tiny populations and huge countries like China. The security council and weighted votes in certain institutions like the World Bank and the IMF compensate for this formal political equality in ways that better correspond to the balance of power and wealth among states, but can hardly be justified by any theory of representation. No formal distinction is made at all between democratic and nondemocratic governments and their delegations to the United Nations. Although some delegations could be seen as quite representative of the views of citizens in their countries and subject to review and replacement, others are quite detached from any representation or accountability to their citizens.

In such a situation of highly imperfect representation, most efforts by NGOs and networks bring a greater diversity of viewpoints and information into international institutions than would otherwise be available. In this sense, transnational social movements can help "undermine rather than reproduce global inequalities" (Smith 2000). Just as firms adapt to "market imperfections," NGOs have developed responses to the political imperfections of representation in international institutions. The voices of NGOs from authoritarian regimes enhance the representation of people whose political participation is limited under harsh authoritarian rule. To the extent that NGOs are holding IO bureaucrats accountable, as Nelson's discussion of the World Bank and Donnelly's discussion of the IMF stress, they also enhance international democratization because very few mechanisms exist to hold international bureaucrats accountable to citizens in the countries they serve.

Yet the structure of representation through transnational advocacy is still inadequate to compensate for the deficit created by the loss of democratic accountability as decisions are made at higher levels. NGOs and networks are informal, asymmetrical, and ad hoc antidotes to domestic and international representational imperfections. The dilemma that transnational NGOs, networks, and movements face is how to continue to pragmatically pursue their policy agendas at the same time that they work to enhance, to the degree possible, their own internal democratic practices and the representation and accountability of the transnational network sector.

Notes

1. According to Bull 1977, an "international society" exists when on the basis of common interests and values, states "conceive themselves to be bound by a common set of rules in their relations with one another and share in the working of com-

mon institutions" (13). We disagree, however, with Bull's emphasis always on a society of *states*.

2. In their survey of international human rights NGOs, Smith, Pagnucco, and Lopez (1998) found that 60 percent of the NGOs received foundation grants to support their work, and 52 percent received grants from government or intergovernmental agencies. Most NGOs list financial constraints as the most significant organizational obstacle they face, far outweighing any other issue.

3. On master-frames, see Snow and Benford 1992.

Bibliography

Aditjondro, George J., ed. 1990a. "Development Refugees: An Indonesian Study with Twelve Case Studies." Country report presented at the Southeast Asia Regional Consultation on People's Participation in Environmentally Sustainable Development, Puncak Pass, Indonesia, 20–22 March, Wahana Lingkungan Hidup Indonesia (WALHI).

———. 1990b. "A Reflection about a Decade of International Advocacy Efforts on Indonesian Environmental Issues." Paper presented in absentia at the Sixth Conference of the International NGO Forum on Indonesia (INGI), Germany, April.

———. 1990c. "Gerakan Lingkungan di Indonesia" (The Environmental Movement in Indonesia). *Suara Merdeka,* 21–25 August.

Albright, Madeleine Korbel. 1999. "Indonesia, the United States, and Democracy." *U.S. Department of State Dispatch* 10, no. 2 (March): 5–8.

Albright, Madeleine K., and Alfred Friendly, Jr. 1986. "Helsinki and Human Rights." In *The President, the Congress and Foreign Policy,* edited by Kenneth Rush and Kenneth W. Thompson. Lanham: University Press of America.

Algappa, Muthiah. 1994. *Democratic Transition in Asia: The Role of the International Community.* East-West Center Special Reports, no. 3 (October) Honolulu, Hawaii.

Alvarez, Sonia, Evelina Escobar, and Arturo Escobar. 1998. *Cultures of Politics. Politics of Cultures.* Boulder, Colo.: Westview Press.

Amnesty International. 1991. *Women in the Front Line: Human Rights Violations against Women.* New York: Amnesty International.

Angarwal, Anil. 1982. *The State of India's Environment.* New Delhi: Centre for Science and Environment.

Angell, Alan. 1994. *International Support for the Chilean Opposition 1973–1989: Political Parties and the Role of Exiles.* Unpublished manuscript.

Arase, David. 1993. "Japanese Policy toward Democracy and Human Rights in Asia." *Asian Survey* 33, no. 10: 935–52.

Aspinall, Edward. 1996. "The Broadening Base of Political Opposition in Indonesia." In *Political Oppositions in Industrialising Asia,* edited by Garry Rodan. New York: Routledge.

Ayres, Jeffrey. 1997. "From National to Popular Sovereignty? The Evolving Globalization of Protest Activities in Canada." *International Journal of Canadian Studies* 16: 107–23.

Ayres, Robert. 1983. *Banking on the Poor.* Cambridge: MIT Press.

Baehr, Peter. 1996. "Mobilization of the Conscience of Mankind: Conditions of Effectiveness of Human Rights NGOs." Presentation made at the UNU Public Forum on Human Rights and NGOs at United Nations University, Tokyo, Japan, 18 September.

Bank of America. 1991. "Less Developed Countries Activity Criteria." *Bank of America Credit Policy Statement,* 22 January (San Francisco): 1–3.

Baumgartner, Frank, and Bryan Jones. 1991. "Agenda Dynamics and Policy Subsytems." *Journal of Politics* 53, no. 4: 1044–74.

Beckmann, David. 2000. "Debt Relief at the Millennium: This Could Be the Start of Something Big." *Commonweal* 127, no. 22 (15 December): 12–14.

Beetham, David. 1991. *The Legitimation of Power.* Atlantic Highlands: Humanities Press International, Inc.

Bell, Peter. 1971. "The Ford Foundation as a Transnational Actor." *International Organization* 25, no. 3: 465–78.

Bichsel, Anne. 1994. "The World Bank and the International Monetary Fund from the Perspective of the Executive Directors from Developing Countries." *Journal of World Trade* 28, no. 6.

Birnbaum. Karl E. 1977. "Human Rights and East-West Relations." *Foreign Affairs* 55, no. 4: 783–99.

Bloed, Arie, ed. 1990. *From Helsinki to Vienna: Basic Documents of the Helsinki Process.* Dordrecht: Martinus Nijhoff Publishers.

Boli, John, and George M. Thomas. 1999. Introduction to *Constructing World Culture: International Nongovernmental Organizations since 1875.* Stanford: Stanford University Press.

Booth, Karen M. 1998. "National Mother, Global Whore, and Transnational Femocrats: The Politics of AIDS and the Construction of Women at the World Health Organization." *Feminist Studies* 24, no. 1: 115–39.

Boswell, Terry, and Dimitris Stevis. 1997. "Globalization and International Labor

Organizing: A World-System Perspective." *Work and Occupations* 24, no. 3: 288–308.

Brandt Commission. 1980. *North-South: A Programme for Survival: Report of the Independent Commission on International Development Issues.* London: Pan Books.

Brecher, Jeremy, John Brown Childs, and Jill Cutler, eds. 1993. *Global Visions: Beyond the New World Order.* Boston: South End Press.

Brecher, Jeremy, and Tim Costello. 1994. *Global Village or Global Pillage: Economic Reconstruction from the Bottom Up.* Boston: South End Press.

Breslauer, George W. and Philip E. Tetlock, eds. 1991. *Learning in U.S. and Soviet Foreign Policy.* Boulder, Colo.: Westview Press.

Brezhnev, Leonid. 1979. *Peace, Détente and Soviet-American Relations: A Collection of Public Statements.* New York: Harcourt, Brace and Jovanovich.

Brown, Cynthia. 1995. "Human Rights and Wrongs—1995." *The Nation*, 25 December, 830–31.

Brown, Michael E., Sean Lynn-Jones, and Steven E. Miller, eds. 1996. *Debating the Democratic Peace.* Cambridge: MIT Press.

Bruno, Kenny. 2000. "Beyond Street Tactics: The Anti-Corporate Globalization Movement after Washington, April 17–18, 2000." Available at www.corporatewatch.org (20 June).

Bryer, David, and John Magrath. 1999. "New Dimensions of Global Advocacy." *Nonprofit and Voluntary Sector Quarterly* 28, no. 4: 168–77 (supplement).

Brysk, Alison. 1994. "Dilemmas of Representation." Draft manuscript.

Brzezinski, Zbigniew. 1983. *Power and Principle: Memoirs of the National Security Advisor, 1977–1981.* New York: Farrar, Straus, Giroux.

Budiman, Arief. 2000. "Menilai Kabinet Abdurrahman Wahid Jilid Kedua" (Evaluating Abdurrahman Wahid's Second Cabinet). *Kompas* (Jakarta), September 13.

———, ed. 1990. *State and Civil Society in Indonesia.* Clayton, Victoria: Centre for Southeast Asian Studies, Monash University.

Bull, Hedley. 1977. *The Anarchical Society: A Study of Order in World Politics.* New York: Columbia University Press.

Bunch, Charlotte. 1993. "Organizing for Women's Human Rights Globally." In *Ours by Right: Women's Rights as Human Rights,* edited by Joanna Kerr. London: Zed Books.

Bunch, Charlotte, and Niamh Reilly. 1994. *Demanding Accountability: The Global Campaign and Vienna Tribunal for Women's Human Rights.* New Brunswick, N.J.: Center for Women's Global Leadership.

Buncher, Judith F., ed. 1977. *Human Rights and American Diplomacy, 1975–1977.* New York: Facts on File.

Byrnes, Andrew. 1989. "The 'Other' Human Rights Treaty Body: The Work of the

Committee on the Elimination of Discrimination Against Women." *Yale Journal of International Law* 14, no. 1: 1–67. Reprint.

———. 1990. "Women, Feminism and International Human Rights Law—Methodological Myopia, Fundamental Flaws, or Meaningful Marginalisation? Some Current Issues." Unpublished manuscript.

Byrnes, Timothy A. 1991. *Catholic Bishops in American Politics.* Princeton: Princeton University Press.

Cahn, Jonathan. 1993. "Challenging the New Imperial Authority: The World Bank and the Democratization of Development." *Harvard Human Rights Journal* 6: 159–93.

Cardoso, Fernando Henrique. 2000. "An Age of Citizenship." *Foreign Policy* 119 (summer): 40–42.

Carothers, Thomas. 1999. *Aiding Democracy Abroad: The Learning Curve.* Washington, D.C.: Carnegie Endowment for International Peace.

Castells, Manuel. 1997. *The Power of Identity.* Vol. 2 of *The Information Age.* Oxford: Blackwell Publishers.

Cavallo, Ascanio, Manuel Salazar, and Oscar Sepúlveda. 1989. *Chile, 1973–1988: La Historia Oculta del Regimen Militar.* Santiago: Editorial Antártica.

Cekal Ramos Membungkam Horta. 1994. "Ramos' Ban Silences Horta." *DeTik* (Jakarta) 25–31 May.

Cernea, Michael. 1986. "Involuntary Resettlement in Bank-Assisted Projects: A Review of the Application of Bank Policies and Procedures in FY 79–85 Projects." Washington, D.C.: World Bank.

Chamberlain, Christopher H., and Martha L. Hall. 1995. *The World Bank's Revised Information Disclosure Policy: A Report on Content and Accessibility.* Washington, D.C.: Bank Information Center.

Charlesworth, Hilary. 1994. "What are 'Women's International Human Rights'?" In *Human Rights of Women: National and International Perspectives,* edited by Rebecca J. Cook. Philadelphia: University of Pennsylvania Press.

Charnovitz, Steve. 1997. "Two Centuries of Participation: NGOs and International Governance." *Michigan Journal of International Law* 18, no. 2: 183–286.

Chatfield, Charles. 1997. "Intergovernmental and Non-governmental Organizations to 1945." In *Transnational Social Movements and Global Politics: Solidarity beyond the State,* edited by Jackie Smith, Charles Chatfield, and Ron Pagnucco. Syracuse: Syracuse University Press.

Chilean National Commission on Truth and Reconciliation. 1993. *Report of the Chilean National Commission on Truth and Reconciliation.* Santiago: Chilean National Commission on Truth and Reconciliation.

Christopher, Warren. 1996. "Remarks by Secretary of State Warren Christopher Prior to Meeting with Members of the Indonesian Human Rights Commission."

Jakarta, Indonesia: U.S. Department of State, Office of the Spokesman, 23 July. File ID 960723-04, EEA.

Clark, Ann Marie, Elisabeth J. Friedman, and Kathryn Hochstetler. 1998. "The Sovereign Limits of Global Civil Society: A Comparison of NGO Participation in UN World Conferences on the Environment, Human Rights, and Women." *World Politics* 51, no. 1: 1–35.

Clark, John. 1987. "A Grassroots View of the Debt Crisis." *Food Monitor* 42: 10–11, 26.

———. 1991. *Democratizing Development.* West Hartford, Conn.: Kumarian.

Claude, Inis. 1966. "Collective Legitimation as a Political Function of the United Nations." *International Organization* 20: 367–79.

———. 1967. *The Changing United Nations.* New York: Random House.

Cleary, Seamus. 1995. "In Whose Interest? NGO Advocacy Campaigns and the Poorest: An Exploration of Two Indonesian Examples." *International Relations* 12, no. 5: 9–36.

Cohen, Margot. 1994. "High Anxiety: Government Proposal Could Crimp NGO Activities." *Far Eastern Economic Review* 157 (September 29): 32.

———. 1996. "New Zeal: NGOs Rally Round Opposition Leader Megawati." *Far Eastern Economic Review* 159 (11 July): 19–20.

———. 1998. "Voice of Ire: Disparate Groups Unite in Cry for Change." *Far Eastern Economic Review* 161 (28 May): 15–17.

Cole, G. H. D., and A. W. Filson. 1951. *British Working Class Movements: Select Documents, 1789–1875.* London: Macmillan.

Collins, Henry, and Chimen Abramsky. 1965. *Karl Marx and the British Labour Movement: Years of the First International.* London: Macmillan.

Commission on Global Governance. 1995. *Our Global Neighborhood.* New York: Oxford University Press.

———. 1999. "The Millennium Year and the Reform Process." Geneva: Commission on Global Governance, November. Available at www.cgg.ch/millennium.htm.

Committee on the Elimination of All Forms of Discrimination Against Women (CEDAW). 1987. *Initial Reports of States Parties: Japan.* March 26.

———. 1994. List of Representatives of States Parties, "Provisional List of Participants." January 25.

Conference of European Churches. 1976. *The Conference on Security and Cooperation in Europe and the Churches.* Report of a consultation at Bruckow, German Democratic Republic (27–31 October 1975). Geneva.

Congressional Record. 1976. 94th Cong., 2d sess. Vol. 122, pt. 12.

Constable, Pamela, and Arturo Valenzuela. 1991. *A Nation of Enemies.* New York: W.W. Norton and Company.

Cook, Don. 1978. "Making America Look Foolish: The Case of the Bungling Diplomat." *Saturday Review,* 13 May, 10.

Cook, Rebecca. 1992. "Women's International Human Rights Law: The Way Forward." In *Report of a Consultation on Women's International Human Rights,* 31 August–2 September, Faculty of Law, University of Toronto, Canada.

Coomaraswamy, Radhika. 1994. "To Bellow Like a Cow: Women, Ethnicity, and the Discourse of Rights." In *Human Rights of Women: National and International Perspectives,* edited by Rebecca J. Cook. Philadelphia: University of Pennsylvania Press.

Corcoran, Paul, ed. 1983. *Before Marx: Socialism and Communism in France, 1830–48.* New York: St. Martin's Press.

Council of Europe, Parliamentary Assembly. 1977. *Implementation of the Final Act of the Conference on Security and Cooperation in Europe.* Debate on the General Policy of the Council of Europe, 27–29 April, Strasbourg.

Covey, Jane G. 1998. "Critical Cooperation? Influencing the World Bank through Policy Dialogue and Operational Cooperation." In *The Struggle for Accountability: The World Bank, NGOs, and Grassroots Movements,* edited by Jonathan Fox and David L. Brown. Cambridge: MIT Press.

Cox, Robert. 1992. "Multilateralism and World Order." *Review of International Studies* 18, no. 2: 161–80.

Detzner, John A. 1991. "Utilización de mecanismos internacionales en la protección de derechos humanos: El caso Chileno." In *Derechos Humanos y Democracia: La Contribución de las Organizaciones No Gubernamentales,* edited by Hugo Frühling. Santiago: Instituto Interamericano de Derechos Humanos.

Development GAP. 1993. *The Other Side of the Story.* Washington, D.C.: The Development GAP.

Dezalay, Yves, and Bryant Garth. 1996. *Dealing in Virtue: International Commercial Arbitration and the Construction of a Transnational Legal Order.* Chicago: University of Chicago Press.

Donnelly, Elizabeth A. "Proclaiming the Jubilee: Global Coalition Demands Further Debt Relief for Poorest Countries." *DRCLAS News* (fall 1999): 11–13.

Donnelly, Jack. 1986. "International Human Rights: A Regime Analysis." *International Organization* 40, no. 3: 599–642.

———. 1989. *Universal Human Rights in Theory and Practice.* Ithaca: Cornell University Press.

Dorsey, Ellen. 1993. "Expanding the Foreign Policy Discourse: Transnational Social Movements and the Globalization of Citizenship." In *The Limits of State Autonomy: Societal Groups and Foreign Policy Formulation,* edited by David Skidmore and Valerie Hudson. Boulder, Colo.: Westview Press.

Draper, Hal. 1985. *The Marx-Engels Chronicle.* New York: Schocken Books.

Drucker, Peter. 1989. *The New Realities: In Government and Politics, in Economics and Business, in Society and World View.* New York: Harper & Row.

Dryzek, John. 1999. "Transnational Democracy." *The Journal of Political Philosophy* 7, no. 1: 30–51.

Dubash, Navroz, Mairi Dupar, Smitu Kothari, and Tundu Lissu. 2001. *A Watershed in Global Governance? An Independent Assessment of the World Commission on Dams.* Delhi: Lokayan; Dar es Salaam: Lawyers Environmental Action Team; and Washington, D.C.: World Resources Institute.

Economist. 1999. "After Seattle: The Non-Governmental Order." *Economist,* 11 December, 20–21.

Edwards, Michael. 2000. "NGO Rights and Responsibilities: A New Deal for Global Governance." London: Foreign Policy Centre.

Ekins, Paul. 1992. *A New World Order: Grassroots Movements for Global Change.* New York: Routledge.

Eldridge, Philip. 1989a. "NGOs and the State in Indonesia." *Prisma* (Jakarta) 47: 34–56.

———. 1989b. *NGOs in Indonesia: Popular Movement or Arm of Government?* Working Paper 55, Centre of Southeast Asian Studies, Monash University, Clayton, Australia.

———. 1995. *Non-Government Organizations and Democratic Participation in Indonesia.* New York: Oxford University Press.

Emmerson, Donald K. 1999. "Exit and Aftermath: The Crisis of 1997–98." In *Indonesia beyond Suharto,* edited by Donald K. Emmerson. Armonk, N.Y.: M. E. Sharpe.

———. 2000. "Will Indonesia Survive?" *Foreign Affairs* 79, no. 3: 95–106.

Eng, Peter. 1998. "A New Kind of Cyberwar." *Columbia Journalism Review* 37, no. 3: 20–21.

Engels, Frederick, Paul Lafargue, and Laura Lafargue. 1963. *Correspondence.* 3 vols. Moscow: Foreign Language Publishing House.

Escobar, Arturo. 1992. "Introduction: Theory and Protest in Latin America Today." In *The Making of Social Movements in Latin America: Identity, Strategy, and Democracy,* edited by Arturo Escobar and Sonia E. Alvarez. Boulder, Colo.: Westview Press.

Escobar, Arturo, and Sonia E. Alvarez. 1992. *The Making of Social Movements in Latin America: Identity, Strategy, and Democracy.* Boulder, Colo.: Westview Press.

European Network on Debt and Development (EURODAD). 1990–91, 1992, 1993, 1994. *Annual Reports.* Brussels: EURODAD.

Fabig, Heike, and Richard Boele. 1999. "The Changing Nature of NGO Activity in a Globalizing World." *IDS Bulletin* 30, no. 3: 58–67.

Falk, Richard. 1993. "The Making of Global Citizenship." In *Global Visions: Beyond the New World Order,* edited by J. Brecher, J. B. Childs, and J. Cutler. Boston: South End Press.

———. 1997. "Resisting 'Globalization-from-above' through 'Globalization-from-below.'" *New Political Economy* 2: 17–24.

———. 1998. "Global Civil Society: Perspectives, Initiatives, Movements." *Oxford Development Studies* 26, no. 1: 99–110.

Fall, Brian. 1977. "The Helsinki Conference, Belgrade and European Security." *International Security* 2, no. 1: 100–105.

Farer, Tom. 1997. "The Rise of the Inter-American Human Rights Regime: No Longer a Unicorn, Not Yet an Ox." *Human Rights Quarterly* 19: 510–46.

Fascell, Dante B. 1978. "Did Human Rights Survive Belgrade?" *Foreign Policy* 31 (summer): 104–18.

FEER. 1994. "Ramos Sighs with Relief as East Timor Conference Ends." *Far Eastern Economic Review* 157 (June 16): 18.

Fifty Years Is Enough Campaign. 1996. "One Year Is Not Enough." Unpublished evaluation.

"Fifty Years of Bretton Woods Institutions: Enough." 1994. *Lokayan Bulletin,* December.

Finnemore, Martha. 1993. "International Organizations as Teachers of Norms: The United Nations Educational, Scientific, and Cultural Organization and Science Policy." *International Organization* 47, no. 4: 565–98.

———. 1996. *National Interests in International Society.* Ithaca: Cornell University Press.

Finnemore, Martha, and Kathryn Sikkink. 1998. "International Norm Dynamics and Political Change." *International Organization* 52, no. 4: 887–917.

Fisher, Julie. 1993. *The Road from Rio: Sustainable Development and the Nongovernmental Movement in the Third World.* Westport, Conn.: Praeger.

———. 1998. *Nongovernments: NGOs and the Political Development of the Third World.* West Hartford, Conn.: Kumarian Press.

Florini, Ann, ed. 2000. *The Third Force: The Rise of Transnational Civil Society.* Washington, D.C.: Carnegie Endowment for International Peace and Japan Center for International Exchange.

Forsythe, David P. 2000. *Human Rights in International Relations.* Cambridge: Cambridge University Press.

Fowler, Alan. 1992. "Building Partnerships between Northern and Southern Development NGOs: Issues for the 1990s." *Development: Journal of the Society for International Development* 1: 16–23.

Fox, Jonathan. 1998. "When Does Policy Reform Influence Practice? Lessons from the Bankwide Resettlement Review." In *The Struggle for Accountability,* edited by Jonathan A. Fox and L. David Brown. Cambridge: MIT Press.

————. 2000. "The World Bank Inspection Panel: Lessons from the First Five Years." *Global Governance* 6, no. 3: 279–318.

Fox, Jonathan, and David L. Brown, eds. 1998. *The Struggle for Accountability: The World Bank, NGOs, and Grassroots Movements.* Cambridge: MIT Press.

Franck, Thomas M., and Edward Weisband. 1979. *Foreign Policy by Congress.* New York: Oxford University Press.

Fraser, Arvonne. 1987. *The United Nations Decade for Women: Documents and Dialogue.* Boulder, Colo.: Westview Press.

————. 1993. "The Feminization of Human Rights." *Foreign Service Journal* 12: 31–34.

Freeman, Marsha. 1989. "Women and Human Rights: A New Discussion." Minneapolis: University of Minnesota MacArthur Program on Peace and International Cooperation, *Working Paper Series 2, No. 3* (November).

————. 1993. "Women, Development and Justice: Using the International Convention on Women's Rights." In *Ours by Right: Women's Rights as Human Rights,* edited by Joanna Kerr. London: Zed Books.

Fruhling, Hugo. 1983. "Stages of Repression and the Legal Strategy for the Defense of Human Rights in Chile: 1973–1980." *Human Rights Quarterly* (November): 510–33.

————. 1989. "Nonprofit Organizations as Opposition to Authoritarian Rule: The Case of Human Rights Organizations in Chile." In *The Nonprofit Sector in International Perspective,* edited by Estelle James. New York: Oxford University Press.

Fruhling, Hugo, and Patricio Orellana. 1991. "Organismos no gubernamentales de derechos humanos bajo regímenes autoritarios y en la transicion democratica: El Caso Chileno desde una perspectiva comparada." In *Derechos humanos y democracia: La contribución de las Organizaciones no Gubernamentales,* edited by Hugo Fruhling. Santiago: Instituto Interamericano de Derechos Humanos.

G-7 Finance Ministers. 1995. "G-7 Economic Communiqué Text." Halifax, Nova Scotia, 16 June.

Garthoff, Raymond L. 1994. *Détente and Confrontation: American-Soviet Relations from Nixon to Reagan.* Rev. ed. Washington, D.C.: Brookings Institution.

Gatehouse, Mike, and Miguel Angel Reyes. 1987. *Soft Drink, Hard Labour: Coca-Cola Workers in Guatemala.* Latin America Bureau.

Geldenhuys, Deon. 1992. *Isolated States: A Comparative Analysis.* Cambridge: Cambridge University Press.

General Council of the First International. 1963–68. *Minutes.* 5 vols. Moscow: Progress Publishers.

George, Susan. 1992. *The Debt Boomerang: How Third World Debt Harms Us All.* London: Pluto Press.

Ghils, Paul. 1992. "International Civil Society: International Non-Governmental Organizations in the International System." *International Social Science Journal* 44, no. 3: 417–31.

Goldberg, Dorothy. n.d. "Personal Journal of International Negotiations about Human Rights." Unpublished and undated manuscript.

Goldman, Ralph M. 1988. "Transnational Parties as Multilateral Civic Educators." In *Promoting Democracy: Opportunities and Issues,* edited by R. M. Goldman and W. A. Douglas. New York: Praeger.

Goldsmith, Edward, and Nicholas Hildyard, eds. 1986. *The Social and Environmental Effects of Large Dams.* Vol. 2. Cornwall, U.K: Wadebridge Ecological Center.

Goldstein, Judith, and Robert O. Keohane. 1993. "Ideas and Foreign Policy: An Analytical Framework." In *Ideas and Foreign Policy: Beliefs, Institutions and Political Change.* Ithaca, N.Y.: Cornell University Press.

Gordenker, Leon, and Thomas G. Weiss. 1995a. "Pluralising Global Governance: Analytical Approaches and Dimensions." *Third World Quarterly* 16, no. 3: 357–88.

———. 1995b. "NGO Participation in the International Policy Process." *Third World Quarterly* 16, no. 3: 543–55.

Görg, Christoph, and Joachim Hirsch. 1998. "Is International Democracy Possible?" *Review of International Political Economy* 5, no. 4: 585–615.

Government of Gujarat. 1979. G. R. No. Misc. RES-1078-Amenities/Part-III/K-5. Gandhinagar, Gujarat. June 11.

Government of Gujarat. Irrigation Department. 1985. Government Resolutions REHAB-Narmada-7082-48-K-5. Gandhinagar, Gujarat. May 30.

Government of Gujarat. Narmada Development Department. 1985, 1987. Government resolutions.

Government of India. 1970. *The Fourth Five-Year Plan.* New Delhi: Government of India Press.

———. 1978. "Report of the Narmada Water Disputes Tribunal." 4 vols. New Delhi: Government of India.

———. 1980. *Tiwari Committee Report on the State of India's Environment.* New Delhi: Government of India Press.

———. 1994. "Report of the Five-Member Group." New Delhi: Government of India. April.

———. 1995. "Further Report of the Five-Member Group." 2 vols. New Delhi: Government of India.

Griesgraber, Jo Marie. 1997. "Forgive Us Our Debts: The Third World's Financial Crisis." *The Christian Century* 114, no. 3: 76–83.

Guidry, John A., Michael D. Kennedy, and Mayer N. Zald, eds. 2000. *Globalizations and Social Movements: Culture, Power, and the Transnational Public Sphere.* Ann Arbor, Mich.: University of Michigan Press.

Gupta, Akhil. 1998. "Peasants and Global Environmentalism: Safeguarding the Future of 'Our World' or Initiating a New Form of Governmentality?" In *Post-colonial Developments: Agriculture in the Making of Modern India,* edited by Ahil Gupta. Durham, N.C.: Duke University Press.

Haas, Ernst. 1990. *When Knowledge Is Power.* Berkeley and Los Angeles: University of California Press.

Habermas, Jürgen. 1986. "Hannah Arendt's Communications Concept of Power." In *Power,* edited by Steven Lukes. New York: New York University Press.

Hall, Rodney Bruce. 1997. "Moral Authority as a Power Resource." *International Organization* 41, no. 4: 591–622.

Harrison, Royden. 1965. *Before the Socialists: Studies in Labour and Politics, 1861–1881.* London: Routledge & Kegan Paul.

Hawkins, Darren. 1996. *The International and Domestic Struggle for Legitimacy in Authoritarian Chile.* Ph.D. diss., University of Wisconsin-Madison.

Helie-Lucas, Marie Aimee. 1993. "Women Living under Muslim Laws." In *Ours by Right: Women's Rights as Human Rights,* edited by Joanna Kerr. London: Zed Books.

Helleiner, Gerald, Tony Killick, Nguyuru Lipumba, Denno J. Ndulu, and Knud Erik Svendsen. 1995. Report of the Group of Independent Advisers on Development Cooperation Issues between Tanzania and its Aid Donors. Copenhagen: DANIDA.

Helsinki Review Group. 1977. *From Helsinki to Belgrade.* London: David Davies Memorial Institute of International Studies.

———. n.d. *Belgrade and After.* London: David Davies Memorial Institute of International Studies.

Hendardi and Benny K. Harman. 1991. "INGI dan Gerakan Demokratisasi di Tanah Air (INGI and the Democracy Movement in the Fatherland)." *Jurnal Demokrasi* 1, no. 1: 9–13.

Heredia, Carlos A., and Mary E. Purcell. 1994. *The Polarization of Mexican Society: A Grassroots View of World Bank Economic Adjustment Policies.* Washington, D.C.: The Development GAP.

Heryanto, Ariel. 1996. "Indonesian Middle-Class Opposition in the 1990s." In *Political Oppositions in Industrialising Asia,* edited by Garry Rodan. New York: Routledge.

Hewison, Kevin, and Garry Rodan. 1996. "The Ebb and Flow of Civil Society and the Decline of the Left in Southeast Asia." In *Political Oppositions in Industrialising Asia,* edited by Garry Rodan. London: Routledge, 1997.

Heyzer, Noeleen, James V. Riker, and Antonio B. Quizon, eds. 1995. *Government-NGO*

Relations in Asia: Prospects and Challenges for People-Centered Development. New York: St. Martin's Press.

Hipsher, Patricia. 1998. "Democratic Transitions as Protest Cycles: Social Movement Dynamics in Democratizing Latin America." In *The Social Movement Society: Contentious Politics for a New Century,* edited by David Meyer and Sidney Tarrow. Lanham, Md.: Rowman and Littlefield.

Hobsbawm, Eric. 1962. *The Age of Revolution.* New York: Mentor.

Holloway, Nigel. 1994. "Seed Money: U.S. Has a Big Message but Little Cash for Asia." *Far Eastern Economic Review* 157, no. 33: 42–43.

Hulme, David, and Michael Edwards. 1997. *NGOs, States and Donors: Too Close for Comfort?* New York: St. Martin's Press.

Human Rights Watch. 1994. *Human Rights Watch World Report 1994: Events of 1993.* The Women's Rights Project.

———. 1995. *The Human Rights Watch Global Report on Women's Human Rights.* New York: Human Rights Watch.

Hunt, Juliet. 1989. "INGI: Meeting the Challenge." *Inside Indonesia* 20 (October): 32–33.

Hunt, Persis. 1971. "Feminism and Anti-Clericalism under the Commune." *The Massachusetts Review* 12, no. 3: 418–31.

Hunter, David, and Lori Udall. 1994. *The World Bank's New Inspection Panel: Will It Increase the Bank's Accountability?* Washington, D.C.: Center for International Environmental Law.

Huntington, Samuel. 1982. "American Ideals versus American Institutions." *Political Science Quarterly* 97, no. 1: 1–37.

Hutchison, Elizabeth Quay. 1991. "El movimiento de derechos humanos bajo el régimen autoritario, 1973–1988." In *El Movimiento de Derechos Humanos en Chile, 1973–1990,* edited by Patricio Orellana and Elizabeth Q. Hutchison. Santiago: Centro de Estudios Políticos Latinamericanos Simón Bolívar.

Hyland, William G. 1987. *Mortal Rivals: Superpower Relations from Nixon to Reagan.* New York: Random House.

Ichiyo, Muto. 1996. "Hope in Kathmandu: Third Major PP21 Program in South Asia." *AMPO: Japan-Asia Quarterly Review* 27, no. 2: 40–45.

ILO Committee of Experts. 1986. *Report of the Committee of Experts on the Application of Conventions and Recommendations.* Geneva: ILO Office.

Ilumoka, Adetoun O. 1994. "African Women's Economic, Social, and Cultural Rights—Toward a Relevant Theory and Practice." In *Human Rights of Women: National and International Perspectives,* edited by Rebecca J. Cook. Philadelphia: University of Pennsylvania Press.

Imig, Doug, and Sidney Tarrow. 1999. "The Europeanization of Movements? A New

Approach to Transnational Contention." In *Social Movement in a Globalizing World*. London: MacMillan.

InterAction. 1999. "Assessment of Participatory Approaches in Identification of World Bank Projects." Washington, D.C.: InterAction. March.

Inter-American Commission on Human Rights. 1985. *Report on the Situation of Human Rights in Chile*. Washington, D.C.: Organization of American States.

International Commission on Large Dams (ICOLD). 1988. *World Register of Large Dams*. Paris: ICOLD.

International Cooperation for Development and Solidarity (CIDSE) and Caritas Internationalis. 1998. "Putting Life Before Debt." CIDSE, Caritas Internationalis, and U.S. Catholic Conference.

International Human Rights Law Group. 1989. *Chile: The Plebiscite and Beyond*. International Human Rights Law Group.

International NGO Forum on Indonesia (INGI). 1986. "Aide Memoire: Second INGI Conference." Noordwijkerhout, Netherlands. 28–29 April.

———. 1988. "Specific NGO Concerns and Recommendations Regarding World Bank-Financed Transmigration Under Repelita IV and V." *Human Rights Forum* (Jakarta) 15: 8–13.

———. 1992. "Aide Memoire: Eighth INGI Conference." International NGO Forum on Indonesia. Odawara, Japan. 21–23 March.

International NGO Forum on Indonesian Development (INFID). 1993a. *Pembanunan Di Indonesia: Memandan dari Sisi Lain* (Development in Indonesia: A View from the Other Side). Jakarta: Yayasan Obor Swadaya dan INFID.

———. 1993b. "Democratisation through People's Participation: INGI Aide Memoires, 1985–92." The Hague, Netherlands. INFID, Working Paper no. 1. July.

———. 1994a. Statement at Ninth INFID Conference. Paris, France. 22–24 April.

———. 1994b. Pertemuan tentang Keputusan Presiden (KEPPRES) (Meeting about the President Instruction). Jakarta: INFID, 21 July.

———. 1996. Statement by the Tenth INFID Conference on Indonesia: Land and Development. Canberra, Australia. 26–28 April.

———. 1998. Statement by the Eleventh INFID Conference on Indonesia: Democratisation in the Era of Globalization. Bonn, Germany. 4–6 May.

———. 1999. Statement by the Twelfth INFID Conference. Bali, Indonesia. 14–17 September.

———. 2000. INFID Statement to the Consultative Group on Indonesia (CGI) and the Government of Indonesia. Jakarta, Indonesia. 1–2 February.

International Women's Rights Action Watch. 1992. *CEDAW 11*. Minneapolis: University of Minnesota, International Women's Rights Action Watch.

———. 1993a. Closing summary read at IWRAW 1993 conference, "Women,

Family Law, and Human Rights and the Convention on the Elimination of All Forms of Discrimination against Women." Vienna International Centre. 14–15 January. Mimeo.

―――. 1993b. Presentation of Miren Busto, Director, Women's Health Program, Santiago, Chile. World Conference on Human Rights, IWRAW Workshop, Vienna. 14 June. Mimeo.

―――. 1993c. 1994 IWRAW to CEDAW Country Reports. Minneapolis: University of Minnesota, International Women's Rights Watch. December.

Jacobson, Harold K. 1979. *Networks of Interdependence: International Organizations and the Global Political System.* New York: Alfred Knopf.

James, Estelle. 1990. "Economic Theories of the Nonprofit Sector: A Comparative Perspective." In *The Third Sector: Comparative Studies of Nonprofit Organizations,* edited by Helmut Anhier and Wolfgang Seibel. Berlin and New York: de Gruyter.

Jane, Wills. 1998. "Taking on the CosmoCorps? Experiments in Transnational Labor Organization." *Economic Geography* 74, no. 2.

Japan Federation of Bar Associations. 1993. *Report on the Application and Practice in Japan of the Convention on the Elimination of All Forms of Discrimination Against Women.*

Jemadu, Aleksius. 1997. "Globalization Boosts Democracy." *Jakarta Post,* 3 June.

Johnson-Odim, Cheryl. 1991. "Common Themes, Different Contexts: Third World Women and Feminism." In *Third World Women and the Politics of Feminism,* edited by Chandra Talpade Mohanty, Ann Russo, and Lourdes Torres. Bloomington: Indiana University Press.

Jones, Sidney. 1997. *Human Rights in Indonesia and East Timor.* Statement to the House Committee on International Relations, Subcommittee on Asia and the Pacific. 105th Cong., 1st sess.

―――. 1998. *Human Rights in Indonesia.* Statement to the House Committee on International Relations, Subcommittee on International Relations and Human Rights. 105th Cong., 2d sess.

Jordan, Lisa. 1996. "The Bretton Woods Challengers." In *Development: New Paradigms and Principles for the Twenty-first Century,* edited by Jo Marie Griesgraber and Bernhard Gunter. London: Pluto.

Jordan, Lisa and Peter Van Tuijl. 2000. "Political Responsibility in NGO Advocacy." *World Development* 28, no. 12: 205–65.

Jubilee 2000 UK. 2000. "New Figures Show Debt Crisis Still Unresolved as Millennium Year Ends." Press release, 22 December. Available at http://www.jubilee.plus.org/media/jubilee2000_archive/endyear211200.htm.

Kalpavriksh. 1983. "The Narmada Valley Project—Development or Destruction?" Unpublished manuscript.

———. 1988. "The Narmada Valley Project: A Critique." Unpublished manuscript.

Kamminga, Menno T. 1992. *Inter-State Accountability for Violations of Human Rights.* Philadelphia: University of Pennsylvania Press.

Kampelman, Max M. 1991. *Entering New Worlds: The Memoirs of a Private Man in Public Life.* New York: Harper Collins.

Katzenstein, Peter J., ed. 1996. *The Culture of National Security: Norms and Identity in World Politics.* New York: Columbia University Press.

Katzenstein, Peter, Robert Keohane, and Stephen Krasner. 1998. "International Organization and the Study of World Politics." *International Organization* 52, no. 4: 645–85.

Keck, Margaret. 1998. "Brazil: Planafloro in Rondônia: The Limits of Leverage." In *The Struggle for Accountability: The World Bank, NGOs, and Grassroots Movements,* edited by Jonathan Fox and David L. Brown. Cambridge: MIT Press.

Keck, Margaret, and Kathryn Sikkink. 1995. "Transnational Issue Networks in International Politics." Paper presented at the ninety-first annual meeting of the American Political Science Association, Chicago, Ill., August 31–September 3.

———. 1998. *Activists beyond Borders: Advocacy Networks in International Politics.* Ithaca: Cornell University Press.

Kedutaan Besar Republik Indonesia (KBRI). 1994. "New Presidential Instruction to Guide NGOs." KBRI-Canberra, Australia, 4 August.

Keohane, Robert O. 1989. *International Institutions and State Power.* Boulder, Colo.: Westview Press.

Keohane, Robert, and Joseph S. Nye, Jr. 1998. "Power and Interdependence in the Information Age." *Foreign Affairs* 77, no. 5 (Sept.–Oct.): 81–94.

———. 2000. "Globalization: What's New? What's Not? (And So What?)" *Foreign Policy* 118 (spring): 104–19.

Kerr, Joanna, ed. 1993. *Ours by Right: Women's Rights as Human Rights.* London: Zed Books.

Khagram, Sanjeev. 1999. *Dams, Democracy and Development: Transnational Struggles for Power and Water.* Ph.D. diss., Stanford University.

———. 2000a. "Towards Democratic Governance for Sustainable Development: Transnational Civil Society Organizing around Big Dams." In *The Third Force: The Rise of Transnational Civil Society,* edited by Ann Florini. Washington, D.C.: Carnegie Endowment for International Peace.

———. 2000b. "Towards Democratic Governance for Sustainable Development: The World Commission on Dams." In *Global Public Policy Networks,* edited by Wolfgang Reinecke. Washington, D.C.: UN Foundation.

Kim, Young. 1999. "Constructing a Global Identity: The Role of Esperanto." In *Constructing World Culture: International Nongovernmental Organizations Since*

1875, edited by John Bolie and George M. Thomas. Stanford: Stanford University Press.

Kitschelt, Herbert. 1986. "Political Opportunity Structures and Political Protest: Anti-Nuclear Movements in Four Democracies." *British Journal of Political Science* 16: 57–85.

Klandermans, Bert. 1992. "The Social Construction of Protest and Multiorganizational Fields." In *Frontiers in Social Movement Theory,* edited by Aldon Morris and Carol McClurg Mueller. New Haven: Yale University Press.

———. 1997. *The Social Psychology of Protest.* Oxford: Blackwell Publishers.

Klotz, Audie. 1995. *Norms in International Relations: The Struggle against Apartheid.* Ithaca: Cornell University Press.

Knight, W. Andy. 2000. "Sovereignty and NGOs." In *Global Institutions and Local Empowerment: Competing Theoretical Perspectives,* edited by Kendall Stiles. New York: St. Martin's Press.

Kompas. 1994. "LSM-LSM Khawatir tentang Keppres" (NGOs Worry about Presidential Instruction). *Kompas,* 19 July.

Koppel, Bruce. 1998. "Fixing the Other Asia." *Foreign Affairs* 77, no. 1: 98–110.

Korey, William. 1993. *The Promises We Keep: Human Rights, The Helsinki Process, and American Foreign Policy.* New York: St. Martin's Press.

Kothari, Smitu. 1991. "Special Issue on Dams on the River Narmada." *Lokayan Bulletin* 9 (3/4).

———. 1995. "The Damming of the Narmada and the Politics of Development." In *Toward Sustainable Development? Struggling over India's Narmada River,* edited by William F. Fisher. New York: M. E. Sharpe.

———. 1996. "Rising from the Margins: The Awakening of Civil Society in the Third World." *Development* 3: 11–19.

———. 2000a. "A Million Mutinies Now: Lesser Known Environmental Movements." *Humanscape,* October.

———. 2000b. "To be Governed or to Self-Govern." *Folio,* 15 July.

———. 2002. *In Search of Democratic Space.* Delhi: Rainbow Publishers.

Kothari, Smitu, Mary Fainsod Katzenstein, and Uday Singh Mehta. 2001. "Social Movement Politics in India: Interests, Identities and Institutions." In *Democracy and Decentralization,* edited by Atul Kohli. Cambridge: Cambridge University Press.

Kothari, Smitu, and Pramod Parajuli. 1993. "No Nature without Social Justice." In *Global Ecology: A New Arena of Political Conflict,* edited by Wolfgang Sachs. London: Zed Books.

Kothari, Smitu, Vijay Pratap, and Shiv Visvanathan. 1994. "On Globalisation and People's Power." *Lokayan Bulletin,* December, special issue on "Fifty Years of Bretton Woods Institutions: Enough."

Krasner, Stephen D. 1985. *Structural Conflict: The Third World against Global Liberalism.* Berkeley and Los Angeles: University of California Press.

———. 1993. "Westphalia and All That." In *Ideas and Foreign Policy,* edited by Judith Goldstein and Robert O. Keohane. Ithaca, N.Y.: Cornell University Press.

———, ed. 1983. *International Regimes.* Ithaca, N.Y.: Cornell University Press.

Kratochwil, Friedrich. 1989. *Rules, Norms, and Decisions: On the Conditions of Practical Legal Reasoning in International Relations and Domestic Affairs.* Cambridge: Cambridge University Press.

Kratochwil, Friedrich, and John Gerard Ruggie. 1986. "International Organization: The State of the Art on an Art of the State." *International Organization* 40, no. 4: 753–76.

Kriesi, Hanspeter. 1996. "The Organizational Structure of New Social Movements in a Political Context." *Comparative Perspectives on Social Movements,* edited by Doug McAdam, John D. McCarthy, and Mayer N. Zald. New York: Cambridge University Press.

Lawyers Committee for Human Rights. 1993a. *The World Bank: Governance and Human Rights.* New York: Lawyers Committee on Human Rights.

———. 1993b. *Unacceptable Means: India's Sardar Sarovar Project and Violations of Human Rights.* New York: Lawyers Committee on Human Rights.

Lembaga Pembela Hak-Hak Azasi Manusia (LPHAM). 1997. "Protes Keras LPHAM Terhadap Pelarangan Kegiatan Seminar Pemily" (LPHAM's Strong Protest toward Banning of Election Seminar Activity). Jakarta: LPHAM, 13 March.

Lembaga Swadaya Masyarakat (LSM) se-Jawa Tengah. 1994. "Pernya Skiapdan Penolakan LSM Jawa Tengah Terhadap Rancangan KEPPRES LSM" (Central Java NGOs' Declaration of Position and Rejection toward Planned Presidential Instruction for NGOs). Surakarta, Central Java, 29 August.

LePrestre, Phillippe. 1995. "Environmental Learning at the World Bank." In *International Organizations and Environmental Policy,* edited by Robert V. Bartlett, Priya A. Kurian, and Madhu Malik. Westport, Conn.: Greenwood Press.

Lessner, Frederick. 1907. *Sixty Years in the Social-Democratic Movement.* London: Twentieth-Century Press.

Lev, Daniel S. 1987. *Legal Aid in Indonesia.* Clayton, Australia: Centre of Southeast Asian Studies, Monash University, Working Paper, no. 44.

———. 1990. "Human Rights NGOs in Indonesia and Malaysia." In *Asian Perspectives on Human Rights,* edited by Claude E. Welch, Jr. and Virginia A. Leary. Boulder, Colo.: Westview Press.

———. 1993. "INGI and International Development Policies." In *Democratisation through Peoples' Participation: INGI Aide Memoires, 1985–1992.* INFID Working Paper 1 (July): 15–20. The Hague: International NGO Forum on Indonesian Development.

Levinson, Jerome. 1992. "Multilateral Financing Institutions: What Form of Accountability?" *The American University Journal of International Law and Policy* 89, no. 1: 39–64.

Lijnzaad, Elisabeth. 1994. *Reservations to UN Human Rights Treaties: Ratify and Ruin?* The Hague, Netherlands: Stitching T.M.C. Asser Institut and Dordrecht, Netherlands: Martinus Nijhoff Publishers.

Lindber, Staffan, and Arni Sverrisson. 1997. *Social Movements in Development: The Challenge of Globalization and Democratization.* New York: St. Martin's Press.

Linz, Juan. 1978. *The Breakdown of Democratic Regimes: Crisis, Breakdown, and Reequilibration.* Baltimore: The Johns Hopkins University Press.

Lipschutz, Ronnie. 1992. "Reconstructing World Politics: The Emergence of Global Civil Society." *Millennium* 21: 389–420.

———. 1996. *Global Civil Society and Global Environmental Governance.* Albany, N.Y.: State University of New York Press.

Lord, Winston. 1994. "APEC Is a Building Block for a Global Approach to Trade." Address to the Asia Society, 28 October, New York.

Lowden, Pamela. 1996. *Moral Opposition to Authoritarian Rule in Chile, 1973–1990.* New York: St. Martin's Press.

Ludwig Boltzmann Institute of Human Rights. 1993. "World Conference on Human Rights, Vienna, Austria, 14–25 June 1993." *NGO Newsletter* 4 (July). Vienna: Ludwig Boltzmann Institute of Human Rights.

Lukes, Steven. 1974. *Power: A Radical View.* London: Macmillan.

Lumsdaine, David H. 1993. *Moral Vision in International Politics: The Foreign Aid Regime, 1949–1989.* Princeton: Princeton University Press.

Lutz, Ellen L., Hurst Hannum, and Kathryn J. Burke, eds. 1989. *New Directions in Human Rights.* Philadelphia: University of Pennsylvania Press.

MacDonald, Laura. 1994. "Globalizing Civil Society: Interpreting International NGOs in Central America." In *The South at the End of the Twentieth Century,* edited by Larry A. Swatuk and Timothy M. Shaw. New York: St. Martin's Press.

Malena, Carmen. 1995. *Working with NGOs: A Practical Guide to Operational Collaboration between the World Bank and Non-governmental Organizations.* Washington, D.C.: NGO Unit, OPRPG, World Bank.

———. 2000. "Beneficiaries, Mercenaries, Missionaries and Revolutionaries: 'Unpacking' NGO Involvement in World Bank–Financed Projects." *IDS Bulletin* 31, no. 3 (July): 19–34.

Marchand, Marianne H. 1994. "The Political Economy of North-South Relations." In *Political Economy and the Changing Global Order,* edited by Richard Stubbs and Geoffrey R. D. Underhill. New York: St. Martin's Press.

Marks, Gary, and Doug McAdam. 1996. "Social Movements and the Changing

Structure of Political Opportunity in the European Union." *West European Politics* 19, no. 2: 249–78.

Martin, Atherton. 1993. Address to the opening session of the World Bank Conference on Overcoming Global Hunger. American University, Washington, D.C., 30 November.

Martin, Lisa. 1992. *Coercive Cooperation: Explaining Multilateral Economic Sanctions.* Princeton: Princeton University Press.

Martin, Matthew. 1994. "Official Bilateral Debt: New Directions for Action." EURODAD Policy Paper. Brussels (April): 1–43.

Marx, Karl, and Frederick Engels. 1969. *Letters to Americans, 1848–1895.* New York: International Publishers.

———. 1975. *Collected Works.* 48 vols. New York: International Publishers.

Mas'oed, Mochtar. 1996. "Globalisation from Below." *Inside Indonesia* 47: 13.

Mawer, Richard. 1997. "Mice among the Tigers: Adding Value in Non-Government Relations in South-east Asia." In *NGOs, States and Donors: Too Close for Comfort?* edited by David Hulme and Michael Edwards. New York: St. Martin's Press.

Maximov, L. 1976. "Fulfillment of the Helsinki Understandings." *International Affairs* (Moscow) 10 (October): 22–31.

McAdam, Doug. 1982. *The Political Process and the Development of Black Insurgency.* Chicago: University of Chicago Press.

———. 1988. *Freedom Summer.* New York: Oxford University Press.

———. 1996. "Conceptual Origins, Current Problems, Future Direction." In *Comparative Perspectives on Social Movements: Political Opportunities, Mobilizing Structures, and Cultural Framings,* edited by Doug McAdam, John McCarthy, and Mayer Zald. New York: Cambridge University Press.

McAdam, Doug, John McCarthy, and Mayer Zald. 1996. *Comparative Perspectives on Social Movements: Political Opportunities, Mobilizing Structures, and Cultural Framings.* New York: Cambridge University Press.

McBeth, John. 1996. "Far from Over: Democrats, Leftists Remain under Political Cloud." *Far Eastern Economic Review* 159, no. 34: 69.

McCarthy, John. 1996. "Constraints and Opportunities in Adoption, Adaption and Inventing." In *Comparative Perspectives on Social Movements: Political Opportunities, Mobilizing Structures, and Cultural Framings.* New York: Cambridge University Press.

McCully, Patrick. 1995. "Update on the Deadly Kedung Ombo Resettlement Fiasco." *Bulletin of Concerned Asian Scholars* 26, no. 4: 85–86.

McLellan, David. 1973. *Karl Marx: His Life and Thought.* New York: Harper and Row.

Medina Quiroga, Cecilia. 1988. *The Battle of Human Rights: Gross, Systemic Violations and the Inter-American System.* Dordrecht, Netherlands: Martinus Nijhoff Publishers.

Mermel, T. W. 1995. "The World's Major Dams and Hydroplants." *International Water Power Handbook.* Sutton, U.K.: IWPDC.

Meyer, David, and Sidney Tarrow. 1998. *The Social Movement Society: Contentious Politics for a New Century.* Lanham, Md.: Rowman and Littlefield Publishers.

Mittelman, James H. 2000. *The Globalization Syndrome: Transformation and Resistance.* Princeton: Princeton University Press.

Morgenthau, Hans J. 1993. *Politics among Nations: The Struggle for Power and Peace.* 6th ed., revised by Kenneth W. Thompson. New York: McGraw-Hill.

Morse, Bradford, and Thomas Berger. 1992. *Sardar Sarovar: Report of the Independent Review.* Ottawa: Resources Futures International.

Mosley, Paul, Jane Harrigan, and John Toye. 1991. *Aid and Power: The World Bank and Policy-based Lending.* Vol. 1. London: Routledge.

Muldoon, Paul R. 1986. "The International Law of Ecodevelopment: Emerging Norms for Development Assistance Agencies." *Texas International Law Journal* 22: 1–52.

Munir. 2000. "The Slow Birth of Democracy." *Inside Indonesia* 63: 4–5 (July–September).

Muñoz, Heraldo. 1986. *Las Relaciones Exteriores del Gobierno Militar Chileno.* Santiago: PROSPEL-CERC.

Muravchik, Joshua. 1991. *The Uncertain Crusade: Jimmy Carter and the Dilemmas of Human Rights Policy.* Washington, D.C.: American Enterprise Institute Press.

Nababan, Asmara. 1996. "Human Rights Belong to Us." *Inside Indonesia* 47: 11.

Nadelmann, Ethan. 1990. "Global Prohibition Regimes: The Evolution of Norms in International Society." *International Organization* 44: 479–526.

Naidoo, Kumi. 2000. "The New Civic Globalism." *The Nation* 270, no. 18 (8 May): 34–36.

Naim, Noises. 2000. "Lori's War: The FP Interview." *Foreign Policy* 118 (spring): 28–55.

Narmada Bachao Andolan. 1988. "Sardar Sarovar Project: An Economic, Environmental and Human Disaster." Unpublished manuscript.

Narmada Control Authority. 1984. *Sardar Sarovar Projects: Land Acquisition and Rehabilitation of Oustees.* New Delhi: Government of India.

Nasution, Adnan Buyung. 1994. "Defending Human Rights in Indonesia." *Journal of Democracy* 5, no. 3: 114–23.

Ndegwa, Stephen N. 1996. *The Two Faces of Civil Society: NGOs and Politics in Africa.* West Hartford, Conn.: Kumarian Press.

Nelson, Joan. 1989. "The Politics of Long-Haul Economic Reform." In *Fragile Coalition: The Politics of Economic Adjustment,* edited by Joan Nelson. Washington, D.C.: Overseas Development Council.

Nelson, Paul J. 1995. *The World Bank and NGOs: The Limits of Apolitical Development.* London: Macmillan.

———. 1996a. "Internationalising Economic and Environmental Policy: Transnational NGO Networks and the Expanding Power of the World Bank." *Millennium* 25, no. 3: 605–33.

———. 1996b. "Transparency, Accountability, Participation: Implementing New Mandates at the World Bank and the Inter-American Development Bank." Informe No. 199. Buenos Aires: FLACSO.

———. 1997. "Conflict, Legitimacy, and Effectiveness: Who Speaks for Whom in Transnational NGO Networks Lobbying the World Bank?" *Nonprofit and Voluntary Sector Quarterly* 26, no. 4: 421–41.

———. 2001. "Transparency Mechanisms at the Multilateral Development Banks." *World Development* 20, no. 11 (November 2001).

Newland, Kathleen. 1991. "From Transnational Relationship to International Relations: Women in Development and the International Decade for Women." In *Gender and International Relations,* edited by Rebecca Grant and Kathleen Newland. Bloomington: Indiana University Press.

Nhlapo, T. R. 1991. "The African Family and Women's Rights: Friends or Foes?" *Acta Juridica,* 135–246.

Nimtz, August H., Jr. 1999. "Marx and Engels—The Unsung Heroes of the Democratic Breakthrough." *Science & Society* 63, no. 2: 203–31.

———. 2000. *Marx and Engels: Their Contribution to the Democratic Breakthrough.* Albany: State University of New York Press.

North Atlantic Council. 1980. *Texts of Final Communiques.* Vol. 2. Brussels: NATO Information Service.

North-South Institute. 1999. *Canadian Development Report 1999: Civil Society and Global Change.* Ottawa, Canada: The North-South Institute.

Nowak, Jerzy M. 1976. "Cooperation between East and West on Humanitarian Issues." *Translations on Eastern Europe* 68273 (26 November). First published in *Sprawy Miedzynarodowe* 9 (September).

Nye, Joseph S., and John D. Donahue, eds. 2000. *Governance in a Globalizing World.* Washington, D.C.: Brookings Institution.

Oberschall, Anthony. 1996. "Opportunities and Framing in the Eastern European Revolts of 1989." In *Comparative Perspectives on Social Movements: Political Opportunities, Mobilizing Structures, and Cultural Framings.* New York: Cambridge University Press.

O'Brien, Robert, Marc Williams, Anne Marie Goetz, and Jan Aart Scholte. 2000. *Contesting Global Governance: Multilateral Economic Institutions and Global Social Movements.* New York: Cambridge University Press.

O'Donnell, Guillermo. 1973. *Modernization and Bureaucratic Authoritarianism.* Berkeley: Institute of International Studies, University of California.

Operation Evaluations Department. 1995. "Learning from Narmada." *OED Précis.* Washington, D.C.: World Bank.

Oxfam International. 1996. "Assessment of IMF–World Bank Debt Reduction Initiative." *Oxfam International Position Paper* (April): 1–9.

Oxfam U.K. and Ireland. 1994. "Structural Adjustment and Inequality in Latin America: How IMF and World Bank Policies Have Failed the Poor." Mimeo. Oxford.

Oxhorn, Philip D. 1995. *Organizing Civil Society: The Popular Sectors and the Struggle for Democracy in Chile.* University Park: Pennsylvania State University Press.

Pacific Asia Resource Center (PARC). 1995. "Statement from 1995 NGO Forum on APEC." *AMPO: Japan-Asia Quarterly Review* 26, no. 4: 18–19.

Paranjpye, Vijay. 1990. *High Dams on the Narmada: A Holistic Analysis of River Valley Projects.* New Delhi: Indian National Trust for Art and Cultural Heritage.

Pasha, Mustapha Kemal, and David L. Blaney. 1998. "Elusive Paradise: The Promise and Peril of Global Civil Society." *Alternatives* 23, no. 4 (Oct.-Dec.): 417–50.

Pathak, Akhileshwar. 1994. *Contested Domains: The State, Peasants and Forests in Contemporary India.* New Delhi: Sage Publications.

Patkar, Medha, and Smitu Kothari. 1995. "The Struggle for Participation and Justice: A Historical Narrative." In *Toward Sustainable Development?: Struggling over India's Narmada River,* edited by William F. Fisher. Armonk, N.Y.: M. E. Sharpe.

Pelikan, Jiri. 1977. "Interview." *Labor Focus on Eastern Europe* 1.

People's Forum on APEC 1996. 1996. Manila, Philippines.

Perrow, Charles. 1970. "Members as Resources in Voluntary Organizations." In *Organizations and Clients,* edited by William R. Rosengren and Mark Lefton. Columbus, Ohio: Merrill.

Peterson, M. J. 1992. "Transnational Activity, International Society and World Politics." *Millennium* 21, no. 3.

Phillips, Anne. 1991. *Engendering Democracy.* University Park: Pennsylvania State University Press.

Piddington, Kenneth. 1992. "The Role of the World Bank." In *The International Politics of the Environment,* edited by Andrew Hurrell and Benedict Kingsbury. Oxford: Clarendon Press.

Pinto-Duschinsky, Michael. 1991. "Foreign Political Aid: The German Political Foundations and Their U.S. Counterparts." *International Affairs* 67, no. 1: 33–63.

Pitanguay, Jacqueline. 1995. "Women's Citizenship and Human Rights: The Case of Brazil." In *A Diplomacy of the Oppressed: New Directions in International Feminism,* edited by Georgina Ashworth. London: Zed Books.

Polanyi, Karl. 1944. *The Great Transformation.* New York: Rinehart.

Pontifical Commission on Justice and Peace. 1987. "An Ethical Approach to the International Debt Question." *Origins* 16, no. 34: 601–11.

Potter, George Ann. 1988. *Dialogue on Debt: Alternative Analyses and Solutions.* Washington, D.C.: Center of Concern.

Powell, Walter W. 1990. "Neither Market Nor Hierarchy: Network Forms of Organization." *Research in Organizational Behavior* 12: 295–334.

Presidential Commission on World Hunger. 1980. *Final Report.* Washington, D.C.

Price, Richard. 1998. "Reversing the Gun Sights: Transnational Civil Society Targets Land Mines." *International Organization* 52, no. 3: 613–44.

Princen, Thomas, and Matthias Finger, eds. 1994. *Environmental NGOs in World Politics: Linking the Local and the Global.* London: Routledge.

Puryear, Jeffret M. 1991. *Building Democracy: Foreign Donors and Chile.* Unpublished manuscript.

———. 1994. *Thinking Politics: Intellectuals and Democracy in Chile.* Baltimore: The Johns Hopkins University Press.

Putnam, Robert. 1988. "Diplomacy and Domestic Politics: The Logic of Two-Level Games." *International Organization* 42, no. 3: 427–60.

Quizon, Antonio, and Violeta Q. Perez Corrall. 1995. *The NGO Campaign on the Asian Development Bank.* Manila: Asian NGO Coalition.

Reed, David. 1992. *Structural Adjustment and the Environment.* Boulder, Colo.: Westview Press.

Reinicke, Wolfgang H. 1999/2000. "The Other World Wide Web: Global Public Policy Networks." *Foreign Policy* 117 (winter): 44–57.

Reinicke, Wolfgang H., and Francis Deng. 2000. *Critical Choices: The United Nations, Networks, and the Future of Global Governance.* Ottawa: IDRC Books.

Rich, Bruce. 1994. *Mortgaging the Earth: The World Bank, Environmental Impoverishment, and the Crisis of Development.* Boston: Beacon Press.

Riker, James V. 1994/1995. "Linking Development from Below to the International Environmental Movement: Sustainable Development and State-NGO Relations in Indonesia." *Journal of Business Administration* 22 and 23: 157–88.

———. 1995a. "Reflections on Government-NGO Relations in Asia: Prospects and Challenges for People-Centered Development." In *Government-NGO Relations in Asia: Prospects and Challenges for People-Centered Development,* edited by Noeleen Heyzer, James V. Riker, and Antonio B. Quizon. New York: St. Martin's Press.

Risse, Thomas. 2000. "Let's Argue! Communicative Action in World Politics." *International Organization* 54, no. 1.

Risse, Thomas, and Kathryn Sikkink. 1999. "The Socialization of International Human Rights Norms into Domestic Practices: Introduction." In *The Power of Human Rights: International Norms and Domestic Change,* edited by Thomas Risse, Stephen C. Ropp, and Kathryn Sikkink. Cambridge: Cambridge University Press.

Risse, Thomas, Stephen C. Ropp, and Kathryn Sikkink, eds. 1999. *The Power of Human Rights: International Norms and Domestic Change.* Cambridge: Cambridge University Press.

Risse-Kappen, Thomas. 1995a. "Bringing Transnational Relations Back In: An Introduction." In *Bringing Transnational Relations Back In: Non-State Actors, Domestic Structures, and International Institutions,* edited by Thomas Risse-Kappen. Cambridge: Cambridge University Press.

Risse-Kappen, Thomas, ed. 1995b. *Bringing Transnational Relations Back In: Non-State Actors, Domestic Structures and International Institutions.* Cambridge: Cambridge University Press.

Robinson, Dan. 1994. "Thailand and East Timor." *Voice of America,* 15 July.

Robinson, Geoffrey. 1996. "Human Rights in Southeast Asia: Rhetoric and Reality." In *Southeast Asia in the New World Order: The Political Economy of a Dynamic Region,* edited by David Wurfel and Bruce Burton. New York: St. Martin's Press.

Rochon, Thomas. 1998. *Culture Moves: Ideas, Activism and Changing Values.* Princeton: Princeton University Press.

Rodan, Garry, ed. 1996a. *Political Oppositions in Industrialising Asia.* New York: Routledge.

———. 1996b. "Theorising Political Opposition in East and Southeast Asia." In *Political Oppositions in Industrialising Asia,* edited by Garry Rodan. New York: Routledge.

Rosati, Jerel A. 1991. *The Carter Administration's Quest for Global Community: Beliefs and Their Impact on Behavior.* Columbia: University of South Carolina Press.

Roychowdhury, Anumita, and Nitya Jacob. 1993. "Was India Forced to Reject World Bank Aid?" *Down to Earth* (April 30): 5–7.

Rucht, Dieter. 1996. "The Impact of National Contexts on Social Movement Structures: A Cross-Movement and Cross-National Comparison." In *Comparative Perspectives on Social Movements,* edited by Doug McAdam, John McCarthy, and Mayer Zald. New York: Cambridge University Press.

Rueschmeyer, Dietrich, Evelyne Huber Stephens, and John D. Stephens. 1992. *Capitalist Development and Democracy.* Chicago: University of Chicago Press.

Ruggie, John Gerard. 1982. "International Regimes, Transactions, and Change: Embedded Liberalism in the Postwar Economic Order." *International Organization* 36, no. 2: 379–416.

———. 1983. "Human Rights and the Future International Community." *Daedalus* 112, no. 4: 93–110.

Salamon, Lester M. 1994. "The Rise of the Nonprofit Sector." *Foreign Affairs* 73, no. 4: 111–24.

Salamon, Lester M., and Helmut K. Anheier. 1996. *The Emerging Nonprofit Sector: An Overview*. Manchester: Manchester University Press.

Salamon, Lester M., Helmut K. Anheier, Regina List, Stefan Toepler, and S. Wojciech Sokolowski. 1999. *Global Civil Society: Dimensions of the Nonprofit Sector*. Baltimore: The Johns Hopkins University Press.

Salzberg, John, and Donald D. Young. 1977. "The Parliamentary Role in Implementing International Human Rights: A U.S. Example." *Texas International Law Journal* 12: 251–78.

Sánchez, Domingo. 1990. "Las resoluciones internacionales sobre Chile: Un desafío para la futura democracia." *Revista Chilena de Derechos Humanos* 12: 61–97.

Sanit, Arbi. 1991a. "LSM dan Kelas Menengah: Arah Baru Pengembangan Strategi Perjuangan" (NGOs and the Middle Class: New Directions in the Struggle of Developing Strategy). Typescript. Jakarta: Pusat Penelitian Pranata Pembangunan. Universitas Indonesia.

———. 1991b. "Hak Berorganisasi di Antara Pemusatan Kekusaan dan Demokrasi" (The Right to Organize Amidst the Centralization of Power and Democracy). Jakarta: Pesat Penelitian Pranata Pembangunan.

Sardar Sarovar. 1992. *The Report of the Independent Review*.

Sasono, Adi. 1989. "NGOs Roles and Social Movement in Developing Democracy: the South-East Asian Experiences." *New Asian Visions* (Jakarta) 6, no. 1: 14–26.

Sassen, Saskia. 1991. *The Global City: New York, London, Tokyo*. Princeton: Princeton University Press.

Save the Children Federation. 1993. "Investing in Health-World Development Report 1993. The SCF Perspective." London. Unpublished paper.

Schittecatte, C. 1999. "The Creation of a Global Public Good through Transnational Coalition of Social Movements: The Case of the Amazon." *Canadian Journal of Development Studies* 20 no. 2.

Schmitz, Hans-Peter. 2000. "Mobilizing Identities, Transnational Social Movements, and the Promotion of Human Rights Norms." In *Global Institutions and Local Empowerment: Competing Theoretical Perspectives,* edited by Kendall Stiles. New York: St. Martin's Press.

Schneider, Cathy Lisa. 1995. *Shantytown Protest in Pinochet's Chile*. Philadelphia: Temple University Press.

Scholte, Jan Aart. 1993. *International Relations of Social Change*. Philadelphia: Open University Press.

Schoultz, Lars. 1981. *Human Rights and United States Policy toward Latin America*. Princeton: Princeton University Press.

Schwarz, Adam. 1992. "NGOs Knocked: Jakarta Extends Ban on Netherlands Aid." *Far Eastern Economic Review* 155, no. 19: 20.

———. 1997. "Indonesia after Suharto." *Foreign Affairs* 76 (July–August): 119–34.

Schwarz, Adam, and Jonathan Paris, eds. 1999. *The Politics of Post-Suharto Indonesia.* New York: Council on Foreign Relations.

Schweitz, Martha L. 1995. "NGO Participation in International Governance: The Question of Legitimacy." *Proceedings of the Eighty-Ninth Annual Meeting of the American Society of International Law,* 5–8 April.

Scudder, Thayer. 1983. "The Relocation Component in Connection with the Sardar Sarovar (Narmada) Project." Unpublished manuscript of *Resettlement Appraisal Mission's Findings.*

Secretary of State for Foreign and Commonwealth Affairs. 1978. Command paper 7126 from the meeting held at Belgrade from 4 October 1977 to 9 March 1978 to follow up on the Conference on Security and Cooperation in Europe. London: Her Majesty's Stationary Office.

Sen, Amartya. 1990. "Millions of Women Are Missing." *New York Review of Books* 37 (20 December): 61–66.

Shaw, Timothy M. 1995. "Africa in the Global Political Economy at the End of the Millennium: What Implications for Politics and Policies?" *Africa Today* 42l, no. 4: 7–30.

———. 2000. "Overview—Global/Local: States, Companies and Civil Societies at the End of the Twentieth Century." In *Global Institutions and Local Empowerment: Competing Theoretical Perspectives,* edited by Kendall Stiles. New York: St. Martin's Press.

Sherer, Albert W., Jr. 1980. "Helsinki's Child: Goldberg Variations." *Foreign Policy* 39 (summer): 154–59.

Sherk, Don, and Elliot Berg. 1993. "The World Bank and Its Environmentalist Critics." Report prepared for the Group of Thirty Commission on the Future of the Bretton Woods Institutions, Washington, D.C.

Shevchenko, Arkady N. 1985. *Breaking with Moscow.* New York: Alfred A. Knopf.

Shihata, Ibrahim F. I. 1994. *The World Bank Inspection Panel.* Oxford: Oxford University Press.

Shulman, Marshall D. 1977. "On Learning to Live with Authoritarian Regimes." *Foreign Affairs* 55, no. 2: 325–38.

Sigmund, Paul. 1977. *The Overthrow of Allende and the Politics of Chile.* Pittsburgh: University of Pittsburgh Press.

———. 1993. *The United States and Democracy in Chile.* Baltimore: The Johns Hopkins University Press.

Sikkink, Kathryn. 1993a. "Human Rights, Principled Issue-networks, and Sovereignty in Latin America." *International Organization* 47, no. 3: 411–41.

———. 1993b. "The Power of Principled Ideas: Human Rights Policies in the United States and Western Europe." In *Ideas and Foreign Policy: Beliefs, Institutions and Political Change,* edited by Judith Goldstein and Robert O. Keohane. Ithaca: Cornell University Press.

———. 1996. "Nongovernmental Organizations, Democracy, and Human Rights in Latin America." In *Beyond Sovereignty: Collectively Defending Democracy in the Americas,* edited by Tom Farer. Baltimore: The Johns Hopkins University Press.

Simmons, P. J. 1998. "Learning to Live with NGOs." *Foreign Policy* (fall): 82–96.

Sinclair, Jim, ed. 1992. *Crossing the Line: Canada and Free Trade with Mexico.* Vancouver: New Star Books.

Skjelsbaek, Kjell. 1971. "The Growth of International Non-Governmental Organization in the Twentieth Century." *International Organization* 25: 420–42.

Smith, Brian H. 1982. *The Church and Politics in Chile: Challenges to Modern Catholicism.* Princeton: Princeton University Press.

Smith, F. B. 1966. *The Making of the Second Reform Bill.* Cambridge: Cambridge University Press.

Smith, Jackie. 1995. "Organizing Global Action: Transnational Social Movements and World Politics." Ph.D. diss., University of Notre Dame.

———. 1997. "Characteristics of the Modern Transnational Social Movement Sector." In *Transnational Social Movements and World Politics: Solidarity beyond the State,* edited by Jackie Smith, Charles Chatfield, and Ron Pagnucco. Syracuse: Syracuse University Press.

———. 1999. *Report on EarthAction Partner Survey.* Amherst, Mass.: EarthAction.

———. 2000. "Social Movement, International Institutions and Local Empowerment." In *Global Institutions and Local Empowerment: Competing Theoretical Perspectives,* edited by Kendall Stiles. New York: St. Martin's Press.

Smith, Jackie, Charles Chatfield, and Ron Pagnucco, eds. 1997. *Transnational Social Movements and Global Politics: Solidarity Beyond the State.* Syracuse: Syracuse University Press.

Smith, Jackie, Ron Pagnucco, and George Lopez. 1998. "Globalizing Human Rights: The Work of Human Rights NGOs in the 1990s." *Human Rights Quarterly* 20: 379–412.

Smith, Shannon L. 1992. *The Politics of Indonesian Rainforests.* Working paper no. 76. Clayton, Australia: Monash University, Centre of Southeast Asian Studies.

Smith, Tony. 1994. *American's Mission: The United States and the Worldwide Struggle for Democracy in the Twentieth Century.* Princeton: Princeton University Press.

Snow, David, Burke E. Rochford Jr., Steven K. Worden, and Robert Benford. 1986. "Frame Alignment, Processes, Micromobilization and Movement Participation." *American Sociological Review* 51.

Snow, David, and Robert Benford. 1988. "Ideology, Frame Resonance, and Partici-
pant Mobilization." In *From Structure to Action: Comparing Social Movement
Research across Cultures,* edited by Bert Klandermanns, Hanspeter Kriesi, and
Sidney Tarrow. Greenwich, Conn.: JAI Press.
————. 1992. "Master Frames and Cycles of Protest." In *Frontier's in Social Movement
Theory,* edited by Aldon D. Morris and Carol McClurg Mueller. New Haven,
Conn.: Yale University.
Soetrisno, Loekman. 1991. "Lembaga Swadaya Masyarakat dan Proses Demokratisasi
di Indonesia" (NGOs and the Process of Democratization in Indonesia).
Makalah disampaikan untuk Seminar Teknologi Tepat Guna (TTG) Bandung
Forum. Yogyakarta. Typescript.
"Statement by the Working Group in Women's Rights of the NGO Forum at the
World Conference on Human Rights" 1995. Mimeo.
Stiefel, Matthias, and Marshall Wolfe. 1994. *A Voice for the Excluded: Popular
Participation in Development.* London: Zed.
Stiles, Kendall W. 1998. "Civil Society Empowerment and Multilateral Donors:
International Institutions and New International Norms." *Global Governance*
4, no. 2: 199–216.
————, ed. 2000. *Global Institutions and Local Empowerment: Competing Theoretical
Perspectives.* New York: St. Martin's Press.
Stokes, Bruce. 1988. "Storming the Bank." *National Journal* 20, no. 53: 3250–53.
Tarrow, Sidney. 1994. *Power in Movement: Social Movements, Collective Action, and
Politics.* Cambridge: Cambridge University Press.
————. 1995. "The Europeanisation of Conflict: Reflections from a Social Movement Perspective." *West European Politics* 18, no. 2: 223–51.
————. 1998. *Power in Movement: Social Movements and Contentious Politics.* 2d ed.
Cambridge: Cambridge University Press.
————. 1999. "International Institutions and Contentious Politics: Does Inter-
nationalization Make Agents Freer—or Weaker?" Paper prepared for the Con-
venor Group on "Beyond Center-Periphery of the Unbundling of Territoriality."
University of California at Berkeley, April 16–17.
Taylor, Bron Raymon, ed. 1995. *Ecological Resistance Movements: The Global
Emergence of Radical and Popular Environmentalism.* Albany: State University
of New York Press.
Thomas, Daniel C. 1997. *Norms and Change in World Politics: The Helsinki Accords,
Human Rights and the Demise of Communism.* Ph.D. diss., Cornell University.
————. 1999. "The Helsinki Accords and Political Change in Eastern Europe." In
The Power of Human Rights: International Norms and Domestic Change, edited
by Thomas Risse, Stephen Ropp, and Kathryn Sikkink. Cambridge: Cambridge
University Press.

————. 2001. *The Helsinki Effect: International Norms, Human Rights and the Demise of Communism*. Princeton: Princeton University Press.

Thomas, Dorothy Q., and Michele E. Beasley. 1993. "Domestic Violence as a Human Rights Issue." *Human Rights Quarterly* 15, no. 1: 36–62.

Thomas, Edith. 1971. "The Women of the Commune." *The Massachusetts Review* 12, no. 3: 409–17.

Thompson, Karen Brown. 1997. *Global Norms Concerning Women's and Children's Rights and Their Implications for State-Citizen Relations*. Ph.D. diss., University of Minnesota.

Thomson, Janice E. 1990. "State Practices, International Norms, and the Decline of Mercenarism." *International Studies Quarterly* 34, no. 1: 23–47.

Tilly, Charles. 1995. "Globalization Threatens Labor's Rights." *International Labor and Working Class History* 47 (spring): 1–23.

Trubek, David M., Yves Dezalay, Ruth Buchanan, and John R. Davis. 1994. "Global Restructuring and the Law: Studies of the Internationalization of Legal Fields and the Creation of Transnational Arenas." *Case Western Reserve Law Review* 44, no. 2: 407–98.

Tsuzuki, Chushichi. 1967. *The Life of Eleanor Marx, 1855–1898*. Oxford: Oxford University Press.

Udall, Lori. 1994. "The World Bank's Revised Information Policy and New Inspection Panel: Public Accountability or Public Relations?" In *Beyond Bretton Woods: Alternatives to the Global Economic Order*, edited by John Cavanaugh, Daphne Wisham, and Marcos Arruda. Boulder, Colo.: Pluto.

————. 1995. "The International Narmada Campaign: A Case Study of Sustained Advocacy." In *Toward Sustainable Development?: Struggling Over India's Narmada River*, edited by William F. Fisher. Armonk, N.Y.: M. E. Sharpe.

————. 1998. "The World Bank and Public Accountability: Has Anything Changed?" In *The Struggle for Accountability*, edited by Jonathan A. Fox and L. David Brown. Cambridge: MIT Press.

Uhlin, Anders. 1993. "Transnational Democratic Diffusion and Indonesian Democracy Discourses." *Third World Quarterly* 14, no. 3: 513–40.

————. 1997. *Indonesia and the "Third Wave of Democratization": The Indonesian Pro-Democracy Movement in a Changing World*. New York: St. Martin's Press.

United Nations. 1957. *Convention on the Nationality of Married Women*, adopted by the General Assembly on 29 January 1957, UN Treaty Series, 309(4468): 65. Reproduced in *The United Nations and the Advancement of Women*. United Nations, New York: UN Department of Public Information.

————. 1980. Report of the World Conference of the United Nations Decade for Women: Equality, Development and Peace, 14–30 July, Copenhagen.

Reproduced in *The United Nations and the Advancement of Women.* United Nations. New York: UN Department of Public Information.

———. 1984. *Convention on the Elimination of All Forms of Discrimination Against Women* (CEDAW). Reprint of United Nations Department of Public Information, Division for Economic and Social Information. Publication provided by International Women's Rights Action Watch, Minneapolis, Minn.

———. 1986. *The Nairobi Forward-Looking Strategies for the Advancement of Women.* New York: United Nations Department of Public Information.

———. 1993. *Vienna Declaration and Programme of Action.* New York: United Nations.

———. 1995a. *Beijing Declaration and Platform for Action.* Adopted by UN Fourth World Conference on Women, 15 September.

———. 1995b. *NGO Forum on Women: Final Report.* New York: United Nations.

———. 1995c. *NGO Forum on Women '95 Bulletin, Final Issue.* New York: United Nations.

———. 1995d. *The United Nations and the Advancement of Women, 1945–1995,* New York: UN Department of Public Information.

United Nations Development Programme (UNDP). 2000. *Human Development Report 2000: Human Rights and Human Development.* New York: Oxford University Press.

United Nations Division for the Advancement of Women. 1996. "International Women's Day, 1996." Available at www.undp.org/fwcw/8march.htm.

United Nations Economic and Social Council. 1946. "ECOSOC resolution establishing the Commission on the Status of Women (CSW)." Reproduced in *The United Nations and the Advancement of Women, 1945–1995.* New York: UN Department of Public Information.

———. 1962. "ECOSOC resolution recommending that Member States make full use of the UN technical assistance and human rights advisory services programmes for the purpose of advancing the status of women in developing countries." Reproduced in *The United Nations and the Advancement of Women, 1945–1995.* New York: UN Department of Public Information.

———. 1994. "General Review of Arrangements for Consultations with Nongovernmental Organizations: Report of the Secretary General." Open-ended working group on the review of arrangements for consultation with nongovernmental organizations. 26 May.

United Nations General Assembly. 1993. Committee on the Elimination of All Forms of Discrimination Against Women. *Report of the Committee on the Elimination of Discrimination Against Women, Twelfth Session.*

United Nations Research Institute for Social Development (UNRISD). 2000. *Visible*

Hands: Taking Responsibility for Social Development. UNRISD Report for Geneva 2000. Geneva: UNRISD.

Unny, Suresh, Gordon Fairclough, S. Jayasankaran, and John McBeth. 1996. "Devious and Deliberate." *Far Eastern Economic Review* 159, no. 47: 16–17.

U.S. Catholic Conference Administrative Board. 1989. "A Statement on Relieving Third World Debt." *Origins, NC Documentary Service* 19, no. 19: 305–14.

U.S. Commission on Security and Cooperation in Europe. 1977. *Basket III: Implementation of the Helsinki Accords.* Hearings, 3 June and 6 June. Washington, D.C.: U.S. Government Printing Office.

———. 1978. *The Belgrade CSCE Follow-Up Meeting: A Report and Appraisal.* Washington, D.C.: U.S. Government Printing Office.

U.S. Department of State. 1978. *Fourth Semiannual Report by the President to the Commission on Security and Cooperation in Europe,* 1 December 1977–1 June 1978. Washington, D.C.: U.S. Government Printing Office.

U.S. Helsinki Watch Committee. 1980. *The First Fifteen Months, A Summary of the Activities of the U.S. Helsinki Watch Committee from Its Founding in February 1979 through April 1980.* New York: U.S. Helsinki Watch Committee.

U.S. House. 1972. Committee on Foreign Affairs. *Conference on European Security: Hearings before the Subcommittee on Europe.* 92d Cong., 2d sess. April 25.

———. 1977. Committee on International Relations. *Second Semiannual Report to the Commission on Security and Cooperation in Europe, December 1, 1976–June 1, 1977.*

———. 1989. Committee on Science, Space and Technology. *Sardar Sarovar Dam Project: Hearings before the Subcommittee on Natural Resources, Agricultural Research and Environment.* 101st Congress, 1st sess. 24 October.

U.S. Senate. 1975. Select Committee on Intelligence Activities. *Covert Action in Chile, 1963–1973.* 94th Cong., 1st sess.

———. 1976. Committee on Foreign Relations. *Establishing a Commission on Security and Cooperation in Europe.* 94th Cong., 2d sess. 23 April.

Uvin, Peter. 2000. "From Local Organizations to Global Governance: The Role of NGOs in International Relations." In *Global Institutions and Local Empowerment,* edited by Kendall Stiles. New York: St. Martin's Press.

Valenzuela, Arturo. 1978. *The Breakdown of Democratic Regimes: Chile.* Vol. 4. Baltimore: The Johns Hopkins University Press.

———. 1989. "Chile: Origins, Consolidation, Breakdown of a Democratic Regime." In *Democracy in Developing Countries: Latin America,* edited by Larry Diamond, Juan J. Linz, and Seymour Martin Lipset. Boulder, Colo.: Lynn Rienner Publishers.

van Tuijl, Peter. 1993. "Conditionality for Whom? Indonesia and the Dissolution of the IGGI: The NGO Experience." Paper prepared for INTRAC Workshop,

"Governance, Democracy and Conditionality: What Role for NGOs?"
     Amersfoort, Netherlands, 4–6 June.

Vargas, María Carolina. 1990. "El caso Chileno en la Asamblea General y la
     Comisión de Derechos Humanos de la Organización de las Naciones Unidas."
     Revista Chilena de Derechos Humanos 12: 31–90.

Vatikiotis, Michael. 1989. "Lobbying the Donors: Pressure Groups Warned about
     Overseas Activities (Indonesia)." *Far Eastern Economic Review* 145, no. 34: 23.

———. 1993. *Indonesian Politics under Suharto: Order, Development and Pressure
     for Change.* New York: Routledge.

Vatikiotis, Michael, and Adam Schwarz. 1989. "Pulp Plan Scotched: Indonesia's
     Biggest Foreign-Invested Project Falters." *Far Eastern Economic Review* 146,
     no. 44: 51–52.

von Gesau, Frans A.M. Alting. 1980. "The Nine and Detente." In *Belgrade and
     Beyond: The CSCE Process in Perspective,* edited by Nils Andren and Karl E.
     Birnbaun. Alphen a/d Rijn: Sihthoff & Noordhoff.

Wade, Robert. 1997. "Greening the Bank: The Struggle over the Environment,
     1970–1995." In *The World Bank: Its First Half Century,* edited by Davesh
     Kupur, John P. Lewis, and Richard Webb. Vol. 2. Washington, D.C.: Brookings
     Institution.

Wahana Lingkungan Hidup Indonesia (WALHI). 1987. "Indonesian NGOs Write
     the World Bank. *Environesia* 1, no. 2: 7–8.

Waltz, Kenneth. 1979. *Theory of International Politics.* Reading, Mass.: Addison-
     Wesley.

Wapner, Paul. 1994. "Environmental Activism and Global Civil Society." *Dissent*
     41, no. 3: 389–93.

———. 1995. "Politics beyond the State: Environmental Activism and World Civic
     Politics." *World Politics* 47, no. 3: 311–40.

———. 1996. *Environmental Activism and World Civic Politics.* Albany: State
     University of New York Press.

Waterman, Peter, Peter Fairbrother, and Tony Elger, eds. 1998. *Globalization,
     Social Movements and the New Internationalisms.* Washington, D.C.: Mansell
     Publishing, Limited.

Weber, Max. 1968. *Economy and Society.* Edited by Guenther Roth and Claus
     Wittich. Vol. 2. Berkeley and Los Angeles: University of California Press.

Weiss, Thomas, and Leon Gordenker. 1996. *NGOs, the UN, and Global Governance.*
     Boulder, Colo.: Lynne Rienner Publishers.

Wendt, Alexander. 1992. "Anarchy Is What States Make of It: The Social Construc-
     tion of Power Politics." *International Organization* 46, no. 2: 391–425.

———. 1999. *Social Theory of International Politics.* New York: Cambridge Uni-
     versity Press.

Wignaraja, Ponna, ed. 1993. *New Social Movements in the South: Empowering the People.* Atlantic Highlands, N.J.: Zed Books Ltd.

Wilkinson, Jens. 1995. "Dealing with a Fiction: The NGO Conference on APEC." *AMPO: Japan-Asia Quarterly Review* 26, no. 4: 6–9.

Willets, Peter, ed. 1982. *Pressure Groups in the Global System: The Transnational Relations of Issue-Oriented Non-Governmental Organizations.* New York: St. Martin's Press.

————. 1999. "Environmental Politics and Transnational Actors in the United Nations." Paper presented at 1999 International Studies Association Conference, Washington D.C., 1–13 February.

Williams, Heather. 1997. "Mobile Capital and Transborder Labor Rights Mobilization: The Case of the Coalition for Justice in the Maquiladoras." Paper presented at the 1997 Annual Meeting of the American Political Science Association, Washington, D.C., 28–31 August.

Wilson, Richard. 1999. "Prosecuting Pinochet: International Crimes in Spanish Domestic Law." *Human Rights Quarterly* 21: 927–79.

Wirth, David A. 1998. "Partnership Advocacy in World Bank Environmental Reform." In *The Struggle for Accountability,* edited by Jonathan A. Fox and L. David Brown. Cambridge: MIT Press.

Wold, Chris A. 1992. "Narmada International Human Rights Panel—Interim Report."

Wolfensohn, James D. 1995. Address to the Board of Governors of the World Bank Group at the Joint Annual Discussion.

Woods, Lawrence T. 1993. "Nongovernmental Organizations and the United Nations System: Reflecting upon the Earth Summit Experience." *International Studies Notes* 18, no. 1: 9–15.

World Bank. 1980. "Social Issues Associated with Involuntary Resettlement in Bank Financed Projects." *Operational Manual Statement No. 2.33.*

————. 1982. "Tribal People in Bank-Financed Projects." *Operational Manual Statement No. 2.34.*

————. 1985. Development credit agreement (Narmada River Development [Gujarat] Sardar Sarovar Dam and Power Project) between India and International Development Association, 10 May. Credit Number 1552 IN.

————. 1992a. Additions to IDA Resources: Tenth Replenishment. Washington, D.C.: World Bank.

————. 1992b. Meeting between IDA Deputies, Executive Directors, and NGOs. 16 September, summary record.

————. 1993a. *Poverty Reduction Handbook and Operational Directive.* Forward by Lewis Preston.

————. 1993b. Disclosure of Operational Information. Washington, D.C: World Bank.

———. 1993c. Bank Procedures, Disclosures of Operational Information, BP 17.50. Washington, D.C.: World Bank.

———. 1993d. The World Bank Inspection Panel, Resolution 93-10. Washington, D.C.: World Bank.

———. 1994a. Report of the Participation Learning Group. Washington, D.C.: World Bank.

———. 1994b. Annual Portfolio Review 1994. Appendix on Resettlement Portfolio. Washington, D.C: World Bank.

———. 1994c. *World Debt Tables, 1994–95: External Finance for Developing Countries,* Vol. 1, *Analysis and Summary Tables.* Washington, D.C.: World Bank.

———. 1995. "NGOS, Bank Set Differences Aside, Call for Full IDA Funding." *World Bank News* 14, no. 37: 10.

———. 1996. World Bank-NGO Review of Bank-supported Policy Reform Programs. Internal memorandum. Washington, D.C.: World Bank.

———. 1997a. *World Development Report 1997: The State in a Changing World.* New York: Oxford University Press.

———. 1997b. *Global Development Finance, 1997,* Vol. 1, *Analysis and Summary Tables.*

———. 1998. "Partnership for Development: From Vision to Action." Washington, D.C.: World Bank.

———. 1999. 1999 Clarifications to Resolution 93-10. Washington, D.C.: World Bank.

———. 2000. *Global Development Finance: Analysis and Summary Tables.* Washington, D.C.: World Bank.

———. 2001. "Adjustment from Within: Lessons from the Structural Adjustment Participatory Review Initiative. "A contribution from the World Bank to the Second Global SAPRI Forum, 30–31 July. Washington, D.C.: World Bank.

World Commission on Dams. 2000. *Dams and Development: A New Framework for Decision-Making.* London and Sterling, Va.: Earthscan Publications.

World Resources Institute, Lokayan, Lawyer's Environmental/Action Team. 2001. "An Independent Assessment of the World Commission on Dams: Preliminary Findings." Washington, D.C.: World Resources Institute.

Yayasan Lembaga Bantuan Hukum Indonesia (YLBHI). 1994. "Surat Terbuka tentang Perampasan Dokumen Delegasi LSM" (Open Letter about the Seizure of NGO Delegation Documents). Jakarta: YLBHI, 29 April.

Zoelle, Diana. 1994. "Reservations and Human Rights Instruments: Can the Convention on Elimination of All Forms of Discrimination Against Women Be an Effective Instrument for Change?" Paper presented at American Political Science Association Annual Meeting, San Francisco, 31 August–4 September.

Zuckerman, Elaine. 1989. "Adjustment Programs and Social Welfare." World Bank Discussion Paper 44. Washington, D.C.: World Bank.

Contributors

KAREN BROWN THOMPSON teaches in the Interdisciplinary Center for the Study of Global Change and in the Department of Women's Studies at the University of Minnesota. She serves as coordinator of the MacArthur Interdisciplinary Program on Global Change, Sustainability, and Justice. Her research interests are in women's and children's human rights, international feminist theory, and gender and citizenship.

CHARLES T. CALL is assistant professor and Global Security Program principal investigator at the Watson Institute for International Studies at Brown University. His interests are security and international policing and Latin America, and he has made trips to the Chechen border and to Colombia for the Human Rights Watch. His book *Calling 911: International Security and the Reconstitution of Foreign Police Forces* is forthcoming.

ELIZABETH A. DONNELLY is a Ph.D. candidate in the Department of Government at Harvard University. She holds an M.T.S. degree in Christian social ethics from Harvard Divinity School and has served as a Maryknoll lay missioner in Lima, Peru. She has worked as a consultant to the U.S. Catholic Conference and the Global Public Policy Project of the Brookings Institution.

DARREN HAWKINS is assistant professor of political science at Brigham Young University. He is the author of *International Human Rights and Authoritarian Rule in Chile;* other recent publications include articles in

Comparative Politics, Political Science Quarterly, and the *European Journal of International Relations.* He has been a Fulbright scholar at the Human Rights Center in Copenhagen, Denmark, where he began work on a project on the evolution of enforceable international human rights norms.

SANJEEV KHAGRAM is assistant professor of public policy at the Kennedy School of Government at Harvard University, where he teaches and conducts research on political economy, sustainable development, democratization, and public leadership. From 1998 to 2000 he was senior policy adviser to the World Commission on Dams and to the international multistockholder initiative in global public policy making. His book *Dams, Democracy, and Development: Transnational Struggles for Power and Water* is forthcoming.

THALIA G. KIDDER is a policy adviser on economics and gender for Oxfam Great Britain, working in Managua, Nicaragua, and Oxford, England. She received her M.A. from the Hubert H. Humphrey Institute of Public Affairs at the University of Minnesota. She was a member and organizing staff of the ACTWU and ULU unions, and worked as ACORN's regional organizing director in Minneapolis. She has participated in exchanges between union women leaders from Mexico and North America.

SMITU KOTHARI is one of the founders of Lokayan ("Dialogue of the People"), a center in India promoting active exchange between nonparty political formations and concerned scholars and other citizens from India and the rest of the world. At Lokayan, he coordinates research and campaigns on political, ecological, and cultural issues and coedits the *Lokayan Bulletin.* He is a member of the Indian Coalition for Nuclear Disarmament and Peace, President of the International Group for Grassroots Initiatives, and has been a visiting professor at Cornell and Princeton universities. He has published extensively on critiques of contemporary economic and cultural development, the relationship of nature, culture, and democracy, developmental displacement, and social movements. He has edited *In Search of Democratic Space, Out of the Nuclear Shadow* (with Zia Mian), *Rethinking Human Rights: Challenges for Theory and Action,* and *The Non-Party Political Process: Uncertain Alternatives* (with H. Sethi).

PAUL J. NELSON is assistant professor in the graduate school of public and international affairs at the University of Pittsburgh, where he teaches and conducts research on NGOs, development policy, and international organizations. Before joining the university in 1998, he worked as a consultant on international NGO advocacy. He is the author of *The World Bank and*

Non-Governmental Organizations: The Limits of Apolitical Development, as well as numerous articles.

AUGUST NIMTZ is professor of political science at the University of Minnesota. He is the author of *Marx and Engels: Their Contribution to the Democratic Breakthrough.* His research interests include African politics, urban politics, social movements, political development, and Marxism.

JAMES V. RIKER is coordinator of the Nonprofit Leadership and Democracy Project of the Union Institute's Center for Public Policy in Washington, D.C. He designs and conducts research and educational and training initiatives that focus on improving nonprofit leadership strategies for effective advocacy on issues of civil society, social justice, and democracy. He is the coeditor, with Noleen Heyzer and Antonio B. Quizon, of *Government–NGO Relations in Asia: Prospects and Challenges for People-Centred Development.*

MARK RITCHIE is president of the Institute for Agriculture and Trade Policy in Minneapolis, Minnesota. He can be reached at mritchie@iatp.org.

KATHRYN SIKKINK is the Arleen Carlson Professor of political science at the University of Minnesota. Her publications include *Ideas and Institutions: Developmentalism in Brazil and Argentina; Activists beyond Borders: Advocacy Networks in International Politics* (coauthored with Margaret Keck); and *The Power of Human Rights: International Norms and Domestic Change* (coedited with Thomas Risse and Stephen Ropp). Her current research interests focus on the influence of international law on domestic politics, especially concerning human rights, transnational social movements and networks, and the role of ideas and norms in international relations and foreign policy.

JACKIE SMITH is assistant professor of sociology at the State University of New York at Stony Brook. She is the coeditor of *Transnational Social Movements* and *Global Politics: Solidarity beyond the State,* as well as numerous journal articles. Her research explores how transnational organizations manage cultural, linguistic, national, and other barriers to organizational cohesion.

DANIEL C. THOMAS is assistant professor of political science at the University of Illinois at Chicago, where he teaches international relations, human rights, and international security. He is the author of *The Helsinki Effect: International Norms, Human Rights, and the Demise of Communism,* and coeditor of three books on international security. His present work focuses on the role of human rights ideas in the construction of the European Union.

Index